Anthropology in the Margins of the State

Publication of the Advanced Seminar Series
is made possible by generous support from
The Brown Foundation, Inc., of Houston, Texas.

School of American Research
Advanced Seminar Series

Richard M. Leventhal
General Editor

Anthropology in the Margins of the State

Contributors

Talal Asad
Department of Anthropology, City University of New York Graduate Center

Adam Ashforth
Institute of Advanced Study, Princeton University

Lawrence Cohen
Department of Anthropology, University of California, Berkeley

Veena Das
Department of Anthropology, Johns Hopkins University

Mariane C. Ferme
Department of Anthropology, University of California, Berkeley

Pradeep Jeganathan
International Centre for Ethnic Studies, Sri Lanka

Diane M. Nelson
Department of Anthropology, Duke University

Deborah Poole
Department of Anthropology, Johns Hopkins University

Janet Roitman
Centre Nationale des Recherches Scientifiques, France

Victoria Sanford
*Institute on Violence and Survival, Virginia Foundation
for the Humanities and Public Policy*

Anthropology in the Margins of the State

Edited by Veena Das and Deborah Poole

School of American Research Press
Santa Fe

School of American Research Press

Post Office Box 2188
Santa Fe, New Mexico 87504-2188
www.sarpress.sarweb.org

Director: James F. Brooks
Executive Editor: Catherine Cocks
Manuscript Editor: Margaret Goldstein
Design and Production: Cynthia Dyer
Indexer: Catherine Fox
Proofreader: Kate Talbot

Library of Congress Cataloging-in-Publication Data:

Anthropology in the margins of the state / edited by Veena Das and
Deborah Poole.
    p. cm. – (School of American Research advanced seminar series)
Includes bibliographical references and index.
  ISBN 1-930618-40-9 (cl : alk. paper) – ISBN 1-930618-41-7 (paper :
alk. paper)
 1. Political anthropology. 2. State, The. 3. Marginality, Social.
I. Das, Veena. II. Poole, Deborah. III. Series.
GN492 .A5923 2004
306.2–dc22

           2003026005

Cover illustration: Door, 1991, spit bite aquatint. © 1991 by Anish Kapoor.

Contents

Acknowledgments   ix

1   State and Its Margins: Comparative Ethnographies   3
    Veena Das and Deborah Poole

2   Between Threat and Guarantee: Justice and Community
    in the Margins of the Peruvian State   35
    Deborah Poole

3   Checkpoint: Anthropology, Identity, and the State   67
    Pradeep Jeganathan

4   Deterritorialized Citizenship and the Resonances
    of the Sierra Leonean State   81
    Mariane C. Ferme

5   Anthropologist Discovers Legendary Two-Faced
    Indian! Margins, the State, and Duplicity in
    Postwar Guatemala   117
    Diane M. Nelson

6   AIDS and Witchcraft in Post-Apartheid South Africa   141
    Adam Ashforth

7   Operability: Surgery at the Margin of the State   165
    Lawrence Cohen

8 Productivity in the Margins: The Reconstitution
   of State Power in the Chad Basin   191
      Janet Roitman

9 The Signature of the State: The Paradox of Illegibility   225
      Veena Das

10 Contesting Displacement in Colombia: Citizenship
   and State Sovereignty at the Margins   253
      Victoria Sanford

11 Where Are the Margins of the State?   279
      Talal Asad

                    References   289
                    Index   321

Acknowledgments

It is a pleasure to offer our thanks to the staff of the School of American Research, Santa Fe, and especially Leslie Shipman, for their marvelous hospitality during the advanced seminar in which these papers were discussed. Our colleagues and students at Johns Hopkins University continue to provide a stimulating intellectual environment—we thank them for the many discussions that have seeped into our writing. We are grateful to Becky Daniels, who cheerfully completed the final task of formatting and consolidating the reference list. And we thank James Brooks and Catherine Cocks at SAR Press for efficiently steering the manuscript through publication.

Veena Das
Deborah Poole

Anthropology in the Margins of the State

1

State and Its Margins

Comparative Ethnographies

Veena Das and Deborah Poole

This book is about margins, the places from which we seek to understand what counts as the study of the state in anthropology. The chapters collected here began as part of a School of American Research advanced seminar. There, we asked anthropologists working on different regions to reflect on what would constitute the ethnography of the state as embedded in practices, places, and languages considered to be at the margins of the nation-state. Although we invited anthropologists whose work focused on regions that have been dramatically affected by recent political and economic reforms, we were interested in moving away from the idea that these reforms had somehow produced a weakening or shrinking of the forms of regulation and belonging that supposedly constitute the modern nation-state. Our analytical and descriptive strategy was to distance ourselves from the entrenched image of the state as a rationalized administrative form of political organization that becomes weakened or less fully articulated along its territorial or social margins. Instead, we asked seminar participants to reflect on how the practices and politics of life in these areas shaped the political, regulatory, and disciplinary practices that constitute, somehow, that thing we call "the state."

As a discipline that itself has often been considered to occupy a marginal voice in Western political theory, anthropology offers an ideal point of departure for the radical rethinking of the state that a view from the margins requires. Anthropology is frequently configured as a discipline that speaks for (or at times with) those populations that have been marginalized by the political and economic strictures of colonial and postcolonial rule. Moreover, ethnography is a mode of knowing that privileges experience—often going into realms of the social that are not easily discernible within the more formal protocols used by many other disciplines. As such, ethnography offers a unique perspective on the sorts of practices that seem to undo the state at its territorial and conceptual margins. The regional or local perspectives of anthropology are also important here, although for somewhat different reasons from those usually implied when anthropologists speak of regional comparisons. The anthropologists in this volume all work in states and regions that are frequently characterized in comparative political theory as "new nations" with "failed," "weak," or "partial" states, and their work speaks in many ways to the particular modalities of rule in Africa, Latin America, and South Asia.[1] Yet, their ethnographies of disciplinary, regulatory, and enforcement practices are framed, not as studies of regional or failed states, but rather as invitations to rethink the boundaries between center and periphery, public and private, legal and illegal, that also run through the heart of even the most "successful" European liberal state. An anthropology of the margins offers a unique perspective to the understanding of the state, not because it captures exotic practices, but because it suggests that such margins are a necessary entailment of the state, much as the exception is a necessary component of the rule.

For reasons having to do with its historical origins as the study of "primitive" peoples, anthropology has traditionally not acknowledged the state as a proper subject for ethnographic inspection. With few exceptions, anthropology's subject, until recently, was understood to be primitive or "non-state" societies. Seen from this perspective, the state seemed distant from the ethnographic practices and methods that constituted the proper, disciplinary subjects of anthropology.

At the same time, however, the language and figure of the state has haunted anthropology. Whether we choose to place the origins of polit-

[handwritten note: What about anthro as a project of knowledge-production for the state?]

ical anthropology w   , Maine ([1866]
2002), or Evans-Prit   order or reason
among the primitive   r that is inherited
from—and indeed p   ite.[2] In this sense,
anthropology has alw   ;ed ways, "about "
the state—even (and   jects were constituted as excluded fi   of administrative
rationality, political order, and authority consigned to the state. We
contend that it is through the language of the state that anthropologists
have traditionally constituted the tropes of social order, rationality,
authority, and even externality for defining their subject. Pierre
Clastres (1974), for example, claimed some thirty years ago that the
rationality and forms of life proper to our nonmodern ethnographic
subjects were best understood as expressions of a collective desire to
fend off the imminent emergence of the state. Here, as in many other
anthropological texts, the state was assumed to be an inevitable or
ghostly presence that shaped the meaning and form that power took in
any given society. The work of the anthropologist, then, became that of
cordoning off the primitive from the domain of stately practices. In this
kind of anthropological practice, as indeed in the early traditions of
Marxist and postcolonial writing, the primitive was constituted as a nos-
talgic site for the discovery of the state form as a universal cultural operator—even when not present, it was seen as waiting on the threshold of
reality, as it were.[3]

Any effort to rethink the state as an object of ethnographic inquiry
must start, then, by considering how this double effect of order and
transcendence has been used to track the presence of the state. On one
level, of course, states seem to be all about order. Thus, in mapping the
effects and presence of "the state" in local life, anthropologists often
look for signs of administrative and hierarchical rationalities that provide seemingly ordered links with the political and regulatory apparatus of a central bureaucratic state. This approach informs much of the
recent turn to the state in anthropological writing (for example,
Ferguson and Gupta 2002; Fuller and Harris 2000; Herzfeld 2001:124–
25; Hansen and Stepputat 2001). Seen from this perspective, the task
of the anthropologist becomes that of first sighting instances of
the state as it exists on the local level and then analyzing those local

manifestations of bureaucracy and law as culturally informed interpretations or appropriations of the practices and forms that constitute the modern liberal state. These parochial sightings of the state lead, in turn, to a more spatially and conceptually dispersed picture of what the state is, albeit one that is still basically identifiable through the state's affiliations with particular institutional forms.[4]

One aspect of thinking of the state in terms of order-making functions is that the spatial and social margins that so often constitute the terrain of ethnographic fieldwork are seen as sites of disorder, where the state has been unable to impose its order.[5] While it is true that political anthropology staked its unique claim for understanding the political precisely by asking how order was maintained in so-called stateless societies such as the Nuer (Evans-Pritchard 1940), it did so by bracketing any reference to the functioning of the actual state—the colonial one—in that very context. As many critics of Evans-Pritchard have pointed out, the segmentary system as a system of balanced force could be presented as embodying the ordered politics of Nuer life, precisely because the disorders caused by the colonial state were left out of the picture (see Coriat 1993; Hutchinson 1996). Although attention to colonial contexts led to increased concern with the state as a factor in the formation of certain types of anthropological subjects (Balandier 1951; Gluckman 1963; Meillassoux [1975] 1981), both political anthropologists (for example, Gledhill 1994; Vincent 1990) and postcolonial and subaltern theorists (see the several volumes on subaltern studies by the Subaltern Collective) have tended, until recently, to emphasize either resistance to the state or the local forms of legal, economic, and cultural plurality that marked anthropological subjects as contained by or articulated with the state.

Given that it is impossible to think of political systems in the contemporary world as inhabiting any form of stateless societies, are we observing simply incomplete—or frustrated—forms of the state in such situations? Or do the forms of illegibility, partial belonging, and disorder that seem to inhabit the margins of the state constitute its necessary condition as a theoretical and political object?

Key to this aspect of the problem of margins is the relationship between violence and the ordering functions of the state. Informed as it is by a particular picture of human nature, European political theology has bestowed the state with both the quality of transcendence and a related monopoly over violence (see Abrams 1988).[6] Max Weber's famous formulation on the criteria for counting a political organization as a state may be worth recalling here. In his words, "A 'ruling organization' will be called 'political' insofar as its existence and order is continuously safeguarded within a given *territorial* area by the threat and application of physical force on the part of the administrative staff. A compulsory political organization with continuous operations *(politischer Anstaltsbetrieh)* will be called a 'state' in so far as its administrative staff successfully upholds the claim to the *monopoly* of the *legitimate* use of physical force in the enforcement of its order" (Weber 1978:54; emphasis in original). Weber also emphasized that use of force in any other type of organization would be considered legitimate only if it was permitted by the state or prescribed by it. Thus, "the claim of the modern state to monopolize the use of force is as essential to it as its character of compulsory jurisdiction and continuous operation" (56). In defining the state as that which replaces private vengeance with the rule of law, Weber was, of course, building on earlier traditions of Kant and Hegel, for whom the state in modernity was defined by clear-cut boundaries between the external realm of law and the internal realm of ethics, and also between the realm of universalistic reason proper to the state and primordial relations proper to the family (for example, Hegel [1821] 1991; Kant [1797] 1965). Inherent in this imagination of the figure of law was the creation of boundaries between those practices and spaces that were seen to form part of the state and those that were excluded from it. Legitimacy, in turn, emerged as a function of this boundary-marking effect of state practices. The violence of warfare contracted between states and police control of the diffused violence of society by force were constituted as legitimate because they were of the state. Other forms of violence that seemed either to mimic state violence or to challenge its control were deemed illegitimate.

In this vision of political life, the state is imagined as an always incomplete project that must constantly be spoken of—and imagined—through an invocation of the wilderness, lawlessness, and savagery that not only lies outside its jurisdiction but also threatens it from within. Kant, for instance, assumed that the ends of government in terms of managing the eternal well-being, civic well-being, and physical well-being of the people were threatened from within because it was "natural" for people to put their physical well-being above their civic well-being and their civic well-being above their eternal well-being. For Kant, this "state of nature" that threatens the civic order was to be transformed by education (Vries 2002). Weber—with whom the theory of the rationalization of the state is most closely associated—similarly treated this process as regrettably incomplete, since the formalism of law had to contend with the demands of popular justice.[7] We wish to emphasize that for these (and other) foundational theorists of the European state form, the state itself was seen as always in danger of losing its hold over the rational organization of governance by the force of the natural from within. Thus, demands for popular justice were interpreted as an expression of facets of human nature that had not yet been mastered by rationality.

And what about the lawlessness and wilderness imagined to reside outside the state? Instructive here is the concept of the state of nature as the necessary opposite *and* origin point for the state and the law. The fact that Hobbes ([1651] 1968), Locke ([1690] 1988), Rousseau ([1762] 1981), and other early theorists of the state imagined the state of nature through the image of America as both a real site of savagery *and* an idealized primordial place suggests that we, too, should think of the margins of the state—the "state of nature"—as located in the space of language and practice where the real spaces or sites that provide impetus to the idea of the state of nature meet the mythical or philosophical origins of the state. Located always on the margins of what is accepted as the territory of unquestioned state control (and legitimacy), the margins we explore in this book are simultaneously sites where nature can be imagined as wild and uncontrolled and where the state is constantly refounding its modes of order and lawmaking. These sites are not merely territorial: they are also, and perhaps more importantly, sites of practice on which law and other state practices are colonized by other forms of regulation that emanate from the pressing needs of populations to secure political and economic survival.

It is important to underscore that at our seminar at Santa Fe, we did not start with the assumption that we had a shared understanding of what would count as the margins. Although all authors wanted to think beyond a simply spatial model of center and periphery, the discussions in Santa Fe made it evident that the relation between sovereign and disciplinary forms of power, as well as the specific genealogies of political and economic subjects, informed our various ideas about the margins. Our conversations led us to formulate these issues around three concepts of margins.

The first approach gave primacy to the idea of margins as peripheries seen to form natural containers for people considered insufficiently socialized into the law. As ethnographers, we were interested in understanding the specific technologies of power through which states attempt to "manage" or "pacify" these populations through both force and a pedagogy of conversion intended to transform "unruly subjects" into lawful subjects of the state. In several cases discussed in this book (Guatemala, Peru, South Africa), marginal populations are formed of "indigenous" or "natural" subjects, who are at once considered to be foundational to particular national identities and excluded from these same identities by the sorts of disciplinary knowledge that mark them as racially and civilizationally "other." In these cases, juridical claims to inclusion are undermined in interesting ways by disciplinary forms of power that destabilize the very discourses of belonging that claim to bind subjects to the state and its laws. In other cases (Colombia, Chad, Sierra Leone, Sri Lanka), the pedagogy of conversion is played out in less settled ways among subjects who have been uprooted or displaced by acts of war. In these cases, subjects are constituted juridically as permanent inhabitants of the same forms of uncontrolled or private justice that undergird sovereign power in the form of war and the exception.

A second, related approach to the concept of the margin that emerged from our papers and seminar discussions hinges around issues of legibility and illegibility. Like other anthropologists, here we begin by taking note of the well-known fact that so much of the modern state is constructed through its writing practices. We recognize that the documentary and statistics-gathering practices of the state are all intended, in some sense, to consolidate state control over subjects, populations, territories, and lives. In our seminar discussions, however, we soon realized that our ethnographies worked against the notion that the state is somehow "about" its legibility. Rather, our papers seemed to point instead to the many different spaces, forms, and practices through which the state is continually both experienced and undone through the *illegibility* of its own practices, documents, and words. Among the sorts of practices we consider are the economies of displacement, falsification, and interpretation surrounding the circulation and use of personal identification papers. Prominent here as well is the tension-filled space of the checkpoint. As a site where assumptions about the security of identity and rights can become suddenly and sometimes violently unsettled, the checkpoint led us to think also about the distinct temporal dynamics surrounding people's interactions with the state and state documents.

Yet a third approach focuses on the margin as a space between bodies, law, and discipline. After all, sovereign power exercised by the state is not only about territories; it is also about bodies. In fact, one may contend that the production of a biopolitical body is the originary activity of sovereign power. Many anthropologists have used the notion of biopower to track the way power spreads its tentacles into the capillary branches of the social. The privileged site of this process has been the growing power of medicine to define the "normal." Yet, the larger issue is the question of how politics becomes the domain in which "life" is put in question. In that sense, the margins provide a particularly interesting vantage position from which to observe the colonization of law by disciplines, as well as the production of categories of pathology through tactics that are parasitical on law even as they draw repertoires of action from it. Our seminar discussions on this set of issues took the notion of the biopolitical state in entirely unexpected directions as strategies of citizenship, technological imaginaries, and new regions of language were analyzed as co-constructing the state and the margins.

These three concepts of the margin all suggest different modes of occupying margins than might be told by a simple story of exclusion. In the remainder of this introduction, we consider how the authors in this book trace these different senses of the margin in their ethnographic work and how in so doing they draw on and rearticulate thinking about the state, sovereignty, and biopolitics in recent political theory. The chapters are not organized around one or the other concept of margins. These three notions are present but have different weights in each chapter. In the following sections, we ask how the logic of exception operates in relation to the margins, how economic and political citizenship is claimed, and how we understand the working of the biopolitical state from the perspectives of regions whose experiences have not normally informed this set of conceptual issues.

LAW, MARGINS, AND EXCEPTION

Recent anthropological work has done much to illuminate the contexts in which war and other forms of collective violence are experienced as either states of crisis or states of exception. Thus, anthropologists have reflected on how the contexts of civil war, general political violence, authoritarian rule, and emergency powers shape people's sense of community, self, and political future (for example, Das et al. 2000, 2001; Feldman 1991; Ferme 2001). At stake here as well has been an extended discussion of the ways in which violence and war shape the very terms in which ethnography can take place (for example, Nordstrom 1995). In this literature, the exception tends to be treated as a bounded entity or form of emergency power, acknowledged as an increasingly frequent, yet somehow aberrant face of the modern states in which ethnographers work.

While our own work has benefited in multiple ways from these sorts of discussions, our concept of the margin goes well beyond the sense of "exception" as an event that can be confined to particular kinds of spaces or periods in time, or a condition that stands opposed, somehow, to "normal" forms of state power. Rather, we draw on the very different approach to the exception articulated by Walter Benjamin, Carl Schmitt, and, most recently, Giorgio Agamben, whose work has been engaged by anthropologists interested in questions of sovereignty and biopower.

In his rethinking of the problem of sovereignty and the exception, Agamben (1998) has resuscitated the figure of *homo sacer,* an obscure figure of archaic Roman law, as the embodiment of "bare life," in order to rethink sovereignty as exercised, not over territories, but over life and death. Further, this life is "bare" because it can be taken by anyone without any mediation from law and without incurring the guilt of homicide. Homo sacer, then, is the person who can be *killed but not sacrificed.* Agamben quotes the words of Pompeius Festus: "The sacred man is the one whom the people have judged on account of a crime. It is not permitted to sacrifice this man, yet he who kills him will

"exception" & ethnography

Agamben

not be condemned for homicide" (71). Bare life, then, turns out to be something constituted in some senses as "before the law." Because homo sacer, this embodiment of bare life, cannot be sacrificed, he is outside the purview of divine law, and because one who kills him cannot be accused of homicide, he is also outside the purview of human law.

We will not go into the questions of historical accuracy here—there are places in which Agamben's text is indeed bare. Examples are offered in a cryptic fashion, but they are not elaborated. For instance, in seventeenth-century texts on sovereignty, it was the father's power over the life and death of the son that represented legal notions of sovereignty (see Filmer 1949), and Agamben rightly draws attention to this idea. But he does not discuss whether the father's exercise of sovereign power is an example of power over bare life, or whether instead the son is to be seen as a legally constituted subject. Similarly, Agamben's discussion of the Habeas Corpus Act of 1679 begs the question whether the person whose "body" is supposed to be produced in court is a legally constituted subject or a bare body stripped of all social and legal marks (Fitzpatrick 2001). All of these are intricate questions. For the moment, what we want to take from Agamben's theory is the implication that law produces certain bodies as "killable" because they are positioned by the law itself as prior to the institution of law.

For Agamben, the figure of homo sacer holds the key to an understanding of sovereignty and modern political and legal codes because of what it reveals of the sovereign's power to resort to a boundless state of exception. Here, Agamben draws on the work of Benjamin ([1978] 1986) and Schmitt ([1922] 1988) to argue that the state of exception provides a theory of sovereignty that is both inside and outside law. Because the sovereign cannot by definition be bound to the law, the political community itself becomes split along the different axes of membership and inclusion that may run along given fault lines of race, gender, and ethnicity or may produce new categories of people included in the political community but denied membership in political terms. The issue is not that membership is simply denied but rather that individuals are reconstituted through special laws as populations on whom new forms of regulation can be exercised. Although the split between inclusion and membership may be clear-cut—as, for instance, in the exclusion of certain races or ethnicities from citizenship—it is well to remember that states of exception, of which war is the classic example, can redraw boundaries so that those who were secure in their citizenship can be expelled or reconstituted as different kinds of bodies. The paradigmatic example of this for Agamben is the concentration camp, where Jews were first stripped of their citizenship and then confined to the camp and subjected to its atrocities. Other examples of such exceptions from "inside" include the internment of American citizens of Japanese descent during the Second World War, or more recent legislation concerning such categories as "terrorist."

Thus, although Agamben presents the figure of homo sacer at least in some instances as if it inhabited some kind of presocial life, it would appear that killable bodies are, in fact, produced *through* a complex legal process of rendering them as bare life (Fitzpatrick 2001). This may explain why one can detect two different modalities of rule in Agamben's conception of bare life. In some places, he assigns it to specific spaces (the concentration camp) and figures of modern life (refugees), as instantiations of how bare life is embodied and acted upon in modern forms of statehood; in other instances, he seems to see bare life as a threat held in abeyance and a state into which any citizen could fall. This latter understanding of bare life as the exception invites attention to one sense of margins that we employ here, as sites that do not so much lie outside the state but rather, like rivers, run through its body.

wm

On one point, however, we differ from Agamben, for we feel that states of exception, differences between membership and inclusion, or figures that reside both inside and outside the law, do not make their appearance as ghostly spectral presences from the past but rather as practices embedded in everyday life in the present. In this volume, then, we suggest two ways in which Agamben's notion of exception frames our ethnographic explorations of the margins. First, our search for the margins often settles on those practices that seem to be about the continual refounding of law through forms of violence and authority that can be construed as both extrajudicial and outside, or prior to, the state. This refounding happens both through the production of killable bodies, as posited by Agamben, and through the sorts of power embodied by figures such as the policeman or local "boss." Like homo sacer, these figures enjoy a certain immunity to law precisely because they are configured as existing outside or prior to the law.

For Kant, Hegel, and other liberal theorists, the origins of law are traced to the foundational and ultimately private (or "natural") forms of law that preceded the state (see Asad 2003). In our ethnographies, this question of the origins of law emerges, not as the myth of the state, but rather in the form of men whose abilities to represent the state or to enforce its laws are themselves premised on the men's recognized ability to move with impunity between appeals to the form of law and forms of extrajudicial practice that are clearly construed as lying outside, or prior to, the state. Examples of such figures include the Peruvian *gamonal*, or local strongman, who represents the state through both particular forms of incivility and modes of violence that are marked as illegal (Poole); Colombian paramilitary forces that act both as an extension of the army and as conduits for the flow of arms to drug lords or plantations (Sanford); and brokers who inhabit the economic frontiers described by Roitman. Such figures of local authority represent both highly personalized forms of private power *and* the supposedly impersonal or neutral authority of the state. It is precisely because they also act as representatives of the state that they are able to move across—and thus muddy—the seemingly clear divide separating legal and extralegal forms of punishment and enforcement. In many ways, these local figures who build their charisma and power through idioms of rudeness, incivility, and threat are similar to the "big men" described by Godelier and Strathern (1991). Like the "big men," they do not so much embody "traditional" authority as a mutation of traditional authority made possible by the intermittent power of the state. Such figures, who appear in different guises in the different ethnographic contexts of the chapters in this volume—as brokers, wheeler-dealers, local big men, paramilitary—represent at once the fading of the state's jurisdiction and its continual refounding through its (not so mythic) appropriation of private justice and violence. In this sense, they are the public secret through which the persons who embody law, bureaucracy, and violence that together constitute the state move beyond the realm of myth to become joined in the reality of everyday life.

Consideration of these personae helps us understand how the frontier between the legal and extralegal runs right within the offices and institutions that embody the state. Das, for instance, offers an example of a policeman, known for his fierce integrity, who comes up against a powerful mafia-like operation and nearly loses his life. Despite the fact that he is a functionary of the state, he, too, is convinced that the judicial process is incapable of pinning the crime on the persons responsible, and thus he proceeds to violate the procedural law in order to hand out what he considers to be substantive justice. The same police officer, when involved in the state's counterinsurgency operations against what are defined as militant or terrorist organizations, is killed by his own trusted deputy, because when police penetrate these militant or terrorist organizations to fight them, the lines between the terrorist and the policeman become blurred. As in Jeganathan's description, so in Das, state practices in emergency zones, or states of exception, cannot be understood in terms of law and transgression, but rather in terms of practices that lie simultaneously outside and inside the law. As an embodiment of the state of exception, the policeman challenges, not this or that law, but the very possibility of law itself (Benjamin [1978] 1986; Derrida 1992; Taussig 1997). By engaging this philosophical dilemma at the origin of the state and law as an ethnographic problem, the authors in this book make clear that this problem of the origin of law is not a ghostly specter from the past, as in, for example, Agamben's appropriation of the figure of homo sacer from Roman law, but rather the result of the concrete practices in which life and labor are engaged (see Rabinow 2002).

A second area in which our work addresses theories of sovereignty and the exception concerns practices that have to do with the securing and undoing of identities. Here, a particular area of interest concerns the documentation through which the state claims to secure identities, but which in practice often circulates in ways that undermine these same identities and assurances. Among the various kinds of documents issued by governments and supposed to act as guarantees of belongingness, passports are the most elite. The majority of the population, however, encounters the state through documents such as ration cards, identity cards, criminal complaints, court papers, birth and death certificates, and First Information Reports filed in police stations. These documents bear the double sign of the state's distance and its penetration into the life of the everyday. Indeed, several scholars have recently argued that it is through these documentary practices that the state makes the population legible to itself, creating what has been referred to as a legibility effect (J. Scott 1998). Trouillot (2001:126), for example, suggests that the legibility effect is the "production of both a language and a knowledge for governance and of theoretical and empirical tools that classify and regulate collectivities." There is indeed a vast literature on the classificatory and cartographic practices of the state that points to the knowledge/power alliance in the new models of governance that arise with the construction of the idea of population (see Appadurai 1996; Dirks 2001; Foucault 1979; Mitchell 1988; Perrot and Woolf 1984; J. Scott 1998; R. Smith 1996).

What interests us here, however, is not how the state makes the population legible to itself but how these documents become embodied in forms of life through which ideas of subjects and citizens come to circulate among those who use these documents. For example, in her chapter in this book, Mariane Ferme notes how state documents shadow and constrict migrants, travelers, and refugees as they move across different sorts of borders and checkpoints. As an example, she tells of a man whose original, and now invalid, Sierra Leonean identity card was based on a false identity and birth date. To claim deterritorialized citizenship as a Sierra Leonean war refugee—and thus to gain certain rights within other, host states—the man must embrace that identity as the only one on which his new status as a refugee can be forged. His identity as a Sierra Leonean citizen, then, exists in an inverse relation to the Sierra Leonean state's ability to secure that identity.[8] In other stories told by Sierra Leonean travelers and migrants, Ferme learns how passports issued by the British during the colonial regime became invalid on independence, thus forcing citizens who were traveling to scramble to acquire new documents within impossibly short time frames, from consulates that did not yet exist. Of particular importance here is the temporal experience of the state. Thus, when the state intervenes to revoke identity papers for seemingly arbitrary reasons, Ferme's informant feels powerless as he is forced to wait months and to postpone scholarships, work, and travel plans in a desperate attempt to acquire new identity papers and conform to the new and seemingly arbitrary demands of the state. In such cases, the law is experienced as a largely arbitrary imposition whose effects are felt as what Ferme describes as conflicting "spatiotemporalities."

Poole's chapter describes similar temporal disruptions in the ways Peruvian peasants engage the state through the endless and seemingly arbitrary flow of paperwork that constitutes their experiences of "justice." In the areas she describes, legal cases rarely reach conclusion, and "justice" itself is more commonly spoken of, not as something that can be obtained, but rather as the ephemeral link that binds peasants to a state whose promise of justice takes the form of endless procedures and the always inconclusive paperwork that drifts among different instances of the judicial system. The pedagogic aspects of the state are manifested here, not through school textbooks on citizenship, but rather through the practices by which subjects are made to learn the gap between membership and belonging. Poole shows that there is some substance to the idea that the spaces these peasants inhabit are marginal spaces, with an absence of roads, schools, or other signs of the presence of the state. What allows the state never to be held responsible to its own promises, however, is the combination of this physical location and other ideas about the "natural" marginality of indigenous peasants.

The temporal configuration and experience of such encounters with the arbitrary power of the state can also be thought of as the highly mobile spaces that Pradeep Jeganathan aptly describes in his chapter as "maps of anticipation." These are spaces where the pedagogic claims and assurances of law and the nation become unsettled by state practices. For Jeganathan, as for other authors in the volume, the military or police checkpoint emerges as a site from which this troubling of expectations and legibilities rubs up against the normalcy of the everyday. Jeganathan evokes the most ordinary of events in the process of a daily commute in the city of Colombo in Sri Lanka: a commuter is stopped at a checkpoint for his identity card. What could this mean in a country that until recently was in the midst of a civil war? Where terrorists, insurgents, militants, or freedom fighters (the appellation depends upon how one reads the conflict) use techniques of terror/martyrdom such as suicide bombings and where security forces, in turn, use similar techniques of terror counterinsurgency, the question, where are the borders of the state? is fraught with uncertainty and risk, for border-making practices run *within* the political and social territory rather than outside it.

This mobility inherent to the spaces and settings in which border-making practices emerge destabilizes the inherently territorial languages of containment and sovereignty that seem to bind the nation to the state. Writing about checkpoints in contested territories in Colombia, for example, Victoria Sanford describes how different military forces compete for control of concrete territories. In these territories that have become in some ways truly "marginal" to the state, the uncertainties of one's own position with respect to the guarantees and protection of state law are further complicated by the deliberately illegible identities and locations of the paramilitaries who are simultaneously of and not of the state. In her reflections on Peruvian checkpoints, Deborah Poole describes how the intentions and even the existence of the state become suddenly illegible during the tense moments when identity cards are surrendered to state officials. Although such spaces are often fleeting and unpredictable—as when someone in a position of authority suddenly stops someone to request documents in the street—they can also become in a sense routinized in the permanency and visibility of physical checkpoints. As Jeganathan points out in his chapter, it is through these "maps of anticipation" that residents of a city or war zone come to anticipate and internalize the unpredictability of violence precisely through the predictability of physical sites where the state exerts its own seemingly arbitrary claims to sovereignty over territories that it clearly cannot control.

The margins so evident in the checkpoint can also present themselves in the bureaucratic routines of modern daily life. Lawrence Cohen provides an example of such a space in his chapter on the techno-scientific imaginary of the operation functions in India. He describes the functioning of a trade in organs that, like the space of the exception, effectively blurs the line between the legal and illegal. Because both the sale and donation of organs by non-kin were legally banned in 1994 in India, surgeons and others who operated in the national and international organ market put pressure on the state to define procedures for authorizing permissible forms of organ donation outside legally defined degrees of kinship. The resulting authorization committees were assigned the task of considering exceptional cases in which organs could be donated outside the sanctioned degrees of kinship. Cohen gives a subtle analysis of the ways these committees operate to create fictions of overwhelming affection between unrelated people in order to allow organ "donations." The public secret, of course, is that the fictions of relatedness and overwhelming affection between recipient and donor are created to cover the illegal sale of organs. Effectively, the structure of exceptions operates to draw a line between membership and inclusion that identifies those citizens who are "bioavailable" and thus could become fictitious "donors" in an underground economy.[9] Moreover, it enables certain discursive forms to emerge in which citizenship is claimed through acts of "sacrifice" on the part of the poor—a point we explore in greater detail later in this introduction.

MARGINS ARE NOT INERT

In the preceding section, we tried to show the intimate connection between law and states of exception. We argued that instead of privileging metaphysical forms of reasoning in understanding sovereignty, anthropology focuses on the workings of the everyday. It is in these processes of everyday life that we see how the state is reconfigured at the margins. Margins are not simply peripheral spaces. Sometimes, as in the case of the borders of a nation's states, they determine what lies inside and what lies outside. Other times, as in the case of checkpoints, they run through the political body of the state. Borders and checkpoints, as we saw, are spaces in which sovereignty, as the right over life and death, is experienced in the mode of potentiality—thus creating affects of panic and a sense of danger even if "nothing happens." Paradoxically, these spaces of exception are also those in which the creativity of the margins is visible, as alternative forms of economic and political action are instituted. To suggest that margins are spaces of creativity is not to say that forms of politics and economics on the margins, often fashioned out of the need to survive, are not fraught with terrible dangers. It is, however, to draw attention to the fact that though certain populations are pathologized through various kinds of power/knowledge practices, they do not submit to these conditions passively. While the work of subaltern historians has done much to emphasize the agency of subaltern groups in important historical junctures, the canonical status of resistance in these studies obscures the relation between these critical moments and everyday life (Das 1989). Even when everyday life becomes the focus of analysis, as in the work of James Scott (1985) on everyday forms of peasant resistance, it appears that agency is seen primarily in acts of resistance. Our emphasis, instead, is on the ways in which the conceptual boundaries of the state are extended and remade in securing survival or seeking justice in the everyday. This does not mean that we consider all kinds of margins to be somehow homogeneous, with categories of minorities, refugees, or immigrants essentially similar. Rather, we take the indeterminate character of margins to break open the solidity often attributed to the state.

Take Roitman's description of economic strategies followed by marginalized youths as they deal with various regulatory processes of the state. With the decline of traditional markets in Chad, it is the emergent markets in drugs, small arms, contraband, and mercenaries that provide opportunities for securing livelihoods in regions devastated by ongoing wars, droughts, and other economic disasters. For obvious reasons, these markets flourish on the borders between nations. Refusing to name these economic opportunities as parts of "informal" or "black" economies, Roitman conceptualizes the youths' strategies as border-making practices in which we witness, not so much the collapse of regulation, but the pluralization of regulatory authorities. Such pluralization leads to an institutionalization of rent extraction by the state, even when this process occurs outside its formal legal procedures. The forms of sociality developed on these borders are, of course, extremely dangerous. But they show that margins, as the literal boundaries of the state, are also the spaces on which the conceptual boundaries of the economy are crafted and extended. Much political rhetoric would characterize such forms of economic activity as "corruption" and interpret it as evidence of the weakening of the state. However, from the perspective of the youths Roitman studies, such strategies of securing livelihood by utilizing the indeterminate character of the borders provide a means of claiming economic rights. At stake is the challenge to state monopoly over taxation or commercial licenses and the effort to appropriate some of these practices to secure economic survival. The pluralization of regulation does not create simply a binary opposition between the state and margins, nor can we say that the state is unable to have its writ over the margins, for it, too, manages to extract rent through this pluralization and extension of conceptual boundaries of the economy. What the consideration of margins enables us to see is how economic citizenship, rent extraction, and multiple regulatory regimes are necessary parts of the functioning of the state, much as the exception is necessary for the understanding of law.

In Ferme's chapter we get further evidence of the "arbitrariness at the heart of *commandement*," which she shows to be characteristic of the colonial state. However, this arbitrariness becomes a resource, as Ferme's informant reveals, for it has facilitated alternative citizenship options for Sierra Leoneans. Migrants exploit emergency measures taken to protect them as war refugees, and in some cases they are successful in using opportunities provided by the capricious and arbitrary laws, forging new forms of economic and political citizenship that sometimes go well beyond the territorial boundaries of the states. For others, such as refugees who are refused asylum or who die in transit, the outcomes are terrible—attesting to the dangers of work at the borders (see Malkki 1995). Thus, for Roitman and Ferme, the possibilities and limits of these new border-bending practices provide an important vantage point for understanding translocal processes through which the state is experienced.

Similar evidence of the creativity of the margins at the political level may be seen in the work of Peace Communities set up by displaced populations in Columbia. Sanford describes how populations displaced by the actions of the paramilitary have tried to create zones of safety, off-limits to both guerrillas and armed personnel authorized by the state. With increasing support from human-rights groups at the national and international level, such communities (again functioning at the literal margins of the state) have reconfigured their spaces to reflect their own imperatives. Their forms of political action use the global rhetoric of human rights. However, instead of making claims through courts of law or international tribunals, they give urgency to the need to secure safety at the community rather than the individual level.

Ashforth's chapter offers another example of the specific local ways in which ideas of justice operate. He argues that an increase in witchcraft accusations among black populations in South Africa ravaged by intolerably high AIDS prevalence and mortality rates is expressed in demands that the post-apartheid state show its responsiveness to the suffering by doing something about both AIDS and witchcraft. But as

Ashforth notes, punishing offenders for performing witchcraft would reinstitute colonial and apartheid-regime prejudices against popular practices of black populations and would criminalize these practices. Thus, witchcraft accusations have to be reformulated as something else—kidnapping, abduction, or murder. The point is that pressure to reconfigure state systems toward different notions of justice is generated from the everyday concerns of those inhabiting a different mode of sociality from that imagined in the rational bureaucratic apparatus of the state. It is interesting to recall here that even in the classic Weberian notion of rationality, law includes lay justice within its processes through the role of the jury, for Weber saw the jury as having taken over the role of the oracle. ("Because of the jury, some primitive irrationality of the technique of decision and, therefore, of the law itself, has thus continued to survive in English procedure even up to the present time" [Weber 1978:763].) Since the "primitive irrationality" that so irritated Weber functions at the heart of state law, one could treat the state, for certain purposes, as lying on the margins of the citizen-body.

Several other authors in this volume argue that a different picture of justice or common good animates activities that take place on the margins of the state. This is not simply a matter of "folk" notions of law and justice versus state-sanctioned ideas of justice. Rather, what is at stake in these sites is formed through the experiences of local worlds— although we must be clear that local worlds and the state do not stand as binary opposites. Even though they are locked in unequal relations, they are enmeshed in one another. Thus, on the one hand, law is seen as a sign of a distant but overwhelming power. On the other hand, it is also seen as close at hand—something to which local desires can be addressed. Thus, Poole shows how peasants in Peru invest their desire for justice in the state, even as the illegibility of the state and its procedures frustrates these desires, in that documents necessary to secure justice tend to drift endlessly between different jurisdictions. We are not saying that populations at the margins are always successful in making the state responsive to their notions of justice or the common good, and we do not wish to romanticize the creativity of the margins. In fact, as Nelson's chapter demonstrates, the same state identified as the perpetrator of terror and scorched-earth policies in Guatemala came to be invested with the desire for justice. What might have been fixed positions, such as victims and perpetrators, came to be highly mobile. The point is not whether the desires, fears, and hopes nourished in the margins and then projected onto the state are somehow more ethical, just, or pure. Rather, the complexity of lived experience inflects notions of justice and law with different kinds of imaginaries from those available in the official sites and representations of justice and law.[10]

The chapters by Das and Nelson provide additional examples of how state law is colonized by other forms of legal/juridical ideas. Das cites the poignant case of widows from the Siglikar community in Delhi whose husbands were killed in the 1984 riots. They tried to claim compensation money awarded to them by the government. The Siglikars lived on the periphery of the city. But more importantly, their notions of community and justice were grounded in different notions of sociality. The government treated the widows as the proper recipients of the compensation, but the dominant opinion in the community was that the fathers of the dead men should have received the money. The conflict was finally resolved by the caste Panchayat of the Siglikars, and the money was divided equally between the disputants. What is interesting is that the agreement was seen as a compromise and was executed on stamped court paper, as if that would make the agreement valid in the eyes of the law. Thus, legitimacy was sought through state law; this compromise was neither attributed to customary law nor treated as a private agreement between the concerned parties. The mimicry of the state to give legitimacy to an agreement that was coercive in many respects might be read as instituting the state as a fetish, but it also attests to community allegiance to the idea of state-instituted law and thus manages to claim citizenship for these communities. Such margins where a different picture of the common good is put into play are not just spaces the state has yet to penetrate: rather, they may be seen as sites on which the state is continually formed in the recesses of everyday life.[11]

In Nelson's chapter, we see how the illusory, trickster-like quality of the state allows it to escape its promissory notes in making justice out of reach for peasant subjects. In her account of postwar Guatemala, Nelson describes how the counterinsurgency state deployed images of the duplicitous or "two-faced" Indian to defend military incursions into indigenous areas, resettlement of indigenous communities into hamlets, and declaration of emergency powers in large sectors of the country. However, Nelson turns this picture of the Indian back to the picture of the state and asks the question, why is it that the state is *also* understood to be two-faced, bamboozling, desirable, deceptive, and dangerous? Thus turning the stereotypical image of the masked mimicry of the state by cunning two-faced natives on its head, Nelson's ethnography of the state puts it on a highly mobile trajectory in which the state is both feared and desired.

Nelson's account would make us highly skeptical of the idea that the state is legible while the populations are illegible. Yet much anthropological theory has concentrated on the ways the state deploys technologies of knowledge and power to make populations legible (Appadurai 1996; Cohn 1987; Trouillot 2001). However, as we say in earlier sections, the very documents through which identity is sought to be fixed themselves acquire a different kind of life as both functionaries of the state and ordinary citizens manipulate them toward different ends. As Poole so effectively demonstrates in her chapter, the possibilities of forgeries and counterfeit documents lead to a suspension of citizens between the poles of threat and guarantee. In turn, one of the modalities in which the state is present in the margins is captured in regions of language that come into existence when access to context becomes fragile. Thus, there is a flourishing of rumor: the state holds that illiterate and poorly educated populations are easily misled. As Nelson argues, the state is seen as two-faced, unknowable, and in many ways the space at which the uncanny is experienced. Yet the state attributes passion (and we might add credulity) to its subjects, thereby constructing itself as "rational," as argued by both Das and Cohen in this volume. In Ashforth's chapter, we find that measures to control HIV transmission are interpreted among black subjects of the South African state as measures to block reproduction of black populations. This interpretation seems to be the legacy of the apartheid regime and its politics of death. Thus, rumors and the aura of suspicion about the state's "real" intentions in instituting policies that involve the body, sexuality, and reproduction need to be understood in the specific local histories of this society. The fact that witchcraft accusations share many characteristics with rumor—its lack of signature (Bhabha 1994a; Das 1998; Geschiere 1997), its perlocutionary force—weaves them into the uncertainty of relations within which the devastating effects of the

AIDS epidemic are experienced. The question is not that rumor is a specifically "subaltern" form of communication, as suggested by Guha (1983), but rather that the state's own mode of representation of its subjects as given to passion rather than reason is turned back on the state, as it were. (See also Nelson's chapter on this point.) The lethal experience of AIDS and its entanglement with accusations of witch-craft, rumor, and panic takes us back to the question of the state as the site on which biopolitics and thanatopolitics are instituted together. We contend that this relation, which is at the heart of the modern state, is much more visible on the margins than at the center. We now turn to these considerations.

BIOPOLITICS AND THE MARGINS

Earlier, we argued that sovereignty is best defined in terms of power over life and death. It is important to underscore that the figure of life is not a piece of animal nature without any relation to law, but is produced by law. As both Agamben (1998, 2000) and Foucault (1976, 2003) have argued in different ways, the state is constituted in modernity through the inclusion of man's natural life into the mechanisms and calculations of power. Despite this agreement about biopolitics, however, there are profound differences in the way these two authors conceive of the rela-tion between biopolitics and thanatopolitics. The negative referent of the new biopolitical sovereignty for Agamben is the figure of homo sacer—life that may be killed but not sacrificed—and the paradigmatic example of that in modernity is the concentration camp. For Foucault, the negative referent of biopolitics seems to be the point at which a cut is made between those whose lives are managed and enhanced and those whose lives are judged as not worth living and who are thus "let die." Both authors seem equally concerned with a seeming contradic-tion in the conception of the biopolitical state—namely, how can a state committed to managing life produce a category of people who are deemed killable. For Agamben, what joins biopolitics with the politics of death is the endless resort that the state has to the state of exception, while for Foucault, the concern is much more with power in the rou-tines of the ordinary and thus the production of the "normal." This is not the place to engage these differences in depth—rather, we use them to direct attention to the way in which the ethnographic method allows us to open up these questions.

As is well known, Foucault's work on biopower replaces the privilege of law and prohibition with an emphasis on tactical efficacy within a multiple and mobile field of forces. He shows that the effects are far-reaching but never stable. His meticulous description of the impact of statistics and the invention of population as an object of knowledge and regulation on changing notions of sovereignty has led to important ways of reconceptualizing the state, especially in shifting the emphasis from territorial jurisdictions to the management of life (see also Perrot and Woolf 1984). Thus, in recent literature we see a proliferation of adjectives used to characterize the state—the *hygienic* state, the *immunizing* state, the *therapeutic* state—each pointing to a different modality for managing life. Simultaneously, the prefix *bio* has become detached from power to signal other kinds of sociality, such as the *biosocial,* as well as other kinds of capabilities, such as *biocapital,* and to refer to new ways of engaging power—for example, patient groups organizing to influence allocation of resources and direction of research for mitigating certain biological conditions. This heterogeneity of ways in which the state is engaged in administering life (and the concomitant letting die), as well as claims that can be made on the state in the regions of life and death by claiming new categories of citizenship, provides a rich terrain in which anthropology can engage the emergent forms of biopolitics (Petryna 2002).

Of course, the *locus classicus* for examining the power of the state with reference to control over populations is found in the literature on epidemics and state formation. As Peter Baldwin (2001) has recently argued, the particular strategies of control developed by the state in Europe in the late nineteenth and early twentieth centuries were closely tied to the issue of management of contagion. Further, concern with regulating the health of populations immediately takes us to connections between metropolitan centers and colonies, for control of epidemics was a necessary condition of overcoming barriers to European exploitation of colonies. Thus, a preoccupation with the health conditions of colonies and techniques of managing disease became part of state repertoires of action. As examples, we might think of the vast legislative changes effected through such acts as the Compulsory Vaccinations Acts, Vagrant Leper Acts, Lunacy Acts, Cantonment Acts, and various forms of Contagious Diseases Acts enacted in this period by

epidemics of colonialism

European states, both in metropolitan centers and in colonies. What is important from the perspective of the colonies is that both public debates on these issues and the scientific rationales given for them constructed the inhabitants of the colonies as credulous, unhygienic, irrational, and in need of discipline. It was Foucault's great achievement to show not only that biopower was about pathologization of populations but also that what was applicable to margins could become generalized and normalized for whole populations. Nevertheless, the continuous production of pathology is an important technique of power—for in this realm, as in those explored earlier, it invites us to look at the intimate connections between sovereign power and disciplinary power.

The management of populations in spaces that Cohen in his chapter calls "just-so modernity" shows that we cannot assume an inexorable logic in the management of life that unfolds in the same manner across all societies. Postcolonial societies such as India and South Africa have specific histories in which the grammar of relationships shapes the way biopolitics is instituted. Thus, the story of modernity becomes complicated in this as in all other spheres (Geschire 1997; Gilroy 1993; Mitchell 2000). Populations, as we argued in the preceding section, may exist only as entities to be administered in the state imaginary, but the inhabitants of these margins are not inert objects: forms of governance, social relationships around different zones of experience, and the cultural genres within which language acquires life generate ways of engaging the biopolitical state that cannot be arrived at through metaphysical speculation. The chapters by Cohen, Ashforth, Das, and Sanford show that although the biopolitical state works with notions of mass bodies in one form or another, techniques of management across these contexts are quite different. Even more important, the ways "managed" populations work with strategies of control to claim citizenship are deeply informed by specific experiences of the state. Thus, while categories of "refugee" and "displaced persons" exist as special legal categories in international instruments that both control them and give them rights, the negotiations effected by Peace Communities to keep both state and guerilla warriors outside their territories surely bear the stamp of their particular experience of violence. Similarly, the management of the AIDS epidemic in South Africa must necessarily address witchcraft accusations as a problem for the state. In the case of

India, the politics of mass bodies was instituted through family-planning programs that included camps for mass sterilization but were also part of a repertoire of charitable and state institutions for other conditions, such as mass health camps or eye camps for cataract operations. Thus, how management of life became an object of politics indeed defines the biopolitical state, but the specific histories are different enough to warrant the observation that this is not a loaded matrix. Perhaps we can illustrate this point with Cohen's specific examples about ways of claiming citizenship through the trope of the operation in India.

Cohen argues in his chapter that three concepts—operability, bioavailability, and supplementability—explain the particular form in which the biopolitical state is encountered in India. Diverse populations at the margins, such as the *hijras* (intersexed, transgendered subjects commonly known as the third sex); bodies treated as a mass in family-planning operations done in medical camps; and sellers of kidneys in the organ trade—all are defined by particular intersections between these three concepts. As Cohen says, the operations become not only a technique and a site instantiating the state but also a form—marking the possibilities and limits of belonging for persons hailed as a mass body—endowed with passions but not reason in the state imaginary. Thus, the pedagogy of converting the inhabitants of mass bodies into ascetic modernizers in possession of reason is specific to the cultural grammar of India within which developmental paradigms have taken shape. The most interesting part of this argument is that through a logic of exception, the generic body of the masses is converted into specific kinds of bodies from whom organs can be retrieved through sale, despite the ban on the sale of organs. The logic of exception helps create the fiction of "overwhelming affection" between buyer and seller, as we stated earlier, despite the public secret that this fiction is created to provide cover to the sale of organs through the mythic form of the gift. The operation itself is seen by marginalized populations as a way of claiming citizenship through the tropes of gift and sacrifice. It is not that the incidence of kidney sales is very high in India, for these sellers are concentrated in specific locales and regions. The possibility of transplantation, however, has enabled discursive forms and networks of talks to emerge at every level, from the domestic to the national.

Brothers talk of selling kidneys to raise dowries for their sisters; wives, to redeem the family from debts. The most marginal of citizens claim that they would donate kidneys to save the lives of ailing national or regional leaders.

The concept of bioavailability, introduced by Cohen, deviates quite sharply from the notion of killable bodies through the scepter of homo sacer—for these are the poor who are not so much killed as allowed to die. Indeed, the rhetorical form used by those who advocate sales is to make these bodies available for medical intervention, but they cast this idea in terms of individual autonomy and care for the poor. This example provides a stunning demonstration of how to move away from metaphysical conceptions of how the exception "operates"—to the task of making the biopolitical state an object of ethnographic investigation. If Foucault's concept of the dangerous individual showed us how law was colonized by disciplines in French forensic psychiatry (Foucault 2003), the concepts offered by Cohen show how gift and sacrifice have not been displaced by commodity forms but rather allow the commodity form to function in tandem with other ways of claiming citizenship.

CONCLUDING THOUGHTS

We can do no better in these concluding thoughts than to refer the reader to chapter 11, in which Talal Asad provides a succinct and provocative commentary on the theoretical issues relating to the state and the margins. Two points of importance may be stressed here. First, Asad argues that the notion of the state in contemporary thought invests it with a life of its own, distinct from both governors and the governed. Because of this abstraction, the state can claim allegiance from both sides. When the relation between the state and the population that is governed is imagined as one in which the state embodies sovereignty independently of the population, it becomes authorized to maintain certain spaces and populations as margins through its administrative practices. Conversely, an imagination of the state as that to which power is delegated, rather than alienated from the subjects, would allow the state itself to be imagined as the margins of the citizen-body. The point is not to show that the state has a fetishist character but rather to show that the imagination of sovereignty can shift the relative position of the center and the periphery: margins move, then, both within and outside the state. Of course, this movement is what makes the margins so central to the understanding of the state. The indeterminacy of the margins not only allows forms of resistance but more importantly enables strategies of engaging the state as some kind of margin to the body of citizens.

Second, Asad introduces the important idea that the formal equality and substitutability of citizens in liberal theory, in fact, rest on uncertainties inherent in the process of abstracting from one given category to another. He gives a beautiful description of how suspicion comes to occupy the space between law and its application, a process that all the chapters engage in, one way or another. This discussion invites us to think of the categories of potentiality, anticipation, and shadows—categories that capture the experience of margins actualized in the spaces of exception. Our imagination of the margins shows them not as inert spaces and populations that simply have to be managed but rather as bristling with life that is certainly managed and controlled but that also flows outside this control. Thus, while we have much to learn from the brilliant contributions of Agamben and Foucault on how natural life comes to be treated as an object of politics, anthropological forms of knowledge do not simply take these categories and apply them to different situations. Rather, in the particular genealogies and histories of the modes of sociality they study, anthropologists show how different desires, hopes, and fears shape the experience of the biopolitical state. The authors in this volume are fully aware of the precariousness of lives on the margins, but they are equally concerned with showing how forms of economic and political action, and ideas of gift and sacrifice that have been relegated to the margins, may, in some moments, also reconfigure the state as a margin to the citizen-body. In one of his political reflections, Agamben says that only by breaking the nexus, at any point between the "vicious entangling of language, people, and state," will thought and praxis be equal to the enormous task "at hand" (Agamben 2000:67–69). The task "at hand," we hope, is that the work done on the margins will be recognized for what it is. It may not be able to break such a nexus once and for all, but it does show that the defeats and victories of everyday life have the ability to return us from the metaphysical to the ordinary. This, at any rate, is how we see the ethnographic objective reconstituted.

Notes

1. The literature on the failed-state thesis is extensive. For critical reviews on this thesis, see, for instance, Bose and Jalal (1997), Dunn (1995), Kohli (1990), Mbembe (2000, 2001), and Pantham (2003). Commenting on the state of theory in relation to the failed-state thesis in Africa, Célestine Monga has this to say: "In recent years the continent has become the El Dorado of wild thought, the best place for daring intellectual safaris, the unregulated space on which to engage in theoretical incest, to violate the fundamentals of logic, to transgress disciplinary prohibitions; in short, to give oneself over to intellectual debauchery" (Monga 1996:39).

2. Recent commentators have noted that anthropology has traditionally neglected the study of the state, but they have failed to notice how the problems of political anthropology were defined within the framework of the state (see, for instance, Fuller and Harris 2000).

3. This imminent or spectral quality of the state was perhaps most clearly articulated by Clastres (1974). Its genealogy, however, can be traced through evolutionist and developmental approaches in anthropology, where such early foundational theorists as Morgan (1877), Maine ([1866] 2002), and Engels ([1884] 1972) held out the emergence of the state as a decisive moment in the progression of cultures toward a condition of civilization marked by writing, private property, and the emergence of the state. Later theorists of "political evolution" expanded on this understanding of historical progression to posit the state as an endpoint in the development of "complex societies" defined as such based on considerations of social stratification, production, and the division of labor (see, for example, Banton 1966; Fried 1967). In these approaches, as in earlier evolutionist models, the state was seen simultaneously as immanent in the logic of social evolution and as a limit condition for the constitution of the anthropological subject. At the same time, emphasis on economic models of social evolution (for example, Wolf 1982) meant that the state per se was not often taken as a subject for anthropological theory. More recent theoretical work has again relied on constructs of the primitive drawn from Clastres (Deleuze and Guattari [1972] 1983:145–85) and Bataille (Taussig 1997) to explore the mobility and immanent character of the state as a "basic formation [that is] on the horizon throughout history." In these theories, the spectral state is envisioned, not as the endpoint of an evolutionary process, as in earlier anthropologies, but rather as a transhistorical "primordial Urstaat, the eternal model of everything the State wants to be and desires" (Deleuze and Guattari 1987:217).

4. On the regional or cultural specificity of modern state practices and effects, see, among others, Abélé (1990); Chatterjee (1997); Coronil (1997); Das (1995); Heyman (1999); Humphrey (2003); Lomnitz (2000); Maurer (1997); Messick (1993); Mitchell (1988); Ong (1999b); Pantham (2003); Sanders and West (2002); G. Smith (1999:195–227); and Hansen and Stepputat (2001). On anthropological approaches to the state as a "translocal" or decentered institutional landscape, see Gupta (1995); Ong (1999a); and Trouillot (2001). For a comparative perspective on state terror, see Sluka (2000).

5. On disorder and marginality in anthropology, see especially Tsing (1993). The idea of a disorderly margin is not peculiar to Western theories of the state. For instance, in *Muqadammah,* a fourteenth-century Arabic text, Ibn Khaldûn argued that Bedouins practiced a form of weakened Islam as compared to urban Muslims because their nomadic character made them distant from regulatory authorities (Rosenthal 1969). There was a marked suspicion of nomads in the administrative practices of colonial rulers, and it continues in postcolonial polities (for a review of these practices, see Rao and Casimir 2002).

6. Though the state was conceptualized as having a monopoly over legitimate violence, it stood in a problematic relation to other kinds of violence, especially sacrificial violence. For example, Dumézil (1956) showed the close connection between the logic of sacrifice and that of punishment in his examination of Indo-European mythology. In anthropology, Taussig has discussed the fetishistic character of the state in relation to its quality of harnessing the power of the dead in the "exchange between the absurd and the official" (Taussig 1997:119). This monopoly over violence contributes to the notion of the transcendent character of the state in the political/theoretical discourse of liberalism.

7. "Modern social development, aside from the already mentioned political and internal professional motives, has given rise to certain other factors by which formal legal rationalism is being weakened. Irrational kadi justice is exercised today in criminal cases clearly and extensively in the 'popular' justice of the jury. It appeals to the sentiment of the layman, who feels annoyed whenever he meets with formalism in concrete cases, and it satisfies the emotional demands of these under-privileged classes which clamor for substantive justice" (Weber 1978:892).

8. For a discussion of how the process of acquiring a new name legally is tinged with the faint taint of criminality, even in the most ordinary of circumstances, see Cavell (1994:27–28). Here is a passage about his experience with a name change at age sixteen: "Probably I did not sufficiently appreciate the irony in thinking what debts the law imagined a sixteen-year-old might have reason to

flee from, but I began to know or know that I knew, that the deed of declaring a name, or making a name, or any questioning of your identity, was being linked with criminality, forged together with it. Quite as if the reasons for being singled out with a name were not just to be traceable in case of wrongdoing, but before that as its ground, to serve notice that identifiable actions, deeds, the work of human beings, are the source of identity, and consequently constitute identity by accusation" (26). Cavell's reflections on the relation between margins, names, and accusations anticipate the experience of checkpoints, which we discuss in more detail below, and show clearly that this experience is not a matter of physical margins alone.

9. It is important to appreciate that the sale could only be possible within a larger context in which there were rich people who operated in an economy with large undisclosed incomes.

10. For a subtle argument on the role of alternative rationalities practiced on the margins in interpreting state terror, see Humphrey's (2003) account of the Buddhist myths of reincarnation used by Buddhists in Mongolia to explain Stalin's regime of terror. In this formulation, the theory of karma is deployed metaphorically to acknowledge the inevitable complicity of the subjects of totalitarian states in regimes of terror—a subtle point that is somewhat similar to Nelson's argument in her chapter. Earlier, Tsing (1993) analyzed the importance of margins as a way of relating disciplinary creativity with forms of life lived at the margins in the context of the state in Indonesia. However, Tsing's idea of margins is strongly influence by spatial models—thus, she defines the margin as a place where state authority is most unreliable and the gap between the state's goals and their local realization is the largest. She contrasts this situation with the project of rule at the center, where state authority is strongest. This way of looking at state and margins, of course, assumes that state goals and authority are transparent in the center, or that the state itself is not invested in maintaining the margins as "unruly spaces"—a point of view critiqued by all the authors in this volume.

11. It may be relevant to point out that while understanding of *process* was always considered central to the anthropology of law, the emphasis was always on arriving at the *rules* thought to be implicit in dispute settlement (see Gluckman 1965; Nader 1969; among many others). A sharp distinction between Western and non-Western forms of law obscured the way in which legal concepts traveled between the different sites on which law was evoked in the same society.

2

Between Threat and Guarantee

Justice and Community in the Margins of the Peruvian State

Deborah Poole

When I first began working in the Andean highlands of Peru in the early 1980s, peasants (and anthropologists) moved from place to place in the backs of large, open, uncomfortable cargo trucks piled high with all sorts of agricultural products, consumer goods, and construction materials. Truck drivers wrote passengers' names and identity-card numbers on pastel-colored forms in triplicate, on the basis of information provided orally by the passengers. Many times during my journeys, the ritual of filling out these forms would give way to laughter as passengers called out names of movie stars or politicians. The forms, with their real and made-up identities, were then given to the Civil Guard officers who manned the numerous police posts set up to intercept contraband and regulate the coca leaf trade. There, the lists accumulated in large, usually rather disorderly piles in the Civil Guard offices. Curious about these tissue-thin, rainbow-hued forms of state control, I would sometimes casually ask what was done with them. The guards assured me that they were seldom, if ever, scrutinized or read. Indeed, it was not uncommon to see some of these lists fluttering about in front of the post, or strewn in the garbage piles out back, in a very public announcement of the arbitrary character of law.

With the escalation of war in the late 1980s, the collection of passenger registries became, not surprisingly, a more serious affair. As violence and uncertainty grew, passenger lists were more intensively scrutinized by the heavily armed, fearful young recruits who manned the numerous military checkpoints that had replaced the familiar Civil Guard posts. For the frightened soldiers, the lists were reminders that an enemy—"a terrorist"—might be hiding among the peasants piled in each truck. From their point of view, the lists served as the only material site from which "identity" could be conjured, not through the science of reading—since, more often than not, the names and numbers on the lists meant nothing to the soldiers—but rather through the instinctual mechanisms of fear.

From the passengers' point of view, however, this mysterious ritual of "reading" the lists carried with it not only all the ominous uncertainty of the war but also all the tangible familiarity of the fluttering, unread, arbitrary, and shifting forms of paperwork that mark the material or lived geography of a state whose form—like the paperwork itself—is never fixed or stable. Within these uncertain geographies where a lack of documents was the most common reason for detention and where documents were often willfully misread, a personal identity card was simultaneously a peasant's only guarantee and his source of greatest vulnerability to the arbitrary power of the state.

In this chapter, I am interested in thinking about this slippage between threat and guarantee as a site along which the legitimacy of state rule is brought into contact with the sometimes arbitrary forms of power that underwrite the sanctity of law. Specifically, I want to think about this moment when the relation between rule and law is rendered tenuous and illegible as a margin in several senses of the word. First, we can think of this "site" of uncertainty as itself constituting a sort of margin along which the legitimacy of state power can be seen to unravel. Second, this "unraveling" often intensifies in those areas—such as the ones I will be discussing here—that are said to be both spatially and socially "marginal" to the nation-state. Finally, and perhaps most importantly, it is a site from which the spatializing idiom of centers and margins itself becomes illegible. In this respect, I want to think about the suspended moment in time that separates threat and guarantee as a "site" that is neither inherently spatial (as is the checkpoint itself) nor stable, as in either predictable or ideologically intentioned. Rather, it is a site that itself is only traceable through (but not equivalent with) the sorts of fleeting instances in which peasant life engages the languages, institutions, spaces, and people who represent justice and the law. In this respect, I see time and mobility as in some senses even more central than space to the twin problems of margins and the exceptions that inhabit (and constitute) those margins.

In thinking about these issues, one of my main concerns will be to question the relationship between the spatializing images and tropes through which the state lays claim to both territory and particular forms of life, and the lived experience of justice as a set of practices through which the state's claims to (territorial and social) inclusion are often rendered illegible and opaque. As an ongoing, unresolved conversation with the state, the idea of "seeking justice" is continually referred to a material geography of centers and margins. In much of the Latin Americanist literature, this geography is described in terms of the allegedly discrete spaces of local and national life. Peasants are said to "encounter" the state when they enter government offices and schools. Peasant communities are similarly imagined to exist at a cultural and social "remove" from a national culture and polity that are imagined to have a tangible (and geographically locatable) "margin" of "inclusion" and "exclusion." Peasant men are "extracted" from their localities through voluntary or forced military recruitment and are "relocated in" the national (or at least "nonlocal") spaces of capital cities, barracks, and patrols. These sorts of territorializing languages— which themselves are, of course, a product of nation-state formation— assume a centrifugal and material model of spatial relations in which a "margin" is imagined as something that can be located, crossed, expanded, or fixed as the outer edge of a given social unit. This notion of a territorial margin (together with the unshakably spatialized model of culture that haunts anthropology) informs the familiar anthropological description of peasant families, households, and communities as distant, removed, and above all marginal to a state that makes "incursions into" their lives in the form of schools, sanitary posts, and the occasional development project.

Of course, some language of spatial marginality is inevitable when speaking of communities whose lives have been constrained and reduced in often quite violent ways by a state whose administration of these populations builds on a whole slew of racial, political, and class-based assumptions about their "marginality." Indeed, "marginalization" is a powerful technique of power precisely because the margin is both a real place where roads do not penetrate, commodities seldom reach, and schools barely exist, and a discursive and ideological position from which people learn how to speak about things like justice to the state and among themselves (Tsing 1993).

What happens to our understanding of both "justice" and "the state," however, if we forget for the moment about resolution and location and focus instead on movement, temporality, and procedure? What happens if, instead of dwelling on the institutional spaces of the judiciary, we think about the endless and unpredictable circulation of juridical paperwork? What happens if, instead of locating the margin of the state somewhere between the urban and rural spaces in which peasants live, we look for it in that odd—and highly mobile—space between threat and guarantee that surfaces every time and every place a peasant hands either legal papers or documents to an agent of the state? In thinking about how the notion of "a margin" conditions people's understandings of the state, I want to focus here, not on the fixed boundaries and territories of a political-economic geography, but rather on this highly mobile, tangible, and embodied space through which the power of the state is felt as the slippage between threat and guarantee.

In discussing these issues here, I will draw on two periods of field research. The first, between 1985 and 1990, includes several periods of both extended and short-term fieldwork in the highland province of Chumbivilcas in the department of Cuzco. Most of the general arguments I offer in this chapter about the privatization of justice and the culture of *gamonalismo* are based on that fieldwork, and on the more detailed historical and ethnographic arguments I have made elsewhere about this particular form of power (Poole 1988, 1994). In the second section of the chapter, I draw on two briefer periods of fieldwork, carried out in 1999 and 2000, on the administration of justice and recent judicial reforms in the department of Ayacucho. When I speak of the broad category of "peasants," I am referring to Quechua-speaking and bilingual (Quechua-Spanish) rural producers from these two regions of Peru. Both regions share certain forms of community and economic organization. Because of poverty levels and poor institutional integration, Peruvian politicians, intellectuals, state agencies, and NGOs consider both regions to have some of the most "marginal" populations in the Peruvian nation-state. Ironically, this classification continues despite the centrality of both regions to the war between the PCP-Sendero Luminoso (PCP-SL), the MRTA, and the Peruvian armed forces (Degregori 1989; Manrique 1989; Poole and Rénique 1992; Stern 1998). As the first territory subjected to emergency power, and as the home of many of the PCP-SL's military leaders, Ayacucho suffered some of the worst human-rights violations during the twelve-year war (Americas Watch 1992; COMISEDH 1990; Comisión de la Verdad y Reconciliacion 2003; DESCO 1989; García Sayan 1987).

I begin with a brief sketch of the Peruvian legal/judicial system. I then look in more detail at the ways in which the slippery boundary between private and state law has been negotiated in two moments in the history of Peru. By tracing some of the continuities between these two rather different historical periods, I hope to show both how the tension between threat and guarantee has figured in the daily lives of Andean peasant communities and how the privatized and often violent justice of the "margins" has figured in the formation (or, more accurately, the continual refounding) of the Peruvian liberal state.

LOCATING THE MARGIN OF THE STATE

Like states discussed in other chapters of this book, the Peruvian state has been profoundly marked by its history as a colonial state. Located on the territorial margins of the Spanish colonial world, the Peruvian viceroyalty itself was, in turn, shaped by a jurisdictional logic that depended on a series of internal boundaries. The first and most important was the jurisdictional distinction between the "Republic of Spaniards" and the "Republic of Indians," each with its own legal code, modes of authority, taxation, and privileges. A second was the formidable geographic divide and distance that separated the Andes—and the even more remote Amazon jungle provinces—from the viceroyal capital of Lima on Peru's central coast. As in the other Spanish colonial states, the institutional and legal form that bridged these different spheres was the *encomienda*. In theory, the encomienda was a grant over

39

Indian labor provided to loyal Spaniards in return for their protection and conversion of the Indians to the "one true faith." Although legally the encomienda did not provide rights to land, it soon devolved into a de facto path to landholding and the eventual emergence of large and semifeudal landholdings, or haciendas. Equally important, the encomienda also served to ground the administrative and colonial state apparatus in the private dominions—and privatized spheres of power—of the indigenous nobles and Spanish *encomenderos* who administered justice, collected taxes, and otherwise regulated relations between the crown and its far-flung colonial subjects. In this respect, the private appropriation of public or state functions can be said to form the historical bedrock of the Peruvian state and judicial system.[1]

Peru gained its independence from Spain in 1821 after a prolonged war in which the country's elites actively resisted any threat to their political and economic privileges as part of the Spanish Empire. During the war with Spain and the ensuing struggle to define Peru's republican identity, the principal factor shaping both politics and the landscape of power in Peru was an intense—and growing—rift between the interests and resources of the coastal capital of Lima and the less prosperous and frequently more progressive regional elites from provinces outside the capital city (Gootenberg 1989; O'Phelan 2001; Walker 1999).

This rift was to have important and lasting implications for the relation between private power and the administration of justice in republican Peru. Indeed, Peru's first constitution, written just two years after independence, sanctified this polarizing divide as a key feature of Peruvian governance. The constitution—and those that followed—provided for a highly centralized government (located in Lima) that would be forever divided between the competing discourses of sovereignty proper to its executive and parliamentary branches. While the executive branch, as in other Bolivarian states, was granted extensive powers of emergency legislative decree, the elected parliament appealed to an explicitly Rousseauian doctrine of popular sovereignty (Aljovín de Losada 2000; Basadre 1997; Loveman 1993; Planas 1998; Stuart 1925).

This language of popular sovereignty integral to the Peruvian constitutional order was intimately and uneasily related to another language of community—in particular, the "natural" or foundational communities of indigenous subjects who formed the vast majority of the population. Although nineteenth-century liberal reforms abolished the distinctive juridical convention of the indigenous republic and outlawed the collective property rights that constituted the basis of the nation's "natural communities" of indigenous subjects, indigenous communities remained until 1855 the basis for collecting the head taxes that helped to finance the liberal state. In this way, the semiautonomous juridical, productive, and political spheres of the indigenous communities came to form both the fiscal basis of the Peruvian state and the perceptual margins of its national "civilization."

In terms of a *spatial* language for representing the nation, then, liberal talk about citizenship and civilization has produced an image of Peru as a nested set of dual oppositions pitting the Creole coast against the indigenous highlands, the civilizing center against the savage periphery. At the center of this imagined state was a national government whose claims to sovereign authority rested on its supposedly exclusive right to make and enforce laws and, in the case of the executive branch, declare states of exception. This claim to sovereignty, however, was rendered curiously illegible by the ways in which the state's own judicial apparatus came to depend on the very forms of natural community and private justice that were spoken of as simultaneously foundational and antecedent to the state. Since the first constitution of 1823, this judicial system has been formed of, essentially, four levels: a supreme court located in Lima; a shifting number of superior courts located in the most important departmental capitals; judges of first instance located in important provincial capitals; and, finally, a unique network of local justices of the peace whose powers range from routine administrative functions (marriage and titling) to the resolution of local disputes and discretionary control of which cases pass on to higher courts (Comisión Andina de Juristas 1999; Instituto de Defensa Legal 1999, 2000).

Today, justices of the peace account for 72 percent of the magistrates in Peru (Comisión Andina de Juristas 1999:9). They are clearly the judicial offices (and officers) with which most Peruvians have the most contact. A significant number of cases, however, are sent on for consideration by higher courts. Thus, although peasants may not often have personal experience with (or in) the spaces and procedures of the higher instances, they understand that their claims do circulate through spaces and procedures "out there" in Lima or the departmental capital. When speaking of this procedure of "advancing" cases to a higher level of authority, peasants borrow the Spanish legal term *deriver,* meaning "to derive" (as in the derivation of a word), as well as "to drift" or "to change course." Indeed, as we will see, the vast majority of legal cases that are "directed" to the next level of the judicial apparatus do indeed seem to drift more or less aimlessly from one office to the next, before finally being returned, unresolved and often years later, to their points of origin.[2]

This image of "drift" is made all the more remarkable by the fact that, like the rest of the Peruvian state, the judiciary is extremely centralized. Appointments at all levels, from supreme court justices to judges of first instance, pass through the executive branch. Justices of the peace are appointed by their corresponding superior courts. In most cases, appointments in the upper courts are for life. At the same time, the judiciary's formal structure provides for a good deal of autonomy on several levels—at least on paper. Justices of the peace and judges of first instance, for example, have discretionary power to direct, or not direct, cases to higher levels of the system.

In many cases, the relative autonomy granted to local judges (and justices) has fostered a sort of de facto—but, until the constitutional reforms of 1993, legally unacknowledged—form of legal pluralism (Brandt 1986; Pásara 1982; Peña Jumpa 1998; Rivadeneyra Sánchez 1991). Justices of the peace are specifically mandated to draw on community tradition to resolve local disputes (Comisión Andina de Juristas 1999, 2000; Inter-American Development Bank 1997:2; Instituto de Defensa Legal 1999, n.d.; Ministerio de Justicia del Perú 2000; Pásara 1979). Because there was no constitutional or codified provision for how (or which) "traditions" should be applied and interpreted, however, in practice, the individual men who held these posts exercised considerable discretionary power over how particular offenses and disputes would or would not be punished.[3]

In the more remote highland regions—including the two where I have worked—the all-important offices of justice of the peace were dominated until recently, not by members of peasant communities with some claim to collective tradition, but rather by men from powerful local merchant or landholding families. As a result, the justices' personal networks of economic and political power were, more often than not, one and the same with the juridical jurisdictions assigned to them as officers of the state. In these cases, the arena of "tradition" upon which judicial authorities drew frequently involved personalized (and, to be sure, "illegal") forms of physical and economic coercion (Manrique 1988; Poole 1988; Pásara 1979). The "shadow" cast by this de facto blurring of "impartial" judicial punishment and personalized or extrajudicial violence was expanded (or perhaps the appropriate metaphor is "darkened") by the fact that justices of the peace and judges of first instance often acted as representatives of several different instances of the state, as well as representatives of the moneyed individuals and families against whom peasants most often sought redress in their legal cases.[4]

It is here, where the discursive (and legal) separation of functions, persons, and offices breaks down, and where the extrajudicial, violent, or private origins of the law become visible, that I seek to locate the "margins" of the state. In many cases, this "frontier" between the legal and extralegal corresponds with territories whose economies and populations might be construed as residing at a physical distance from the centers of political and economic power. In other cases, however, this frontier runs through the very heart of those offices, institutions, and individuals who seem to embody the very center of the central state.

In my previous work, I have attempted to unpack this idea of the margin or frontier through a consideration of the figure of the *gamonal*. Derived from the name of a vigorous high-mountain or tundra plant that grows through parasitic runners and roots, the *gamonal* is most succinctly defined as a highly personalized form of local power whose authority is grounded in nearly equal measure in his control of local economic resources (Burga and Flores Galindo 1987; Mariátegui 1925), political access to the state, willingness to use violence (Manrique 1988), and the symbolic capital provided by his association with such important icons of masculinity as livestock, horses, and a regional bohemian aesthetic (de la Cadena 2000; Poole 1988, 1994).

The particular feature of the gamonal that I want to underscore, however, is his historical status as representative of both the state and the principal forms of private, extrajudicial, and even criminal power that the state purportedly seeks to displace through law, citizenship, and public administration. Thus, gamonales in the regions where I did my fieldwork would commonly rule in two apparently distinct landscapes of power—the traditional agrarian estate, where the gamonal served as magistrate, police officer, and jailer, and the modern liberal state, where the same man often served as legislative representative and civilizing agent for the "primitive" (and for the most part disenfranchised) indigenous populations who formed the majority in his home district.

Elsewhere I have focused on the performative aspects of both violence and masculinity as defining features of a regime of power that is attached, in important symbolic as well as material ways, to the body (and person) of the gamonal. Here I would like to pull away from the person of the gamonal himself and focus more closely on the mercurial qualities of gamonalismo as a site that reveals the place of the margin in the logic of the state. Peruvian intellectuals, politicians, and urban people in general have long seen both the gamonal and gamonalismo as evocative symbols of the dangers and illicit and excessive forms of power believed to lurk along the territorial and political frontiers of the Peruvian nation-state. Thus, during the 1920s and 1930s, highland middle-class and mestizo intellectuals known as *indigenistas,* as well as socialist intellectuals in Lima (Mariátegui 1925), denounced gamonal violence. Half a century later, gamonalismo was a rhetorical and political target for the left-wing military government of General Velasco Alvarado. More recently, the authoritarian culture of gamonalismo has been cited as a factor contributing to the political violence of the 1980s (Degregori 1989; Manrique 1989; Poole ed. 1994; Poole and Rénique 1992).

Today, to speak of—or to accuse someone of—gamonalismo is to speak of a type of illicit force that is at once vaguely "premodern," uncontrolled, and shamefully rude (that is, uncivilized). In Cuzco, these qualities are emphasized by comparing the gamonal to the more "cultured" or "decent" landowners who govern their lands and peons without excess. The quality of rudeness forms the center of the gamonal's mythic persona in two senses for the bilingual (and "bicultural") gamonal—as I have argued elsewhere at greater length (Poole 1988)—incorporating both the idea of the indigenous primitive (or

"natural man") whose state of nature precedes the state, and the countervailing mystique of the illicit criminal whose power somehow
escapes the "long arm" of the state. At the same time, it was the
gamonal who historically monopolized access to the national state, in
the form of appointed offices (for example, subprefecture) and even as
elected parliamentary representatives.[5]

I want to focus for a minute on the rudeness of the gamonal and,
by extension, that form of power known in Peru as gamonalismo. As a
personal characteristic, "rudeness" suggests both ignorance (or lack of
education) and an exceptional sense of self-centeredness (or lack of
civility). Both position the gamonal and the form of power he represents somewhere just outside the acceptable boundaries of social
behavior. In the language most often used to denigrate persons of both
gamonal and rural origins in general, he is denied the status of a
"decent" person. As Marisol de la Cadena (2000) has argued, the label
"decent" (decente) carries a heavy racial load in the Peruvian Andes. Not
to be recognized as decente is to be at once unsocialized and dark,
rural and Indian, unwashed and impure. In addition to its racial connotations, however, lack of decency also connotes lack of civility and
thus a certain distance—though not exclusion—from the social contract that makes up "decent" society. Rudeness, moreover, can be either
unintended (through ignorance) or intentional (through arrogance).
It can refer to either the savage, as a person who has not yet entered the
social state, or the individualist, as someone who has deliberately
removed himself from the constraints of social manners.

It is precisely this ambiguous mixture of threatening savagery and
seductive individualism that forms the mystique (and threat) of the
gamonal. Once we read this character back onto the gamonal's equally
ambivalent role in the constitution of the Peruvian state in its territorial
hinterlands, it becomes possible to imagine the gamonal as somehow
both originary of the state (as in the "state of nature" that precedes and
stands opposed to the state) and threatening to it (as in that ultimate
individual, the criminal) (see Benjamin [1978] 1986).[6] As judge or justice of the peace, the gamonal embodies the state, yet he also marks the
spot where the state's rationality and jurisdiction fade into the uncon-
trollable (and unseen, hence secret) dominions of extrajudicial force
and violence. At the same time, in his "other" role as local authority,

45

judge, or schoolteacher, the gamonal is very much a part of the ongoing, day-to-day constitution of "the state."

PRIVATE JUSTICE AND THE JURIDICAL STATE

The originary and boundary-marking qualities of classic gamonalismo emerge clearly in a 1920s judicial case from Ayacucho. In the case, Samuel Torres, a nonindigenous rancher from Chapi in the district of Chunqui (La Mar Province, department of Ayacucho), attempted to press charges against the *hacendado* Hernan Carrillo for the crime of whipping (ADA 1920). The case, which lasted for nearly a decade, is interesting primarily for what it tells us about the rather byzantine administrative histories of such cases. The first denuncia was addressed in April 1920 to the prefect of the department of Ayacucho, whose seat was in the departmental capital of Huamanga (Ayacucho). In detailing the charges, Torres tells of the various abuses he allegedly suffered at the hands of Hernan, "son of don Benjamin Carrillo, hacendado of Chapi." According to Torres, Carrillo entered his ranch along with seven other men. Then, Torres continues:

> [W]ithout giving me any motive, Carrillo ordered that I be arrested, an order that was carried out by his accomplices, who made use of the firearms they carried with them to threaten me with shots. Once seized in the corridor of my house, I was dragged by Carrillo and his accomplices to the patio where they laid me on the ground and whipped me villainously, as the medical certificate that accompanies this document attests. (ADA 1920:f. 3v)

The men then stole a horse, pocketknife, and revolver from Torres. Torres also denounces Zaragosa Aspur as the "instigator of the criminal acts" and requests that the "penal sanction also be brought to bear on her, so that she might return to me the gray mule that belongs to me and which had been unduly *[indebidamente]* dispatched to Chapi by [another accused man] Avelino Nuñez, because the said beast is still there on her ranch." He then comments that "my own attempts to get them to mount an investigation in Chungui have been sterile because of the influence [*ascendiente* or ascendancy] that Carrillo has over this district" (ADA 1920:f. 3v).

In Torres's accusation against Carrillo, the lawmaking power of the gamonal is all too clear. Carrillo, who holds no office, is said to "arrest" Torres and to head a band of accomplices who act as his "deputies" and punish Torres for some offense. Carrillo is also portrayed as having a firm hold—or great "ascendance"—over the entire judicial and state apparatus of the region:

> Because Sr. Fiscal, as you know, the political and judicial authorities are held in sway by those who impose themselves with the title of gamonales who are those who subjugate the laws of the land *[avasallan las leyes patrias]*. As a result of the unfounded fears of these *[gamonales]* I have been unable to get the justice of the peace in Chungui to carry out his duty by taking any measures in my complaint. For that reason I then went to the capital of La Mar, traveling more than thirty leagues, but there too I was unable to obtain justice from the local authorities who claimed that the law was new, that the Subprefect did not know about it [the law], that the Judge of First Instance did not exist, that the Town Mayor was absent, and thus that nobody could hear my case. From that state of despair, I arrived to this city [Huamanga] dragging myself along after the whipping, and I went to the Fiscal Agent who informed me that he was not required to denounce deeds that were not done in his jurisdiction, and that I should therefore return to La Mar and file my charges with the Fiscal Agent of La Mar, an office that does not even exist. That is my despair: that justice does not reach me *[no me alcance justicia]*. (ADA 1920:ff.11-1v)

The route followed by Torres's case is both complex and highly typical. To give a quick idea of the case's course: The day after charges were filed in the prefect's dispatch in Huamanga, the case was remanded to the subprefect in La Mar (a journey that would have taken several days at best in 1929). This subprefect then ordered the governor of the Chungui District to "gather the animals and things taken by Don Hernan Carrillo and send this evidence to the Judge of the First Instance so that he might organize a hearing." In the meantime, Torres filed more paperwork, increasing the charges against

Zaragoza and adding to the list of his stolen property. Torres next approached the public prosecutor (*fiscal*) in the superior court in Huamanga, only to have his case again returned to the judge in La Mar. This judge, in turn, wrote to the subprefect (in La Mar) that the accused did not belong to his jurisdiction (Chungui) and that he thus required a special order from the subprefect to act on the case. The papers were then sent to the governor of Chungui, where they rested untouched for nearly a year before being sent once again to the superior court in Huamanga. The superior court then directed the case back to the justice of the peace in Chungui, who directed it to the judge of the first instance in Ayacucho, stating that "the personnel in this dispatch excuse themselves from the case because of spiritual relations [that is, *compadrazgo*] with the accused, Hernan Carrillo."

The case follows a similar itinerary over the next eight years, moving back and forth no fewer than twenty times between Ayacucho and La Mar, where it circulates among virtually all the authorities of that province. At all levels, the *expediente's* routings, or "driftings," include not only judicial authorities but also such administrative officials as subprefects and prefects, none of whom fulfill any explicit judicial role. Finally, in April 1926, six years after the events in question, Torres writes that he has been unable to get a single person to testify against Carrillo, "because as a feared gamonal in the highland regions of Chapi, Chungi and other places, he impedes [*dificulta*] the appearance of witnesses by threatening to inflict all sorts of harm to them [if they testify]. They are terrified by his conduct and his antecedents are hateful [*destestables*]" (ADA 1920:f.61). In February 1927, Torres's case is then raised for a fifth, and final, time to the superior court, where it remains, untouched, until October 1929, at which time it is *archivado* (closed without resolution).[7]

During the nine years that elapsed between Torres's first *denuncia* and its "archiving," Torres's case "drifted," at least once, through every instance of the Ayacucho state government. This "drift" was propelled, in large part, by fear of a gamonal who, far from having to "direct" the documents along their path, needed only to sit in Chungui and allow the papers to move along their course. Because Carrillo was a feared gamonal, his "lawmaking" powers were largely reactive and hence officially invisible. The passive (or deflective) agency of the gamonal surfaces most clearly in the testimony of witnesses who respond to questioning about Carrillo's crime by speaking of other, local cycles of robbery and animal theft. Thus, when asked about the incident in question, witnesses respond with detailed accounts of either their own complaints about animals that have been stolen by Torres or others, or their own understanding of a cycle in which Carrillo robs from Torres, who robs from Zaragoza, who robs from Carrillo, and so on. Rather than opt for silence, the witnesses in Torres's case answer in the local language of vengeance—what Kant calls the "reciprocal justice" that exists in nature. In this way, they hope perhaps to deflect the accusations against the feared Carrillo, while at the same time sneaking in a plea for the return of their own stolen livestock. Two points are worth emphasizing here. First, none of the witnesses refer to the criminal charges of whipping and robbery being brought against Carrillo in this case (and about which they were interrogated). Instead, the witnesses undertake their own sort of "directing" (or "detouring") of the case away from the feared Carrillo.

Second, it is precisely this "detouring" or avoidance of the gamonal that causes the charges to loop back against Torres himself so that in the end, *Carrillo* is able to construct a defense that includes criminal charges against *Torres* for the theft of Carrillo's (and others') animals. As with the passenger lists with which I began this chapter, Torres's legal paperwork quickly slips into that uneasy space between threat and guarantee. By accepting and recording the testimony as evidence supporting the justice of Carrillo's "arrest" of Torres, the administrative and knowledge-gathering power of the state incorporates and partially legitimizes the ulterior logic of a judicial culture based on reciprocal acts of "self-made" justice. Such reversals of justice were common at the time. In other legal cases I have reviewed from the Cuzco and Ayacucho archives, it was not at all uncommon for those filing the original charges to end up doing time in jail.

Peruvian national imagination (and the state's own representations of itself) conceives of jurisdictions like Chungui where gamonales ruled (and in many instances still rule) as hinterlands lying just beyond some imaginary boundary of the state. The nation-state, in other words, is conceived of as a centralized administrative and political community whose density decreases as one moves toward its territorial margins and

49

away from the administrative centers of Lima and the departmental capitals. What such cases as Torres's make clear, however, is that the gamonal's power lies precisely in his ability to reach across the distinct jurisdictional boundaries that define the nested territorial structure of the state. Indeed, the "long arm" of gamonal power is closely allied with—and, in some cases, one and the same with—the "long arm" of the law. From the gamonal's (and the peasants') perspective, then, there is little distinction between the margin and the center of the juridical state: for the gamonal, the essence of "law" resides in its necessary privatization and, hence, infraction, just as the sovereign's power resides in the exception. Seen from this perspective, the "law" as a guarantor of rights always already contains within it the threat of an arbitrary power even when physical violence may not be present.

Within liberalism, both the state and its law are explained and justified by reference to the mythical history of emergence and transformation that occur when individuals come together to form society and leave the "state of nature." This point of origin is not just inscribed in the annals of liberal theory. It surfaces each time the intimate relation between law and enforcement, between the rationalism of juridical procedure and the violence of the state, between the person of the objective judge and the punishing person of the jailer, is brought into consciousness. As one prominent liberal theorist put it while writing about the necessary grounding of law in violence, "Every legal order must conceive of itself as emerging out of that which is itself unlawful" (Cover 1995:118). Indeed, Kant himself, who was very clear that the origins of justice and law lay in what he called "reciprocal coercion," cautions us regarding the inherent danger of dwelling on this point of origin. "The origin of the supreme authority," Kant writes, "is not open to scrutiny by the people who are subject to it....Whether as historical fact, an actual contract...originally preceded the submission to authority or whether, instead, the authority preceded it and the law only came later or even is supposed to have followed in this order—these are pointless questions that threaten the state with danger if they are asked" (Kant [1797] 1965:84).

As a form of private and partial power that constitutes "law," "authority," and "sanction" at the margins of the public and "impartial" state, gamonalismo raises this secret of the coercive (or lawless) origins of power in the juridical state. At the same time, as Torres's case makes clear, gamonalismo is also rooted in the forms and language of juridical and legal process. It is therefore neither an alternative form of sovereignty that exists "beyond" the margins of the state nor a sovereign power that either mimics or "contaminates" the state—for both these terms imply a point of departure that is somehow exterior to the state. Rather, this relationship between the Peruvian state and its violent, extrajudicial, primitive, or natural "margins" is simultaneously both *accepted* and *denied* as a more or less constant and central feature of the judiciary, and indeed of "the state" in general. To return to my opening question, we might say that this double assertion is made each time the order "to present your documents" is issued (and understood) as both a threat and a guarantee.

RECONFIGURING THE MARGINS

As a recognized form of local power, gamonalismo flourished in the 1920s, 1930s, and 1940s, when highland landowners exerted a notable influence in the national parliament. As "politicians," the gamonales were accepted in the civil life of the nation; as "landlords" and local rulers, they were exiled to the far-off reaches of the indigenous highlands. Moreover, in both political discourse and the public imagination, the spatial distancing of gamonalismo was matched by its removal in time to a "premodern" era, when abusive, private power had not yet been replaced by the bureaucratic rationality of an idealized modern state. Thus, gamonalismo was widely understood as a problem that would be eliminated by the eventual modernization and territorial consolidation of the administrative state. Successive state reforms targeted the abuses of the gamonales, most dramatically in the early 1970s when the military government headed by General Juan Velasco Alvarado effected an agrarian reform whose principal rhetorical and ideological target was gamonalismo. By eliminating large landholdings and abusive local powers, Velasco promised to rationalize production and attain equity in the distribution of land. In short, by targeting gamonalismo, the military reformers hoped to modernize a state in which private interests were seen to dominate over the common public good. In isolating the gamonales as "premodern" and hence exterior to the modern state, however, the military reformers failed to address the protean forms that such modes of power assume in response to shifting state priorities and agendas. Thus, although agrarian reform was widely believed to have put an end to gamonalismo, strikingly similar forms of privatized, abusive, and violent authority remain at the core of public life and political practice. In many highland districts, for example, descendants (or replicas) of gamonales have retained their hold on local power through the administrative, political, and ideological (educational) positions they hold within the Peruvian state (Poole 1994).

Velasco was not the only state reformer to target such forms of local, "premodern" power. Similar concerns with eliminating privatized forms of power and privilege have driven the continual demands and projects for modernization of the judicial system in Peru. Although the judiciary, as a set of institutions and procedures, has in many respects been one of the most stable components of the modern Peruvian state, it has nonetheless been a permanently contested site of state and lawmaking. It has, for example, been a recurring target for reforms aimed at eliminating the corruption and privilege through which this intimate association of public power and private interest becomes visible.

The most recent and in some respects the most radical such reform was scripted as part of the sweeping neoliberal reforms of the 1980s and 1990s. In documents charged with the moral language of rooting out corruption and decay, US-AID, the Inter-American Development Bank, and the World Bank spearheaded reforms in two areas. They moved to "streamline" the administration of justice in the twenty-six superior courts located in Lima and the larger departmental capitals. This was to be accomplished by modernizing obsolete organizational structures, separating administrative and judicial tasks, and depoliticizing the appointment of judges and the judiciary (Inter-American Development Bank 1997; Ministerio de Justicia del Perú 1994; USAID 1999). As interpreted by the Fujimori regime (1990–2000), however, this well-meaning move to make justice "more efficient" resulted in the de facto control of judicial appointments and procedures by an increasingly authoritarian executive branch. This aspect of the judicial reform has been the subject of much public discussion and debate, both under Fujimori and during the democratically elected government of Alejandro Toledo (García Sayan 1996; Ortíz de Cevallos 1999).[8]

In addition to streamlining judicial procedure in the higher courts, recent judicial reforms have also called for expanding "judicial coverage" to the approximately one-third of the population who in 1997 were considered to lack adequate access to the national judicial system (Inter-American Development Bank 1997:2). To address this problem, the reforms envisioned the creation of new arenas of arbitration that would be overseen by the national judiciary but would not be directly part of it. In urban areas, the government and its international sponsors created Conciliation Centers modeled on US and British experiments in neighborhood dispute mediation (Fitzpatrick 1988; Harrington 1985). In rural areas, the reforms moved to replace or complement the traditional justices of the peace with newly devised (or revised, depending on the region) systems of customary law and community-based dispute resolution. While the apparent intent behind both proposals was to provide increased access to justice by allowing poor people to bypass the national judicial system for petty claims and local disputes, the end result appears to be the creation of a shadow legal system that is both of and not of the state.

Several things interest me about this latest round of attempts to eradicate corruption and inefficiency from the Peruvian judicial system. The first concerns the ways in which the reforms articulate understandings of the jurisdictional and conceptual boundaries of the state and its law. One of the reformers' primary concerns, for example, has been to provide a more solid institutional framework for the 3,700 justices of the peace who handle the great bulk of Peru's petty claims, local disputes, and domestic violence cases. In framing their arguments for how and why the *justicia de paz* should be reformed, however, proponents of reform argue that the justices' *separation* from the state must be overcome:

> The functioning of this judicial service [that is, the justicia de paz] occurs in the most remote places in the country, where the State, through its Judicial Power, has not managed to institutionalize the ordinary system of administration of justice. This gap has traditionally been covered by community authorities, having evolved to the point of legal recognition of the figure of Justice of the Peace in the Provisional Statute decreed by General Jose de San Martin on October 8, 1821.
> (Comisión Andina de Juristas 2000:9)

The point the reformers miss here is that the "ordinary system of administration of justice" is, in fact (and *by law*), grounded on the ambiguous jurisdictional and legal status of justices of the peace who act necessarily as representatives of both "public" and "private" justice.

My second point of concern has to do with the reforms' base in a new calculus of exclusion and their consequent move away from the older paradigm of modernization. According to this more familiar understanding of development, state building was "about" the need to progressively incorporate marginalized territories and populations into the modern center of the state (and its capitalist economy). In this view of the state and development, the "margin" represents a zone of instability and danger precisely because it lies outside both the control and territory of the national state. For modernization theorists, the solution to this problem was a simple one: the state would progressively cannibalize and modernize these areas. In recent neoliberal reforms, however, this dynamic of inclusion has been effectively reversed. As in earlier reform projects, development agencies have unveiled the public secret that the poor do not receive justice in the national judicial system. Rather than move to reform the system to make it more inclusive and hence "just," the new generation of reform projects suggests that poor people should be asked to avoid the judicial system as a court of first instance and to turn instead to a network of "informal" dispute-resolution centers with hazily defined ties to the national judicial and legal system.

These reforms, however, conceived in Washington and Lima, are implemented in territories with historical traditions of jurisdiction, procedure, and governance that are, as we have seen, already both at odds with and deeply embedded in the judicial structure of the state. Given this landscape and historical experience, the very claim that offices or officials are enacting "justice" or making "decisions" that will not be shared with "the state" is rendered unintelligible. In addition, as we have seen, even the basic principle of justice is, for many people, best understood as the modes of anxiety and indistinction that separate the security of the state as a guarantor of rights from the uncertainty of the state as enforcer of law. In sanctioning the move toward informal models of justice, the judicial reform reconfigures these traditional spaces of indistinction as part of a new political order in which exclusion from the state is made to appear as an asset, a means through which justice can be more readily obtained. Thus, for example, both urban and rural reforms are designed as "informal branches" of the state judicial system.[9] Many Conciliation Centers, for example, are actually located in offices either within or adjacent to (or known to belong to) the judicial branch. Yet, as voluntary "reconciliation" centers, they do not share the powers of enforcement that mark the judiciary as an arm of the state. Their relationship to the law is thus reminiscent of the private forms of "self-made" or "reciprocal" justice that have always been configured as anterior to the state. At the same time, it is known that they do contain a certain ill-defined institutional relationship with the law of the state.

These forms of ambiguity emerge in different ways in the urban and rural projects implemented in Ayacucho as part of the judicial reform process. The urban project was implemented in response to the national Law of Extrajudicial Conciliation (Ley de conciliación extrajudicial, law number 26872; on the application of this law in Ayacucho, see Arce Vilar and del Solar Retamozo 1998), mandating the creation of conciliation processes for informal and extrajudicial dispute resolution. The resulting centers are like petty claims courts. Cases are resolved through mediation, and both sides of the dispute must agree to the terms and sign a document stipulating the terms of the agreement. Lawyers or trained paralegals (mostly university students) act as mediators. The Centro de Conciliación (APENAC) where I worked in Huamanga handled two types of cases: *judiciales* and *extrajudiciales*. The former were cases that could have qualified for hearing in the state judicial system; the latter included cases that never would have become formal judicial cases. In many instances, they were cases the superior court had "directed" to APENAC. The overwhelming majority of both types of cases involved complaints of domestic violence against women and failure to provide child support. The national courts were thus freed from the escalating load of domestic violence hearings, while women, the most frequent victims of this form of criminal violence, were shuttled into a system where no legal sanctions could be brought against their attackers.[10]

Because conciliation hearings and agreements do not bear the sanction of the law (or, in the case of the urban Conciliation Centers where there is no formal sense of community at work, any sanction whatsoever), APENAC personnel are required by law to do follow-up "home visits" to check whether stipulations agreed to in mediation are being met. This requirement turns out to be the biggest problem for APENAC workers, who observed that "these sort of people tend to move a lot," both within the city and between the city and the country-side. Several workers noted that people intentionally gave false addresses.

This urge to hide is heightened by people's very clear understand-ing that although APENAC presents itself as a nonjudicial institution, it is logistically and institutionally connected to the superior court, which oversees its operations and houses its main office. APENAC workers told me that people "are afraid of the institution [APENAC]...because they confuse us with the judiciary *[poder judicial]*." Thus, for people liv-ing—and moving—in the poor neighborhoods of Ayacucho, the effort to create sequestered forms of informal mediation separate from the state actually results in a greater contamination by the state. It is no secret that the mediation centers have been created by the judiciary and are therefore a "part" of the judiciary. Even for people who might otherwise not hesitate to file litigation in the court system, entry into a reconciliation center with no observable legal status smacks of other, more familiar forms of justice. As one couple explained to me, the APENAC offices "reminded" them of the judicial offices in their provin-cial hometown. Here, of course, a key issue is the familiarity of the spaces themselves, with their institutional furnishing, didactic wall hangings, and sharp division between public spaces and secret cham-bers. Another is the idea that justice is necessarily and always both of and not of the state. APENAC's claims to autonomy from the state thus become illegible to people for whom "justice" has always occupied the slippery space between threat and guarantee.

Similar forums for promoting dispute arbitration have been imple-mented in rural Ayacucho, where reforms coincided with a broader set of initiatives designed to "reinsert the state" after a twelve-year war dur-ing which nearly 90 percent of Peru's highland population lived under special states of emergency. The cumulative effects of living under mili-tary rule affected understandings of community in many subtle—and not so subtle—ways. Local authorities—who were once controlled by strict community hierarchies and traditional systems of rotating positions of authority—often continued to assert special powers even after the lifting of the emergency. Other communities split along religious lines, due to the greatly increased presence of Protestant sects after the war (Gamarra 2000). Finally, many communities emerged from the war with the armed vigilante, or *ronda,* organizations that had been formed to control incursions of Shining Path militants and military (Coronel 1999a, 1999b; Degregori et al. 1996). Following the war, the rondas—renamed "Auto-Development Committees" in an attempt to deflate their obvious political and jurisdictional autonomy from the state—took over much of the daily work of enforcing social and moral order in the communities. Like other forms of "customary law" in the region, the rondas, which modeled their policing, organizing, and modes of address on those used by the national armed forces, based their particular form of power on their claims to be both of and not of the state. The forms of legal transgression intrinsic to police enforcement (Benjamin [1978] 1986; Derrida 1992; Taussig 1996) were thus, in the case of the rondas, magnified by their position within two ambiguously connected, yet conceptually distinct legal landscapes.

Within this complex political landscape, one of the most successful projects for the reinvention of community-based justice was the Nucleos Rurales de Administracion de Justicia, or NURAJ, put together by IPAZ, a local NGO in Ayacucho, with funding from the World Bank, British Council, US-AID, and PAR (Fujimori's agency for assisting populations displaced by the war) (IPAZ n.d., 1998). I worked at a NURAJ in a "resistant community" of approximately 10,000 people in the Huanta highlands.[11] Because of its proximity to a principal Shining Path corridor, the community was severely affected by the war. Many people left for the cities. Others remained, sleeping in caves or in their fields. Today, community members refer to the war euphemistically as "the time of problems" *(la época de los problemas).* Among other things, this time serves as a sort of judicial black hole, during which much of the legal paperwork, documentation, and community records simply disappeared. Indeed, every case I heard argued in the NURAJ included problems with paperwork (titles, deeds, documents) that had been either intentionally destroyed or lost during the war. In theory, the NURAJ meets once a week, on market day when more people are in the town center. In 2000 it was headed by seven men and two women from surrounding communities.[12] The most common types of litigations the NURAJ heard were child support cases (involving principally payment of food), animal theft cases, and land disputes (Coronel 2000b; IPAZ n.d.).

The NURAJ itself was housed in a wing of the Community House *(Casa Comunal)*, established in the main residence of an old hacienda. The NURAJ was thus physically associated with both the collective space of (local) governance and, perhaps more importantly, the private spaces of the gamonal who, until the mid-1970s, had once controlled the community's labor and land. Beyond its obvious symbolic association with the form of "justice" controlled previously by the gamonal, when speaking about the NURAJ, people often mentioned its fixed location. Before the war, disputes were resolved in situ by community authorities. As one man explained to me, "In the older customs, the authorities *[varayuq]* walked from field to field, and it was there, in the place of the offense, that they solved whatever problem came up." Now, he continued, "the written documents come to the NURAJ [and pass] in front of authorities who represent both the state and the community." Rather than physically trace boundaries—as in the older practice of walking the boundaries while resolving disputes—in the new "tradition," jurisdiction is marked by documents that move in and out of the NURAJ and through the hands of its authorities. Indeed, in people's descriptions of legal cases, "justicia" and the movement of paperwork were clearly linked. The NURAJ's work was described to me as "piling up [or gathering] papers" *(juntando papeles)*. Although NURAJ leaders consciously and purposively avoided forwarding cases to higher judicial instances, in the NURAJ cases I heard, the most common outcome was to send people off to the city in search of paperwork issued by the state and without which the NURAJ could not resolve the cases. As with the urban Conciliation Centers, the NURAJ cannot resolve cases if both parties are not present (compared to the state judicial system, in which cases can be resolved without litigants present).

The NURAJ's principal tie to the state judiciary thus centers on the paperwork itself. The other link, of course, is NURAJ members' references to laws in the civil and penal codes when deciding cases. NURAJ authorities are instructed to administer justice according to "customary laws," at the same time being careful not to violate the civil and penal codes. They are not, however, empowered to enforce these laws. Nor do they openly interpret them in the proceedings, although, in the cases I observed, they did frequently refer to them by number and page. In all cases, copies of the penal and civil codes were visible on the table that separated "judges" from litigants.

As in the Torres case discussed above, claims brought to the NURAJ are often "resolved" (or derailed) through inclusion of other accusations. One land dispute, for example, was "resolved" after it devolved into another set of accusations against the principal defendant, Don Pablo, "who has another problem to solve, because when he was drunk at the fiesta he fell and on falling, broke don Erasmo's violin. That's why the owner of the violin is also here with us." In the state legal system, these two cases, which the NURAJ ruled on jointly, would have had to be filed separately and through different channels.

Other disputes over land rentals center on incorrectly executed documents. In one such case, over a rent-to-buy agreement *(anticresis),* the document itself was found to be "missing a key clause, because that person who copied the document did a miswriting *[hizo un tinterillada]*." *(Tinterilladas*—from the Spanish *tinta,* meaning "ink"—are made both easier and more common by the language barrier separating Quechua-speaking peasants from the Spanish legalese in which the petty scribes known as *tinterrillos* write their documents.) Because the original "had been burnt in the time of problems," the claimants were ordered to go to Huanta for additional corrected copies. "You have to come here with your document in hand," resolved the NURAJ authorities. "Everything here is done under the cover of a document *[todo se hace bajo un documento]*."

CONCLUSIONS

I began this chapter by thinking about the tense unity of threat and guarantee that emerges each time a peasant is ordered to show personal documents. I have ended by asking what "law" and "justice" mean for peasants being asked to enforce a form of community whose juridical status is both excluded from and dependent on the state. It is precisely in these sorts of opaque semantic and cultural domains, where threats bleed into guarantees and "community" is made to straddle the line between the judicial and the outlawed, that we should look for the link between the margins of the state and the particular regimes of sovereignty, citizenship, and regulation through which the state defines and controls its territories and populations. For many peasants with whom I have worked, the idea of a *unified* state seems to be most intimately experienced in the procedures and channels through which juridical paperwork circulates. As they well know, these familiar routines of judicial procedure, paperwork, and oral denuncias (official complaints made to police or the courts) take place along the same deeply historical divide through which the modern, efficient, and juridical procedures of the state are differentiated from the traditional, inefficient, and extrajudicial practices associated with tradition, community, and the periphery of the state. In this respect, these juridical forms are inseparable from the shadows cast by the forms of violent authority and privatized power through which public interest and the law have historically been enforced.

Peasants who enter into legal disputes are shuttled back and forth between different instances of the Peruvian judicial system. They are accustomed to hearing that the legal papers in which they have placed their trust and invested their resources are invalid because the scribe, lawyer, or notary who drew them up did so incorrectly. As anyone who has perused the legal archives of highland Peru can well imagine, many peasants would be surprised to learn that legal cases can, in fact, be resolved—rather than simply archived (or closed) for reasons having to do with either private "influence" or some seemingly arbitrary judicial time limit. Indeed, in one study conducted in the late 1980s, a vast majority of highland peasants who were or had been involved in legal cases declared that they simply did not know whether their cases had been resolved (Pásara 1988:84). For these rural aspirants to justice, legal suits are things filed in person and at great cost. Once legal documents leave the local setting of scribes, legal advisers, and notaries, however, their course through the Peruvian judicial network is at once mysterious and beyond the control of those filing the suits. Justice, in other words, is a "right" that proceeds, as it were, on its own (and sometimes forever), but only rarely does it come back to benefit one's own family or life.

In such contexts, it is not hard to understand why "justice" itself is often not valued as an attained state of equity or compensation, but rather as the constellation of languages and social practices through which claims on the state can be continually reasserted. As a language of dispute—and contention—"justice" in all liberal states involves the struggle to discern and enforce the slippery boundary that distinguishes private and public interest. In Peru, this struggle has historically been waged along the simultaneously rhetorical and legal divide between *el Peru real y el Peru legal* (Basadre 1931).[13] This popular expression invokes two sorts of "divides": between reasoned judicial procedure and extrajudicial or "frontier" justice and between the public officeholder and the private individual who holds that office. As an image of the nation, this image of two parallel countries or states speaks to a commonsense understanding that things like justice and disinterested public service are inherently fictional yet nevertheless very real parts of what "the state" is all about. Whereas in much democratic theory the attainment of a democratic society is presumed to require a banishment of private regulatory services (corruption) and lawmaking (frontier justice), in this real politik of the Peruvian peasant, the state is understood to be both disinterested and corrupt, just and coercive, participatory and removed.[14] It is precisely the tension between these countervailing—and, for us, contradictory—understandings of the state's moral project that explains why, despite their experience with the heavy hand of state repression, the marginalizing practices of state agencies, and the unbelievable ravages of market economies, peasants—perhaps more than any other sectors of Peruvian society—continue to believe in and fight for justice and democratic reform.

Finally, I want to note the curious division of labor between the abstract principle of "the law" and the concrete materiality of the "documents" through which law is given form. The principle of law is offered as a threshold against which (or above which) illegal or corrupt practices are defined as "outside" or "above" the law. Law is likewise ascribed a rationality whose transparency and universality is grounded in its ostensible legibility or transparency (as in the neutrality of the "letter of the law"). At the same time, although the state and NGOs assure them that "the law" is universal and impartial, peasants—like many other Peruvians—negotiate their daily lives as a series of calculations involving individuals and spaces that everyone knows exist "outside the law." They understand—but only partially accept—the fact that legal cases are settled according to personal connections and money.

More interesting for our discussion of the margins of the state, they also clearly understand that the "letter of the law" is rendered curiously illegible, or opaque, through the very processes and procedures that produce the documents that are its material expression. Small wonder then that "law" itself—unlike documents, whose shadows obscure all proceedings—is assigned little, if any, agency in determining the outcomes of the judicial proceedings that take place within the margins of the state.

Notes

Research on judicial reform in Ayacucho was made possible through the support of a Faculty Development Grant from the Graduate Faculty of Political and Social Research at the New School University. The research would not have been possible without the gracious support and friendship of Jefrey Gamarra, Wilfredo Arce, Pepe Coronel, and other researchers at IPAZ, with which I was affiliated during my time in Ayacucho. My research on judicial reform has also benefited from conversations with Isaias Rojas Perez, at that time of the Institute de Defensa Legal in Lima. Earlier research on gamonalismo in Chumbivilcas was made possible through fellowships from the University of Michigan Society of Fellows and the Social Science Research Council.

1. Although, as I have argued here, the privatization of the state in Peru has its roots in the colonial order, private power is not unique to either "colonial" or "postcolonial" states. In fact, the *problem* of private interest or "corruption" emerges only with the formation of liberal constitutional states based on the fiction of public interest. Illustrative here is Jeremy Bentham's ([1830] 1962:76) description of the constitutional regime as a "system of corruption by law." The point for anthropology would be to think about particular styles and forms of privatization (or corruption) and how these, in turn, shape the historically and culturally particular forms of illegibility or indecipherability that emerge from the necessary (and universal) tension between the discursive ideals of "justice" and the lived realities of judicial process. On the encomienda and the privatization of regulatory functions in the Latin American state, see especially Lomnitz 2000:11–30. On privatization of power in African postcolonial and neoliberal states, see Bayart (1989), Mbembe (2001), and Hibou (2002).

2. This idea of documents "drifting off" into the upper levels of the judicial system provides an interesting contrast with *derecho,* meaning at once "law" and "right" and, in its adjectival form, "straight" or "direct."

3. Today, much of the debate on customary law in Peru, as in Africa (Mamdani 1996) and elsewhere in Latin America (for example, Gow and Rappaport 2002), centers on the use of traditional forms of punishment. "Traditional punishments" imposed by justices of the peace in rural Ayacucho ranged from whipping and walking a prescribed number of times around the community on bare knees, to imprisonment and different forms of community service. The PCP-SL used these same kinds of punishments in "people's trials" that also claimed to be "customary law" administered through the party.

4. This is particularly true if we consider that the relevant social person is often the family rather than the individual who holds office. It thus becomes meaningless to claim that a judge "separates" his judicial authority from administrative affairs when his father, brother, or sister may well hold some other state office in the same town or region. The archives in both Ayacucho and Cuzco are packed with cases too numerous to mention that were declared null after authorities and litigants were unsuccessful in finding a single judicial authority who was not related to the accused.

5. In this, the gamonal can be seen as a distant relative of the indigenous nobility who acted as "brokers" between Spanish and indigenous or local political and legal systems during the colonial period. Like the gamonales, these *curacas,* or "brokers," often used their privilege as nobles to construct forms of highly abusive personal power (Larson 1988; Stern 1983).

6. The Spanish word most often used—in both Spanish and Quechua—to describe the gamonal is *prepotente,* meaning "arrogantly powerful" or, more literally, "prepowerful."

We might therefore say that the gamonal is both excessively powerful, and hence beyond the reach of the state, and rudely powerful, thus suggestive of a form of power that precedes—and is hence foundational to—the state.

7. In this regard as well, Torres's case is completely typical. Of the more than one hundred court cases I reviewed in the departmental archives in Huamanga, only a handful had achieved a resolution or ruling. This pattern becomes even more extreme in regions such as southern Cuzco or Huancavelica, where gamonales monopolized political offices to an even greater extent than in Ayacucho.

8. Within the country, the most common reason given to justify the reforms was the frequent loss of paperwork, which somehow seemed to disappear as it moved through the system, and the length of time and resulting waste of both time and money involved in very long judicial cases. Following Fujimori's fall from

power in November 2000, the transition government gave priority to the problem of executive control over judicial appointments. Other aspects of the reform, however, will undoubtedly survive the transition. For critical perspectives on the judicial reforms as carried out by the Fujimori government, see, for example, García Sayan (1996) and Ortíz de Cevallos (1999).

9. The judicial system in Ayacucho includes eight judicial districts (that do not coincide with administrative districts) headed by a superior court in the departmental capital of Huamanga. The superior court, which has two *salas* and six *vocales* and is presided over by a president appointed by the executive branch, handles nearly 80 percent of the caseload in the department, or approximately 10,000 cases per year. A simple case involving child support can last two or three months. Two hundred and fifty justices of the peace handle petty claims, local disputes, and domestic violence cases. In 1999 a new law mandated election of justices of the peace by popular vote.

10. Domestic violence cases involve potential criminal charges and therefore are first heard by the police, who decide whether the cases should be handled in *conciliación* or by the courts. Although the Peruvian government recently created a special female police section to receive domestic violence complaints, it had not yet been implemented in Huamanga at the time of my fieldwork.

11. Communities in Ayacucho are classified as resistant, returned, or relocated, depending on their response to the war. Resistant communities include a significant percentage of original inhabitants who remained during the war. Returnees are populations and communities that moved elsewhere (usually to Lima or Huamanga) during the war and then returned. Relocated communities are new populations formed of several smaller communities either after or during the war in an effort to create stronger defenses against the PCP-SL and the Peruvian armed forces. All three types of communities are heavily dependent on state aid. See Coronel 1999a, 1999b, 2000a.

12. This is an entirely new role for women in the community, since women "traditionally" did not serve in any formal decision-making capacity in such disputes. Community members often pointed to women's participation in response to my questions about how the NURAJ differed from earlier modes of dispute resolution, before the war. Despite all the talk about women's participation, women were singularly silent in the NURAJ sessions I attended.

13. "Legal Peru and real Peru." In Spanish, the word *real* carries an interesting double connotation, meaning both "real" or "actual" and "royal" or "monarchical." On the construction of similar divides in the legal cultures of other Latin American countries, see O'Donnell (1999).

14. The "frontier justice" associated with gamonales and their "hinterlands" is more than just the "self-made" or "reciprocal" justice of the Kantian state of nature (Kant [1797] 1965:76–84). Rather, "frontier justice" takes shape through the complex interweaving of the judicial procedures, aimless "driftings," and reasoned "evidence gathering" of the state, and the coercive practices, silences, and reciprocal justice of the gamonal. Frontier justice—like the frontier itself—forms a region where the margins of the state become blurred and illegible. As this form of illegibility becomes inscribed into the documents and judicial procedures that flow from this zone, the "margin" of the state moves into the very heart of the judicial offices of the state itself.

3

Checkpoint

Anthropology, Identity, and the State

Pradeep Jeganathan

On January 31, 1995, cadres of the Liberation Tigers of Tamil Eelam (LTTE), arguably one of the most sophisticated militant groups in the world, exploded a massive bomb in the heart of Colombo's financial district. Hundreds died, and nearly a thousand people were injured. Several steel and glass towers were reduced to blackened shells. The direct consequences of this explosion, even though important in many ways, do not concern me here. Rather, I am concerned with another kind of consequence of this event.

Let me explicate that concern with an example. The headquarters of the Sri Lankan air force sits a few miles south of the financial district, at a busy intersection named Tunmulla. In a holdover from another time, the headquarters is surrounded by upper-middle-class homes of prominent Colombo citizens. The bomb downtown did not directly affect this neighborhood. Yet, in the wake of that event, residents renewed with vigor their efforts to have the military installation, which had been part of the area for many years, removed. Why so? The next bomb, they thought, might blow up right next door. That assumption was not unreasonable. Six years previously, a similar bomb had exploded at another military complex, the Joint Operations Command

(JOC), located nearby in another upper-middle-class residential neighborhood. Every new bomb that explodes in the city renews the possibility of more violence in areas like Tunmulla. Such places are remapped, again and again, into new spatial arrangements. New cartographies, predicated on the anticipation of violence, come into being.

In Colombo, bombs, like people, are given names—from the Pettah bomb, which killed 150 people in the Pettah bus station in the summer of 1986, through the JOC bomb, which devastated an entire neighborhood in 1990, to the Wijeratne and Dissanaike bombs, which killed politicians in the intervening years. A bomb is named after its "target": a military installation, government office, hotel, airport, or politician. And once the "target" of the bomb has been "determined" after the event, all other destruction accompanying the event is folded into that one "thing" the bomb is thought to center on, such as the JOC or the Central Bank. That "target," in turn, becomes the name of the bomb. There can arise then, in the wake of the relocation of these transgressive events into the social, cartographies of targets, which are, in turn, cartographies of anticipated violence, mappings of a terrifying future.

A map of targets, as lived by the residents of Colombo, would include a whole host of sites, such as military installations like the air force headquarters, homes of prominent and therefore vulnerable politicians, ports and airports, and shopping malls. But such maps are not indiscriminate; such maps of anticipation have a particular logic, constituted by tactics of preparation. For example, such maps do not include schools, universities, stadiums, or playgrounds in the city, since the LTTE has never attacked such sites and has not, therefore, made them visible as "targets." The targets could be further classified into "hard targets" that are "well secured," such as the president's official residence, and "soft targets" that are hardly "secured" at all, such as buses and trains. One could, in fact, extend these labels to "fixed targets," such as buildings, and "moving targets," people. One could argue that Neelan Tiruchelvam, a senior colleague and renowned liberal intellectual, was a soft, moving target: he was blown up by a suicide bomber in July 1999, just outside the International Center for Ethnic Studies (ICES), which he directed and had founded.

It is possible here, then, to produce what would be recognizable, in anthropological discourse of an ethnographic map of Colombo, as a map of targets, organized spatially, classified through some social logic. Such a map filters and flickers as implied targets do, for what might be subject to "violence" shifts—and the targets themselves move like shadows across the landscape of the city.

Targets are marked by "checkpoints." Colombo is a city of checkpoints. Sri Lanka itself is a territory of checkpoints—large or small, important or minor, confused or precise, official or unofficial. At its most basic and ordinary, a checkpoint is staffed by low-ranking soldiers, men or women, who stop the flow of traffic, usually vehicular but quite often pedestrian, to ask questions of those who pass by. The questions turn around matters of identity, and I shall return to these questions in some depth at the end of the chapter. But before I do, let me try to constitute in a multilayered way the "checkpoint" as an anthropological object.

The checkpoint lies at the boundaries of a target. As such, it delineates and focuses attention on the target. If the logic of the anticipation of violence creates a plethora of shifting targets that flicker and move like shadows across the landscape with each explosion or threat, then the checkpoint is an attempt by an agency of the state to control that flickering movement, to announce in no uncertain terms: "This is a target." The irony of this situation must be more than apparent. Such "checkpointed" targets might be the president's residence in the city or the residence of the commander of the army. But checkpoints also govern entrances/exits from the city, delineating the city itself as a target. The checkpoint configures practices of anticipation in a double way. On the one hand, to pass through a checkpoint is to remember why checkpoints exist—it is to recall the possibility of a bomb. The few who are, in fact, carrying or have some knowledge of a bomb would also, I imagine, anticipate its explosive impact. But on the other hand, there is another kind of anticipation—that of the soldiers checking the flow of traffic and people, asking questions. They are anticipating violence in another way.

In the larger work of which this essay is a chapter, my attempt has been to account for the location of "violence" in the lived world. That has been an anthropological project, the endpoint of which has been the attempt to produce ethnographies that are adequate to the object, "violence." One of the fundamental claims of the larger work is that "violence," taken as an anthropological object, is not self-evident. Such a claim is made, certainly, from within an analytical tradition that questions the self-evident character of any category, but a focus on violence has strongly underlined this question. Violence, I suggest, is only visible in the cusp of things, at the moment of its emergence as violation, before its renormalization and relegitimation. After it is well named and known, it carries only traces of its temporal past. It ceases to be a violation and fades from view, or remains only a "well-understood" legitimate force.

This fleeting, shifting violence that concerns me is in the lived world, embedded in fields of recollection and anticipation, fields that move in both temporal directions, past and future. Each recollection of "violence" can also be a moment of anticipation of "violence" to come and, as such, forms the conditions of possibility of the emergence of "violence" in the lived world.

This larger project is also concerned with anthropology as a form of knowledge. The fleeting object of violence also raises questions about the security of its apprehension. The "checkpoint," taken as a site of anthropological inquiry, is a telling exemplar of these concerns and claims about violence and also the epistemological concerns of the self-conscious anthropologist. As such, I will stay with the checkpoint, ethnographically, for much of this chapter, attempting to draw insights through those descriptions. I do not, however, offer a "thick" or well-secured description of these anthropological sites. That is tangential to my path here; I am attempting only to think through checkpoints to the margin of the state.

The most prominent checkpoint in my everyday life in Colombo is the Baudhaloka Mawatha checkpoint. It is 300 yards or so from Tunmulla, where the air force headquarters stands. Its location interrupts a major road that houses a series of state facilities. The Sri Lanka Rupavahini Corporation, which comprises TV studios, telecast towers, and transmitters, and the Bandaranaike Memorial International Conference Hall, a major convention center, are both farther down the road from the checkpoint. By the side of the checkpoint itself are spacious "official" residences of senior state bureaucrats—arranged in order of their rank. The governor of the Central Bank's official resi-

dence lies at the first section of this road, right near the Tunmulla intersection and next to the army commander's residence. Hence the
checkpoint. When in Colombo, I take great care to avoid this checkpoint, navigating alternative routes, weaving in and out of the terrain of
targets. Another checkpoint is situated north of this one, again on a
major road, which curves by an airfield. That road is unavoidable, and I
am often stopped there.

Let me step back a moment, delineating the qualities of the checkpoint as anthropological object and embedding it in webs of local
signifying practices. The checkpoint's location, its size, the demeanor
of the soldiers, the very nature of checking itself, all are enmeshed in
such webs.

Let me give depth to this observation by contrasting the
Baudhaloka Mawatha checkpoint with another checkpoint, far away in
the war zone, near the prized natural port of Trincomalee, perhaps the
most contested city in the whole of Lanka. When you turn at the
Habarana junction, the last outpost of Sinhala colonization on the dry,
hot plains of Nuwarakalaviya, and drive across the almost uninhabited
scrubland to the east, you know that the war is near. Government
troops have cleared huge swaths of scrub on either side of the road so
that approaching enemy cadres will have no cover. Every quarter mile
are sentry points, not checkpoints but small tin-roofed bunkers occupied by a lone private, who watches the road and the hard, brown
plains before him.

You reach the checkpoint I have in mind much later, after two
hours of travel on this road. You turn north at the entrance to the town
of Trincomalee and head toward Nilaveli, the beach of moon sand, one
of the very finest I have walked on. The checkpoint on the Nilaveli
road, which bisects shining fields of marsh, soft mud, and water, is itself
a target. Its occupants watch for their enemies. The troops are edgy,
quiet; they know that the stakes are high. Pedestrians from local villages
may pass by with a word, a look, a wink, or a smile. A resident told me
that the soldiers, who are well disciplined, like civilians to smile at
them. If you do not, they will be annoyed. The troops did not smile at
me—I was an outsider. I did not have that option. Soldiers at the
Baudhaloka Mawatha checkpoint, to move the contrast back to the city
where I began, may not smile either, but they are more relaxed. They

do not expect the checkpoint itself to be attacked. In a curious way, their work has become routinized. A sign that reads "Thank you for your cooperation" greets you as you approach, and it even includes a tasteful advertisement for something as ordinary as toothpaste or a mentholated balm. The very embedding of checkpoints in differential ways indexes, I suggest, the terrain of anticipated violence. Each is a nodal point in that map of anticipation, each reconfigured by it. I can think of no better place where the state performs the magic of its illegibility with such breathtaking precision. (On "magic" and "illegibility," see Veena Das's chapter in this volume.)

"May I see your ID?" is the first question one is asked at a checkpoint. It is asked very politely and cautiously, by a soldier in fatigues with a large, visible automatic weapon slung over his back. The question is the same in Colombo and Trincomalee.[1] Not having an ID card is the privilege of foreigners or careless citizens, who then have added questions to answer. A passport may be proffered and deemed acceptable, but it is the national identity card (NIC) that is requested, not any other form of identification. It is a small, yellow, laminated paper. On one side is a photograph, the date of issue, a long unique number, and the signature of the bureaucrat responsible for issuing the card. On the other side is written, upon a series of dotted lines, the name, sex, date of birth, place of birth, occupation, and address of the holder. This card, unlike a passport, has no expiry date on it, so its renewal is difficult to enforce. My card is old, issued in 1982, just before I took a national university entrance examination. It lists my occupation as student, my place of birth as Colombo, and my address as my parents' house, located in a residential district in the city. There is nothing else on this card; there is no line for "nationality," "race," "ethnicity," or another such classificatory category. After asking for my ID and looking it over, the soldier usually returns it to me and waves me on. Sometimes he may ask a question such as "Do you still live at this address?" or say, "This card is very old." Rarely do the questions get more intense. Once, at another checkpoint, I was arrested.

Several months after I had written this description, I realized that I had missed something on the card. I was amazed, for I had examined my card and several other cards carefully while writing the description. What I had missed is a small rectangle at the bottom of the card that states in Sinhala, "The Registration of Fersons Act, No. 32 of 1968." During a presentation of this paper at ICES in Colombo, a distinguished human-rights attorney explained to me, in the course of providing comments on my work, that the Registration of Persons Act had made the NIC possible. It was only after I had taken notes, reread the notes, and reexamined the card that I realized that the title of the act was written on the card. In legal terms, the act and the act alone secures this card; yet this detail had been illegible to me, as it is to a large number of my fellow citizens.

The act itself is fascinating (see Government of Sri Lanka [1972] 1998). Most stunning is that it has little to do with establishing identity, in relation to persons, in a random and regular way. Rather, the act is about maintaining a book: a numbered register of persons who are citizens of Sri Lanka. The card is a certificate of registration. A commissioner, the registrar, is charged with maintaining the book, the register. To my mind, this is clearly the other half of the project of enumeration, which is carried out in the census.[2] For if the census counts persons and then classifies them in accordance with a certain logic, thereby aggregating them into well-known fields, how is the state itself to produce a disaggregating practice? By recording a name and address in a book and issuing a certificate with a photograph—a kind of receipt of that entry. Hence, there is no need to aggregate identity—Sinhala, Tamil, and so on—on this certificate, for that is not the work it does in relation to the "population" practices of the state.

This certificate, under conditions unenvisaged in 1968, becomes the card that every Sri Lankan citizen carries on his or her person for purposes of identity. But a reading of the act makes it crystal clear that no provision of the act requires people to carry the card. Section 15(1) specifies that "the holder of an identity card shall, on a request made by the Commissioner or any other prescribed officer, produce the card at such time and place that shall be specified in such a request, and permit it to be inspected" (Government of Sri Lanka [1972] 1998:7). The card need only be produced with prior notice, so it need not, under the law, be carried on one's person. Note that the place of production itself must be specified in the request, together with the time. This is to be an individuated request; it has to be, since this document is a document of individuation, as I have argued above. It is not possible, therefore, to declare a checkpoint as a specified "place" a priori, where at "all" times such a card should be shown by all "citizens." Furthermore, only the commissioner and his officers may make such individuated requests. And while Section 5(2) of the act allows for wide delegation of power, each of such "agents" must be "subject to the general direction and control of the Commissioner" (Government of Sri Lanka [1972] 1998:3), not the commander of the army or the secretary to the ministry of defense, who command troops at checkpoints. In November 2001, a handful of human-rights attorneys explained that they shared my interpretation of the law.[3] They said that several supreme court justices had indicated that the court eagerly awaited a test case so that the illegality of ubiquitous checkpoints might be elaborated upon in judgment. (No postcolonial Sri Lankan regime has ever ignored or countered a direct order of the supreme court.) But that was a fine question of law. Not only was this situation not widely known at the time in popular or scholarly circles, but also nearly every critical intellectual I knew had acquiesced to the illegible magic of the checkpoint.

The checkpoint is, I wish to suggest, more central, more constitutive of the epistemological architecture of modernity than is at first apparent. I shall try in the rest of this chapter to discuss this centrality, returning as I must to the state and its margin at the end. As a beginning, let me suggest that a checkpoint is a place where we who have seen, heard, and felt destruction, terror, pain, and death and who anticipate with uncertain anxiety that which is to come to us and ours, sense for a moment a stilling of that foretelling of death, a moment where returning to that ever-so-familiar way of reading and writing will allow foreknowledge and therefore safety. This, of course, is a fantasy. Nevertheless, it is a crucial one for many. It is worth noting that checkpoints are not uniquely Sri Lankan. In fact, after 9/11 they seem to be more widespread than before, all over the world. For example, every domestic airport in the United States is a giant checkpoint.

I draw several strands from my brief description of checkpoints in Sri Lanka. The first begins with a reiteration; I have already tried to underline the point that the checkpoint works betwixt and between the recollection and anticipation of violence; it is that place in the lived world that acknowledges the emergent quality of violence without producing a normalization that is also its effacement.

The second strand is the relationship of the checkpoint to the state, which is crucial to the concerns of this volume. While on the one hand, the relationship of the checkpoint to the state is sutured through its very location in a temporal field of recollection and anticipation, it is also located at the margin of a spatial field, which it defines. It may be useful here to contrast a checkpoint with a sentry or guard post, or even an immigration post. The latter seems to mark boundaries that are well mapped and defined; it marks the boundary of the state, implying different forms of citizenship and subject on either side. A checkpoint may be different, for it operates within a given state, with a regime of citizenship and subjection. It is mobile in particular ways, for recall that it is required by targets, which themselves are constituted by anticipations. A checkpoint—in the way it emerges here—is located perhaps, not at the boundary of the state, but at its shifting, fluid margins. Yet the very existence of a checkpoint, as an operational entity and a concept, challenges the clarity of the boundary, blurring its distinctiveness. The boundary might also be a margin.

This marginal location of the checkpoint is mapped again through the identification card, which, as I have described, is the illegible, illegal demand of the checkpoint. The point is not only that checkers at the checkpoint demand this card; it is also that all those who anticipate this demand then carry this card. This, I submit, is an observation that should give pause.

What is the form of subjection implied by this practice? It is not simply that the state has a project of enumeration and individuation. This has been noted earlier, and undoubtedly the identification card can be understood as such. As I also noted, in the Sri Lankan context, that has nothing to do with checkpoints as described, logically or historically. It seems to be a more general point. The production of the ubiquitous "picture ID" at US domestic airports, it seems now, has the same logic. It extends the uncertain, fluid margin of the state to one's wallet.

The bringing of these three elements together—the checkpoint, the card, and the subject—then forms a new space for reflection. The citizen who carries a card, anticipating that it will be checked, is subjected through that very act. It ties the citizen to the state, the card always pointing toward the margin of the state. How is this triangulation to be fully thought through? There are undoubtedly many ways to think through these margins, and several authors in this volume offer insights far more acute than my own.

To reflect on this triangulation, on my way of grasping something of the state's margins, I return to the process of checking itself, asking for a conceptualization of the question that is being asked. At its heart, the question is this: "Are you an enemy of the state, and does your enmity extend to violence upon it or its citizens?" This question is surely a specific form of a more general question: "What is your political identity?" Elaborated, the question might be something like this: "Do you represent a politics that lies outside the bounds of the state, that is an insurrectionary one, that in its deployment and operation may explode a bomb in the vicinity of a well-known target?" If the soldier decides that the answer is yes, then he may detain you.

But the crucial question is this: How would that be decided? How can an account of political identity, which might be an adequate answer to this question, be obtained by quick and polite interrogation? My concern here, let me hasten to add, is with the logic of the question, not with the success or otherwise of these interrogations. It is my claim that following the logic of the question may take us some distance in our appreciation of the "checkpoint."

The answer to the "What is your political identity?" question, I argue, is read off a series of interpretations of what are taken to be social or cultural signs on the card. In this, it seems to me, the soldiers participate in the work of anthropology, which through its disciplinary provenance marks privileged access to, and makes authoritative claims about, the "cultural," undergirded, or secured, perhaps even simultaneous with the "social." If the soldier can be seen in one sense as asking an anthropological question, let me qualify quickly that I do not see him as an anthropologist, for he is not a disciplinary practitioner. What I want to analogize here is the form of the question, "Who are you?"

The blanks on the card—as in "name........" and "occupation........" —are written in both Sinhala and Tamil. These are both official languages of Sri Lanka at present. However, the blanks are filled out in one language, as one might expect. My card is filled out in Sinhala. This, from the point of view of deciphering the sociocultural, is significant, since some cards are filled out in Tamil. A card filled out in Sinhala—cards are handwritten—would mean, of course, that the official who wrote it out could write Sinhala. It would not be certain that he was "Sinhala" in the classificatory sense of the census, since by the state's own rules, all state bureaucrats must have some proficiency in Sinhala. That is to say, bureaucrats who are Tamil, in a classificatory sense of the census, may well write Sinhala script. But in the north and east of the country, more often than the south, administrative affairs are conducted in Tamil, so a card written in Tamil may well have originated in the north. The address and place of birth on the card are also crucial. They place the holder on a map of Lanka, north, south, east, west. But none of this information gives a "conclusive" reading of the holder's social-cultural identity, since one can be born in the south, have a card written in Sinhala, and be thought to be "Tamil," or vice versa. Or one might be a Muslim who speaks Tamil but is not "Tamil" as such. The name might well prove a clincher. It can be read, again with an anthropological eye, for the sociocultural: Sinhala names, Tamil names, Muslim names, and so on. These readings, too, can confound— or not. Anthropological logics can often be quite effective.

But what I want to draw attention to is not the confounding (or not) as such—which is to say, not the possibility of the sociocultural being so radically heterogeneous that it defies easy classification, a position of one critique of social scientific knowledge, best known as a critique of essentialism.[4] That is not the position I take or wish to develop. Rather, my concern is with *the play* of the two questions. That is to say, the play between the first question, "What is your political identity?" which is logically prior to the second question, "What is your social/cultural identity?" It is crucial to think of the situation as play, for even after the second question is answered, let us say securely, as in "a Tamil from the North," this does not answer the first question securely. If it did, then the state would simply have to arrest all persons answering "a Tamil from the North." This is logically possible and would then call for a characterization of fascism, but even so, it would not answer or put the elaborated form of the first question to rest in a secure way. (Even after the Nazi state arrested its Jewish citizens, it still could conceive of enemies.) Given the state of this play, then, the answer to the second question only allows a return to the first in a circular way.

In two brilliant and increasingly well-known essays, the political philosopher Etienne Balibar theorizes this state of play that modern beings—that is, we and our interlocutors—operate (see Balibar 1991, 1994).[5] His formulations, I suggest, will illuminate my navigation of these checkpoints. The modern citizen, Balibar argues, is defined by the unique confluence of equality and the sovereignty of that collective equality. The citizen is the conceptual representation of this confluence, but that duality is an irreducible contradiction. The play is between equality on the one hand and the particular expression of sovereignty, freedom, or liberty on the other. *Equaliberty* is a neologism that Balibar coins to capture this play, which results in the production of an unpredictable excess. Forms of subjection are forms of this excess. To be a citizen is also to be a subject, doubly, paralleling here, of course, Foucault's empirico-transcendental doublet of Man (Foucault 1970:318; see also Balibar 1991:51). The citizen is that abstract being of equality who, with the demand of freedom in an insurrectionary sense, or its granting, as a right, in a constitutional sense must be subject in the double sense of self-subjection and being to that field Balibar calls "community." In this formulation, "community" is irreducibly modern, since its very form is produced by a play between two modern conditions of "Man," equality and liberty. This community then can take the specific form of the nation, an "ethnic" group, or a political party. The community itself might make claims to egalitarianism, or it might well be hierarchical; that is not crucial to its constitution. What is crucial is the claim that it mediates between equality and freedom. Subjection, in other words, is that which mediates the contradiction of citizenship.[6]

Let us return to the checkpoint. Consider the two, necessarily double, operations of subjection. The first is both inscribed and reinterpreted by the agents of the state on the document of identity. There is some social-cultural identity that corresponds to some community, which might be marked as a mix of both ethnic and regional produced in the reading of that card. Then there is the cardholder, the navigator of the checkpoint. His self-subjection may or may not match that of the state's—but it does exist in some form: when once arrested at a checkpoint, with a detailed map of the country that aroused suspicion in my bag, I claimed to be a scholar working at a renowned research center, which, of course, was only one such community I could claim. For the checkpoint to do the work it claims—that is, check identity—the double play on both sides of the divide must match up: the soldier and I (or whoever is checked) must agree on the resultant answer of the irreducible play between citizen and subject. In this case, it did not work; I was arrested.

But in most cases it seems to work: most people pass through checkpoints without disagreement, their identities "checked," just as many ethnographies are written by disciplinary anthropologists. Surely we now see the precarious nature of this agreement between checker and checked. For each citizen, to position his political affiliation in terms of alliance or enmity with the state is also then to work through his own subjection—and that result, clearly, is not fixed. Surely, militants on bombing missions will carry false papers. Many who do not, who are in fact arrested, do not intend to commit projects of violence upon the state. Yet the checkpoint persists. The high and almost unimaginable stakes of the massive explosion it entails keep it in place, a testament, not to what it can tell us about the identities of those who pass through it, but to what it cannot, given the irreducible contradictions of citizenship, which are the irreducible contradictions of politics itself.

Those contradictions of politics define, in terms of this chapter, what I take to be the margin of the state. For the state takes its domain to be that of politics—in Balibar's terms, constitutional politics. The field of counterpolitics that presses against the state's domain is what he calls insurrectionary politics. Where they meet might well be the margin of the state. Such margins, I have argued, are marked by checkpoints that ask questions of identity, social and political, with recourse to the documentary practices of the state. Such margins of the state are not fixed, I have argued. Not only are they mobile, in as much as targets are lived and mapped in fields of anticipation and recollection, but they also blur the clarity of the state's boundaries. An identification card, carried in a pocket or bag, and all the other paper associated with it, which is elsewhere—consider what one would need to replace a lost card—are mediators of that margin, the tiny compasses that have written upon themselves, that very contradiction of politics, which itself is, of course, a miniature map of the margin of the state, guiding us back to the checkpoint.

Notes

This chapter has gained much from extended discussion at the School of American Research in Santa Fe and the International Center for Ethnic Studies in Colombo. I am grateful to Diane Nelson, Deborah Poole, Veena Das, Talal Asad, Lawrence Cohen, Radhika Coomaraswamy, Justice P. Ramanathan, Jeevan Hoole, and Dileepa Vitharana for their careful comments and questions. I am also indebted to Desmond Fernando, PC, for his comments and for several personal communications afterward.

1. This question is not the same in Vavuniya, which has a different "documentary regime," given its differential location in a field of anticipation. Vavuniya is a special case, yet what is at stake there is also a document that depends upon other documents, an iteration.

2. On the logic of the census, see Cohn's (1987) classic essay.

3. An activist human-rights group founded by Amara Hupuarachichi in the wake of several discussions surrounding the NIC is in the process of publicizing these contradictions in the media and challenging them before the Human Rights Commission and the supreme court, and through direct action. Malathi De Alwis and I are active members of this group.

4. This position is well known; perhaps Inden (1990) could be taken as a good example of it. My thoughts on essences owe much to David Scott's (1999:9) questions, even though my own critical direction may diverge from his.

5. My reading of both essays is indebted to Vivek Dhareshwar's engagement with them (see Dhareshwar 1995a, 1995b).

6. In an earlier work, I attempted to work through this contradiction by reading Marx's "The Jewish Question"; see Jeganathan (1994). I am now persuaded, given Balibar (1994:46), that Marx is incorrect on this point.

4

Deterritorialized Citizenship and the Resonances of the Sierra Leonean State

Mariane C. Ferme

> The State...is a phenomenon of intraconsistency: It makes points
> resonate together...very diverse points of order, geographic, ethnic,
> linguistic, moral, economic, technological particularities.
>
> —Deleuze and Guattari, in *A Thousand Plateaus*

Since the 1990s, political theorists of the state have had a field day in Africa—a continent that has been the setting for scholarship on the collapsed, privatized (Hibou 1999), criminalized (Bayart, Ellis, and Hibou 1997), shadow (Reno 1995, 1998), and even forgerer state, or state as agent of deception *(l'état falsificateur).*[1] The more innovative contributions have sought to depathologize scholarly discourse on the state in Africa, by rethinking "corruption" within the framework of alternative political idioms, for instance (see Bayart 1981), and in the context of the historical legacy of colonialism in contemporary African politics (for example, Bayart 1993; Cooper 2002; Geschiere 1997; Mamdani 1996). In particular, the civil wars in Liberia and Sierra Leone (and the flow of refugees they sent in flight toward neighboring countries, with destabilizing effects in the region) underscored the porousness of African border zones and brought to the fore the need to reflect on the state at its territorial margins. Liberia and Sierra Leone were referred to as "shadow states"—that is, states characterized by "the emergence of rulers drawing authority from their ability to control markets and their material rewards" (Reno 1995:3), especially

through the exploitation of precious resources. According to Reno, this control over wealth allowed the shadow state to disregard the absence of international recognition of its sovereignty and of other standard entanglements of legitimacy. Among other things, the shadow state could produce statelike enclaves in resource-rich parts of its territory, with their own regulatory practices. For example, Sierra Leone's Kono region, where the country's richest diamond veins are located, had its own security, licensing, and pass system to control the movements of a large and potentially restless population of young male dia-
m   o   n   d
diggers—and this for well over two decades before the onset of the civil war. But as long as shadow states need to control natural and mineral resources that bring hard currency to survive, they also need to control the territorial enclaves where these resources are located. Whether the state controls these enclaves itself or temporarily cedes the right to do so to private businesses, it still exercises its prerogatives as an apparatus of capture that operates through specific places, and hence on the territory—the classic site or location of sovereignty. This is the case no matter how selectively this apparatus is activated in practice (Deleuze and Guattari 1987:432ff.).

Thus, even semiprivatized, semicriminal states achieve a measure of "integration"—in Deleuze and Guattari's terms—at least enough to produce what Timothy Mitchell has called a "state effect." One way a state effect is produced is by the drawing of boundaries, for instance, between state and society, or state and economy, urban and rural, in ways that make the state appear as an "inert 'structure' that somehow stands apart from individuals, precedes them, and contains and gives a framework to their lives" (Mitchell 1999:89). This is partly because the state is a "translocal" institution "made visible in localized practices" (Gupta 1995:376). In this chapter, I examine the relationship between two sets of practices that interpolate between local and translocal—even global—scales on which the resonances constitutive of a state effect are produced, with special reference to Sierra Leone. These are first some of the legal and administrative practices in which various states (including Sierra Leone) have engaged, having as their object Sierra Leonean citizens and their movements as migrants, travelers, and more recently war refugees. Among these practices are those of control over territory (including its delimitation with borders, their policing, and so on) and populations (for instance, through the issuing of identity documents or restrictions over mobility).

But the bulk of the chapter situates such practices in the context of the experiences of Sierra Leoneans affected by them, and those who engage in border- and identity-making and -crossing practices of their own. These social actors, and their relationship to Sierra Leone and various host countries where I have encountered them, highlight ways in which forms of belonging characteristic of citizenship are deterritorialized, particularly through the figure of the immigrant and the war refugee. Broadly speaking, then, this chapter addresses problems in the biopolitical management of populations and territory, in this case specifically through the production of a social body—that is, counting, tracking, and identifying citizens with identity documents (see Foucault 1994:67–85)—as well as through control of flows of humans and goods at state borders. These practices have effects on citizen-subjects, who, in turn, shape the terms of this engagement in critical ways. Because this part of my analysis focuses on ways the state apparatus reterritorializes and works as a point of resonance beyond its borders, much of it deals with Sierra Leoneans outside their national territory.

ARBITRARINESS AND THE LAW

In what ways are the laws and workings of the (supra)state arbitrary? For one thing, they are experienced to be so by people who find themselves consistently disadvantaged by them: the law appears then as a well-guarded secret that exists to serve the interests of particular categories of people. There is also arbitrariness in the ways laws are applied—a problem not so much in the law itself as in its enforcement. But a further way in which the law and state rule are seen as arbitrary— one experienced by the Sierra Leoneans encountered in the course of my research—is that the state can arbitrate, decide, or create situations in which competing interests or interpretations of the common good obscure the threshold between legality and illegality. The antecedents for this arbitrariness are found in colonial rule, as others have pointed out (for example, Mamdani 1996; Mbembe 2001).

Under colonial rule in Sierra Leone, conflicting statutes setting the boundaries between the colony (ceded in 1807 to the British Crown by the Sierra Leone Company) and the protectorate (declared in 1896 over the adjoining hinterland—a much vaster territory) triggered flows of people and goods across internal border regions. Thus, rural people inhabiting neighboring villages separated by the invisible border between protectorate and colony experienced apparently arbitrary differences in treatment by the state's agents: on the protectorate side, taxation was announced in 1896, the same time foreign rule was established, and was enforced beginning in 1898 without exemptions; on the colony side, taxes were established a full century after the inception of colonial rule—later than in the protectorate—and with exemptions. The choice was clear for those wanting to avoid taxes. But it was in the domain of courts and the application of different bodies of law that ordinary people most felt the arbitrariness of jurisdictional boundaries, for in the colony they were subjects of the British Crown under English law, whereas in the protectorate they were subject to native courts and the oversight of summary justice meted out by the Frontier Police (Fyfe 1962:545). While under ordinary circumstances, people in the protectorate seeking legal redress felt that they could be better served by the colony courts, during the 1898 anticolonial "tax war," the situation was reversed. Of the 158 people convicted of murder after the rebellion was suppressed (Fyfe 1962:588–89), chiefs in the colony were hanged for treason as Crown subjects, whereas protectorate rulers were tried as external enemies and suffered a variety of punishments, including exile and imprisonment. Finally, the different treatment of slavery (legal in the protectorate until 1927, outlawed from 1787 on the colony's "British soil") produced the strategic back-and-forth movement of a population set in motion by all that this boundary implied.

Far from being ignored, the dividing line represented by the protectorate-colony border, and the differences in jurisdiction that came with it, gave rise to new meanings and uses. And these border practices were not circumscribed to rural inhabitants of the Sierra Leonean hinterland. The Frontier Police—and the composite colonial state on whose behalf they acted—invented their role as they went along. They had the vague mandate of keeping the peace in a vast territory while being explicitly forbidden to interfere with the rule of local chiefs and the courts. Police could not even protect citizens of the colony in the protectorate, because they were outside British jurisdiction. Often posted in small numbers to remote areas, far from the supervision of their European superiors, members of this paramilitary body took on roles that ranged from standing by while local witch hunts produced dozens of casualties, to taking on abusive enforcement roles in stamping out domestic slavery and enforcing taxation (see Fyfe 1962:487, 506–07, 515). Furthermore, uncertainty about where the border between colony and protectorate lay periodically produced incidents that highlighted the social and political effects in practice of apparently abstract matters of law.

The twentieth century brought legal reforms that made British policies on either side of the border more consistent and eventually unified colony and protectorate under a single jurisdiction through a series of constitutional reforms initiated in 1951. But, to paraphrase Mitchell, the "border effect" of the British colonial state's policies in the area continues to resonate in internal divisions within postcolonial Sierra Leone. In this aspect, Sierra Leone appears to be a classic "bifurcated state" inherited from the "decentralized despotism" of colonial rule (Mamdani 1996), where on the one hand the colonial (and postcolonial) state exercised "customary" power, through native authorities, over tribalized peasant subjects in the rural hinterland—a hinterland that overlaps with the former protectorate. On the other hand the colony mostly overlapped with the Freetown peninsula and therefore corresponded to spaces where the colonial state held "civil" power over British subjects—urban-based citizens and non-Africans subject to modified forms of metropolitan law, and peasants subject to hybrid, intermediate jurisdictional forms. However, this would be a reductive, all too literalist reading of the state's territorializing power—its power to express in spatial terms specific forms of control—given the many ways in which the colonial state, however multiple and disorganized its practices, produced an effect of cohesion in the experience of its subjects.

In the extreme, colonial power exercised a form of absolute control over the body of the colonized, with its indiscriminate use of the "right to kill and make force prevail. Exercising command thus meant to compel people to perform 'obligations.' It also meant, as in an army, to proceed by orders and demands. *Commandement* itself was simultaneously a tone, an accoutrement, and an attitude" (Mbembe 2001:32).

One could go further and say that the colonial state was "a *state*ment, an ongoing assertion: it [gave] voice to an authoritative worldview, sometimes backed by (open or concealed) displays of might" (Comaroff 1998:342), and in this capacity it was effective even when it lacked organizational unity, when it appeared to sow the seeds of "collapsed" or "shadow" postcolonial states. In other words, I would tend to disagree with the "totalitarian" reading Mbembe gives of both the colonial and postcolonial successor states, given that one needs to take into account the distinction between "state effect"—including the phantasmatic constellation in which the state project is couched, thus projecting a totalizing image of itself—and the extent to which it may or may not be integrated at particular times and in particular sites.

Successor states held on to the absolute rights claimed by colonial rule, including the "right to kill," and exercised them often with the same impunity. The power of the postcolonial state in contemporary Sierra Leone manifested itself in the periodic declaration of emergency curfews, among other things. These were most recently justified by the government's provision of security in the context of the civil war and were accompanied by an escalation of abuses linked to "checking documents" (on the linkages between states of generalized insecurity, checkpoints, and the fetishism of documents, see also the chapters by Poole and Jeganathan in this volume). Under normal circumstances, blocking the movements of populations to inspect documents was linked to predictable sites and incidents (for example, the border crossing, the airport arrival lounge, the commission of an infraction), but under states of emergency, the sites of arbitrary blocks multiplied. Thus, as reported in Freetown's *The New Breed* (July 7–13, 1993), a soldier's demand that a citizen produce an identity card and pay a fine for leaving his house at night (during the curfew), even though he had left only to relieve himself in the outhouse in back, escalated into the citizen's death. I mention this example as a caricature of the routinized, socialized character that the portrayal of the state's "absolute power" takes on in contexts in which it should not have to be invoked.

The prosecution of the soldier who committed this killing belies the fact that his gesture was far from illegal—it was authorized, as such gestures always are, under the emergency stipulations of the Sierra Leonean constitution. Furthermore, it belies the fact that, increasingly, such gestures are not only a feature of emergencies but are also experienced in ordinary life, a feature of the commandement in post-colonial Africa (Mbembe 2001). In Sierra Leone and elsewhere, then, the arbitrariness at the heart of commandement became socialized—it became a feature of the popular and political imagination and an inseparable attribute of the state as an apparatus of capture and appropriation. However, this arbitrariness was unable to hinder practices of mobility and self-fashioning among actors seeking, under different circumstances, to redefine themselves according to alternative logics of belonging—whether religious or political or in relation to humanitarian discourse. It is paradoxically the latter, despite its refusal to be beholden to the logic of sovereign states, that has facilitated the search by Sierra Leoneans—migrants, refugees—for alternative citizenship options. This they have done by exploiting emergency measures taken elsewhere to protect them as "war refugees"—for instance, in countries to which they flee, where such "states of emergency" have been used to lift restrictions on immigration. Such practices highlight the limits *and* flexibility of citizenship in the new era of rights heralded by global humanitarianism.

Critiques of liberal-democratic models of the political (for example, Carl Schmitt) have underscored their weakness in failing to recognize that ultimately sovereignty is about the power to suspend the (ordinary) rule of law. Though in practice the decision on what constitutes an exception usually becomes relevant only in emergency situations, Schmitt saw it as a general concept in the theory of the state, to the extent that he redefined state sovereignty as being "not about the monopoly to coerce or to rule, but as the monopoly to decide" (Schmitt [1922] 1988:5–13). Sovereignty is therefore always a borderline concept, one that must be legally circumscribed through provisions that grant only certain offices or bodies the right to decide upon—and hence declare—the exception, but it limits temporally the duration of states of emergency that are usually the pragmatic result of constitutional exceptions, without hampering them with particular laws. The decision is provided for in law, but at the moment of its exercise, it is not of the law—it must transcend the law as an included but external moment/provision of legality. The sovereign is the legally sanctioned outlaw.

Thus, the border between norm and exception, legality and illegality, is precisely where, according to Schmitt, the ordinary business of sovereignty is transacted. One is not aware of the sovereign in ordinary circumstances, only in emergencies that call for a decision about exceptions. If a sovereign body is to remain legitimate—and Schmitt's critics hardly ever pay attention to the great care he paid to legitimacy—it must revert to the rule of law once the emergency is over. Ultimately, Schmitt was more interested in democratic forms of sovereignty than in totalitarian ones, but he saw the contradictions embedded in the weak models of sovereignty being developed by the liberal, parliamentary democratic regimes of Europe in the interwar period.

Schmitt's notion of the legality or illegality of the state can be tested at the various points of intersection along geographic borders where Sierra Leonean citizens and refugees clash with the law in the state's multiple resonances. Borders are sites for the territorial manifestation of state sovereignty in its classic sense: where practices of inclusion (of certain categories of citizens) or exclusion (of unwanted others) take place. But even where state authority is diminished, where sovereignty is in question and regulatory practices are not visibly displayed except in an arbitrary manner, encounters with borders still tell us much about the shifting contours of state *interests* in different subjects and territories. Indeed, the arbitrariness with which the state displays and imposes its interest in different bodies of subjects is compounded by the complicity of those very subjects, whose practices of self-fashioning produce unpredictable (and sometimes equally arbitrary) outcomes. For the effort to comply with arbitrary and capricious laws often produces unpredictable outcomes. This is true, too, when the arbitrariness is only apparent—in other words, when it is the product of opaque intentions and appears to protect the interests of the privileged few who are "above the law" or whose interests are best served by existing laws.

In his political writings, Foucault has shown the intimate links in modern Europe between the erection of state borders and the production of a social body through the control of populations. Indeed, he argued that in modern times there has been a "shift of accent" (Foucault 1994:67) from territorial states to states interested in regulating populations through ordinary and ubiquitous mechanisms that produce specific kinds of knowledge—the census; birth, marriage, and death records—at the same time that they enable the delivery of services to populations. Foucault saw this modern form of power as producing biopolitical regimes where states control populations in increasingly intimate spheres of their bodily existence, to the point of producing new forms of subjectivity and even life.

On the face of it, biopolitical regimes appear very distant from Sierra Leone, which, with its neighbor Liberia, has had the distinction of being dubbed "the basket case of Africa" in matters ranging from the viability of the state to chances for a lasting peace after a decade of civil wars (see Moran and Pitcher 2003). The argument against the applicability of a biopolitical model to Sierra Leone is that the state as a regulatory and governing apparatus has failed to such a spectacular extent here that one can invoke neither governmentality nor older contractual, juridical models of sovereignty. Instead, I argue that a hybrid of these two models applies to postcolonial states like Sierra Leone and, more generally, that postcolonial Sierra Leone's political subjects are more at home in the "control" models of the state espoused by Deleuze and Guattari—who see the state as an apparatus of capture, integrated more as a network than an organism—than in the purely biopolitical ones spawned by partial readings of Foucault. Postcolonial states like Sierra Leone work more according to the logic of code than life-forms, discontinuity and resonances than organisms, and as such are fundamentally at odds with the supposedly organic models of the biopolitical. The modal form of relatedness in a digital system is the network, within which the state can carve out an area of control without compromising the whole system, as opposed to the interdependent integration of (pre- or post-genomic) organisms and their component parts (see Riles 2000).

Paradoxically, the biopolitical administration of life and over the living, and the incompleteness of its projects, paves the way to different constructs of the national or supranational subject-citizen. Sierra Leoneans with whom I have worked, in and outside their country, are subject to discontinuous forms of state and supranational interventions, which, while apparently random and arbitrary, make up an experience that as a whole reinforces their "being Sierra Leonean"—constituting resonances that might produce a sense of shared nationality when they find themselves elsewhere. As I show below, this reinforcement of a national identity is not bound up with clearly marked territorial boundaries but rather with a lingering, deterritorialized fetishism of the origin, of belonging. Thus, for example, one can have the paradox of Mohammed, a Sierra Leonean I met in Egypt in 1993 and who eight years later was admitted into the United States as a "war refugee," thanks to the intervention of a humanitarian organization—even though he had not lived in Sierra Leone since 1961, let alone directly experienced the upheavals of the 1991–2002 civil war. Indeed, his transformation over the years into a devout Muslim whose main community of belonging was based on religion had been so thorough that he had even shed his original name. This situation points to another "layer" in the integration of the state, for in the post–civil war context, it is the global humanitarian apparatus that often intervenes with statelike forms of governmentality—producing demographic data on populations, issuing identity documents, delivering health care and other services—that reconstitute a deterritorialized Sierra Leone through the assemblage of the country's refugees and migrants.

The emergent figure of the refugee in contemporary political debates—replacing the traditional "citizen" attached to the land by blood and territoriality and, in the process, representing "the extreme phase of the separation of the rights of man from the rights of the citizen" (Agamben 1998:133)—raises crucial questions about the juridical implications of deterritorialization. People become refugees at territorial borders between states (otherwise, humanitarian organizations classify them as IDPs—internally displaced persons—a category predicated on other kinds of intrastate boundaries). And it is often at the border that exceptions to the rule of inclusion/exclusion that necessarily define the limits of citizenship are made. Additionally, refugees in humanitarian camps raise the question of territoriality and boundaries in ways that highlight the "borderline" nature of sovereignty as the decision about the exception, for it is under the conditional, temporally bounded, and regulated vigilance of a sovereign state that a territory within it can be created—a territory over which the state shares control with, say, the United Nations High Commissioner for Refugees or other humanitarian organizations (see Malkki 1995:38). Thus, the refugee is the negative image through which new modes of citizenship can be perceived (and, too, a new generation of rights linked to them), and the border, both conceptual and territorial, is a privileged site for eliciting certain kinds of legal practices.

Refugees experience in practice the exclusionary nature of state sovereignty in relation to the state from which they have fled but also in relation to the host state, where they are treated as barely included exceptions without citizenship rights (see Malkki 1995:162–64). Furthermore, a neglected aspect of the forms of exclusion set in motion by violence and warfare is their impact on host populations. Refugees confront citizens with the limits of their own rights and sometimes become catalysts for processes of nation building among their hosts. The exclusions included in the normal exercise of state sovereignty are highlighted by the presence of refugees in part because states often contain them in camps near territorial borders, as was the case with large camps for Liberian and Sierra Leonean war refugees in the "Parrot's Beak" region, where the two countries and Guinea join borders (see Henry 2000:87, 2002). Among other reasons, states choose these locations to isolate the potential logistical and other problems represented by refugees and sometimes to channel the international humanitarian resources that normally concentrate around refugee camps into underdeveloped frontier zones, where host states have an interest in better controlling their own citizens and interests. Thus, Liisa Malkki points to the Tanzanian government decision to locate a major camp for Hutu refugees of the 1972 Burundian civil war in an uninhabited, "forbidding" region in order to use refugee labor to develop the area for agricultural use. The refugees understood that their role in the area was to develop the frontier (Malkki 1995:40–44, 121–24). In some cases, this process produces situations in which refugees interact with citizens of a foreign state, and familiarity is established rapidly because of shared histories, languages, and cultures—as with refugees from the Liberian and Sierra Leonean civil wars in Guinean camps—but new tensions arise because their presence highlights the marginality of host populations within their own countries.

That the flight of refugees from Sierra Leone can be, as Mohammed's case suggests, more the product of imagination than historical fact is precisely part of the argument here: postcolonial Sierra Leone as a state is first and foremost a state of the imagination—albeit one that has "real" effects such as points of legal decision, coercion, rights of life and death, and so on. This is especially true of post–civil war Sierra Leone, where international media and humanitarian interventions have projected on a global stage this particular state's "resonances." Since its inception in 1991, the civil war in Sierra Leone has been notable first for its invisibility on the global scene, and from 1996 on, for the attention paid by the international media and humanitarian organizations to the youthfulness of the perpetrators of violence, the mutilated bodies of their victims, and the role of global diamond and criminal interests in the prolongation of the war. These images have helped propel Sierra Leone to the top of the charts of humanitarian interventions, to the extent that despite its relatively small size and population (fewer than five million inhabitants), it has been the theater of the largest deployment of UN peacekeepers anywhere in the world (more than 17,000 troops), has the highest concentration of NGOs, and has seen an investment of funds by the global humanitarian apparatus that dwarfs the country's gross national product (see Ferme and Hoffman 2002:27–28).

This major exercise in humanitarian intervention and international aid has not merely supported the state apparatus: it has become a key point of integration of the state, resonating from the global to the local level. In the process, these interventions have become factors in the very processes of destabilization they seek to ameliorate, while producing more "points of resonance." For instance, donors or lending agencies such as the World Bank and the IMF make aid to African states conditional upon human-rights reforms in ways that manage to undermine the old system of legitimation, but without monitoring the thorough implementation of reforms. Thus, the old is destroyed, but the new political forces that may emerge in its place are never given a chance to become strong enough to subvert corrupt regimes (Bayart, Ellis, and Hibou 1997:19). These interventions have contributed to the loss of central power in African states and to their privatization—the contraction or redeployment of state sovereignty in many parts of Africa (Hibou 1999), perhaps even altogether privatized sovereignty, through forms of "private, indirect government" that prolong by new means colonial forms of rule (Mbembe 2001:80–85). Such perspectives on the postcolonial African state rightly link the privatization of the state to the increasing involvement of larger and larger parts of the state apparatus in criminal activities that have brutal effects on the populations inhabiting particular territories.[2] In Sierra Leone, complicities among state actors acting for private gain and global business interests, especially around precious mineral resources, have been at work mostly in diamond-producing areas, which in wartime were placed under the effective control of private security firms acting in lieu of the state (see Reno 1997a, 1997b). However, since the 1990s, privatization has taken on positive connotations too, with PPPs, "public-private partnerships" among states and business interests, becoming key discursive and pragmatic vehicles for development policymaking in Africa. Their main institutional framework is NEPAD, the New Partnership for African Development, a body whose neoliberal premises are exposed by the eclectic mix of private enterprises, states, NGOs, and international humanitarian organizations that have chosen to channel through it activities ranging from business investments to development aid.

Humanitarian organizations' practices of registration—in wartime and postwar settings—of multitudes of refugees, internally displaced people, combatants, and civilians, in order to identify those in need of development, health aid, and food relief, fall within the biopolitical order within which so-called failed states do not operate consistently. In Sierra Leone, then, supranational mechanisms for regulating populations succeeded where the state failed. For example, a range of registration, counting, and identification exercises took place after January 2002, when the war was declared officially over, so most Sierra Leoneans have acquired multiple identification documents and registrations in overlapping exercises of "hyper-identification": preparations for the first postwar national census; the drawing up of voter lists for the May 2002 national ballot; the drawing up of lists of chiefdom electors for the 2002–2003 chiefdom elections; DDR (disarmament, demobilization, and reintegration) programs; and so on. Everyone has multiple IDs, each entitling the holder to something different, and each corresponding to a name on a different agency's list.

And yet the Sierra Leonean state has not been entirely unsuccessful in its practices of governmentality, especially in regulating fiscal behaviors that others have identified among the key "boundary-marking" practices of the state (Roitman 1998). Thus, for most of the decade leading up to the civil war, the "SAPped" (Structural Adjustment Program–debilitated) 1980s, when the Sierra Leonean state's ability to deliver services or health care, or even to carry out a census, had deteriorated so much that the state could only engage in such practices when they were mostly organized and bankrolled by international agencies (for example, the UN-sponsored 1985 population census), taxes, fines, and fees were collected with impressive regularity in rural areas. Indeed, well into the 1990s, the annual tax receipt was the only identity document valid for travel within the country issued with any regularity, as one national identification scheme after another failed or was not implemented. The receipt vouched for a man's identity and residence (it documented a tax on "adult heads of households"—generally male). It included the man's name and village/chiefdom of residence, along with the amount paid and the signature of the chief collecting the tax. Since the receipt could be issued only by a chief or his representative, it amounted to an endorsement by the local authorities that the bearer was a person in good standing in the area. As such, the tax receipt and the fiscal practices it stood for acted precisely as one of the "local" points of resonance that made fiscal governmentality an aspect of the overall "state effect."[3] Though this scheme, too, failed to achieve full compliance—and left open the issue of how to keep track of people who were not required to pay taxes, such as the young, old, and female dependents of those (mostly male) "household heads"—men who did not have their tax receipts did not dare travel the "failed" Sierra Leonean state's main roads for fear of running into harassment by the police at checkpoints.

In the section that follows, I turn to a more detailed analysis of precisely this aspect of the "state effect," namely, the ways in which individual Sierra Leoneans (in this case those living in the diaspora) have refashioned their sense of belonging to the Sierra Leone nation-state in their encounters with the deterritorialized arena of international legal and humanitarian intervention, sometimes exploiting it in unpredictable manners.

REFUGEES, MIGRANTS, AND THE LIMITS OF CITIZENSHIP

When I met him in Cairo in 1993, the "elder" of the resident Sierra

Leonean community, Mohammed Mussa Ibrahim (not his real name), had no prospects of immigrating to America, even though he had taught himself English to improve his employment prospects in a country that was suffering serious economic setbacks as a result of the 1991 Gulf War. The war-linked exodus of expatriate workers from Persian Gulf states—and the related decline in remittances—had significantly affected the livelihoods of many Arab-speaking Africans in Cairo, whose seasonal employment in the oil-fueled gulf economies supported their semilegal existence in Egypt. As noncitizens, they could not legally work in Cairo, and though the particular group I got to know had originally entered the country as scholarship students at al-Azhar University—one of the eminent institutions of higher learning in the Muslim world—their scholarships had long since ceased to be adequate to support them.[4] Thus, Mohammed joined a growing number of noncitizen West Africans who lived in precarious conditions—having ceased to be al-Azhar students, either because they had graduated or had been forced to drop out to support themselves, and yet not being able to find adequate employment to move on and leave the country. Their movements were circumscribed too, because with respect to their earlier lives as fully registered students with official papers, travel out of the country now could very well leave them stranded and unable to legally reenter. For Sierra Leonean students in particular, the absence of any diplomatic representation in Cairo presented a further problem, making them dependent on the mail, or on increasingly rare visits by staff from the embassy in Saudi Arabia (in 1993, no one had come for more than two years). Finally, the fact that many in Mohammed's older generation were men who had arrived alone, and had married Egyptian women and had families, was an indication of crucial gendered and generational dimensions of this precarious existence at the margins of legal and political citizenship. In Egypt as elsewhere, paternity determines citizenship, so Sierra Leonean men have no hope of becoming citizens or passing their citizenship on to their Egyptian-Sierra Leonean offspring.

Hence the paradox of the case of Sheku, a Sierra Leonean whose mixed parentage created a rather different citizenship conundrum than did Mohammed's. Sheku was born in Cairo of an Egyptian mother and a Sierra Leonean father and grew up both in Egypt and in Sierra

Leone. When we met, he was a cosmopolitan and well-educated student in the first year of a health administration master's program at the American University of Cairo (AUC). He had paid for his much more expensive private education at this international English-language university with money earned on a summer job as a translator in the Arabic department of Christie's auction house in London and with odd white-collar jobs taken during school holidays in Egypt and Saudi Arabia. Yet, as a noncitizen (because his Egyptian birth and Arabic mother tongue were products of maternity rather than pater-nity), Sheku, too, could rely only on his active enrollment status as a student to get the proper papers needed to travel out of the country.

The much younger Sheku (he was twenty-seven years old when we met in Cairo) had already decided that he wanted to go to America. Born in Egypt, educated in Sierra Leone between the ages of eight and twenty, then flown back to Cairo to attend university, Sheku had come somewhat closer to his American dream after leaving Cairo University, where he had begun his studies, and enrolling instead at AUC. By con-trast, Mohammed was about fifty, and in many ways he represented a different Sierra Leonean generation. He had arrived in Cairo in his late teens or early twenties with virtually no formal schooling, and his heav-ily accented Arabic was the only international language he spoke. He had left Sierra Leone in 1961, only a few weeks after the country had become independent of British colonial rule, and had traveled three years overland before arriving in Egypt—a country he remembered leaving only to go on pilgrimage to Mecca. Yet both these men had to become "Sierra Leonean war refugees" before they were able to move to the United States under the auspices of humanitarian NGOs devoted to supporting refugees.

During the second half of the 1990s, the international humanitar-ian mobilization triggered by the civil war enhanced the prospects of Sierra Leoneans emigrating to diasporic communities in the United States, Europe, and elsewhere. Sheku, Mohammed, and other Sierra Leoneans in Egypt were part of the deterritorialized "resonances" that suddenly made their putative origins in an African state at war a ticket to their American dreams. The fact that for Sheku, born in Egypt, and Mohammed, born in Sierra Leone, the fetish of territorial origins still operative in the international order of things worked along the axes of paternity and birth respectively underscores the multiple ways in which the articulation of blood, birth, and territory works to deterritorialize and reterritorialize the state. Always the lucky one, Sheku arrived in the United States in 1999, having won one of 55,000 Diversity Immigrant Visas granted through an annual lottery according to an utterly American logic of the gift, "profitlessness," and excess, which Bataille (1989: esp. vol. 1, pt. 1; vol. 3) so perceptively linked to true sovereignty. Sheku was issued an Alien Registration Receipt Card, also known as a "green card," which official US government Web sites helpfully describe as no longer green but pink with blue security marks. Note that for the United States too—as for the Sierra Leonean state—the link is made between fiscal matters and the incorporation of potential citizens: the green card is a "receipt." Thanks to his lottery luck, Sheku might not have to live for years in vulnerable states of illegality or legality limited by partial rights, as was the case with Mohammed and many other Sierra Leoneans I met in the United States. Thus, if the modality of the postcolonial African state is an arbitrariness of rule inherited from its colonial antecedents—as Mbembe argues—the modality of other empire-states can also be the decision to leave the matter of citizenship for some limited number of applicants to the randomness of luck and the lottery. For Sierra Leoneans like Mohammed, a green card will be found at the end of the ordinary, more circuitous and time-consuming, bureaucratic channels.

Empires new and old have sometimes delegated the most recent arrivals into their territories to policing borders and ports of entry, so in some ways Mohammed's first job in America, as a refugee screening travelers in the Phoenix, Arizona, airport, was only the most recent version of an ancient strategy. What has made more marked the paradox of a person without the right to permanently reside in a country—let alone rights of citizenship—providing a form of "border security" is that in the age of air travel, this task has moved from distant land frontiers or ports at the edge of the sea to the heart of our cities. International airport employees in Mohammed's precarious position with respect to citizenship and employment work to screen others in very similar positions to their own—people whose fates are different only because of aspects of their documentation. These make the difference between being able to reside in a country and find employment there—if only at half the hourly pay of better-educated citizens, as was the fate of Mohammed after the 9/11 tightening of security regulations that cost him his airport screening job. Others never step on the state's sovereign territory to enjoy more or less of the benefits of citizenship. Instead, they remain trapped in the *zones d'attente*—the airport buildings and rooms where asylum seekers, refugees, and other "aliens" with irregular documentation remain without rights while waiting for decisions to be made on their fates. In these places, they sometimes feel the state's policing force without the mitigating restraint of the law. For example, in early 2003, ZAPI 3, one of Charles de Gaulle International Airport's several *zones d'attente pour personnes en instance* (ZAPIs, waiting areas for persons with pending applications and judgments), came under inquest and public scrutiny for episodes of police brutality against foreigners (Zappi 2003; see also Agamben 1998:175).

But Mohammed's short-lived employment in the airport security business was only one of the ironies of his predicament. Another was that, as mentioned earlier, although he arrived in the United States under dispensations granted to refugees of the Sierra Leonean civil war, Mohammed had not resided in Sierra Leone for some forty years. Nonetheless, his American journey was made possible because for several years the US attorney general had designated Sierra Leonean citizens as having the right to "temporary protected status," or TPS.[5] TPS grants to nationals of specific states—or aliens with "no nationality" residing in the United States who last resided in those states—permission to regularize their positions and hence legally reside or work in the United States. A special emergency provision explicitly targets those "in nonimmigrant and unlawful status" (Department of Justice 1997:59736–37), including those whose applications for refugee status have already been denied by the US government. Like all emergency procedures, then, TPS designation suspends laws that would ordinarily apply to Sierra Leoneans who want to enter and remain in the United States, and as long as it is renewed, it grants them (and people from other designated countries) the right to remain and work in the country regardless of the conditions under which they entered.

However, it takes more than laws to facilitate the movement of multitudes reclassified as "refugees" (always individualized as "special cases") or exceptions by humanitarian discourse (always carefully counted in annual TPS extension documents). In 1997, when TPS began, a maximum of 4,000 "nationals of Sierra Leone (and aliens having no nationality who last habitually resided in Sierra Leone)" were estimated to be "in nonimmigrant or unlawful status and therefore eligible for Temporary Protected Status" in the United States (Department of Justice 1997), but by 2002 that figure had been reduced to an estimated 2,209 eligible individuals (NILC 2002). Here again the logic of deterritorialization intrudes, for to those Sierra Leoneans who still need to go through the regular channels and apply for a visa to enter the United States from their own country, other obstacles loom large. At several points during the civil war, and continuing in its aftermath, there were no routine American consular services in Sierra Leone (and sometimes no US diplomatic representation at all). Sierra Leoneans seeking visas to travel to the United States must first find their way to Abidjan in Côte d'Ivoire. As the Freetown press routinely points out, this situation excludes all but the wealthiest and most cosmopolitan (internationally connected) Sierra Leonean citizens from attempting to enter the United States legally, as they must risk wasting the airfare and costs of staying in Abidjan while their visa applications are processed without the certainty of success—a different kind of lottery and risk from those resulting in Sheku's green card, which also underscores the fact that in practice there are obstacles to mobility other than legal proscriptions.

Nor is the international traffic in visas and the desire to immigrate a one-way street from poorer to wealthier countries. During the latter part of the civil war, Solomon Musa, the head of the Sierra Leonean immigration service, was imprisoned in a Hong Kong jail. Freetown's *Progress* newspaper reported on August 27, 1999, that he was "still languishing [there] for the illegal sales of Sierra Leonean diplomatic passports to Hong Kong citizens." The desirability of passports from a small African country mired in civil war for wealthy Asians may be difficult to understand, even as an extreme manifestation of the "weakness for foreign passports" among Hong Kong businessmen on the eve of the colony's 1997 transition from British rule to reunification with mainland China (see Ong 1999b:1). Uncertainties about the potential hazards of the transition from British rule—under which capitalist accumulation and labor circulation were relatively unfettered by government intervention—to one of the last "actually existing" socialist regimes may have made Hong Kong elites rather unselective about their pursuit of multiple citizenships. Perhaps, too, Hong Kong businessmen were aware of the economic opportunities offered by the exploitation of Sierra Leonean natural and mineral resources. However, it would be a mistake to see this passport story linking a Sierra Leonean immigration official seeking private gain and Hong Kong businessmen in search of double citizenships as merely an ironic, fateful coincidence in the order of things in the age of globalization, for both sides of this encounter are linked by their unsettled locations at the opposite spatiotemporal extremes of a single British Empire.

Indeed, it was the interpolation of these edges of empire with another "empire," the United States, that shaped the improbable alliance between wealthy Hong Kong citizens and Sierra Leonean immigration officials. For despite his own immobilization in a Chinese jail, Mr. Musa's activities were embedded within a transnational project of his own, one not unlike those of the more mobile Chinese citizens who brought about his downfall. Indeed, proceeds from the sale of diplomatic passports financed the comfortable relocation of his wife and children to the United States—a relocation facilitated by the US government designation of Sierra Leoneans under TPS. Furthermore, even though in this case a state agent acted illegally to grant documents to people who were not entitled to them, just as often the dynamics were reversed, and citizens found themselves dispossessed by the arbitrary withdrawal of their rights and documents by state agents, or they manipulated their paperwork to circumvent these agents in the pursuit of traveling papers.[6]

So far, the different circumstances under which Mohammed and Sheku entered the United States from Cairo as "Sierra Leonean refugees" have highlighted some of the ways in which the Sierra Leonean state is territorialized even under deterritorialized conditions, for it can cast its shadow onto American soil through the assemblages of its refugees, who as deterritorialized lines of flight (quite literally in flight from Sierra Leone) nonetheless undergo "all kinds of reterritorializations and redundancies—redundancies of childhood, village-life, love, bureaucracy, etc." (Deleuze and Guattari 1987:89). At the same time, this process can produce deterritorialized vectors of belonging to the nation-state, so as refugees in America, Sheku and Mohammed perhaps are now more "Sierra Leonean" than they were in Cairo—at least according to official state documentation. In the process, American officials have sometimes unwittingly engaged in practices that have magnified previous bureaucratic errors and forgeries to change the identities they have been so careful to document. Thus, I mentioned earlier that I could only guess Mohammed's age to be around fifty when we met in Cairo. I did so after the fact because when I met him bearing an unfamiliar name but a very familiar face, I discovered that he was a close relative of my first Mende language teacher, a fellow graduate student in the United States, and one of my closest Sierra Leonean friends—a Freetown nurse who had moved to London before the civil war. Mohammed had left Sierra Leone as Jusu L., but on the way he had taken on the name of a Nigerian patron who had inspired him and his two traveling companions to go to Cairo for a higher religious education at al-Azhar University. This patron also found them work to finance the trip ahead and, more importantly, made arrangements for Jusu and friends to have a scholarship at al-Azhar waiting for them once they arrived in Cairo.

For many years, I had known Mohammed's father and siblings in rural Sierra Leone. When I returned there after my visit to Cairo and told them I had met him and reconstituted their side of his story, it became clear that he was born well before 1949, the birth date he gave me. But this was the only birth date Mohammed knew, and when I had expressed doubts about his age, he had provided as supporting evidence an expired Sierra Leonean passport. In addition to the 1949 birth date, the passport gave Mohammed's "newer" name, although, as we shall see below, the transition from his birth name—listed on the passport with which he had left Sierra Leone—to his new identity was not as unproblematic as changing his birth date. Each document legitimized the issuing of successor documents, so erroneous initial information (the date of birth) or changed information (the name) was reproduced or magnified. By the time Mohammed arrived in the United States with only Red Cross "refugee" papers, the need to reconstitute his birth certificate so that he could apply for a green card had moved the name Mohammed, a name acquired as an adult in an act of religious conversion and loyalty, back in time to his birth. Thus, the question of Mohammed's Sierra Leonean provenance and his status as an "alien having no nationality who last resided in Sierra Leone" were deceptively clarified and fixed in new documents by the humanitarian organization that brought him to the United States, and thereafter by American authorities in the process of issuing him a new birth certificate. In the process, his (changed) name was also inextricably linked to his (wrong) birth date in a falsified document of birth and origins. L'état falsificateur, the state as agent of deception, indeed!

As Jusu/Mohammed told the story of his journey out of Sierra Leone, his name change was a gesture of gratitude toward the Nigerian man who had given spiritual direction to a trip that had begun as an impulse to see the world. But from that encounter onward, it became a focused quest for a Muslim religious education and for the concrete means to attain it. His account was essentially a narrative of conversion, and his name change was a natural way of signaling the profound transformation he experienced. But the circumstances under which Mohammed's generous patron had traveled to Sierra Leone in the first place, and the circumstances of Mohammed's visit to him, bespoke a pattern of mobility not only linked to the religious imagination and to historical Muslim networks such as those of the Tijaniyya Sufi order to which both of them belonged. It also was a mobility made possible by the fact that their respective homelands in northern Nigeria and southern Sierra Leone were linked by their common belonging to the British imperial political economy, despite the distance separating them. Within this empire, people like Mohammed's patron were set in motion from far-flung corners by colonial policies "discriminating against indigenous entrepreneurs" in Sierra Leonean diamond mining in order to undermine potential internal challenges to the state's authority over resource-rich areas (Reno 1995:50).

At the border crossing between Chad and Sudan on the main road toward el-Obeid (Sudan), Mohammed and his fellow travelers were stopped on grounds that they were "too young" to travel on their own. This was a significant and highly charged border crossing—one situated on the overlapping topographies of ancient land routes taken by West African Muslims on the pilgrimage to Mecca and the political economy of the postcolonial Sudanese state and the massive, intensive cotton-growing scheme inherited from its colonial predecessor. The

Gezira Scheme required large labor inputs, and "the largest farm in the world under one single management" (Yamba 1995:68ff.) gradually came to shape the Sudanese colonial and postcolonial state's efforts to control for this purpose the multitude of West African pilgrims passing through on land routes to Mecca. It was this latter dimension—the state's opportunistic policing of potential labor traffic over the border, reducing entries when the scheme was doing poorly while trying to entice migrants to settle under better circumstances—that probably resulted in Mohammed's exclusion on grounds that he and his companions were "too young" for unaccompanied travel. Eventually Mohammed managed to illegally cross the border with the support of a Chadian Muslim who was moved by the story of his quest for an al-Azhar education.

When Mohammed went to the Egyptian embassy in Khartoum to get a visa for his trip to Cairo, "history" caught up with him. Up to that point, he had managed to travel across the newly independent states of West Africa while still enjoying to some extent the mobility that had been possible in the large territorial expanses of colonial empires with variable interests in policing their internal borders. Often these policing efforts were linked to particular fiscal or labor needs (as in the case of colony-protectorate borders in Sierra Leone discussed earlier, and in the Sudanese case). But in Khartoum, Mohammed encountered a different instantiation of the Sierra Leonean state within terms still framed by its former colonial ruler. The Egyptian embassy informed Mohammed that his British passport was no longer valid, and he was directed to the British embassy to have a new one issued. At the British embassy, the three-year "British Commonwealth" passport that Mohammed had been issued in Sierra Leone was declared invalid, and he was given one week to secure new identity papers and a passport from Sierra Leone. In issuing this direction, the British embassy in Khartoum—and the Sierra Leonean state it represented in the absence of its own diplomatic mission—placed Mohammed in a vulnerable position on the margins of legality, with only one week to regularize his position.

The British Nationality Act (1948), under which Mohammed's first passport had been issued, had granted him in theory easy access to other Commonwealth countries under colonial policies that saw in such movement the key to economic prosperity in the imperial economy (see Mukwaya 1997:4). Indeed, diamond mining in Sierra Leone and cotton farming in the Sudan were among the projects that benefited from such population movements, as we have seen. But with the independence of many African colonies from the mid-1950s onward and the "darkening" skin hues of what once was known as "the White Commonwealth," on the one hand Britain began to enact increasingly restrictive legislation to control access to its own territory by former colonial subjects, and on the other hand the new nation-states began to regulate their borders with their own immigration laws. Some of these laws were directly triggered by the weakening reciprocity in Britain's policy toward Commonwealth citizens and the former colonial power's increasingly selective approach to granting citizenship rights. For example, the 1948 Nationality Act and 1962 Commonwealth Immigrants Act specified that British subjects in newly independent states who found themselves excluded by new citizenship laws had the option of remaining British. This provision, under the guise of protecting them from becoming "stateless," gave communities such as white settlers or Asians in African states the privilege of retaining UK citizenship. The other side of this provision was that in the process of decolonization these communities had more options when it came to citizenship than did people of African descent, who because of their race (disguised in language about birth and descent) were turned automatically into citizens of the newly independent states without any choice in the matter (see Mukwaya 1997 for a discussion of the Ugandan "Asian question" from this perspective). The Commonwealth Immigrants Act of 1962 also made the issuing of Commonwealth documents valid for travel to the United Kingdom conditional upon applying for selectively issued work vouchers. Later immigration laws introduced distinctions between "patrial" and "non-patrial" British subjects—to distinguish those with a parent or grandparent born in the United Kingdom from those (mostly nonwhites) who could not meet this requirement—that justified granting *partial* citizenship rights to some and rather fuller ones to others (see Hope 1997).

Mohammed unwittingly got caught in the changes enacted by the 1962 Commonwealth Immigrants Act and its radical restriction on his movements as a Sierra Leonean national. Some thirty years later, when he told me his story in Cairo, one could still hear his surprise at the arbitrariness he perceived in the way in which his passport's validity and the rights it secured him were altered. His "British" passport, which was supposed to have a three-year validity, was taken by an embassy bureaucrat, who without a word shortened it to one week "because Sierra Leone is now independent, and you can no longer have a British passport. So you have one week to get yourself the proper passport. And there was no Sierra Leone diplomatic mission there." Because of the difficulties involved in securing the proper documentation by mail from Freetown and London, the need to earn money for this process and the rest of their journey, and complications linked to the fact that Mohammed wanted his new passport issued in his new name, he and his two friends ended up remaining in Khartoum for more than nine months. He recognized that the problems linked to his name change were of his own making, so he did not resent the delays this caused. But he experienced the reduction within a few seconds of a vital document with a three-year validity to a temporary, one-week paper as an arbitrary act. He had taken his original passport to be guaranteed by the laws in force at the time it was issued. He assumed that any changes in policy would not affect already existing documents and considered that ex post facto invalidation to be arbitrary and unjust.

The former colonial state's unilateral suspension of rights and documents and its exclusionary practices produced illegalities beyond its borders by transforming a citizen of the British Commonwealth with a valid traveling document into a stateless person. The exclusionary practices that accompany even more ordinary transactions between states and citizens were exacerbated by the transitional nature of the very questions of national belonging on which Mohammed's identity documents depended in the shift from colonialism to independence. In order to get new passports and earn enough money to continue their journey, Mohammed and his friends waited for nine months and two weeks, while the correspondence, forms, money, and photographs circulated among London, Freetown, and Khartoum. One factor lengthening the wait was the absence of a developed infrastructure for diplomatic representation for the newly independent Sierra Leonean state and its reliance on the embassy of its former colonial ruler. Another factor was the ambiguous legal status of Mohammed's new name. He and his friends experienced, as a loss of time carefully measured in its passing (nine months and two weeks), their impotence in the face of bureaucratic powers and the international order of things and their reduction to an illegal status (their criminalization) as a result of the Sudanese, British, and Sierra Leonean states' doings.

By the time Mohammed finally reached Cairo in 1964, his change of identity became once again a stumbling block. The documents that he had so carefully carried from Nigeria to ensure that he would be awarded a scholarship became an impediment in that direction, since they were issued in his birth name, a name that no longer appeared in his (new) passport. This situation caused a further six-month delay in his receipt of the scholarship that would allow him to begin his studies, although he was able to prove with his earlier passport in hand that he was the same person with a different name in his new document. Mohammed's delays were partly linked to historical contingencies in the wider world (the changing international order of the 1960s, available travel and communication technology in Africa, and so forth), partly to changes in his own identity, and partly to educational and other socioeconomic circumstances that prevented him from traveling faster.

As Sheku's contrasting story makes clear, there were marked generational differences in the experiences of other West Africans in the diaspora who made their way to Cairo as migrants, refugees, or business travelers. Mohammed stood for the almost classic figure of the young person moved to travel by wanderlust, and taking his time to gain experiences along the way, only to undergo a life-transforming religious conversion on the road, which then gave his movements a specific goal. His narrative did not dwell on the bureaucratic mishaps or delays that he and his traveling companions encountered while covering the considerable land distance (and several border crossings) between Sierra Leone and Nigeria. It was only *after* his encounter in northern Nigeria with the patron whose name he now carries, after his religious reawakening gave him the urge to do something with himself and acquire a "proper" advanced education that would give him the necessary fluency in Arabic to read advanced religious and philosophical texts in the Islamic tradition, that the temporal impediments to his journey and the very detailed accounting for wasted time loomed large in his narrative. By then he was in a hurry to get where he was going, so his account of document mishaps in Chad, Sudan, and Egypt were peppered with expressions such as "We started the paperwork to apply for a new passport…in order to get through all this it took us nine months and two weeks. Nine months and two weeks in Khartoum" and "But in Cairo I encountered another problem…. So it took me six months to get a scholarship once I cleared up the business of my name. I showed them the old passport, it is Jusu L., the new one, it is Mohammed Mussa Ibrahim, both are the same person, I changed names." In Mohammed's account of his encounters with border guards and other state authorities, his feeling of powerlessness in front of the agents of the state was always expressed as a conflict of spatiotemporalities, as an excessive amount of time spent in a particular (other) state or space, rooted in immobility for a long time, his mobility disrupted because of yet another problem arising with his passport.

By contrast, Sheku, the binational son of a mixed marriage, apparently at home in Europe, the Middle East, and Africa, even though in the end just as foreign and displaced in Egypt as Mohammed was, gave a very different account. He, too, ran into "roadblocks" put up by the Egyptian government to favor its own citizens. He had wanted to study medicine, an elite subject requiring entrance examinations, at Cairo University. Because the bulk of his schooling had been in Sierra Leone, he was not allowed to enroll without doing a preparatory year. Even when he placed first in his class in the final exams, he still was denied a scholarship to medical school. While waiting for something to clear the impasse, he decided to take advantage of an opportunity to perform the Umra (a minor pilgrimage to the holy places in Saudi Arabia). While there, he stayed on a few months to meet up with his grandfather, who was coming from Sierra Leone for the hajj. His family had political connections with the government in Sierra Leone (his uncle was a minister), and his grandfather introduced him to another minister on hajj with him. Through the minister's influence with the Egyptian ambassador to Sierra Leone, Sheku managed upon his return to Cairo to find a scholarship to go to medical school.

Thus, through the deterritorialized displacements of Sierra Leonean–Egyptian diplomatic, religious, and business interests, and the political and family connections among Sierra Leoneans at home and abroad intersecting in Saudi Arabia, the matter of Sheku's university scholarship and "foreign" status was solved—at least temporarily. His privileged socioeconomic background in Sierra Leone was a key factor, pointing to yet another aspect of the workings of the state's territorializing tendency, namely, its role in the reproduction of class differences and the difference class makes in access to the rights of citizenship. These differences are, in turn, key elements in unequal access to educational opportunities and the mobility to which such education gives access. Thus, while Sheku's flawless standard Arabic and English and his family connections in the United Kingdom gave him access to a legal, well-paying summer job at Christie's in London, Mohammed worked illegally as a "foreigner" without working clearance in Cairo, giving remedial private lessons to schoolchildren at home. But the outcomes of their encounters with state bureaucrats and agents were not always radically different: after two years at Cairo University, Sheku's scholarship was abruptly terminated due to a technicality, and he found his university studies interrupted for three years. Like Mohammed and so many others when they encountered the legal and bureaucratic apparatus of the state, Sheku came up against the arbitrary reduction of the duration of a document—in this case, the Egyptian government document granting him a fellowship.

With the assistance of his Egyptian mother and another very good summer job, he was able to save enough money for tuition at the American University in Cairo—where his foreign status made no difference as long as he could cover the fees—and came closer to his dream of moving to America. But for him too, it was ultimately the random lottery and the designation "Sierra Leonean refugee" that had to intervene to transform the fantasy into a landing on American soil.

Other West African students I met in Cairo fell somewhere between the extremes represented by Mohammed and Sheku. Many of the more recent arrivals who were not partly Egyptian like Sheku had followed family connections to expatriate Arabic speakers or Muslims in their countries, such as Lebanese traders. Some of them had been raised in these people's houses. For these young men, other Arab countries had sometimes been intermediate points in their journeys. Even among the younger generation, it was mostly men who had come to Egypt—the younger Sierra Leonean women were either the offspring of mixed marriages contracted by an earlier generation of African male immigrants or the rare wife whose husband's seasonal employment in Gulf states had enabled him to bring her from "home." Some of these men had been sent as domestic workers to relatives in Lebanon by their West African–based employers, and there they managed to begin their education before being granted scholarships to come to Egypt. Others had worked as couriers in illicit international businesses, such as diamond smuggling for the Lebanese or money laundering for illicit Saudi interests. Having acquired fluency in Arabic and links to Arab states (not to mention Muslim religious networks) in the process, they were now enjoying the fruits of their labor by advancing their education in modern Egyptian universities. Many younger students had bypassed the official scholarship route and funded their studies with income from these business ventures. Some had bought passports rather than face the delays of official bureaucratic channels.

Note that the practice of buying passports usually amounted to "buying time" and did not necessarily entail falsification of the kind that landed Solomon Musa, the Sierra Leone immigration official discussed in an earlier section, in a Hong Kong jail. He had engaged in falsification of documents and identity by granting diplomatic passports to Hong Kong businessmen who were not diplomats. He had falsified their occupations, if not their names (as Sierra Leonean authorities had suspected Mohammed of doing when he applied for a new passport under a different name and when he went to claim his scholarship). But in most cases I came across, "buying passports" meant using money to lubricate bureaucratic channels, to expedite paperwork—hence buying time. As Mohammed pointed out when we met in Cairo, he had *paid* for his name change by waiting nine months and two weeks in Khartoum while a new passport was being issued.

The journeys of many others I met in Cairo seemed to be shorter and quicker, partly because air travel was more accessible in 1980s and 1990s Africa—especially for urban-based people—than it had been in the 1960s for Mohammed, an illiterate rural teenager. But the journeys were sometimes no more straightforward. The mode of transportation was more direct, but the travelers often had to engage in detours they neither planned nor wanted because of arbitrary interventions of state agents or bureaucrats at crucial spatiotemporal junctures. These travelers, too, had experienced stretches as illegal workers, dangerous brushes with criminals or the police in foreign countries, and summary expulsions with the excuse that they carried "invalid" documents. In particular, the fact that they used air travel for each leg of their trips deferred for them questions about national belonging that for Mohammed were raised differently every time he crossed successive land borders. They had to face these questions only when departing and arriving at "sanitized" customs and passport checkpoints at foreign international airports. Because these are shared with all categories of passengers, including the elite who can afford rapid air travel, these "checkpoints" may appear to be run according to more efficient, less arbitrary principles than remote land border crossings.

But the state's control over territory and time, even in these zones of apparently rapid transit, becomes apparent as soon as a "problem" is found in a traveler's documents. Some of the young men in Cairo told harrowing stories about being isolated in the much less sanitized environment of separate rooms or buildings, to which only state authorities had access, in the zones d'attente of the Charles de Gaulle Airport in Paris. There, once again, the state took control over time. Once confined in these "waiting areas," as the term zone d'attente implies, the men lost control over the time they had cleverly "bought" by paying for an airline ticket instead of other means of transport, by expediting their passport and visa applications, and so on.

CONCLUSION

The state's control over territory and populations is often experienced as control over space-time—the duration of passports, visas, scholarships, residence and work permits, and so forth. One key additional "state effect," then, is the state's capacity to appear eternal—indeed "thinglike" in its eternity—in its powerful determinations of who might and might not have access to what, in its role as gatekeeper, even when the door or gate its agents guard appears to be democratically and transparently open to the deserving among the multitudes. In "Before the Law," a much analyzed section in *The Trial,* Kafka portrays "the man from the country" arriving to consult the law and finding the door open but watched by an imposing guard, who tells him that he may go in if he wants but will not be able to get past other doors or guards inside. The man ends up waiting for the rest of his life, outside the open door to the law, to be granted permission to enter. Law, too, operates this way then, apparently open but playing for time (and with time) to limit access and determine the outcome of cases. Who "has time" to bring a court case, for instance, against a government that unlawfully denies one a document or access to a territory? If one has money, one pays for a lawyer's time—carefully clocked to the minute at hourly rates—to follow through a case. Otherwise, one invests enormous amounts of one's own time and knowledge. But even then, education is key: it is significant that Kafka portrays the man in a lifelong wait to gain access to the law as a peasant, not an urban dweller. The man from the country in Kafka's story is Mohammed, not Sheku. But ultimately both of them simply got up and went to a different door, even though in Kafka's story, the guard tells the man from the country, just before he dies, that this particular access to the law had been there exclusively for him and would after his death close forever.

Thus, if the "state effect" and "law effect" are partially operative on the level of controlling narratives of lived time and literally making people wait (Mohammed, for his passport and then his scholarship; Sheku, for his scholarship), they are also about singularizing relations with people. States control populations and territories, and supranational entities such as humanitarian organizations and international bodies like the UN, the World Trade Organization, and so on, exercise other governmental forms of control, but they often do so through a logic of singularization. Passports and other documents tend to place people within "populations" (the census is a good example, classifying people as it does by age, occupation, and so forth), but they also serve to singularize identities and fix them in time—rigidly so, in fact, since a single passport cannot accommodate the multiple names that over the course of a person's life span often signal important identity transformations. Instead, each change requires a new passport. The state allows the individual to change name, marital status, appearance, and so forth, but it can accommodate only a single facet at any given time and requires the document to be changed with every change in identity. The US attorney general argues for renewing Sierra Leone's TPS designation on the basis of specific estimated counts of individual "eligible applicants" and on the claim that refugees from particular areas are "special cases" at any given time and, as such, deserve to be treated as exceptions to normal immigration laws. The whole logic of the decision on the exception—if we take seriously Schmitt's argument that it has to serve as a *general* theory of the state's authority and not merely as applying to "states of emergency"—is one of singularization, for each exception must be decided on a case-by-case basis and not for an entire class of phenomena.

In this process of singularization, the state effect works differently on different citizen-subjects. The issue of race came to the fore in my discussion of changing UK immigration laws in the transition from an almost exclusively "White Commonwealth" to a slightly more café-au-lait one once the South Asian colonies attained independence in 1947–1948 (triggering the Nationality Act of 1948) and ending with the African independences in the 1950s and early 1960s (which brought about the 1962 and 1968 Immigration Acts). Finally, the 1971 Immigration Act, a prelude—perhaps a prerequisite?—to Britain's joining the European Union, explicitly distinguished between white and nonwhite citizens of the United Kingdom and colonies by requiring a "direct link of descent by blood with the UK" in order for former subjects to gain access to its territory (Hope 1997). But another singularizing effect acts along the axis of gender.

The fact that matters of citizenship are determined according to paternity in Egypt and Sierra Leone, or that taxation in rural Sierra Leone applies only to (mostly male) heads of household, means that male and female subjects experience the "state effect" differently in these contexts. The Egyptian mothers of Sheku and those like him who are noncitizens despite being born of mixed marriages suffered the effects of the state's exclusionary practices in the most intimate spheres of their lives. They experienced them as the sudden disruption of their domestic and affective lives, a kind of deterritorialization of the heart when a short visit back home by a foreign husband and an Egyptian-born child—as the journey that took Sheku to Sierra Leone at age eight was supposed to be—became a twelve-year separation. The sudden illness and then death of Sheku's father during their journey to Sierra Leone left the son in the hands of his paternal relatives for the rest of his formative years, with his Egyptian mother unable to get him back. My stay in Cairo was punctuated by encounters with other such mothers, who in the knowledge that I would be going from there to Sierra

Leone plied me with names, pictures, and messages for stranded children from mixed marriages, children who sometimes suffered more than others the uncertainties and displacements of the unfolding civil war.

Aspects of Mohammed's and Sheku's bureaucratic and legal entanglements are common to the migrant experience, and in some ways this is precisely the point: if all states, no matter how close they appear to be in their functioning to modal parliamentarian, totalitarian, or socialist (and so on) states, subject their citizens to a greater or lesser extent to the "blockages" and detours, the loss of time experienced by these and other Sierra Leonean migrants and refugees, then weighing in on the relative strength or weakness of a state, or whether it is "solid" or "shadow," is a somewhat misplaced effort. Furthermore, though Mbembe may be right to argue that the regime of impunity developed in colonial and postcolonial African states became a historically specific phenomenon because of the ways in which it was grafted onto the political economy and (socialized) memory of slavery and the forms of racism it generated, it would be misleading to draw the conclusion from this argument that there is such a thing as a state that does not act with impunity. All states, as Deleuze and Guattari point out, are integrated "intra-consistently" at different points and on different levels, and perhaps to different degrees—depending on the context and historical moment—in ways that constitute more a system of resonances that produce an overall "state effect" (in Mitchell's words) than something of consistency in the other sense of the term, something with a certain firmness, even solidity. Even the "weak" Sierra Leonean state made its effects felt locally as well as on the global scene and produced an interiority as well as an exteriority in the experiences of its citizens— including those, like Mohammed, who had spent the better part of their lives out of its territory. For "it is a vital concern of every State…to control migrations and, more generally, to establish a zone of rights over an entire 'exterior,' over all the flows traversing the ecumenon" (Deleuze and Guattari 1987:385; see also Sassen 1998), and it is at the very least in this sense—in the exterior and at the global level—that the state operates as an apparatus of capture. This does not mean that the state is reducible to foreign policy "or a set of relations among States" (Deleuze and Guattari 1987:360), because in its exterior manifestations it is always also pulled toward internalizing and appropriating locally. It is always situated between different polarities. Among these, the urban-rural polarity is a key one upon which many others are mapped in order to produce the "state effect"—hence Kafka's representation of the man denied access to the law as being "from the country," not to mention Mamdani's bipartite model of postcolonial African states as polarities between mostly urban citizens having access to "The Law" and rural subjects ruled by native administrations through the colonial invention of customary law.

But the state effect is also ecumenical in its reach. The absence of a Sierra Leonean embassy in Khartoum in the 1960s or in Cairo in the 1990s slowed efforts by holders of that country's passports to secure traveling or identity papers. But the closure of the American embassy in Freetown during the 1991–2002 civil war and its aftermath also brought about spatial detours and added (wasted) time for US citizens in Sierra Leone, who had to travel to Abidjan or Conakry to regularize their papers. Their experiences of such complications may not have been as traumatic as they were for Mohammed, the man from the country, or for some of his fellow Cairo-based Sierra Leoneans, who literally died there while waiting for a chance to return "home" to Sierra Leone, or even for the Cairo-born Sheku. The point remains that both Sierra Leonean and American citizens are subject to these forms of capture once they find themselves in the ambiguous zones devoid of rights that all states produce. In these ambiguous zones there are also possibilities for flight, and it is here that the reconstitution of subjectivity beyond the categories of citizenship, refugees, and migrants can unfold.

Notes

I thank Deborah Poole and Veena Das for inviting me to join in April 2001 the collegial and productive atmosphere of their advanced seminar at the School of American Research in Santa Fe, for which an earlier draft of this chapter was written. I am grateful, too, for their feedback and for that of the other seminar participants, especially Janet Roitman, as always a close reader and robust critic. For comments on later versions, I thank Peter Geschiere, and the reviewers for the SAR Press. As always, Luca D'Isanto was there when it most mattered with his exemplary analytical clarity. I alone am responsible for the final outcome.

1. On the idea of l'état falsificateur, see Hibou (1997).

2. See Michel Galy (1998) for the Liberian case, understood as a "per version" of the relationship with the "war machine" that Deleuze and Guattari argue must ultimately remain separate from—albeit susceptible to being captured by—the state apparatus.

3. See Ferme (1998:563–65) and Fyfe (1962). Fanthorpe (2001:380) discusses early-twentieth-century policies of the colonial state in this regard and the use of tax receipts as identification during that period.

4. Sierra Leonean students in Cairo were organized in the Sierra Leone Student Union (SLSU), a group with some four hundred members. Of these, just under fifty were officially enrolled at al-Azhar. By comparison, there were about 340 Senegalese students among the 6,400 foreign students at the university (al-Azhar University 1991:26–40). Many of those not officially enrolled either were lapsed students or were in the process of acquiring the necessary competence in Arabic and educational qualifications to gain admission to the university.

5. The designation of Sierra Leonean citizens under TPS began in October 1997 under then Attorney General Janet Reno (Department of Justice 1997:59736–37). Like all emergency provisions, TPS designation must be revised regularly, in this case annually. In September 2003, Sierra Leone's TPS status was revoked, effective May 3, 2004, by the Department of Homeland Security, under whose jurisdiction such matters now fall (Federal Register 2003).

6. Passport dealings of the sort attempted by Mr. Musa became more difficult with the introduction in May 2001 of state-of-the-art, falsification-proof, and machine-readable passports in Sierra Leone. For a conceptual and material history of the passport, especially with reference to the state's relative interest in surveillance of populations and their mobility within its territory (for instance, between rural and urban areas) as opposed to beyond national borders, see Torpey (2000).

5

Anthropologist Discovers Legendary Two-Faced Indian!

Margins, the State, and Duplicity in Postwar Guatemala

Diane M. Nelson

The subject is here "beheaded," "lost in the crowd," yet the
transsubjective mechanism which regulates the process (games…
carnivals) is clearly of a symbolic nature: it can be unearthed by
means of the act of interpretation.

—*Slavoj Žižek,* Enjoy Your Symptom!

In December 1996 the Guatemalan state and the URNG
(Guatemalan National Revolutionary Unity) guerrillas signed a peace
treaty ending thirty-five years of civil war. The official end of the war
unleashed an explosion of organizing around Mayan rights, reincorporation of refugees, women's issues, environmental concerns, and historical reincorporation of memory—especially how to remember the
war. I have recently noticed the violence being explained as the result
of *engaño* (deluding, beguiling, duping)—by the army, the government, the guerrillas, the NGOs, or even the person telling the story.
Some attribute their survival to *their* ability to dupe others, to live with
"two faces." But often people explain their own actions as based on
engaño, a result less of their own will than of someone else's will working on them. I do not want to suggest that people really are duped by
some beguiling, insidious power. Rather, I am curious why the concept
of duping explains things to people now.

In this chapter I explore this idea of duping to frame the puzzle of
the state at its margins. The metaphors of core and periphery, capital

and border, position the less powerful—the poor, women, indigenous people—struggling, as bell hooks (1984) put it, to move "from margin to center." Dictionaries define the center as something that contains power and control, the point around which anything revolves, from which ideas and influences emanate, to which many people are attracted—in other words, the traditional notion of the sovereign state. More recent thinking has displaced the state into various apparatuses, the broken landscape of civil society, a network rather than a node (Althusser 1971; Gramsci 1989; Castells 1989). Following this de-centering and the epigraph from Žižek, I propose the metaphor of the sideshow as my "act of interpretation" to think about people's experiences of engaño, of being lost in the crowd. I draw from a number of theorists who deploy a similar theatrical or carnivalesque model (Bakhtin 1984; Boone 1999; Geertz 1980; Guha 1983) or who focus on the magical, fantastic, or imaginative aspects of the state (Brown 1995; Coronil 1997; Hansen and Stepputat 2001; Rose 1996; Taussig 1997). I want to explore the simultaneous suspicion, uncertainty, fascination, and desire that surround the state, while keeping in mind Foucault's warning: "[P]erhaps the state…does not have this unity, this individuality, this rigorous functionality, nor, to speak frankly, this importance." (1991:103)

A margin is a border or brink. Emily Martin imagines certain people who seem to live on the outskirts, in traditional unchanging places, as actually the ones "inhabiting an exposed cusp…feel[ing] acutely the raw impact of forces of change." Academics like myself, based in the global north, are not necessarily on the forefront of changes. In fact, we may be marginal, as Martin says, "the last to learn about some of the profound shifts shaking most of our major institutions." (1994:8–9) Here I discuss a "marginal" place—Guatemala—and one of its margins, a highland village called Joyabaj and its even more marginal hamlets, at a marginal time—a period between war and (hopefully) peace. I also explore the margin between the state and its subjects, that fraught cusp between the life of the collective and the life of the individual.

Stringing together a series of stories about engaño and two-faced Indians to explore the state more as sideshow than center attraction, I am interested in the uncanny sense of duping as being acted on from outside. I am curious how the Guatemalan state, which carried out genocide in the early 1980s and is grossly inefficient and corrupt, still exerts a strange, ambivalent appeal for its subjects, becoming the guarantor of Mayan rights and peace accords (COPMAGUA 1995). As Slavoj Žižek asks, "[H]ow does an empirical, positively given object become an object of desire; how does it begin to contain some X ...something which is 'in it more than it' and makes it worthy of our desire?" (1989:119). I suggest that the state seems fixed (static), a condition or form of being. However, when we explore its operations at the margin, it is actually ecstatic (X-static), coming out of stillness, a mobile force (sideshows are all about mobility). Dictionaries define *ecstatic* as "subject to ecstasy," and my inquiry is moved by this double entendre of "subject to"—the idea that a self is acted on by an outside force in order to become a subject at all (Butler 1987, 1993; Hegel [1807] 1977). Stories about duping assume a double—two faces, two lives, this double move that is the entry point to identification. While the gruesome state violence of Guatemala's civil war may seem aberrant, people's experiences on this cusp may aid in understanding subjection more generally and capture profound shifts that affect us all.

THE TWO-FACED INDIAN

A catechist is in his second hour of speaking in Maya-K'iche' about martyrs. He links the martyrdom of the biblical Israelites with Jesus Christ, then with the 1980 assassination of the local priest, and finally with the recent state-sponsored genocide of the "Mayan people." He is a corn farmer who also migrates to pick coffee, and unlike most men his age, he wears *traje* (traditional clothing). It is July 2000, and this is the first day in a week of mission work connected to the Vatican's Jubilee Year. Genocide is not part of the standardized lesson plan distributed by the Church.

I am sitting on a dirt floor covered with pine needles in a schoolroom in an outlying hamlet of the highland Guatemalan town of Joyabaj and feeling a bit surprised when he uses the term *Maya*. It is usually associated with urban-based, white-collar indigenous activists. In fact, when I had asked the indigenous mayor *(alcalde indígena)* of Joyabaj whether there were "Maya" in the area, he looked puzzled, then asked if I was looking for a museum.[1] As I do some deep "hanging out" (that is, sleeping in the school), I learn that the Guatemalan Mayan Language Academy (ALMG), an indigenous-run, autonomous state agency, is providing the village with culturally sensitive curricular materials in both Spanish and Maya-K'iche'. All three official teachers in this public school are local K'iche' speakers. Some have been involved in Mayan revitalization efforts for many years, and several are studying "intercultural education" through a National University extension program taught by Mayan activists I know from earlier work in Guatemala City. The program is partly sponsored by USAID (United States Agency for International Development).

Domingo González, the president of the hamlet's improvement committee, had just returned from a seminar on Mayan rights in Guatemala City, also partly funded by the Guatemalan government and USAID. In fact, while the community (and Mr. González, also a corn farmer who migrates to pick coffee) seems very out of the way, it is connected in multiple ways with the government. The state, in turn, is represented in the person of Mr. González when he returns to the hamlet. He frequently visits the departmental and national capital, seeking funds and material support for education and road building. Indigenous intellectuals created the ALMG in the early 1980s, and they struggled for a decade to gain legal recognition for the academy. In 1990 it became an autonomous state agency. At the seminar on Mayan educational rights, Mr. González heard a presentation by Dr. Demetrio Cojtí Cuxil, one of the founders of the ALMG and now vice minister of education. Here was the state in the person of a Mayan man. As Mr. González described it:

> [T]here were people from all over the country, the twenty-three languages all had representatives. Those Kaqchiqueles, from Chimaltenango, they are really *adelantado* [advanced]. There was the *viceministro* who gave a talk. His name is Cojtí. He's a doctor! We don't have any doctors, lawyers, engineers here. We need to work more on education so our children can learn and come back, like they do there. Cojtí started his speech speaking perfect Kaqchiquel, it was very smooth. Then he went right into Spanish—he has accomplished so much, but he hasn't lost his language! You'd never know he's a doctor! He was very humble.

Mr. González tells me that the catechist who spoke of martyrdom was the driving force behind getting a road built to the hamlet, organizing state funding and community labor crews. The catechist also organized the community-controlled bilingual school and served several terms as a minor elected official in Joyabaj. Where is the state, and where are its margins in these movements of people, projects, and money through the countryside? How could the same state accused of genocide against the Mayan people be embodied by indigenous men and women when local people arrive in the capital, or when the state arrives in marginal hamlets via representatives of the ALMG (as well as indigenous soldiers)? Are these simply masks to hide the state's "real" face?

Several days later I learn from the catechist that he was a leader of the hamlet's civil patrol—the army-run militias responsible for atrocities during the war. "I have two faces," he said. "One I show to the army, the other I show to my people."

This image of two faces appears in many ethnographies of postwar Guatemala (González 2002; Green 1999; McAllister 2002; Zur 1998) as people explain how they survived the government's counterinsurgency campaigns. The civil patrol system, instituted in 1981, was quite diabolical, inducing community members to surveil, incriminate, and punish one another. This system gave the military state some distance from these crimes, which, in turn, warped and undermined community solidarity. Throughout much of the country, but especially in indigenous communities, every single man from age fourteen to sixty was incorporated into the patrols. In some cases, leaders were former soldiers or military commissioners whose faces already pointed toward the state (although sometimes these same people used their military experience to train local youths as guerrillas). In many cases, however, the army laid this onerous task on respected local leaders, often catechists, cooperative members, or schoolteachers. Compared to other dirty wars in Latin America, Guatemala's counterinsurgency war was exceptional for its almost total incorporation of civilians.

Many nonindigenous (ladino) Guatemalans I have interviewed seem to believe that the indigenous people, a majority in Guatemala, are hiding something—often plans for revolt, rape, and plunder. Guatemalan state policy seems to assume that indigenous people are untrustworthy and must be controlled through any means necessary.

The thirty-five years of civil war (and continuing divisions between indigenous highlands/margins and the nonindigenous city/center) are often read as proof that the Indians (represented in tourism literature as alluring and welcoming) are actually attempting to penetrate and overcome the urban core. Homi Bhabha (1994b) reminds us that these stereotypes (stereo as dual, not mono) of masked mimicry and two-faced natives undergird colonial power relations and had already appeared in the form of "noble savages" with cannibalistic tendencies in European sideshows some five hundred years ago (Hulme [1986] 1992).

In Joyabaj, as elsewhere, masked men do enact scenarios of revolt, sly resistance, and counterinsurgency during the yearly festivals. Fabulously costumed dancers perform among food stalls, Ferris wheels, and bingo and video tents interspersed with processions that move local saint figures around town. It is easy to get lost in the crowd, mesmerized by the battle between Moors and Christians (transposed to the indigenous Tecún Uman versus conquistador Pedro Alvarado) or the struggles of exploited *mozos* (field hands) to rid themselves of their masters through serpent venom in the Baile de la Culebra (Snake Dance). Played by indigenous men behind blond, fair-skinned masks, year after year Alvarado wins, and the master is brought back to life by his shaman. But these outcomes are not static. They are open to multiple acts of interpretation (Tedlock 1992).

The title of this chapter, "Anthropologist Discovers Legendary Two-Faced Indian!" is a carnylike attempt to lure in readers. But it is misleading. Anthropologists do not "find" two-faced people in untouched hinterlands. The very ideas of margins or duplicitous natives are products of states and colonial capitalism. The two-faced Indian is a figure of myth and legend produced by the traversals of the state through labor regimes, tax and marriage laws, and counterinsurgency protocols. Žižek suggests that we can unearth the transsubjective mechanism that regulates such processes. I hope to trace the processes here by searching for the state at its margins in the figure of the two-faced Indian and by asking, in turn, why the state is *also* understood to be two-faced—simultaneously desirable, deceptive, and dangerous? A play of masks, a theater, it moves about the countryside like a terrifying and alluring circus, appearing to ventriloquize its demands through local people who seem *engañado* (duped). But it also, strangely, constitutes a site of agency.

To push this insight, I use the metaphor of the sideshow: connected to boardwalks, carnivals, midways, sideshows are marginal things, geographically, temporally, morally, and categorically. The image of the sideshow evokes the unsettled, mobile, and powerful but not always successful state effect that (through "freaks" like two-faced Indians) is monstrous and simultaneously normalizing. It is a metaphor, but everyday experiences of the state are like the carnival coming to town. We blessed souls living outside totalizing state institutions like prisons can mostly go about our daily lives as if the state were not there. It is easy to ignore how deeply regulated our lives are by state functioning. However, there are times when—Boom!—the state suddenly arrives (via the "Hey, you" of the police, a jury summons, being called to war), and it is all-engulfing, terrifying, full of promise. Mariane Ferme reminds me that sideshows are also like the state in that the experience is often deathly boring: long lines and sharp disappointment in the failure of the show's awesome promises.

I have discussed elsewhere how the state seems desirous of "fixing" or holding still everything, from people to meanings, and how its confusing legitimacy may rest in part on its promise of "fixing" in the sense of repairing (Nelson 1999, 2003). But I find the sideshow a productive metaphor for thinking about the state because it focuses on mobility, and because it mimics the experience of moving through the strange mix of now and then, here and there (medieval Spanish dances performed in Joyabaj), distraction and fascination, rationality and fraudulence at a carnival midway to show how the state is simultaneously magic and banal. This strange mix is a central puzzle in many of the chapters here: Poole questions why Peruvians turn to the law, knowing that they will never win their cases. Ashford ponders witchcraft beliefs concerning AIDS and the state (supposedly the site of modernizing rationality) as it fails to address this crucial crisis (and the role of road shows). He asks, what if the state was read as a witch? Ferme, like Jeganathan and Roitman, examines the centrality to the "state effect" of traveling, borders, floating populations, and circulations, and Cohen describes mobile body organs as part of the (w)hole.

Historically, sideshows have been vital passage points for the lethal transnational brews concocted in colonial "laboratories of modernity" (Cesaire 1972; Driscoll 2000; Rabinow 1989; Stoler 1995), where humans like Squanto, Ota Benga, and Sarah Bartmann were displayed (Bradford and Blume 1992; Gilman 1985). As I discuss the relation between Maya and the state, I want to keep this history in view. During the war, and increasingly after 1996, the Guatemalan state is expressed through circulation and by its appearance in apparently marginal indigenous places, not as an outside, external power, but as embodied through local people taking on dual roles, such as the catechist, the Mayan vice minister, and Mr. González. Its power is less in any static central place than in its mobility through these other bodies. This process may explain the stereotypes of indigenous people as duplicitous, untrustworthy, and sly (González Ponciano 1999), and perhaps why the state is also seen as two-faced, deceptive, yet simultaneously alluring—a site and stake of struggle (Althusser 1971:147).

Binary dichotomies obviously reduce the complexity of lived experience, yet images of two-facedness and a truth hiding behind a mask abound in analyses of postwar Guatemala and post–cold war globalization (the nation-state is simply a mask for the International Monetary Fund [IMF] or "empire"). The Guatemalan political scientist Carlos Figueroa Ibarra (1991) also figures the state as dual through the metaphor of the centaur—both rational and bestial—a carnivalesque figure (see also Jonas 2000; Kantorowicz [1957] 1981). Rather than rely on a dual model by asking whether this is true or false, I ponder why *doubles* and *duplicity*, with their attendant uncertainty and suspicion, are such alluring terms. Focusing on mobility via the sideshow trope plays up, as do the other chapters here, the crisscrossing of apparent boundaries between state and margin, center and periphery, ethical and criminal, city and country, modern and traditional. Carnivals (like the state) travel through the Guatemalan countryside, setting up in highland villages for each town's titular fiesta. Midways (like the state) are aimed at picking your pocket, seducing you into circulating your money as you yourself are circulated. Like the state, the marginality of the sideshow may lie in its suspicious merging of legitimate entertainment and stealing.

But there is another face that is like the state: sideshows are popular, cheap entertainment. Everyone I know in Joyabaj goes to the carnival when it comes to town. The state, too, can seem accessible to the "popular classes" via public services of education, transportation, communication, and health care. I argue that moving through the sideshow illuminates the doubling experiences of desire and identification, belief and subjectivity, awfulness and the everyday, and the simultaneity of suspicion and giving oneself over that characterize the margin between the state and us. Duplicity always suggests a double. To jump ahead, could the something extra that makes the state so "magical" be the effect of a double bind? That it simultaneously must be embodied in the flesh *(carne)* of those who represent it yet it transcends the individual body (*carne-vale,* "farewell to flesh") to represent the body politic?

THE STATE-EFFECT AND INDIGENOUS ORGANIZING

This chapter grows out of my research on the relations between the Guatemalan state and the Mayan cultural-rights movement. Beginning with studies I conducted in the mid-1980s of the counterinsurgency war in the countryside (Nelson 1988), in 1988 I began to follow the surprising rise in Mayan organizing—surprising because the scale of destruction has been called genocidal (CEH 1999; Sanford 2003; Schirmer 1998), seeking to destroy in whole or in part the indigenous population. The United Nations Commission for Historical Clarification (Comisión de Esclarecimiento Histórico [CEH]) reports that 93 percent of the human-rights abuses it investigated were carried out by the army and the state-sanctioned paramilitary civil patrol. More than 200,000 people were killed, and 1,000,000 people (one-eighth of the population) were displaced. The CEH singled out four areas of the country where genocidal actions occurred, including Joyabaj, home of the self-identified, two-faced indigenous man.

In the early 1990s I followed Mayan organizers from the highlands to the capital city, where they were struggling for inclusion *in* that very state. Trying to understand this situation as the binary of state versus civil society, or the ladino (nonindigenous) state versus the indigenous people, left me confused. Information, identifications, *mestizaje* (genotypic and cultural "mixing"), class distinctions, and, of course, transnational forces such as gringa anthropologists, structural adjustment packages, and images of modernity crosscut these supposedly clearcut lines. As Das and Poole point out in chapter 1, we must go beyond those approaches that focus only on the repressive practices of the state and that think of margins as being only about the clear-cut dynamics of inclusion and exclusion.

The current Mayan movement is a long-term political project (Bastos and Camus 1995, 2003; Grandin 2000; Fischer and Brown 1996; Cojtí Cuxil 1991, 1995, 1996) that also responds to the horrors of the war and to transnational indigenous-rights activism. It focuses on codifying cultural rights, stimulating pan-ethnic organizing, and rethinking relations between Maya and ladino. The term *Maya* is an invented tradition, deployed since the late 1980s by Mayan intellectuals to name the majority indigenous population more commonly identified by place of origin or language. By 2003 *Maya* was generally accepted in the cities by ladinos and Maya alike, appearing in press reports, government rhetoric, World Bank reports, and ethnographies. However, some critics contend that the urban-based movement, which includes the state-funded ALMG and several Mayan government ministers, is elitist, out of touch with the more "authentic" indigenous culture of the rural highlands it seeks to revitalize. Increasingly, activists are represented as two-faced manipulators. The supposed center-margin relationship between the formal institutions and political projects of the organized Mayan movement and the apparently organic, lived experience of highland villages like Joyabaj may give rise to the traversals that make duplicity such a powerful discourse.

THE TWO-FACED STATE

The margins of the state are often depicted, as in James Scott's wide-ranging *Seeing Like a State,* as sites that have yet to be mapped, miniaturized, fixed, understood. They are outside state control, grasped more through myth and stereotype than accurate information, full of often contradictory figures resisting state rationality. People do not have last names, taxes are irregularly collected, and native guides are few and untrustworthy. While Scott balks at any impulse to romanticize, he seems, like many others, to see the margins as spaces outside full state control (and thus as sites of possible resistance) but that nonetheless will be penetrated by that state.

My first sense of highland Guatemala (in 1985) was definitely as a place distant from modern statecraft (Nelson 1999). It was far away from the state geographically, infrastructurally (many places were and are inaccessible by road), and superstructurally. It was hard to find out what happened there, as the state worked to dupe observers—wavering between denying massacres and claiming that "only subversives" were being killed, not "people." Local identity seemed very strong, expressed in village-specific dress; deeply held identifications within a matrix of spiritual understandings, temporality, and kinship structures tied to specific landscapes; structures of local authority; and geographic isolation (Adams 1998; Tedlock 1992; Watanabe 1992; Wilson 1995). Human-rights and anthropological explanations for both the brutality and governmentality of army actions there—from massacring, selective killing, and rounding up nomadic displaced people and ensconcing them in "modernist" planned model villages, to the massive investing in infrastructure projects, especially roads—rely on the model of a state penetrating zones formerly closed to it.

Ideas of "authentic culture," margins outside state control, and the two-faced Indian simultaneously fit colonial stereotyping and disrupt standard understandings of identity. Careful historical work on Guatemalan ethnic identification shows that it has always been "intercultural" and crosscut by class and caste relations. Ideas, institutions, and individuals have been highly mobile throughout the national territory and beyond for five hundred years (Bastos and Camus 1995; Grandin 2000; Hale 1997; Loucky and Moors 2000; C. Smith 1990; Warren 1998). For example, Carol Smith (1990) argues that in the past five hundred years it is hard to find a time when the Guatemalan highlands were not closely interconnected with both colonial and postcolonial state formation. From the Spanish settling indigenous allies from central Mexico throughout those highlands to facilitate assimilation and tribute payment, to centuries of indigenous military service and articulation to the various plantation systems, the divide between highland margin and state center has long been breached.

In fact, Joyabaj, where I "found" the two-faced Indian, has been a *finca de mozos* for close to one hundred years (CEH 1999; Oglesby 2001; Remijnse 2002). Just as different areas were given over to export monocrop cultivation—*fincas de café, banano, azucar, algodón* (plantations of coffee, bananas, sugar, cotton)—Joyabaj produced *mozos:* field hands for seasonal work on Guatemala's South Coast plantations. The same ladino family that acquired vast tracts of land in the hot coastal low-lands also bought up land around Joyabaj. In return for farming what had been their communally held land, individuals and families had to migrate to cut cane during the harvest season. The state regulated these transactions through landholding, labor, vagrancy, and other laws and their violent enforcement.

The reeducation phases of counterinsurgency that followed the army's scorched-earth campaigns of the late 1960s and early 1980s suggest contradictory understandings of "the Indian." On the one hand, indigenous people are seen as manipulated by guerrillas—duped by revolutionary promises of a chicken in every pot. Those who survived the army massacres needed to be taught a lesson, as they were several times a day, starting at 6 a.m., in the army-controlled resettlement camps known as "model villages" (Nelson 1988; Sanford 2003; Wilson 1995). As an army colonel in Nebaj told me in 1985, "They've had a bad cassette put in their heads. Our job is to change the cassette." Similar to the liberal period when it "produced" migrant workers, here the state becomes the manipulator, creating the kind of Indian it wants.

Images of the state as manipulative and indigenous people as empty puppets waiting for outsiders to put the cassette in vie with the other counterinsurgency fear—that indigenous people are two-faced. It is not enough to have them report to the state through patrol duty, schooling, or forced labor, because you never know what they are saying behind your back. In the areas where the guerrilla struggle was especially powerful, the army was stationed in most outlying hamlets. Intensive surveillance and vigilance networks constantly traversed the apparent border between public and private, and a variety of carrot-and-stick mechanisms were set up to try to align the two faces, to ensure that the one shown to "the state" was the same as that shown to "the people." These are checkpoints, as Jeganathan points out, dense sites for both fixing and mobility.

It has been twenty years since the worst of Guatemala's counterinsurgency violence. The civil patrols were disbanded eight to ten years ago, and the catechist now petitions the state for road-building aid and serves in the Joyabaj mayor's office. Most of the young men and women I talk to remember, as children, hiding in the mountains from army soldiers or seeing family members killed. Now, however, they seem more interested in talking about Bruce Lee and how to get to the United States.

The state has been theorized as "difficult to study" (Abrams 1988), a set of apparatuses, or masks without a face. It is clearly present in this hamlet, but it is a bit hard to get a handle on. Thus, this "marginal place" is good to think with, as this is where the state grapples with deployment, effects, articulations, resistances, and "execution" of policy. The grisly pun is meant to keep the effects of state violence in play. The army suddenly and inexplicably abandoned its outpost in Joyabaj in mid-2000. Recent mudslides in Joyabaj uncovered a clandestine cemetery behind church buildings previously occupied by the army. The police were called in to oversee the exhumation. On this apparent margin, we can contemplate the odd concatenation of the state as repressive and the state as the site and stake of struggle, as disciplinary and governmental, as duplicitous.

WHO'S DUPING WHOM?

Many people in Guatemala blame duping (engaño), or being acted on by another power, for the apparently contradictory actions of fellow citizens. In February 1999 the CEH named General Efraín Rios Montt a party to genocide in Guatemala's civil war. After taking power in a coup in 1982, his government oversaw scorched-earth campaigns and massacres. To the shock of many, a few months after the CEH findings, a member of Rios Montt's political party was elected to the presidency, and Rios Montt himself was elected head of the national congress. He is now set to run in the 2003 election. I and other outside observers felt stunned that the same population massacred under his earlier regime would willingly vote for him fifteen years later. What should be a static position, a single face (resentful victims), becomes uncannily mobile. It is tempting to fall back on duping to explain this apparent anomaly. I was similarly stunned when some indigenous peasants requested the reanimation of the civil patrols in June 2002.

In turn, exiles returning from years outside the country comment on how hard it is to organize compared to the 1970s. Many blame this situation on the magical-seeming power of consumerism, evangelical churches, and a few crumbs from the government (some infrastructure; a paid position) to bedazzle and distract those formerly open to critiques of structural inequality and the violence deployed to maintain it. Rather than think for itself, *el pueblo* seems to be acted on by these outside forces.

The state also appears as a duplicitous actor in accounts of the lynchings and mob violence that have killed and wounded dozens of people in the last few years. Suspected thieves and rapists, Japanese tourists taken for devil worshippers, and suspected gringa child snatchers have all fallen victim. Explanations of this panic behavior often rely on the sense that the mob is acted on by state-backed provocateurs. In 1994, for example, a North American woman, accused of kidnapping a child to sell its organs, was beaten and left for dead in a highland indigenous village (Adams 1996; Kadetsky 1994). A number of commentators placed the attack in the context of the deployment of United Nations peacekeepers. They claimed that it had been planned and incited by the Guatemalan state as a means to frighten off foreign human-rights observers. The presence of road workers in the crowd and the slowness of police and the army to respond to the attack suggested the state's sinister role. In the spring of 2000, a young Japanese tourist and a Guatemalan guide were lynched in a different highland indigenous village. Again the state was blamed, this time for spreading rumors (via radio broadcasts and public schoolteachers) that devil worshippers were targeting the region (Burrell 2000). Here the state takes on immense power to magically induce hundreds of men, women, and children to act against their better judgment. Indigenous people incited to lynching evoke Ashford's description in this volume of witchcraft controlling your actions without your even knowing it. The state, through provocateurs, radio broadcasts, or promises of gain, controls its citizens the way a sideshow magician manipulates his ventriloquist dummy.

Seeing like a two-faced Indian, rather than a state, makes the explanations more ambivalent. When the catechist calls himself two-faced, it is a story of taking some agency in an impossible situation—the state may think that it makes him do what it wants, but he knows that he has another face. In July 2000 I discussed the lynching of the Japanese tourist with a Mayan teacher from northern El Quiché, who said, "But lynchings come from the United States. The word *lynch* comes from a white man killing a black." In the past three years there have been at least two lynchings in Joyabaj. In both cases the victims were Guatemalan men. They were, according to witnesses, well-known thieves and murderers. Precisely because of the often lamented "rule of impunity"—that is, because the state refused to move against these men—local men and women say that they took matters into their own hands and punished them, hanging the reputed murderers in the central square of a hamlet.

The reasons for General Efraín Rios Montt's popularity and reelection, despite his complicity in genocide, are also multifaceted. They include class identification among his supporters (Rios Montt was a poor ladino child from the highlands who worked his way up through the military), his paternal style, a certain populism and attention to indigenous representation in his party, the promise of Protestant discipline and moral rectitude, and mobile memorializations of the war (things did improve in particular areas during his de facto government). I do not want to posit a rational-choice reading to oppose that of duping. As we know, those of us who think that we are not duped (we know the guy is a war criminal) may err in thinking that Rios Montt's supporters are simply fooled by his empty promises.

TWO FACES, THE MAYA AND ECSTATIC IDENTIFICATIONS

What does it mean to live with "two faces" between the state and one's people? This is an untenable yet widespread effect that frequently leads to charges of manipulation and duping, to horrific violence and freakishly hybrid identifications. Mayan struggles to create a state-backed agency like the ALMG have turned indigenous people into state representatives when they visit Joyabaj or speak at USAID-sponsored seminars attended by improvement committee members from a tiny hamlet. They are also blamed for duping people. Like the church, the school, and the family, the ALMG and the state-related Mayan movement are puzzling, confusing, in part because they are both ideological state apparatuses and sites for resistant social movements.

To add to the confusion, geography, networks, even the availability of spare time influence these identifications. When I interviewed the alcalde indígena in Joyabaj, he complained about ladinos in the area who called him an *indio*. He said, "I am not one of those because they were people who lived here a long time ago...naked, without schooling. Now there are schools in all the hamlets. There are only *naturales* here." I asked whether there were any Maya in the town. "Like in a museum?" he asked. "Here there aren't any of those, like from before. But there is an organization in Guatemala City. People who have their degrees....There is a Grupo Maya here....They talk about how we can all be united, how to come together....When I leave here [retire from being mayor], I'm going to become a Maya." Where is the state? Where is the margin? Will he be duped as he becomes a Maya, or were the schools that made indios into naturales the sites of duplicity?

Anastasia Mejia is a member of the Joyabaj Grupo Maya. Several people described her as the founder of the group and a Mayan priestess. We found her in her shoe store on the main plaza, busy preparing the Indigenous Queen contest for the annual fair and selling shoes to the young ladina woman who had been chosen Queen of Sports. She was younger than I expected, quite pregnant, and a bit wary of us at first. She was very busy attending to her customers and what seemed to be a constant stream of people "seeing about something."

Mejia became a Maya in Costa Rica. She got involved with a group of Guatemalans there who had formed the Maya League and were studying esoteric literature, music, and social change. Some of them had ties to the URNG member organization ORPA (Revolutionary Organization of the People in Arms). During that time, she began to suffer several of the illnesses that presage a calling to become a diviner or curer. Ms. Mejia says that a Dutch woman working for a European Union–financed development agency offered to help pay for trips to Guatemala so that she could apprentice herself to a day keeper. She was initiated and in the late 1990s returned to Joyabaj. She and her husband lived with her parents until they could get their feet on the ground. She seems well respected and is involved in a number of projects to support Mayan cultural survival. However, she chafes at the gender attitudes of local indigenous leaders, including the alcalde indígena. She is also frustrated with her parents, who want her to concentrate on having more children and who constantly rib her husband about who "wears the pants" in their relationship. She has worked with the Rigoberta Menchú Foundation and was involved with the formation of COPMAGUA, the Mayan organization formed by the state to oversee implementation of the Peace Accord on Indigenous Identity in 1996. However, she complains about the duplicitous way the men in COPMAGUA treated the women: "Ooh! I was so mad at what happened there! They came and told us what to do, and we just kicked the men out—we really got *brava* [bold, angry]! A meeting was called to form the committee for the women's forum. But they already had the list of women they wanted. The women they chose were all very young, very inexperienced, no training, *muy sumisas* [very pliant]. They said, 'Please, stop making problems. The foreigners are going to come, and we just need to get the list to get the project going.' We refused. They invited me for other meetings, but I couldn't go, and I pulled away after that."

Now she helps support her family with the shoe store and works on a variety of local issues. She said, "The Maya Committee, we are facing a lot of obstacles. In a lot of ways I think it's because I'm a woman. I wonder why there are so many problems. They say I'm a *bruja* [witch], that I'm not from here, that I'm a *manipuladora* and just want to make money. I don't want anything to do with that—how could they think that?"

Throughout Guatemala, Mayan women working for gender equity in the cultural-rights movement are accused either of duping or of being duped (or acted on) by outside interests. Many Mayan men claim that international feminism, even a lesbian conspiracy, is using these women. Mayan women, who are struggling to be loyal to their ethnic as well as gender identifications, counterattack by saying that the true Mayan man honors equality. They draw on the origin story of the holy books of the Pop Wuj, in which women are made simultaneously with men and of the same substance. Thus, they say, men who argue that women are secondary are actually dupes of the sexist Christian Bible and ladino machismo.

In addition to the claims against Ms. Mejia, the committee just lost its treasurer, a local woman who "all of a sudden went to the US." Just as Ms. Mejia traversed Central America to become a Maya, Joyabaj (true to its patron saint, the Virgen de Tránsito [Assumption]) is a major point of passage. As Joyabaj is a finca de mozos, almost every man older than thirteen from the northern hamlets has worked on the southern coast sugar plantations (Oglesby 2001). Most of them hate it and struggle to find ways to make ends meet without having to go down to the coast. In interviews with these mozos, Liz Oglesby and I found that after back-breaking labor, often continuously for more than two months, and after paying the plantation for their food and lodging, they would return to Joyabaj with maybe Q500 (about $100). Increasing numbers, indigenous and ladino, are looking to the United States as a better deal, a way to save up money for a home or car. The hamlets of Joyabaj, like hamlets all over Latin America, often show a conspicuous absence of young men. Remittances from migrant labor in the United States are increasingly the major source of foreign currency for many Latin American countries. The Guatemala-based Banco Metropolitano acknowledges, in ads for its convenient outposts in California, Chicago, and Florida, that Guatemalans working in the United States are "central to the development of their families and of Guatemala." A private but state-regulated company, Banco Metropolitano is one of millions of spaces through which human beings and the expression of human labor circulate through the apparent divides between north and south, across national state-patrolled boundaries. This is another apparently marginal circuit, a sideshow to the big issues of political economy. Yet remittances (and the state, ethnic, kinship, and gender relations that make them possible) are absolutely central to the nation-state and the transnational order.

In Joyabaj, it is very hard to ask about the migration process because curious gringos are suspected of being *la migra* (border patrol). One's interest is read as an attempt to dupe people into admitting how they dupe the state and its borders. However, it seems to cost a mind-boggling $3,000 (US) to make the trip. People sell goods, even land, and turn to family members or people already in the United States for loans.

Late one afternoon in the hamlet, we sat in a family's patio, where Liz and I heard a fascinating story about failed duplicity on the way to the United States. Only eighteen years old but a wonderful storyteller, Juan recounted in stirring detail how the coyote he had paid to get him through Mexico to the US border had "enrolled" him in a school in Chiapas, southern Mexico. There, over the course of several weeks, the students learned how to erase the telltale signs of "Guatemalanness" so that their practice would fit the theory of the false Mexican identity cards they had purchased. Armed with new clothes, geographies, family histories, and slang, they embarked on the several-day bus ride toward the northern border. Juan recounted several thrilling brushes with the law as Mexican state officials tried to trip him up in long interrogations that showed (to me) their truly amazing grasp of the tiny cultural details that differentiate Guatemalan from Mexican Maya. A belt buckle, a certain way of blowing your nose, a slip-up in terms (*coche* means "pig" in Guatemala but "car" in Mexico) could give you away. They made it as far as Mazatlán, where one of his buddies got them all caught. They spent several weeks in a Mexico City jail with people from all over the world, from the Americas and the Caribbean to China and Africa, before being sent back to Guatemala. Juan is gearing up to go again, and instilling the same desire in his younger friends, who hang on his every word like careful ethnographers and practice their Mexican accents.

Which state is Joyabaj on the margins of? The US and Mexican states are both intriguingly potent here, through remittances, through fantasies of wealth and risk, through USAID funding for indigenous revitalization and education, and, of course, through my person, able to travel unrestrictedly while local youths risk their lives to visit "my" country.

DO WE ALL LIVE IN A STATE OF TWO-FACEDNESS?

These postwar stories tell of people trying to do more than merely survive on the exposed cusp of a marginal place: a road-building catechist lecturing on martyrdom; a woman trying to be Maya while accused of witchcraft and manipulation; indigenous kids training themselves to wear a second (Mexican) face. Laying these stories side by side, like a carnival midway we have been walking through, points to the mobility among Guatemalan, US, Mexican, and other state officials; highland Maya; ladinos; and gringa anthropologists.

In turn, the state, like a sideshow, has two faces: one legitimate, the other criminal, corrupt, and murderous; one rational, the other irrational and magical. In one the state is the people, our representative; in the other the state is against the people, constantly assessing the risk of our rebellion, always ready to repress. With one face the state is regulator, creating and maintaining standards by normalizing; with the other it is a freak show functioning precisely through its abnormality, its awesomeness, its massive differentiation from the everyday.

I have tried to describe the double fascination and terror embedded in these narratives about duplicity that posit both indigenous people and the state as two-faced. This doubleness seems especially powerful when the "margin" takes on the "center's" role of punishment, road building, welfare, civil patrol surveillance, and investigations of duplicity (as in Mexican state officials, as part of NAFTA protocols, ferreting out Guatemalans passing as Mexicans) and when indigenous people are the state, functioning as soldiers, civil patrollers, government ministers, teachers, or unofficial finance ministers and economic support (as migrant workers). Here the difference between victim and perpetrator blurs; the potential subversive power of the margin wavers. Indigenous people struggle to maintain two faces, to preserve some autonomy against the state even as they are the state's agent in their hamlets. Ladinos, the alcalde indígena, and state officials of various nations worry about being manipulated by Mayans.

Why the proliferating anxieties of being acted on emanating from so many different sites? Diana Fuss suggests that identification itself may feel magical or freakish because it is "profoundly unstable and perpetually open to radical change…[it] is, from the beginning, a question of relation, of self to other, subject to object, inside to outside" (1995:2–3). And, I would add, of state to margin and margin to state. The allure of the duping narrative may be a symptom—a writing on the symbolic flesh of the body politic—that is groping toward the seemingly magical, X-static effect of identification as a "detour through the other that defines the self" (Fuss 1995:3). In this chapter I have explored two uncanny aspects of two-facedness: that identity is not static, but always moving, and that the effect of an internal subjectivity itself comes from being acted on from the outside.

MOBILITY

Mobility (like walking through the sideshow) is central to the state as it detours through the margins and as indigenous people detour through the state via the state-instituted civil patrol, reeducation camps, ALMG, and COPMAGUA. They also detour through NGOs supported by other states; a woman becomes a Maya while detouring through Costa Rica; mozos become central to the state's political economy by detouring through the plantation system and by duping state-instituted border checkpoints to labor in the north; citizens detour through state responsibilities such as policing and become lynch mobs; and gringo anthropologists detour through Guatemala to write about indigenous people, the margins, and the state. In all this traversing, where exactly is the two-faced Indian? Is one of those faces "real" and the other a sham? Or is the self effect, like the state effect, precisely in the continuing movement between them?

Karl Marx reminds us that the value of money is not internal to it. The value is materialized in our effective social activity. "Cut off from all relation to circulation [money] would not be money, but merely a simple natural object" (in Spivak 1988:163). Similarly, to understand the state at the margin means acknowledging that its effectivity comes from its mobility, its circulation. This mobility is ambivalent, like the stereotype, always double. A two-way street, it is not just a one-way activity of the state on the margin or of external actors on the Guatemalan state. Instead, the state effect emerges from a multiplicity of exchanges. The X that is in the state and in the two-faced Indian, that gives duplicity its charge, is this constant mobility, its X-stasis.

ACTED ON

Where is the state? Like the "real" (as opposed to the two-faced) Indian, it seems to be nowhere. When we look for it, it melts away. We see only its effects, never "it," and those only as they are incarnated in human action. The state (like Kantorowicz's King ([1957] 1981) and Poole's account here of *"el Peru legal y el Peru real"*) has two bodies. One is the individual who carries out the deeds of the state—as soldier, bureaucrat, representative—through everyday, ordinary actions. The other is the body politic that transcends the flesh (carne-vale) into the larger social forms of incorporation. This pivot point midway between the life of the individual and the life of the species is the exposed cusp, the margin this volume explores.

I have been describing the (often terrifying) general experience of identification as unfixed and mobile and of two bodies in one—the conundrum of the social or the state in/as the individual. Žižek describes the experience as the "agency of the big Other" and sees it present in two mutually exclusive modes. In one it functions as a hidden agency, pulling strings, running the show. This is precisely the conspiracy theory of the two-faced state or indigenous subversive. It presupposes that the subject presumed to know, a manipulative intentionality. This reading can quiet and strengthen our attempt to make sense of the world, or it may become terrifying paranoia. But Žižek also suggests that this agency of the big Other is present in an exactly opposite way, as pure semblance, as nothing, but whose appearance is essential and must be preserved. This is how he explains the parades of Eastern European socialism. The long lines of happy people are a spectacle for the gaze of this Other, although neither the people nor the party believes that they are happy, and everyone knows that no one else believes. It is an essential appearance that rules our lives. Here the subject is supposed not to know (Žižek 1992:38–41). What is monstrous, terrifying, and perversely enjoyable about this second mode is that it hints at "a traumatic shock for the symbolic universe" (Žižek 1992:22) by acknowledging that there is something that lies exterior to it.

Traversing carnivals and sideshows, we play games of chance, go on rides that fling us about, and shudder in horror at the freaks. We submit to forces outside our control. We are "beheaded, lost in the crowd." These may be domesticated versions of our submission to the terrors of the world: implacable government counterinsurgency; the inevitability of collaboration; the obscene arbitrariness of the market; the simultaneous demand from outside mixed with our internal desire to cross the heavily guarded borders maintaining global inequalities. Discourses about the two-faced Indian and duplicitous state are creepy but also alluring because they describe these subjectivizing, carnivalesque experiences of mobility and being acted on. The state lives via two bodies. It and we are only subjects as we are subjected to another mobile force coming from outside. But even as it may fling us into paranoia, the two faces story is also reassuring because it fits Žižek's first mode of conspiracy theory. It posits a subject presumed to know, something we can interpret. For the catechist, "the people" know that the face he shows the state is one of many; for those who warn of duping, the nonduped know better.

What is the state? A site and stake of struggle (Althusser 1971). But it is also a traumatic thing, an excess X-statically exuding from people's banal everyday actions but never reducible to that. It may be inaccessible to interpretation. Perhaps the sense of something radically evil just outside our grasp is also the state effect. A woman who worked with the CEH said, "I have interviewed people who carried out massacres, and I have read everything I can find on why people would do those things, how training can dull you, how you fear for your own life, how you come to believe it's for a higher ideal, that the person you're killing or torturing somehow deserves it, but none of that explains what I encountered in that work. I feel I confronted some *thing* radically evil."

We gropingly acknowledge that our reliance on the consistency of some big Other is an illusion, that there is duplicity without a duper. Perhaps the state is the Thing Žižek describes that "'holds together' the social edifice by means of guaranteeing its fantasmatic consistency... [O]ur relationship to the Thing becomes *antagonistic:* we abjure and disown the Thing, yet it exerts an irresistible attraction on us; its proximity exposes us to a mortal danger, yet it is simultaneously a source of power" (1992:123).

The chapters in this book suggest that what appears marginal is often vital, that attention to the exposed cusp reveals more than attending to the settled static center, that what seems exceptional (like Guatemala's brutal state) may be more like the rule. People living on the exposed cusp in Joyabaj dupe and feel duped because they are double, living simultaneously their lives and the state's life as "it" is dispersed, acting through their bodies. Living in the wake of counterinsurgency violence, Mayan organizing, and capital's demands for mobile labor, they seem freakish yet also normal, teaching us "about some of the profound shifts shaking most of our major institutions" (Martin 1994:9). Duping is not "in" the state or the two-faced Indian or the Mayan movement any more than value is "in" money, to be dispelled through interpretation or finding the "real" face. It is "in" our mobility as we walk through the sideshow, in our effective social activity even as we are acted on by forces outside our control. This is the simultaneous horror and fascination in the state at its margins, but also its (and our) source of power.

Notes

Thanks to Deborah Poole and Veena Das for all their work in creating the workshop and this book and to the School of American Research and all the seminar participants. Peter Geshiere, Ben Orlove, Deborah Poole, and the SAR

Press editors were generous with careful and useful comments. I am indebted to Elizabeth Oglesby, Simone Remijnse, and Anastasia Mejia for much of the fieldwork and these ideas. Fieldwork was funded by Lewis and Clark College. Lots of my thinking has happened with Tom Boellstorf, Greg Grandin, Bob Goldman, Ramón González Ponciano, Deborah Heath, Marcia Klotz, Carlota McAllister, Bill Maurer, Lee Medovoi, Irma Velasquez Nimatuj, and Paula Worby. Special thanks to everyone in Joyabaj. Thanks to Donald Moore for "fixed" and fluidary attention and to Ranjana Khanna for going to the fair. I owe a special debt to Mark Driscoll for every kind of exchange (emphasis on *kind*).

Quotes are from interviews conducted with a range of people including Mayan organizers, Guatemalan state officials, development workers, and popular-organization activists beginning in 1985. I spent a year of fieldwork in Guatemala, 1992 to 1993, supplemented by stays of one to three months in 1996, 1998, 1999, 2000, 2001, and 2002 (my total time in Guatemala was more than five years). Unless otherwise indicated, all quotes are from author interviews, and all translations are mine.

1. In Guatemala, *indigenous* refers to more than twenty ethnic-linguistic groups, including K'iche' and Kaqchiquel. I use the term *gringo* to refer to North Americans in Latin America because it acknowledges an identity formed in relation. Joyabaj has a dual civil government system, with a mayor elected through a nationally supervised process and an alcalde indígena selected less formally, primarily by indigenous people.

6

AIDS as Witchcraft in Post-Apartheid South Africa

Adam Ashforth

In 1999, in a scene replayed tens of thousands of times in recent years in South Africa, a relative appeared at the Khanyile family's door in the shack settlement of Snake Park on the outskirts of Soweto to inform them of a funeral. A cousin in a town not far off had passed away. He was a young man, in his late twenties or early thirties, and had been sick for some time. In their message announcing the funeral, the dead cousin's parents specified nothing about the illness, other than to say that he had been sick for some time. The relative visiting the Khanyiles, however, whispered the cause: *isidliso.*

The Khanyile family took note. *Isidliso,* also known as "black poison," is an evil work of the people they call witches or, in the Zulu language of the Khanyile household, *abathakazi.* Along with whatever treatments the deceased relative might have secured from medical practitioners in his town, the family knew without being told that he had been taken to traditional healers to combat the witchcraft manifest in the form of isidliso. All Khanyile family members, except one, concurred with the diagnosis. Moleboheng, twenty-seven and skeptical, thought that the cousin's story was "nonsense."[1]

"He died of AIDS, obviously," Moleboheng told her mother after the cousin left. (She was far too polite and sensible to say this in front of the relative, for then the relative would have reported to others that her family was starting rumors.) Mama Khanyile conceded the possibility of AIDS, although that did not necessarily rule out isidliso. Her view was that the AIDS, if indeed it were AIDS, must have been sent by someone. Someone had wanted to see the young man dead and had used witchcraft to send AIDS or isidliso to kill him. Moleboheng still insisted that the idea was nonsense, as she did whenever her mother started to talk of witchcraft. In this, as in most things pertaining to witchcraft, the daughter and her family agree to disagree. She knows that among "Africans" in South Africa, her way of looking at things is in a distinct minority.

As the AIDS epidemic sweeps through this part of Africa, suspicions of witchcraft fan out among those in the epidemic's wake. The epidemic of HIV/AIDS is also an epidemic of witchcraft. But the implications of a witchcraft epidemic are quite different from those of a "public health" crisis, at least as such things are conventionally conceived in established discourses of social and political management. For when suspicions of witchcraft are in play in a community, problems of illness and death transform matters of public health from questions of appropriate policies into questions concerning the fundamental character and legitimacy of public power in general—questions relating to the security, safety, and integrity of the community, the fundamental purposes for which public power is supposed to exist.

Of course, not everyone will be persuaded that witchcraft is in play when people fall sick and die from HIV/AIDS. Many, like Moleboheng, will resist the invocation of witchcraft as an explanation. But virtually everyone here who identifies as "African" will find him- or herself forced to confront the *possibility* of witchcraft, as Moleboheng was. The question this chapter considers is, How might the fear of AIDS as witchcraft influence the character of the post-apartheid state?

In post-apartheid South Africa, the primary problem of public power can be summarized as the task of creating, through the transformation of a racist and oppressive state, a system of institutions and procedures not only represented on paper (in the preamble to the constitution) as the expression of "democratic values, social justice and fundamental human rights" but also resonating with a popular sense of trust in law and government as effective instruments of service to the public and justice. Despite the "small miracle" (Mandela's phrase) of democratic transformation to date, the South African state still has a long way to go before the legitimacy of governance can be taken for granted as a cultural foundation of political power. And with the HIV/AIDS epidemic following so closely on the heels of democracy, the government's response to the crisis will surely affect the long-term health of the political system. Yet if even a significant minority of people afflicted with the disease interpret their suffering in terms of "witchcraft," the political implications will be such as are rarely found in political science or public administration textbooks. My argument in this chapter is that the AIDS epidemic will affect the long-term legitimacy of democratic governance in this region, as much through the way the government manages the witchcraft problem as through the way it protects citizens from the ravages of a virus.

THE AIDS EPIDEMIC AS PUBLIC HEALTH CRISIS

Since 1990, the South African Department of Health has conducted annual anonymous surveys of blood tests of pregnant women in antenatal clinics around the country. The survey suggests a terrifying rate of increase in HIV infections in the late 1990s. At the end of 1996, the overall prevalence of HIV among women of childbearing age (fifteen to forty-nine) was estimated at 14.7 percent. At the end of 1997, it was 16.01 percent. At the end of 2000, the seroprevalence rate for HIV among pregnant women was 24.5 percent (Department of Health 2001). In KwaZulu-Natal, where prevalence is highest, the rate of infection in 1999 was estimated at 36.2 percent (Department of Health 2001). Estimates drawn from this survey data suggest that more than 4.7 million South Africans are currently infected with HIV. That figure is likely to double by 2010 (Abt Associates 2000:7).

South Africa faces a huge increase in mortality in the years ahead. The decimation has already begun. UNAIDS estimated that 250,000 people died of AIDS in South Africa during 1999. City officials in Durban and Johannesburg announced in May 2000 that the number of deaths in 1999 was more than twice that of five years earlier (Jordan 2000). Statistics South Africa, the official statistics office of the South African state, predicts that the death rate will continue to rise at

20 percent per year (Thomas, Masego, and Khupiso 2001). The Medical Research Council estimates that 6,500,000 people will die of AIDS by 2010 (Bradshaw et al. 2001:25). Life expectancy in South Africa is expected to drop from age fifty-five in 2000 to age forty by 2010 (Bradshaw et al. 2001:25). Less than 50 percent of South Africans alive today, according to a UNAIDS estimate, will live to see their sixtieth birthdays (Joint United Nations Programme on HIV/AIDS 1999). Moreover, people ages twenty to thirty-nine, normally the most economically productive years, are dying in the greatest numbers (UNAIDS and World Health Organization 1998).

By any measure, this wave of death approaching South Africa is a social and economic disaster. It is also a potential political disaster for the new democratic regime. So far, the record of the ANC government in South Africa regarding AIDS has not been impressive. When the ANC took office in 1994, the importance of addressing the AIDS issue was recognized at the highest levels of government. The new government endorsed the strategy of the National AIDS Co-Ordinating Committee of South Africa (NACOSA), established under the National Party in 1992, to prevent HIV transmission, reduce the impact of infection, and mobilize resources in the anti-AIDS battle (South Africa 2000). But the history of the ANC government's anti-AIDS efforts since 1994 is the story of one distraction after another. The first was a long-running scandal over the funding of an anti-AIDS musical, *Sarafina II*. The major part of the AIDS budget, 14.2 million rands of European Union funds, was promised to the ANC-aligned producer of the Broadway hit *Sarafina*. In an inquiry by the Office of Public Protector into the commissioning of the play, which revealed much incompetence in administration but no "bad faith" or outright corruption, the play was criticized as simplistic and misleading. According to the Public Protector's report, "The only message that came across clearly, when we attended the play, is that one must use a condom when indulging in sexual activity, otherwise one is bound to contract AIDS and die" (South Africa Public Protector 1995:1).[2] The *Sarafina II* saga was followed by controversy over the cabinet's support of development of a supposed anti-AIDS miracle drug named Virodene, whose use had been banned by the Medical Research Council and whose only active ingredient turned out to be an industrial solvent.[3]

Following the Virodene scandal, the next distraction in AIDS politics was a 1999 proposal—dropped in the face of outrage by health-care workers and AIDS activists—for legislation mandating compulsory notification of family, health-care providers, and sex partners of HIV-positive patients. Then, in April 2000, in the midst of a storm of protest over the government's refusal to provide anti-AIDS drugs to pregnant women and rape victims, President Thabo Mbeki intervened in the AIDS debate to question whether HIV was really the cause of AIDS and to announce the empanelment of a council of experts to debate the causes of AIDS.[4] Mbeki's intervention was denounced worldwide and led to his subsequent retreat from public discussion of HIV/AIDS. In January 2001, the Health Department began a pilot program, quietly issuing the antiretroviral drug Nevaripine to pregnant women. A year later, however, the ANC government challenged a court ruling requiring provision of drugs to HIV-positive pregnant women and resisted calls to declare AIDS a national emergency. At about the same time, an anonymous document arguing that the AIDS crisis was a plot concocted by multinational pharmaceutical companies, rumored to have been authored by Thabo Mbeki and his close ally Peter Mokaba (who subsequently died of AIDS), circulated through ANC branches.

The failure of South African governments to stem the spread of AIDS in the second half of the 1990s is a cruel political irony. Although the danger of AIDS was well recognized in the country by the end of the 1980s, even with the best of intentions, the white National Party government, lacking the trust of the people, would have been incapable of stemming the tide of the disease. The National Party government's first response to HIV/AIDS was that it was a disease of foreigners and homosexual men and thus not deserving of serious attention. By 1988, however, government officials recognized the potential for a widespread epidemic among the black heterosexual population, and basic AIDS-awareness and -prevention programs were initiated (Grundlingh 2001). By 1990, clinics were issuing free condoms, and AIDS-awareness campaigns had been launched in black townships. However, my friends in Soweto at the time used to joke that AIDS stood for "American Invention to Discourage Sex." Doubting that the "apartheid regime" would ever act in the true interests of black people, they insisted that the free condoms were really intended to reduce the black birth rate in order to secure white domination. Having never buried anyone who died from a disease named AIDS, they doubted the reality of the condition.

In the aftermath of apartheid, few public institutions in South Africa were capable of speaking to black people in a way that was granted the authority of truth. (The main exceptions were churches, but churches have proven notoriously inadequate in preaching *safer* sex messages when their primary doctrines specify abstinence.) The message of AIDS awareness could only be preached by a government that was responsive to the people and trusted by them—that is, by a democratic government. When such a government arrived in 1994, however, the opportunity to tackle the disease was missed. The official excuse for these failures was that "resources at all levels were limited" (Department of Health 2000:10).

As the death toll mounts in the coming years, the government's performance in handling, or mishandling, the AIDS epidemic will be judged severely. Policies relating to protecting the integrity of the blood supply, educating people about the dangers of exchanging bodily fluids, sponsoring research, subsidizing treatments, and caring for the dying and their children will all be scrutinized for signs of failure of political will and action. Njongonkulu Ndungane, the Anglican archbishop of South Africa, foreshadowed the tone of such scrutiny in September 2000 when he issued a statement saying that history would judge the government's inaction on AIDS "as serious a crime against humanity as apartheid" (*South African Press Association* 2000). And the trope of governmental responses to AIDS versus apartheid as rivals for the status of crimes against humanity has become a staple of polit-ical discourse. For example, on March 21, 2001, in commemorations of the Sharpeville Massacre in Langa, Cape Town, opposition Pan Africanist Congress speaker Costa Gazi lambasted the ANC government's handling of the epidemic and claimed that it had cost far more lives than apartheid ever did (Own Correspondents 2001a). The consequence of these failures in the long term could be a fundamental loss of trust in government.

In addition to failing to take adequate measures to prevent the spread of infection in the late 1990s, the ANC government has failed miserably in providing leadership in reducing the stigma associated with HIV/AIDS. Despite great volumes of pious sentiment, no significant ANC leaders have emerged as persons living with AIDS, and the party has resisted any effort to publicize the HIV status of its leaders. The first South African officeholder to publicly comment on a family member's HIV status was Thomas Shabalala, an Inkatha leader and former "warlord" of the Lindelani squatter settlement. He announced to the KwaZulu-Natal legislature in January 2001 that his daughter had died of AIDS.[5] In an interview in March, Shabalala explained his decision to make the family's tragedy public: "You know how it is—if you don't tell people the truth, they become suspicious. They try to come up with explanations, which raises unnecessary suspicions such as someone had put muti on [bewitched] the children—which is not good" (Kindra 2001).

The consequences of the HIV/AIDS epidemic for democratic governance could be dire. Even when interpreted in conventional terms of social and political management, the potential threat to political legitimacy is immense. The question I want to address now is, How might these implications be complicated by an interpretation of the disease as "witchcraft"?

AIDS AS WITCHCRAFT

Cases of premature death or untimely illness in Africa are almost always attributed to the action of invisible forces, frequently those described as "witchcraft."[6] A disease or complex of symptoms better suited than HIV/AIDS to interpretation within the witchcraft paradigm would be hard to imagine. In Africa, the diseases most commonly associated with AIDS are tuberculosis, wasting, and diarrhea (National Institute of Allergy and Infectious Diseases 2000). None of these ailments are new. All have long been interpreted in terms of indigenous categories, including witchcraft. The time between infection with HIV and the onset of AIDS symptoms varies widely, as does the length of time a patient might survive with the disease. Once infected, a person can remain without symptoms for ten years or more, making it difficult to pinpoint the source of infection. How might we make sense of this situation if we took seriously some of the commonplace hypotheses of the witchcraft paradigm?

The central questions that the witchcraft paradigm answers in relation to the meaning of suffering—Why me? Why now?—are acutely posed in relation to illnesses associated with AIDS, particularly as the Who is to blame? question arises no matter how the disease is interpreted (Farmer 1992). While AIDS-awareness campaigns in South Africa, as elsewhere on the continent, spread the message of a dangerous epidemic of sexually transmitted infections and knowledge of the impact and dangers of the disease become widespread, the deaths are only just beginning. Few HIV-positive people, even those with symptoms of AIDS, know for certain that they are infected. And it is extremely important to remember that symptoms associated with AIDS do not present themselves as familiar forms of sexually transmitted disease. Thus, it is pointless to inquire into such things as "traditional" understandings of and treatments for sexually transmitted infections, except to interpret the impact of AIDS-awareness discourse. The actual symptoms—coughing, diarrhea, wasting, and so on—resonate within an entirely different realm of experience from sex. For generations, healers have identified these ailments as resulting from witchcraft.

In my experience, when someone dies in Soweto and the symptoms suggest AIDS (whether or not a medical practitioner has made an HIV/AIDS diagnosis), the most frequent form of witchcraft blamed is isidliso (a Zulu term; sejeso is the Sotho equivalent—both terms derive from the root verb "to eat").[7] Isidliso is usually translated as "black" or "African" poison in order to distinguish it from mere toxic substances such as Rattex and other popular poisons. The term is commonly invoked in connection with slow, wasting illnesses or those affecting the lungs, stomach, or digestive tract. It seems to me that isidliso is one of the most common afflictions produced by the witch's craft these days. Typically, the poison is said to take the form of a small creature lodged in the gullet or a snake moving up and down inside the abdomen (Farrand 1988:101). Sometimes it seems to be a crab; other times a frog or a lizard. I have even heard it said that the substances dispatched in this form of witchcraft can take a man's form and devour a person from the inside out (Ashforth 2000:ch.14). Oosthuizen reports (1992:100), after surveying healer-prophets of the African Independent Churches in Soweto and Durban, that regarding isidliso, "the consensus is that the victim becomes thin, loses appetite, coughs continuously as if he/she has tuberculosis, vomits (blood in some cases), and becomes dark in complexion. The affliction disturbs the heartbeat."

Sent by the witch through *muthi* (mixtures of herbs and other magical substances, such as animal fats) adulterating food or drink, isidliso is said to consume the witch's victim slowly, creating all manner of hardship and pain along the way. Families fracture, friendships break, lovers leave, jobs disappear—all as a result of isidliso. Although spoken of in English as "poisoning," the dangers of isidliso are not generally understood in the limited terms of modern toxicology—a point that should also be borne in mind in African discussions of "poison," as the English term serves as a useful bridge between quite different conceptions of the agency inherent in material substances. This poison, despite acting through the medium of food or drink, is directed toward particular victims not by chemistry but by interaction with the intention of the witch. Another person can eat the food poisoned for my benefit with no ill effects; it will kill me. Isidliso can even afflict a victim while he or she sleeps: the witch places the muthi in food consumed in a dream or sends poisoned food into a dream (Ashforth 2000:186). It is no surprise then, that isidliso is greatly feared. Once inside its victim, the isidliso results in a battle to the death, and the victim must engage a powerful healer to repel it. The more powerful the witch, the stronger the isidliso and the more protracted the struggle for cure. For one who is not strong, however, the battle itself can kill. Although I do know people who have self-medicated by purging their bodies with emetics, generally when such affliction is suspected, treatment by a professional healer is required.

An indication of the significance of isidliso in the era of AIDS can be gauged from studies of attitudes toward tuberculosis, another rampant epidemic in southern Africa. In a 1998 pilot study of traditional healers in Natal regarding their treatment of HIV and tuberculosis, twenty-four healers were asked for their diagnosis "if a patient reports chronic cough, chest pains, and blood in sputum." Eighteen healers responded *"isidliso."* Six diagnosed TB. Those who reported TB suggested that "the difference between isidliso and tuberculosis is that isidliso is curable by traditional medicine, and a patient coughs sputum without bloodstains, while on the other hand tuberculosis is not curable by traditional medicine, and a patient coughs sputum with blood stains." This distinction appears to emerge more from the exposure of healers to TB-awareness programs and their desire to answer questions correctly than from "traditional" healing practice. The healers apparently all agreed that isidliso cannot be passed from one person to another but, is rather, "man-made TB caused by a person mixing a poison with somebody's food" (Gcabashe 2000).[8]

It is important to distinguish between modes of interpreting symptoms, such as the coughing up of phlegm (which might be a sign of witchcraft in action), and modes of interpreting "diseases," such as those named AIDS or TB by doctors. Traditional healers, like ordinary people, generally have great respect for the powers of Western medicine. However, they tend to distinguish between diseases that doctors can treat and those that require "traditional" or "African" methods. Nobody would seriously consider taking a victim of a car accident to a traditional healer, for example. However, after the physical injuries healed, someone might take the patient to a healer, or to a Christian faith-healing "prophet," to deal with the ultimate source of the misfortune. Similarly, healers tend not to claim greater power than doctors in curing TB or AIDS as such, at least not once they understand the clinical nature of the disease.[9] However, they do insist that isidliso can be cured only by traditional or spiritual methods. And I would venture to suggest that every traditional healer or prophet in this part of the world claims the ability to cure isidliso. (Of course, when the patient dies, as most do, the healer's failure is less a function of his or her incapacity than a sign of the awesome power of the witch or the patient's failure to follow the healer's prescriptions.) While Western medicine pronounces that AIDS cannot be cured, thereby eliminating a potential "natural" counterexplanation to the witchcraft hypothesis of "man-made" illness, the course of the disease has its ups and downs, such that intervention by "traditional healers" can very often seem, at least for a time, efficacious.

When suffering and misfortune are understood in terms of witchcraft, incurable diseases are hard to imagine. For if illness and death are caused by the action of others, healing is a matter of a struggle between the curative and restorative powers of the healer and those of the "evil forces." As in any power struggle, success cannot be guaranteed in advance, but neither can failure. The powers to which healers are believed to have access, in varying degrees, in southern Africa include powers inherent in substances, powers bestowed by the healer's ancestral spirits, powers possessed by the ancestors of the afflicted, and, ultimately, power represented by the triune god, particularly in the form of the Holy Spirit. From the perspective of the believer, in the face of such an awesome array, it is absurd to say that a particular disease, such as AIDS, is undefeatable.

In my experience talking to people in Soweto about the current AIDS epidemic in South Africa, most people now know about the disease and would not say that AIDS itself is witchcraft. If pressed to find some supernatural dimension to the epidemic, people are more likely to offer gloomy disquisitions on the eternal sufferings of Africa or to suspect the work of God as punishment for immorality. Confronted with the symptoms of respiratory disease and wasting, however, virtually everyone suspects isidliso. Yet even if AIDS is interpreted along "Western" lines as an incurable disease caused by a virus spread by the exchange of bodily fluids—most often in sexual acts—the witchcraft hypothesis still frames the questions, Why me? and Why now? in terms of the question, Who?

Interpreting symptoms associated with AIDS in terms of the witchcraft paradigm by no means precludes the notion of a sexually transmitted infection.[10] For example, while it may be accepted that the disease is transmitted through sex with an infected partner, it does not necessarily follow that the origin of the misfortune lies in that particular person. That is to say, while the virus might be contracted from a man's illegitimate love affairs, the witchcraft responsible for his infection could have been sent to him by his mother-in-law, a jealous neighbor, his wife, or another person motivated by jealousy and hatred to perform malicious occult action. Moreover, AIDS-awareness campaigns—highlighting the dangers of exchanging bodily fluids—present a story immediately recognizable to anyone conscious of the hazards of witchcraft and sorcery being wrought with blood, hair, nail clippings, and other bodily excretions. This message resonates powerfully with various notions and practices concerning pollution, dirt, and "heat" (Verryn 1981), although "taboos" associated with such matters are not strong among contemporary South African youths. Contemporary practices of healing, health maintenance, and self-medication place a premium on practices of cleansing internal organs and expelling contaminating matter (including witchcraft agencies) by means of purgatives, emetics, and enemas. By analogy, a person aware of the dangers of contamination through sexual contact might well reason—without needing to be taught by mischievous traditional healers, as is usually assumed—that the risk of AIDS can be reduced through deliberate emission of sexual fluids, preferably into that paragon of purity—the virgin. The explosion of child rape, coterminous with the growth of AIDS awareness in the late 1990s, suggests that many men could be adopting such reasoning, though I must confess I have never spoken to anyone nor seen report of anyone who has medicated himself in this way.

A curious homology also exists between the way HIV is represented in popular discourses of AIDS awareness as an invisible agent working in mysterious ways (such that, for example, a person can seem healthy but still be sick) and commonplace understandings of witchcraft in Africa. The language of viruses "attacking" the immune system parallels the common talk of witchcraft as an attack, as does the fact that the victim of the virus, as the victim of the witch, is said to be in a constant struggle against invisible forces depleting his or her life. Moreover, witches are particularly keen on attacking the generative capacities of families and lineages, so an affliction that specializes in fertile victims and is passed through sexual contact is tailor-made for their craft. Even an awareness of the length of time that elapses between infection and the onset of symptoms is conducive to witchcraft hypotheses, for everyone knows that witches' hatreds are deep and their memories long in communities throughout urban and rural South Africa where neighbors have lived, loved, and hated one another for generations. Hence, with jealousy the primary motive for the witch's evil, the sexual character of the disease is a fertile field for presumptions of witchcraft. One might almost say that if AIDS did not exist, the witches would have to invent it. Thus, as the number of cases increases, so must the number and power of the witches. As the number and power of the witches increase, so grows the need for protection. And in the face of evil wrought by malicious individuals, the desire for justice grows.

WITCHCRAFT AND THE SOCIAL IMPACT OF AIDS

According to all the epidemiological data, the persons most likely to be infected with HIV/AIDS are young adults (with women typically ten years younger than men at the onset of the disease) (UNAIDS

2000). Most black households in South Africa have no health insurance and little in the way of income or assets to bear the extra strain of illness. Under such circumstances, if an illness or death arouses suspicions of witchcraft, it is likely to strongly exacerbate existing tensions within a household as well as between members of that household and other relatives. The survivors will be faced with the question, *Who* is responsible? Even in families where witchcraft is not a general preoccupation, when serious illness strikes, people find it difficult to resist the supposition that "evil forces" *might* be at work. And the general ethic is that when someone is ill, it is irresponsible not to explore all possible avenues of cure.

In my experience of these situations, suspicions of witchcraft—which come to a head at the time of death and burial—cause families and friends of the deceased to seek clues in recent quarrels with relatives and neighbors or other likely suspects. Unless the perpetrator is obvious, old grudges and grievances are resurrected and minutely reexamined in search of probable cause for the crime. Actions or gestures that once seemed innocent (such as the loan of an article of clothing or the gift of food) can suddenly turn into ominous portents that were foolishly overlooked at the time. When the illness and suffering are protracted before death, such as they are with AIDS, families and communities fearing witchcraft have sufficient time to tear themselves apart under the strains of suspicion.

A suspected witchcraft-related illness or death tends to exacerbate tensions between the household and members of the surrounding community. Neighbors are also suspects. Community relations become stressed, for neighbors wonder who among them might have been responsible for the misfortune in the victim's house. They always have their ready suspects. With whole families falling into dire straits, neighbors worry that those afflicted will be jealous of those not afflicted, and thus more likely to wage wars of witchcraft against the unscathed. Moreover, since traditional healers promise to treat witchcraft by turning evil forces back upon the witch who dispatched them, the fact of a person dying can also be a sign of his or her guilt, evidence of being hoist by one's own evil petard.

Perhaps the most distressing feature of the witchcraft interpretation of AIDS is that as young and productive members of a household succumb to the disease, their children, if they are lucky, become the wards of grandmothers. Because older women in a community are presumed to be the most inclined to jealousy and at the same time have the least capacity to resort to violence, grandmothers have a long history in these parts of attracting suspicions of witchcraft (Ashforth 2000:82). The dynamics of relations between grandmothers and their daughters-in-law are already complicated by mutual fears of witchcraft, and the fact that many households are dependent upon a grand-mother's pension while the young people are dying is a sociological time bomb.

A family suspecting witchcraft as the cause of illness will be under increased financial pressure, as they will feel the need to consult tradi-tional healers and make feasts for their ancestors. In contemporary South Africa, so-called traditional medicine is typically far more expen-sive for ordinary families than Western medical treatment. To line up the full panoply of spiritual forces needed to ward off an attack of a dis-ease such as AIDS, a family needs an extended course of treatment with a traditional healer—costing typically the equivalent of one month's wages for an industrial worker. In addition to the healer's fee, success cannot be guaranteed without the hosting of an ancestral feast, the cost of which can run to another couple of months' wages. Few have this sort of cash readily available without imposing on relatives and friends. Despite strong norms of sharing and mutual responsibility in African families, such burdens breed resentment. When the initial treatments are found to fail, as they will, pressure mounts to try other healers and modes of remedy until all avenues are exhausted.[11] Few have the resources to support these treatments through to the last resort, espe-cially as those receiving income are burdened with ever-increasing costs. In families I have known coming to terms with an untimely death, a sense lingers that if only the right healer had been found (along with the money to pay for treatments), death could have been averted.

As the suffering associated with witchcraft/AIDS worsens in a fam-ily, and as "traditional" herbal, spiritual, and ritual remedies fail, the pressure on a victim's kin and friends to find and neutralize the social source of illness grows. Knowing that *someone* is responsible for all the misery increases the desire for justice. If the witch can be identified and neutralized, his or her evil work will cease, and a cure will ensue. But justice is not easily attained. In the absence of justice arises the desire for revenge. But the desire for vengeance on the part of people who are already victims is a desire that must be delayed, repressed, controlled. It is a desire that can be acted upon only with stealth and secrecy.[12] For people filled with such vengeful desires, witchcraft is an obvious solution and an appealing prospect. Their neighbors, relatives, and other associates will know that such people, victims of witchcraft, will yearn for revenge and thus be more inclined to perform witchcraft themselves. Such people should be treated with caution, if not shunned completely.

AIDS stigma is exacerbated by the interaction between official discourses of AIDS awareness and popular fears of invisible pollution surrounding death. The primary message transmitted in AIDS-awareness campaigns is that AIDS is an incurable, terminal disease. In recent years this message has been reinforced by a gathering tide of untimely death, a tide that is rapidly becoming a tidal wave. Dead bodies have customarily been treated with great care, respect, and reverence in Africa. This regard for a dead body stems not only from memory of the departed and a tribute to his or her human dignity but also from a sense that the presence of death can be dangerous and polluting, bringing upon the unwary all manner of misfortune. When people attend funerals and return from graves, they are careful to undergo brief ritual cleansing procedures. These days most people have difficulty articulating quite what these procedures are meant to achieve, but few would willingly ignore them. Dead bodies are dangerous entities, and the cemeteries where they congregate are dangerous spaces.

To name a disease as incurable is tantamount to saying that a person with the disease is already dead. So when a complex of symptoms is named as HIV/AIDS (or if the diagnosis is made in the absence of symptoms), the sufferer becomes a sort of living dead person. This category of person has no place in "traditional" discourses of health and illness. Death, for most people in this context, is understood less as an event than a process—a movement into another domain, a process of becoming that other kind of being commonly termed an ancestor. Ancestors for most people—even many Christians whose churches frown upon traditional practices—are not simply an abstraction from past relationships or mere objects of "belief" and veneration. Ancestors are a real presence in the lives of family members, differing from the living in ways akin to unborn children—invisible, to be sure, though nonetheless present and real and capable of making their presence felt. And the process by which a person becomes an ancestor, through death, is as difficult and as dangerous as birth.

Given that a wide range of customs, rituals, and hygienic practices are premised upon the presumption that dead bodies are a source of dangerous pollution, questions must arise about the dangers of pollution emanating from a terminal patient before the moment of actual death. Though African customs surrounding death suggest that the terminally ill may be dangerous, African traditions teach little about what these dangers might be. Western medical authorities insist that with the exception of bodily fluids, the AIDS patient is harmless. But Western medicine knows nothing of the dangers presented by the person of the dead. People in contact with an African AIDS victim, then, may know that they have a minimal risk of catching HIV, which they know is a virus transmitted through sex, yet may still fear that contact with this living dead person could expose them to an unknown and indefinable form of pollution, perhaps bringing misfortune similar to that of the pollution emanating from the already dead.

The point here is not that "African traditions" teach these things. On the contrary. In the absence of authoritative traditions, people are forced to figure out the dangers for themselves. Clearly, they have figured out that acknowledging AIDS is a dangerous matter. To talk of a "stigma" attached to AIDS in contemporary South Africa without understanding the mystical dimensions of witchcraft and pollution is, in my view, to risk misunderstanding both the nature of community power relations and the impact of the epidemic. For even as they lie dying, most people do not know that they or their loved ones have the disease. Nor would they want to know, or be wise in so desiring. This willful ignorance arises not simply from fear of the name *acquired immunodeficiency syndrome,* nor from shame over the sexual licentiousness that presumably gave rise to the infection in the first place. After all, hardly a family in the country does not have children giving birth to children, sons being sought to support their offspring, fathers finding long-lost progeny they secretly sired many years back, or mothers with children by different fathers. Sexual misdemeanors are shameful sometimes, but also commonplace. And while the disease was first registered in South Africa among white homosexuals, nobody identifies it now as a "gay disease" or stigmatizes its victims for their sexual orientation. The silences and stigma associated with symptoms of the diseases decimating villages and townships in the wake of HIV/AIDS, however, make much more sense if their occult dimensions are taken into account.

With cases of witchcraft, silence and discretion are the norm. No one wants to publicize the fact that they have been cursed. Such publicity would be not only embarrassing but also dangerous, because it would enable the witch to learn about efforts being made to counteract his or her occult assault. Such knowledge allows the witch to redouble his or her efforts or to seek out other avenues of attack. For this reason, traditional healers typically enjoin their clients to silence. (And when the cure fails, the client's breach of silence is one of the first excuses proffered for failure.) The essence of curing witchcraft is to engage in a struggle with the witch by employing all the spiritual and medicinal powers of the healer in league with the ancestors of the victim. Any compromise of this struggle can be fatal. And as someone once said regarding another war, "Loose talk costs lives."

WITCHCRAFT, JUSTICE, AND DEMOCRACY IN THE AGE OF AIDS

Although a great deal more ethnographic work would need to be done to delineate the precise contours of meaning associated with AIDS in different communities throughout South Africa, for the purposes of discussion, let us assume that the HIV/AIDS epidemic in black townships and villages is likely to stimulate suspicions of sorcery, fear of witchcraft, and a general sense of spiritual insecurity as more and more people die at an early age of painful, debilitating, and incurable infections that resonate with indigenous categories of interpretation broadly subsumed under the rubric "witchcraft." The question I want to address now is, What might this mean for democratic governance, the rule of law, and human rights?

For people who live in worlds where witchcraft is experienced as a real and present source of danger, managing the problem of witchcraft typically involves two distinct though interrelated strategies: counteracting the unseen forces of supernatural evil on their own terrain through ritual action, and neutralizing the social source of that evil, the witch. The first strategy typically involves healing rituals, prayers, and consultations with diviners, prophets, priests, or other experts in spiritual succor. While such rituals and healing practices can have public implications, they are usually conducted in private, or in "semi-private" family or communal settings such as religious congregations (Oosthuizen 1992).

From the point of view of public policy, as it is ordinarily conceived, the issues raised in relation to anti-witchcraft action as a form of healing have mostly to do with registration and regulation of healers, the recognition of "alternative" healing practices and therapies, environmental protection relating to the harvesting of medicinal plants and animals, and the protection and exploitation of indigenous biological knowledge and substances. In post-apartheid South Africa, the ANC government has committed itself to "integrat[ing] the activities of the public and private health sectors, including NGOs and traditional healers, in a way which maximizes the effectiveness and efficiency of all available health care resources" (South Africa Department of Health 1997). To do this, the parliament has proposed establishing a national register of traditional healers, recognizing their rights to issue medical certificates and receive reimbursement from health insurance companies (Select Committee on Social Services 1998). Despite much pious sentiment and endless "stakeholder" meetings, little progress has been made. Given that the final authority for a healer's activities and the source of the healing gifts lie in the domain of unseen spirits, and considering that many ailments healers treat are considered to have an origin in domains of occult forces, it is difficult to see how bureaucratic regulation of this sector could be effective.

The second line of anti-witchcraft strategy, however, the attribution of responsibility for evil to particular individuals, is inherently public and political, as it always involves the making and contestation of accusations within a public domain, even one of limited scope. Indeed, the effort to mobilize resistance to persons deemed witches, to struggle for justice and punishment of enemies of the community, can be fundamentally constitutive of the political sphere within communities, as people debate such basic issues of community life as who belongs and who does not, and who are the rightful and effective leaders of public action (Auslander 1993; Willis 1970). The AIDS epidemic, experienced as a result of witchcraft, inevitably raises questions about justice, legitimacy, and community power in villages and townships that will surely have political implications for the state as a whole.

To date, most people living with a fear of witches have not begun to insist that government address matters of witchcraft. I would submit that this quiescence signifies more a lack of a sense that democratic government is supposed to respond to the needs of the people than it does the importance of the issue of witchcraft. If cases of witchcraft are not dealt with in the formal legal system, however, people subject to fears of witchcraft are likely to take independent action, which can pose significant problems for the legitimacy of the legal system as the state seeks to police those who would police witchcraft.[13] In post-apartheid South Africa, the risk for the state generally is less that of losing legitimacy than of failing to develop a sense of trust in the legitimacy of institutions purportedly representing the rule of law.

When efforts to manage the social dimensions of witchcraft result in "informal" judicial procedures that result in punishment of witches, the modern state is placed in the position of having to prosecute the perpetrators of community justice. In the past decade or so, hundreds of people in South Africa have been killed as witches, and the problem of witchcraft violence has become part of the national political agenda (Delius 1996; Minaar, Wentzel, and Payze 1998; Niehaus 1997; Commission on Gender Equality 1998). Modern jurisprudence tends to take a rather simple view of the problem of witchcraft violence: arrest the people responsible, charge them with whatever crimes are relevant—kidnapping, assault, and murder are the most common—then accept as a plea in mitigation of sentence a sincere belief in witchcraft (Nel et al. 1992). In addition, and beyond the courtroom, procedures can be established to protect those accused of practicing witchcraft. Community mediation can be encouraged to help overcome the social tensions that might underpin conflicts expressed in terms of witchcraft, and public relations efforts can be mounted to defuse the urge to publicly point out witches.[14]

In the absence of a dramatic improvement in physical and financial security, however, such procedures will do little to satisfy those who see witches as destroying the health and prosperity of their communities.[15] With witchcraft, as with all radical evil, there is no middle ground: you are either for the witches or against them, just as in the days of apartheid one was either for "the people" or against them. There can be no compromise. In a context where state provision of services is inadequate while inequalities thrive (on a continent where the prosperity of the ruling economic and political elites often seems to be consumed at the expense of the masses), the failure to act against witchcraft is potentially serious for the legitimacy of political and juridical institutions. Moreover, where there is scant trust of officialdom, suppression of witch- finding and punishment can very easily lead people to see the authorities' protection of accused witches (who are generally already convicted in the court of public opinion) as evidence that those occupying powerful state positions are using witchcraft for their own nefarious purposes to "eat" the birthright of the people (Geschiere 1997:ch.4).

In South Africa during the 1980s and 1990s, suspicions that authorities were protecting witches became a staple of politics in regions governed by the former homeland authorities. As the Ralushai Commission reports of the Venda Homeland: "To politicize rural communities, the revolutionary forces chose witchcraft and ritual killing to destabilize these communities. One finding is that the reason why this route was chosen was due to the fact that the revolutionary forces were fully aware that the local communities were dissatisfied with the manner in which such cases were being handled by the authorities, for example, as witches could not be tried, the government was seen as a protector of witches" (Commission of Inquiry into Witchcraft Violence and Ritual Murders 1996:270). There is no guarantee that the present regime will remain immune to this taint.

The challenges to democratic governance posed by life within the witchcraft paradigm, challenges that can only be exacerbated by the AIDS epidemic, take three broad forms. First, there is the demand from people living within the witchcraft paradigm for governmental response to harm caused by witches. Related to this is the correlative suspicion that government is in league with the witches against the interests of the people. This is a different kind of legitimation problem from those commonly found in liberal democracies.

Second, in communities where a witchcraft paradigm informs understandings about other peoples' motives and capacities, life must be lived in terms of a presumption of malice. In other words, it is dangerous to ignore the possibility that anyone, even one's most intimate relations, can despite all appearances be poised to commit the most abominable crimes against you and yours. Given the possibilities of occult harm, peaceful community life requires constant vigilance against and protection from witchcraft attack, as well as efforts to minimize the impact of social jealousy, and procedures to defuse the desire for vengeance. I would argue that, particularly in urban multicultural communities, this presumption of malice makes it difficult to build networks of trust and that this situation has practical implications for civil society and the building of social capital, especially when a high prevalence of misfortune (such as the present epidemic) makes suspicions of witchcraft all the more plausible.

Third, practices of interpreting the nature of power within the witchcraft paradigm put a premium upon the penetration of presumed secrecy in order to reveal the hidden source of evil manifested in particular misfortune. In political life, the tendency to see evil forces manipulating visible appearances and conspiring to pervert the institutions of public power is both extraordinarily difficult to disprove and extremely destructive of trust in the legitimacy of those institutions. Within the witchcraft paradigm, the tendency is to presume that the secret source of power lying behind appearances is inherently evil. If misfortune is widespread, as in the AIDS epidemic, the plausibility of witchcraft interpretations is enhanced, and the legitimacy of public power is, in turn, diminished. Under apartheid, this evil was apparent and obvious. It was responsible for the suffering of all black people. In the post-apartheid era, the meaning of misfortune is not so easy to construe. Yet misfortune is every bit as palpable now as it ever was and, with the increasing death toll from AIDS, will be even more so.

Notes

1. Moleboheng gave me this story by phone and e-mail. For an account of my connection with Soweto, which began in 1990, see Ashforth (2000).

2. For an account of this fiasco, see the Public Protector's report presented to parliament on January 26, 1995 (South Africa Public Protector 1995:1).

3. For background links on this story, see the *Electronic Mail and Guardian*, http://www.mg.co.za/mg/za/links/sa/virodene.html.

4. Mbeki's intervention occurred after reportedly spending late-night sessions surfing the Internet, researching AIDS and visiting sites promoting the views

of so-called AIDS dissidents such as Peter Duesberg of Berkeley, who deny that HIV causes AIDS (McKie and Beresford 2000). For an example of the sort of material he would have encountered, see Geshekter (1999).

5. In May 2001, an ANC MP, Ruth Bhengu, became the second politician to describe the personal impact of the disease when she told the National Assembly that her daughter was HIV-positive. Judge Edwin Cameron has long been the only prominent person to be open about being seropositive.

6. Many Africans object to the terms *witch, witchcraft,* and *witchdoctor,* arguing that they are both derogatory and misleading. This is undoubtedly so, but the words are impossible to avoid. Not only are the English words common in African usage, but indigenous terms such as the Zulu *ubuthakathi* have long been inflected with notions deriving from Europe as much as Africa. Nor is it possible to insist on definitional clarity and precision without obscuring the ways the words are actually used in everyday practice. I prefer to use the terms loosely, much as my friends in Soweto do, while seeking to tease out what they might mean from investigation of context. I also want to stress that the personal manipulation of evil powers spoken of as "witchcraft" is only part of a more general condition of spiritual and existential insecurity that is related to, but not reducible to, insecurities arising from poverty, violence, and disease (Ashforth 1998a). The literature on "witchcraft" both in Africa and elsewhere is immense, and little purpose would be served in trying to survey it comprehensively here. Evans-Pritchard's book on witchcraft among the Azande (Evans-Pritchard 1937) is the grandfather of witchcraft studies in Africa. Virtually everything since relates to his work in some way or other (Douglas 1970). The doyen of recent studies is Peter Geschiere (1997). For a recent sample of work about the issue on the continent, see the essays in *African Studies Review,* volume 41 (1998) and Moore and Sanders (2001).

7. Zulu speakers also refer to these matters as *idliso,* referring to the substances used in poisoning, as distinct from *isidliso,* referring to the condition of being poisoned.

8. See also Wilkinson, Gcabashe, and Lurie (1999).

9. Some healers do make blatant claims to cure AIDS, but they generally tend to be circumspect rather than confront Western medical science head-on. For example, in a news item headlined "AIDS Cure Ploughed up as a Weed," Credo Mutwa, a famous South African healer and former proprietor of a Soweto theme park, praised the healing powers of an indigenous herb known as *Sutherlandia:* "I don't claim this is the cure [for AIDS], but what it does to

people is amazing. Men and women who have been sent home to die are alive now because of an ancient African herb." Asked whether he thought that there would ever be a cure for AIDS, the well-known visionary said, "It's right there in the violated plains of my fatherland. It is being ploughed up as a weed" (Own Correspondents 2001b).

10. In this regard, AIC adherents are in a more favorable position because the healer-prophets in these churches do not usually charge for their services, or do not charge as steeply as traditional healers. Participation in the AICs, however, involves a major commitment of time and lifestyle. See Oosthuizen (1992).

11. For an exposition of the psychological dynamics underpinning this sort of action, see Scheler (1961).

12. For an example, see the transcript of my interview with the former mayor of Soweto. When I pointed out the connection between witchcraft and democracy, the mayor acknowledged that witchcraft was the "biggest problem" and that the city council ought to be looking into it (Ashforth 1998b:524–527).

13. For a discussion of informal policing of witches and the dilemmas of recognizing the realities of witchcraft facing the legal system, see Harnischfeger (2000) and Mavhungu (2000). For an attempt to reconcile the claims of "tradition" and "modernity" in relation to courts and witchcraft, see Chavunduka (1980).

14. In July 2000, the Commission on Gender Equality claimed that its "Witchcraft Roadshows" have had just such an effect in the formerly violence-plagued Northern Province of South Africa (Commission on Gender Equality 2000; Hill and Black 2002).

15. For an example of this sort of attitude, see Ashforth (2000:97ff.).

7

Operability

Surgery at the Margin of the State

Lawrence Cohen

"If you work for the city, the operation is free."
> —*Graffiti scrawled on bathroom door of coffeehouse,*
> *San Francisco, 2001*

This sentence, which I discovered while writing this chapter, oddly evokes the stakes for citizens I engage here. Its specific referent was a 2001 decision by the San Francisco Board of Supervisors to include sex-change operations as health benefits for city employees (Associated Press 2001). Here I would only foreground the indexicality of the comment, the way "the operation" in its generality and lack of reference comes to stand for something far more particular, the way we dwellers of this city, in knowing just *which* operation is meant, somehow commit to the relevance of the general form. I write in the United States in the aftermath of Operation Infinite Justice and its successors, a chain of operations marking the unending state of exception of the new war on terrorism (Agamben 2001). Though I take up matters at an arguable remove from either urban or imperial American politics, the *form* of the operation as both sovereign gift and exception seems ever more necessary to engage.

To pursue one way into an anthropology of the operation, I turn to the particular intimacy of operative form for certain marginal actors in relation to practices constituting the state and their affiliation to it.

Discussing three kinds of surgeries—hijra (sex-change) operations, kidney-selling operations, and family-planning operations—that circulate not only as technical assemblages but also as ubiquitous public sites in contemporary India, I will argue that operative form is critical to what one might term the presence of the state in relation to its political margins. Each operation presents quite different historical and analytic challenges, but all share what I argue is a dominant and critical form. I will suggest that this form emerges in the instantiation of a governmental order we might call "as-if modernity."

In its bare bones, the ground of my argument runs as follows: (1) Bureaucratic elites and their client labor force comprising state planning and welfare agencies reproduce a colonial and nationalist structuring of their target as "the masses"—that is, as subjects capable of passion but not reason. (2) Planned development as the dominant logic of Indian modernity presumes a process we might call Weberian—that is, ascetic—modernization, and population control (as opposed, for example, to agronomy) becomes its metonym. (3) The development project as a critical form instantiating the state is faced therefore with a fundamental contradiction: it is organized around a transformation of reason and will in the production of ascetic moderns, but it takes as its material for transformation a population it constitutes as radically disjunct from reason itself. (4) The operation, in the instance of tubal ligations and vasectomies, becomes a means by which the development state can reimagine its conditions of possibility given this contradiction. Sterilization produces a body that performs *as if* it had undergone a transformation of reason, *as if* it were inhabited by an ascetic will. (5) The operation becomes not only a technique and a site instantiating the state but also a form marking the possibilities and limits of belonging for persons hailed as this mass body. As such, it is not only a matter of the politics and life-making of sterilization in itself but also a *general* form.

My work to date has focused not on sterilization but on a very different set of conjoined procedures, nephrectomy (the removal, or in this case extraction, of a kidney) and transplantation. This chapter centers on a set of concepts (operability, bioavailability, and supplementability) that have emerged in the course of this work, concepts that help me link questions of forms of life (new practices of recognition) and forms of exchange (medical entrepreneurship and relations of care under Indian neoliberalism) to what I am calling operative form. I develop these concepts along the following lines. To be supplementable is to be able to receive a gift from the sovereign state in the form of another's body. To be bioavailable is to be that body, contingently mattering as an articulation of markets, relations of affection and disaffection, and the presence of a technical apparatus. And to be operable is to be that body *not only* as such an articulation: it is to be that body as a countergift to the state, in some cases as a sacrifice resurrecting a failing or absent sovereign. From a different perspective, to be operable is to be assimilated to norms of modern citizenship and its constitutive will—despite oneself—through a radical, here surgical, act of subsumption.

Left unto itself, the case of transplantation even in the context of its critical link to sterilization in South India will not foreground the general form of the operation adequately. So I introduce a third operation, foreshadowed in my opening: the open secret of the hijra operation, the castration and penectomy that seals a third-gendered hijra (eunuch) status as ritually, sexually, and, as we will see, politically distinct. As sterilization produces a citizen-body that acts *as if* it were modern, castration produces a politician-body with a similar *as if* relation to the contractual narrative of modern statecraft.

"If you work for the city, the operation is free." What sort of freedom is it, demands this thesis inked to a bathroom door, to have one's relation to the polis defined by an operation as the form of the sovereign gift?

THE OPERATION AND ITS INTIMACY

We are awash in operations. Since 1997 I have been writing about the transplantation of a kidney and the social and imaginary relations between persons that it appears to remake. My focus, in tandem with the extensive work of my colleague Nancy Scheper-Hughes (1996, 2000), has been on the transplant's relevance for the everyday life, substantive and imaginary, of the poor. I have argued that despite the relative infrequency of the transplant operation in the lives of most poor in India and the still greater infrequency of the much discussed sale of a kidney in these lives, attention to both the practice and form of the market in organs is a critical anthropological task. There are many reasons for this relevance, and among these the most central for my discussion are what I term *bioavailability* and *operability*.

Bioavailability is a feature of the dispersed and flexible logic of late capital and labor in relation to the changing technical possibilities for redistributing human tissue. During the twentieth century, more and more live human tissues became available for extraction from one body followed by infusion or implantation into others, and both routine and end-stage medicine became increasingly reliant on tissue transfer to replenish blood and enable certain surgeries (through transfusion) and to replace failing organs (through transplantation). One can schematically represent the emergence of the transplant era in terms of three technical shifts. First, in the case of renal transplantation early in the century, surgeons developed mechanical techniques for safely and effectively extracting, transporting, and grafting tissues. The work of surgical pioneers like the Lyonnais researcher Alexis Carrel revealed a limit to mechanical innovation in the body's tendency to reject foreign tissue. In most cases, only very close relations were possible tissue donors, and even then with great likelihood of graft rejection.

Second, through the development of transfusion medicine as defensive technology over two world wars and the science it made possible, immunological techniques for recognizing degrees of tissue relatedness at the subcellular level were developed. Tissue rejection could be minimized through screening, and an effective transplant medicine came to depend on the stabilization of large populations as bioavailable recruits to ensure the likelihood of a match (Cohen 2001). The only postwar population both large enough and available enough to enable a transplant medicine was that of the almost-dead, bodies still and yet barely alive because of the development of the ventilator in the face of polio. For this population to be rendered bioavailable, as the work of Margaret Lock (2002) richly illustrates, two technical problems required solution. New ways of conceiving of these bodies as more or less dead needed to be articulated and acceded to, thus the emergence of "brain death." And new rhetorics and understandings of organ donation as "saving a life," despite the limited promise of risky, imperfect, and frequently experimental procedures, needed to be publicized.

But it was the third technical shift, the development and manufacture of effective immunosuppressant drugs, that made possible both the globalization of the transplant operation and the emergence of multiple bioavailable populations, not only the almost-dead. With the Sandoz (later Novartis) corporation's invention of cyclosporine and its use in tandem with other agents, close matching of transplant tissue was no longer essential, and clinics around the world began in the 1980s to turn to multiple, usually smaller, and more easily mobilized populations. What characterized the mobilization and stabilization of bioavailable populations in this era was the flexibility of these processes. As far more persons could serve as donors, bioavailability was no longer determined solely by consanguinity or brain death but additionally by economic need, political vulnerability, and frequently gendered moral demands of prestation. Clinical efficiency and competitiveness were dependent on flexible entrepreneurship and often on brokers able to recruit new groups into bioavailability (Cohen 2001).

Thus, both Scheper-Hughes and I have chronicled an extraordinary range of marked donor populations in and across different places and moments. In my own field and archival work, I have begun to delineate as bioavailable groups ranging across space and scale: from poor relations to wives to migrant labor, from indebted weavers after a boombust cycle in the power-loom sector to small peasants struggling with diminished productivity after the adoption of cotton monoculture, from prisoners in China to evangelicals in America, from men in rural villages to women in urban slums. These groupings share little except their contingent bioavailability, organized variously around the loving or charitable gift, the commoditized sale, or the authoritarian or piratical forced extraction or seizure.[1]

Studying transplantation as a critical engine and index of bioavailability foregrounds certain relations and not others. What matters in delineating structures and genealogies of bioavailability is an articulation of vital technique with neoliberal entrepreneurship. Ethical conversation hovers around utility and the fragile claims of deontology. The law and other instances and agencies of the state are reduced to passive or complicit (or at most weakly regulatory) players.

Operability demands a different calculus. For now, I will define it as the degree to which one's belonging to and legitimate demands of the state are mediated through invasive medical commitment. To develop the concept, and thus why I think it can be fruitful to juxtapose different kinds of operations (beyond their subdisciplinary relevance for an anthropology of surgery), I turn to a finding from my earlier work on organ transplantation in South India and specifically to interviews with women in several slums of Chennai (formerly Madras) who, in the face of chronic indebtedness, had sold kidneys to a clinic run by Dr. K. C. Reddy.

Organ transplantation expanded quickly in southern and western India with the advent of cyclosporine. Local bioavailability was characterized by specific relational vectors (parents to children, brothers to sisters and brothers, wives to husbands, and asymmetric gifts from poor relations and family servants), the expanding recruitment of urban and rural poor as sellers, and very little use of the new brain death. Transplantation was profitable and advertised the hypermodernity of a clinic: numerous centers were set up in Chennai, Mumbai (Bombay), and Bangalore, and these began to compete for stable bioavailable populations. In the southern state of Tamil Nadu, bioavailable populations were recruited from urban Chennai slums and rural towns near the city of Erode. Chennai sellers were predominantly women, and Erode sellers, recruited for Bangalore clinics, were predominantly men. Though clinic directors I interviewed differed widely in their estimates of the relative number of family donors versus paid unrelated donors, most agreed that the majority of donations, until paid donations were outlawed in 1994, were commercial.

What intrigued me in Chennai during my 1998 interviews was the ubiquitous presence for these women of a *prior* operation: specifically, every one of the almost thirty sellers with whom I spoke had had a tubal ligation, the "family-planning operation." The matter of the first operation came up in interviews because the women were informed, early on in enlisting, that in order to sell a kidney, they had to have the family-planning operation for health reasons. But each, in turn, related that she had already had *that* operation (Cohen 1999).

The very instance of this requirement suggests the need for a concept of operability. The rationale for prophylactic tubal ligation as minimizing future risk to a now compromised renal system appears to have far less to do with demonstrated risk than with a paternalistic medical value machine mandating tubal ligation for poor and low-status women whenever possible.

But there is more than paternalism at stake here. I was struck not only by the ubiquity of the prior operation but also by what I would call its intimacy, its identity with or proximity to the everyday. Cecilia Van Hollen's work (1998) on poor women's often extensive use of available obstetric and prophylactic technology in Chennai has suggested that in Tamil Nadu in the 1990s, both the agency and governmentality of urban slum dwellers—their commitment, in other words, to state intervention in their lives—were mediated through invasive medical technology. Kalpana Ram (1998) has examined the forms of political subjectivity and citizenship that women's enlistment in health development articulates, and Darren Zook (1998) has contributed to a broader genealogy of development and docile bodies in Tamil Nadu. My reading of accounts of the prior operation is in conversation with this literature, which might offer the operation as but one instance of governance. But my specific effort has been to focus on the formal and material instance of the operation in itself.

Operability and bioavailability reflect two interlocking families of exigency that constitute subjects and deploy life. A person is hailed through nephrectomy—the extraction of a kidney—as a bioavailable source of newly scarce tissue for the often financially better-off but dying. The point here again is that this interpellation operates flexibly in specific and dispersed points of production and exchange. One is hailed *either* because of one's identity with a recipient, whether that be affective or immunological, *or* because of one's difference from him or her, usually given one's marginality across lines of class or gender or other political subordinacy.

A person is hailed through the family-planning operation as a premodern and precapitalist breeder, for whom appeals to modern or bourgeois asceticism will be inadequate. In other words, the operation works under a patronizing logic presuming that the proper subjects of development are peasants or slum dwellers marked by excessive passion and limited reason, prone thus to pathology rather than discipline of the will. Thomas Hansen locates the genealogy of such pathology in what he terms nineteenth-century British colonialism's "double discourse"—of an imperial subject split between reasoning elites and passionate masses—and its extension in the "antipolitical" governance of the Nehruvian state and its separation of a sublime realm of culture and reason from the debased space of subaltern politics (1999:32–35, 50–57). The cure lies in what Sudipta Kaviraj (1988) and other political theorists after Gramsci have termed the passive revolution of the Indian state, a process of formal subsumption in which the impatient techniques of the modern state are justified by the persistence of pre-capitalist (un)reason (Prasad 1998). The operation is thus necessary to remake one's mindful body in accordance with the demands of developmental modernity, to remake one as if one were a modern, bourgeois subject. Arguably, if the operation becomes the form through which marginal, premodern subjects can secure some form of modern participation in the nation-state, it may become a critical desideratum.[2]

Ultimately, one must contend with the intimacy of the surgical in practices defining the making of contemporary subjects on the margin in *multiple* registers: in the conjoint terms of bioavailability and operability. To put it otherwise, biopolitics at the margins of the state is constituted surgically in two ways: as the flexible disaggregation of the class subject into its flexible worth as bioavailable life and as the passive revolution subsuming the underdeveloped subject into the bodily exigencies of the modern order as operable citizenship.

LOGICS OF EXCEPTION

Government General Hospital sits across the Poonamallee High Road from Madras Central Railway Station in Chennai. Most patients and caregivers enter the grounds from the gate closest to the station, near Emergency and Triage. The old main gate is farther to the east. Entering here, one first passes the morgue. Then the way branches: to the right is the hospital, and to the left, the Madras Medical College. In the middle is the central administrative building with the medical college director's office. Though once the primary route of access, the arched open doorway leading into this building is now seldom used by those seeking care. The panoptic location of the centralized government administrator is reduced to surveying death: in appearances, a forensic state. The live action is over at Emergency.

In 2000, Tuesdays are one of the exceptions: not to the forensic state but to its lack of animation. The central wing is slightly busier: a few more patients enter by the old gate. The authorization committee for the state of Tamil Nadu meets each Tuesday in the director's office to regulate this state of exception, literally so, for the authorization committee determines who may be excepted from the 1994 law that restricts the giving of one's kidney while one is alive. Families of persons needing a kidney to go on living, their donors or more often sellers, and, in the case of sellers, the agents who broker the deals all gather in the passageway outside the office, waiting. The reasons for attempting to buy a kidney vary, but they frequently include some variant of the following: "How can I put a family member at such risk when I can just buy a kidney?" The need of kidney-buying families to look elsewhere may of necessity be framed as a series of impossibilities: "Our son is sick. They say I am too old. His brother has young children, and his wife will not let him. His sisters are unmarried; it would be difficult for them to have the operation. It would be hard for them to get married in that case."

Several Indian states have set up authorization committees per the provisions of the Transplantation of Human Organs Act of 1994 or variants of the act passed in some states in succeeding years. The act provides for procedures to define and determine "brain death" in order to create a supply of organs through procedures consonant with best practice in Europe and North America. It stipulates that solid organs cannot be bought or sold and that only four classes of relations—parents, children, siblings, and spouses—can give them. One of the authors of the act, R. R. Kishore, former chief medical officer of India, noted in an interview with my student and colleague Malkeet Gupta and me that spouses, though usually not "biologically" related, were included in the Indian law as an acknowledgement of what he termed "culture." The authorization committees were set up to consider exceptions to the four permitted classes of relatedness and to allow families to demonstrate the proper degree of relatedness.

Exceptions were variably defined but almost always included some extension of legitimate degrees of kinship along the lines of "affection." Families would claim that the seller was a distant relation, or a dependent who wanted to discharge a deep debt in exchange for years of loving patronage. These claims were made through a formalized structure in which "affection" would be isolated, named, and measured.

The available language of affection in relation to the expert committee inevitably jarred. In an interview, the transplant surgery team at

Government General Hospital read to me the acknowledgments of a popular manual on transplant medicine written by an American author. The author thanked his family, utilizing instead of kin terms the formalized language of bonds of affection used to regulate the ethics of kidney donation. It was an inside joke and, in its retelling, was offered to suggest the falseness of such language to the ear and heart. There was more to the moment, of course: if an *American* was aware of the falseness of the language of the ethical, why was I, another American, seeking out the falseness in *Indian* transplant surgery when I could have done so as easily back home? Conversely, if, despite the transnational joke, the American author could turn his wife and children into abstract loci of regulated affection, the real violence was there in America. Here it was clear: We all know it's a scam, but you guys scare us. You really believe this language. Why else would so many of you keep flying over to audit how ethical *we* are?

Committee sessions were, of course, closed. I reconstruct some of their dynamics from interviews in two cities (Chennai in Tamil Nadu and Bangalore in Karnataka) with current and former committee members, government ministers, patients, brokers, sellers, transplant physicians, journalists, lawyers, and the police. The presumption of virtually everyone interviewed was that *very few* cases brought to the authorization committee were what they technically claimed to be and that money and not "affection" was the critical variable. Most committee discussions centered on nonrelatives and the affection they might lay claim to. In general, exception to the law through nonrelatives' ties of affection might be established along two allowable axes: the bonds of friendship based on identity and translatability and the bonds of enlightened patronage—usually a domestic servant or former domestic servant offering a kidney to an exemplary employer, a relation that to the extent it reproduced legitimate kinship was seen to place an enormous debt on the servant. These two axes came together in the figure of the poor relation, the persona most often crafted by families and brokers for the committees.

As transplantation becomes more widely available in India, in state after state, a cycle of unregulated entrepreneurship, coercive or exploitative practice, accusation and counteraccusation, scandal, and calls for state action is set in motion, leading the state legislature to pass some variant of the 1994 law. In this context, new authorization committees follow their mandate strictly at the outset. Transplant physicians, hitherto accustomed to a fairly streamlined process of diagnosis, linking the patient to a broker, identifying a seller, testing, and operation, described their and their patients' frustration during these initial periods. Dr. Sunder of Bangalore's Lakeside Hospital, for example, angrily told me of grandparents denied the opportunity to save the lives of their grandchildren and of patients dying because of the lack of previously easy access. He implied that the committee in the state of Karnataka had barely deviated from this draconian pseudoethical rule, forcing his colleagues and him into constant and desperate appeal. Sunder cited a famous example of a similar "ethical" measure that wreaked havoc on the lives of patients. Pulling an article by British philosopher Janet Radcliffe-Richards from a desk drawer, he pointed out a passage describing the tragic case of a British man prevented by the British government from buying a Turkish man's kidney. The Turk was selling his kidney to pay for an operation for his ailing daughter. The state's maneuver, in the doctor's retelling, killed both the British kidney patient and the Turkish girl. Such examples, and Radcliffe-Richards's arguments more generally (Radcliffe-Richards et al. 1988; Radcliffe-Richards 1998), are as widely circulated among transplant physicians internationally as is the immunosuppressant cyclosporine.

Despite the production and circulation of such narratives, the evaluative criteria of the authorization committees quickly shift from zero to almost infinite exception. Within months of a committee's establishment, new procedures are established and routinized—on the committee's side for the generous interpretation of documentation and interview, on the family's and seller's side for the production and performance of legitimate forms of relatedness. As brokers and physicians learn how to master the new administrative forms, they discover quickly that the committees, in fact, make it *easier* to conduct business as usual—efficiently and legitimately mobilizing the transfer of kidneys from the poor to the sick—while avoiding the possibility of scandal. Sellers are coached, in many cases, in answering questions committee members might ask. These questions are fairly standardized, and a properly finessed appointment with the committee usually produces an approval. The exception becomes the norm.

Committee members and former members I interviewed in both cities gave four reasons for their ability to create such fictions of legal relatedness in approving these cases.

1. *Ethical.* To cite one former Tamil Nadu authorization committee head and ex-director of Madras Medical College, "How could we let this poor chap go off and die?" Committee members expressed a conflict between their role as appointed officials interpreting the law strictly and their conjoined professional and *human* responsibilities. I belabor the obvious to note that "poor chaps" within the frame of identification are always organ recipients, never donors. Identification seldom extends to the seller or indeed to the majority of persons with renal failure who cannot afford the triple cost of the operation, the immunosuppressant medication, and, if the organ is purchased, the organ itself. Where the law frames the citizen against the demands and potentialities of the operation, everyone the same and no one entitled to buy or sell, the committee presumes an identifiable citizen-patient able to be operated upon and to *receive* tissue, and it attempts whenever possible to allow for the flow of tissue to that body as both a medical and an ethical responsibility on its part. The ethical is exceptional in its framing of bioavailability as a good beyond the law's presumption of the sameness of citizens. This state of exception is entered into through an act of recognition premised on sympathetic identification.

Though buyers and recipients more generally are for the most part wealthier than sellers and donors more generally (Scheper-Hughes 2000), many recipients are not well-off, and they draw upon nonmonetary and often fragile networks of influence and patronage to subsidize family operations. Identification with and of the citizen-patient is therefore not simply a function of class but has much to do with which side of the operation one can locate oneself on. Let us redefine *operability* here. We can term such ethical recognition—the ability to be given or to imagine being given a transplant organ as a constitutive feature of one's citizenship—an incidence of *supplementability,* and the ability to have an organ *legitimately* taken or to imagine this as a feature of one's participation in the state, an incidence of operability. The two sides of the operation are neither mutually exclusive nor restricted to the matter of transplants. In the case of the family-planning operation, one either identifies with the sterilizing authority acting on behalf of a public threatened by a phobically constituted Malthusianism, in which case sterilization supplements one's imaginable future, or one identifies one's civic person with the body sterilized. For the state committee, the incitement of the subaltern's bioavailability generates a space of exception constituted as ethical for both sides. The bureaucrat-physician *identifies* with the buyer's need and alternately ignores the seller or— particularly if the seller is female—*imagines* the sale of an organ as the minor exception preventing her from the more traumatic violation of prostitution. Again and again, nephrologists on and off the committee suggested that if people were not allowed to sell their kidneys, they would have to sell their *entire bodies.*

2. *Formal.* Committee members noted again and again that they were empowered only to evaluate the evidence of the documents submitted and the formal interview with both donor and recipient; they did not have the power to create further evidence to assess claims of relatedness. Relatedness was a specific performance to be evaluated on the basis of formal criteria and attending to specified sites: the document, the interview. Brokers learn what will be asked and prepare documents and sellers accordingly. Success or failure is limited to the formal space and time of performance. Operability, under the formal parameters of the law, is dependent upon the ability to perform one's identity with a more privileged buyer; supplementability, upon the ability to choose a good performer and performance director in anticipation of the state's parameters of identification.

The second logic of the exception secures the ethical claim of the first: any other ethic besides that recognizing an equitable exchange of needs through the twin processes of identification and imagination is put under erasure as exceeding the formal possibilities of articulation. Whatever other story besides the state's ethical response to the desperate need of patient and seller through the necessary space of exception might hover behind the iterative performance of this narrative is relegated to the inarticulateness of the informal. The formal sector is revealed less as a space of law than as the portion of a political subject's performance that can be constituted as legitimate speech. Here the committee's practice of granting exception is acknowledged as false recognition, but necessary if the debased space of the political and the unreason of the masses are to be evaded. Though the pure play of need that comes to frame the ethical seems to generate a Hobbesian space of contract and Warre that the logic of the formal would eschew, the iteration of formal norms secures what Hansen calls the sublime and James Ferguson the antipolitics machine (1994).

3. *Sovereign*. Committee members in several cases spoke of political pressures from ministers and members of the legislative assembly, who pushed them to aid a powerful or well-placed constituent. Supplementability was achieved by mobilizing social networks to generate a political space of exception. This exception appears doubled, an extralegal political exception to the expert committee whose task is to generate legitimate exceptions. In practice, however, there is little distinction between a space of sovereign exception—the politician's extralegal request—and the legal structure of formal exception, among other reasons because committee members are political appointees. Formal norms and sovereign exception overlap, apparently similar to what Agamben has referred to as the expanding zone of indistinction (1998).[3]

One could frame the authorization committees as exemplifying this expansion, but in a particular way. With the passage of the Transplantation of Human Organs Act, the state locates itself against the market in bioavailability save for the committee's flexible power of exception. As this exception quickly expands to become all but identical with the signature of the state, a situation much like that proposed by Agamben appears to consolidate. To the extent that one is bioavailable, one is constituted as zoe, as bare life, in a space of exception that simultaneously refuses one's status as the supplementable bios of the citizen-patient. Operability—one's ascension *to the polis* through the operation— is not at stake in a figure that reduces citizenship to bioavailability.

Yet the work of brokers and buyers, validated by the committee, collapses bioavailability and supplementability into a zone of indistinction less than it performs a fiction of indistinction through relatedness abetted by the operability of sellers asserting more than their consensual commodification. The fiction is that donor and recipient are already so intensively transactionally and ethically connected (*biomorally* linked, in the phraseology of McKim Marriott) that the donor's constitution as an organ and tissue bank remains distinctly a matter of the polis and its norms under the sign of the gift. The fiction goes beyond the fictive kinship invented by persons seeking to get through the checkpoint of the committee, encompassing both real and fictive "gifts of life": it is a matter of the gift of life in itself.

The logic of bioavailability—the current conjuncture of technique, market, and order of kinship and care—differentiates bodies into donors and recipients, ranged along flexibly articulating axes of class, gender, and countergift. The brokered work of exception today sustains this relation by collapsing the difference between donors and recipients into a fiction of relatedness. Such a fiction applies not only to the procedures of committees such as those that legitimate the claims of nonrelatives to be related. More generally, fictive kinship is widely materialized by a global logic of bioavailability that *mandates* that relations of caring and being cared for can be translated into the imperative to donate tissue and the narrative of the "gift of life." The fiction of relatedness, in other words, operates as much within the domain of kinship as outside it.

4. *Degenerate.* Finally, one former member said that he left the committee because of the constant presence of bribes, invoking the fourth reason, the always-difficult-to-substantiate ground of "the nexus," of a criminality so pervasive as to render forensic analysis unthinkable, for any given account of interest is always itself interested. By *nexus*, I mean the popular social theory in both everyday conversation and popular and learned media in India that everything is linked to everything else through relations of barely hidden profit and influence. News articles and market and scholarly analysis feature ubiquitous accounts of subterranean "vested interests" that inflect all social and economic relations (*Hindu* 1998, 2000). When in 1997 and 1998 I followed several emerging transplant scandals in Delhi and Jaipur, I encountered dense cycles of accusation and counteraccusation, portraits of a world in which rival clinics run by rival industrial barons enlisted rival political and police assemblages to manufacture rival forensic accounts of medical malfeasance.

The sensibility of the nexus, shared by many bureaucrats, physicians, journalists, and others with whom I spoke in Chennai and Bangalore, reframes the indistinction between law and nature that we can hear in the talk of sovereign exception as all but solipsistic indistinction between forensics and criminality, significance and redundancy. Everyone is operable, for everyone is subject to the nexus; everyone is supplementable, for everyone is part of it. Such indistinction frames the terror of moments of social panic, such as the 1996 kidney-stealing panic in eastern Uttar Pradesh in northern India, where persons across class and community feared that their children's kidneys—and lives—were threatened by mysterious shape-shifting agents and suspected organ stealers were sighted everywhere (Cohen 1998).

FARMERS AND EUNUCHS

Rentachintala became a non-place on the Internet long before it was invaded by the global forensic vanguard. A village in Andhra Pradesh's Guntur district near the border of the impoverished Telegana region, it was long known as the hottest inhabited place on earth. Its weather was regularly featured on CNN and other Web sites. Its more recent claim to fame occurred when a local reporter for the Telegu daily *Eenadu* wrote a short story about the large number of poor Reddy-caste farmers—more than one hundred—who had gone to far-off Delhi to sell kidneys. Saye Sekhar, a reporter for the national English-language daily the *Hindu,* noticed the story and himself went to Rentachintala, where he wrote an expanded report on what became India's newest kidney scandal. Sekhar wanted to photograph several of the sellers and got the village police to help him round up sellers, though no one locally was sure if they had done something they could or should be charged with. The resulting photograph featured around the country. Five farmers (all men) were lined up, their shirts off, their flanks—and scars—toward the camera. Behind them stood two policemen, proud and with bigger and fatter bodies than the more emaciated sellers. It was the classic crime photo, and behind the lineup was the local police station's chart—a modified chalkboard—of crimes committed in the area.

By Sekhar's own account, the men were humiliated by this exposure. They had gone to Delhi in secret, in most cases not telling their wives or other family members the real reason for the trip. "She never would have let me go," one farmer later told me. A man from a neighboring town had heard through a friend of money to be made in Delhi and had gone to sell his own kidney. He was told that he did not have healthy kidneys but that he could bring in more money by recruiting others. Delhi had recently been through a major kidney scandal of its own—local men accusing clinic doctors of tricking them into the operation—and clinics and brokers were setting up more carefully structured chains of recruitment. The Guntur broker-to-be knew only his contact, not which hospital or doctor the kidneys were going to. The farmers from Rentachintala he recruited knew even less. They were put up in safe houses, and they waited. Some were operated on right away, some asked to wait, and many sent back and told that they would be contacted as soon as a patient was ready. Uttar Pradesh, where many suburban Delhi clinics were located, was just setting up more formalized authorization committees and parallel procedures, and procedures of exception had yet to be routinized: scandals hovered.

Like the predominantly female sellers in Chennai, the Rentachintala farmers sold kidneys to get out of debt. The money was gone, and they were still in debt, minus a kidney and in many cases with no access to adequate postoperative care. Most reported generalized weakness and a reduced ability to work as a farmer. Sekhar was at times sympathetic to this situation. Other times, when he and I returned to Rentachintala, he took pains to disprove it. We were walking through the village; a seller was drawing water from a well. "Quick, take a picture," Sekhar grabbed my arm. "He says he is too weak to work. But look, he is hoisting that heavy *lota*." The nexus vied with expectations of village credulity in Sekhar's mistrust. On the one hand, the farmers might be encouraged to play up their weakness to benefit certain unstated parties at the expense of others. On the other hand, villagers confused kidneys with testicles, other operations with castration. Complaint might be based in such misunderstanding.

The sources of indebtedness were different, tied to a cycle of dam building; the promotion of new high-yield cotton varieties; the inability of small farmers to rotate crops; dependency on large farmers' control of pesticides, credit, and state officials; and liberalization of pricing, exacerbated by drought. Incidents of farmers' suicides, related to the same structures of debt, were fairly frequent in the state and generated modest political capital for survivors. The kidney-selling scandal was framed as the newest wrinkle in human abjection. Local and national politicians came to the village. The state health minister set up a fact-finding commission. Sekhar called several ethicists, talking heads who could be counted upon to frame the events as symptomatic of larger rot. He hoped that the Chennai office of the *Hindu* would notice: he did not want to be stuck forever in Guntur. The farmers reported wave after wave of experts and politicians, but no support—financial, legal, medical—of any kind. Sekhar asked me whether I wanted to use the police to round up the sellers again for another group photo. I declined, and he got a local studio to take a photo of me instead for a story on the international attention Rentachintala was receiving.

In Rentachintala, all known sellers were men; in Chennai, most sellers were women. Despite accounts of weakening, similar to reasons given in Chennai for the unwillingness of most men to have the operation, a significant number of Rentachintala men were recruited. Rural men were more bioavailable, and rural women less so for many reasons. The temporality of debt differed radically, not the constant and slowly mounting indebtedness of the Chennai households but cycles of crop failure or price collapse with sudden and massive debt in peasant households where men's corporeal sense of themselves was bound up in their land and its future. Whereas men in Chennai routinely asked me whether selling a kidney would make them sterile, and the rare interlocutor invoked the coercive surgeries of the 1970s Emergency, men interviewed in Rentachintala refused any suggestion that they had been in a position to think beyond the emergent state of the present when they decided to go to Delhi. Most said that in the very temporality of the present, it had been a mistake to sell a kidney: they were now weak, and they worried that they might not be able to work again. It was hard to know how to interpret talk of a mistake, standing in line behind the journalists and the police to elicit a confession. What was clear was that the gendering of a person's bioavailability was in several senses a matter of time. In particular, the state of emergency for small peasants contrasted sharply with the everydayness of debt spoken of in the Ayanavaram and Ottery slums. The male operation was framed in terms of emergency, whether the economic crises that demanded male bioavailability or the lingering memories of emergency sterilizations of the 1970s that stood against the possibility of everyday male operability.

"If I had known about MGR's disease then," said a woman in Chennai who had sold a kidney and later regretted how little money she had received, *"I would have given him both of mine"* (Cohen 1999). The late Tamil Nadu chief minister M. G. Ramachandran, a former film actor and populist hero known as MGR, developed end-stage renal disease in late life and went to New York for a transplant; his niece donated. Throughout the state, renal failure is known as MGR's disease. Pictures of the late chief minister hung all over the woman's flat. But *both* her kidneys? One could never offer enough to MGR, framed as he had been as the ultimate source of *dana,* the gift. MGR was beloved as the good sovereign, the constant donor to the poor, the classic figure of the king as paradigmatic giver so useful to Indian anthropological debate and here mediated through the popular Tamil cinema. The imaginary demands of the countergift are infinite.

Yet MGR does die, despite his supplementability through the unstinting love of the Tamil nation, and times change. The era of the populist deployment by latter-day sovereigns of the apparent largesse of development capital is over, at least in South India, replaced by hybrid varieties of neoliberal sovereignty articulated with the development state. Andhra Pradesh chief minister and booster N. Chandrababu Naidu is in many ways the cynosure of the New South, famed for soliciting Internet business and other technical and telecommunications outsourcing. A hero to the new technocracy and its diasporic extensions, Naidu is framed more ambivalently at home. The Rentachintala "scandal" hit state politics not long after Naidu had convinced Bill Clinton (then US president) to visit his capital of Hyderabad, and it was used by critics and opponents to stabilize a different image of his rule—Naidu the elitist, whose policies have abandoned the flow of dana and who is forcing the poor, as a result, to literally consume themselves. The running joke at the time went, "What's Naidu's newest Web site? Saleofkidneys.com!" (Akbar 2000).

The operation reanimates the leader in a time marked as *after.* While I was working in Ayanavaram, a story from Iran was widely circulated in India. According to this story, supporters of the Iranian revolution in the religious center of Mashhad had pledged to sell their kidneys to raise the reward and extend the *fatwa* for killing writer Salman Rushdie. President Khatami was up for reelection, and his continued administration threatened to erode further the purity of Ayatollah Khomeini's vision of and commitment to a self-respecting and culturally independent Islam. At the same time, émigrés in Paris and elsewhere continued to challenge the revolutionary state by pointing out the current practice of kidney sales in Iran and suggesting that revolution was turning men into eunuchs.

The eunuch has persisted and reemerged as a critical figure of the political in various sites globally and in India. In earlier work on northern Indian political satire, I described a mode of representing the political relation between the politician or the police and the *janata,* or people, as sodomitical, with the implicit or explicit referent of castration (Cohen 1995a). In political speeches widely circulated on cheap cassettes, figures associated with the Hindu right "family," particularly orators like Sadhvi Rithambara and Bal Thackeray, have assaulted the enemies of the nation as eunuchs, hijras.[4]

In the last year of the twentieth century, hijras were put up for a series of municipal and statewide elections in central and northern India and won several of them (*Times of India* 2000b, 2000d; *Statesman* 2000). Even the eunuchs' backers were surprised: their stratagem in local multiparty politics in recruiting hijras (eunuchs, intersexuals, the "third gender") as political spoilers did not encompass robust expectations of victory (Singh 2000). The new hijra politicians were quick to contrast their own honesty and courage with the venality and weakness of their opponents, whom they called the "real eunuchs" (Mukerjee 2001). In so doing, they drew upon the ubiquitous feature of provincial political discourse just mentioned, the disparaging of a political rival as castrated or effeminate, that had stabilized as national ideologeme with the growing popularity of Hindu "communal" blocs and the parallel decline of the centrist Congress Party (Anandan 2001; Patwardhan 1994).

The actual number of hijras in prominent elections during this period remained small. But the unexpected literalization of the once merely rhetorical politician-as-eunuch caught the attention of media agencies (*Hindustan Times* 2001). It was cast as an event-form (Das 1995; Rabinow 1999:171–79) by political commentators bemoaning the collapse of meaningful democratic life or asserting the fragility of its persistence in the presumed desperation of voting in the most

marginal of social beings (*Times of India* 2000c). And as the first generation of hijra politicians proved to be signifiably more able and efficient
than their detractors and even some of their supporters had feared, the
appearance of the sovereign eunuch came to mark not so much the sick-
ness of modern political life as its potential redemption. The hijras'
repeated claim that they were incorruptible because of their renuncia-
tion of manhood, and thus the impossibility of having sons and the consequent need to earn for them, began to appear less audacious.

In the form of this event, a reversal was effected. Unlike ordinary
politicians, hijra politicians could not be accused of *pretending* to sacrifice their own family's interest for the greater good: their sacrifice,
embodied in the iterated fact of their castration, was legible as the very
sign of their difference. Ordinary eunuchs were revealed as the real
leaders in the same movement that revealed ordinary leaders as the
real eunuchs. To put it differently, the embodied *sign* of the operation—both as presence (the wound, the scar) and absence (the hijra's
"hole," her lack of male genitals)—came to have a paradoxical relation
to the embodied *effect* of the operation: the modern sovereign's inability to constitute filial relations with ordinary citizens. Eunuchs publicly
bear the sign of the operation and in so doing secure the electorate's
trust and the possibility of authentic sovereignty, of being *ma bap*,
mother and father, to the people. Politicians are those who hide their
personal appropriation of the commonweal under false gestures of kinship and thus bear the effect of the operation. Their inability to create
meaningful bonds of sovereign filiation through proper giving proves
the wounded state of contemporary sovereignty to which the eunuch's
scar bears witness. Sovereignty is cut open: the operation extends
beyond the dyad of operator and operated. Its signs and its effects pursue unnatural courses.

The moment of hijra electoral capital may be short-lived; more
recent efforts to define hijras as male under the law and to prevent
them from mobilizing electoral seats reserved for women are part of a
broader set of controls that may limit future eunuch wins (*Hindu*
2003). Still, the language of the new hijras, and the surprise of their
move from the presumptive margin to the center of the state under the
sign of operability, deserves some attention. Such surprise accedes not
only to the non-hijra account of hijra abjection but also to the hijra's

own *nautak,* her drama of a wretchedness caused by society and merit-
ing societal patronage (Cohen 1995b). Yet despite this double position-
ing on the margin, hijras have for decades demanded formal
recognition as citizen-eunuchs: to vote and to be counted and to do
and be so *as* hijras. Recent contests over hijra electoral gender and
their definition as male reenact a longer contest, by no means over.

What it means to enact citizenship as a hijra is what is at stake here.
Hijras use the shame and double threat (to recognize signs of sexual
difference in a child and claim it as hijra and to reveal the site and pres-
ence/absence of their wounds/genitals and render men impotent and
hijras themselves) their appearance presupposes to beg or coerce
money and to protect themselves from harassment. They demand their
jajman, their right of support from local shopkeepers, sometimes
claiming that it is "you men who made us this way," implying that
frequent sodomizing in boyhood made them what they are and in
effect forced them to have the operation and reduced them to this
state. This sense of abjection converted *through the operation* into a legible right in others (the operative wound as the legitimation of the
demand for support) extends to jajman mapped onto the nation itself.
For example, eunuchs may call their holes "all-India passes," allowing
them to pass onto trains and across the nation without anyone daring
to stop them. I have also heard the operative mark called a "passport,"
in the context of travel to and from Bangladesh and an imagined trip to
America. National claims are not always demands. When in the early
1980s Indian cosmonaut Rakesh Sharma was about to join a Soviet
crew to become the first Indian in space, hijras launched a press
campaign calling on India to put a hijra in space instead. For Sharma to
go up in space was but an empty gesture of a satellite nationalism, but
for India to put the first hijra into space would be to reclaim the
ground of history.

Hijra politicians have stressed hijra difference as central to their
political integrity. Far from hijras being the weak and corrupt villains of
political critique, they emerge in both their own and many popular
accounts as having cut away the ties that bind them to others and being,
because of their operations, the only bodies truly able to materialize a
democratic polity. Madhu Tiwari, a college-educated hijra who lost an
election in the Haidergarh district in Uttar Pradesh against Chief
Minister Rajnath Singh, nevertheless drew large crowds and significant

attention by accusing her famous rival: "I am not going to win. But I will surely tell people that they should choose the real eunuch instead of these politically impotent people....We are eunuchs. We have no caste, gender or religious bias. Our philosophy cuts across all kinds of people. We also have no family or ambitions which can lead us to vested interests or corruption" (Mukerjee 2001). The refrain—of hijras escaping the nexus because of their excision of family—has become frequent. Shabnam Mausi, the first hijra elected to a post not reserved for a woman, noted in her inauguration speech in the Madhya Pradesh State Assembly: "The politicians merely make noises and issue platitudes. They never work for the welfare of the common people....I have no family of my own. My electorate is now my family" (*Statesman* 2000).

Though without family, Shabnam claimed the prime minister himself as a brother. Reporters interviewing her while she visited the city of Gorakhpur to stump for fellow hijra Asha Devi, elected mayor in November 2000, noted: "Shabnam Mausi said that eunuchs could serve the people better than any male or female politician because they had no near and dear ones as their family members. The people of the country are their family members, she claimed. However, she regarded prime minister Atal Behari Vajpayee, without naming him, [as] her elder brother, who could not lead a family life and is serving the country" (*Times of India* 2000a). Vajpayee, India's prime minister, has not married, and despite a quiet if well-known relationship with his "adopted" children and with women, he maintains the charisma of a worldly ascetic. Against the national politician Bal Thackeray, head of the Shiv Sena Party and frequent hijra-baiter, who had called Vajpayee impotent and a eunuch at about the same time, Shabnam claimed him as something else, as *counterabject,* as the one redeemable politician in his almost operable asceticism.

Hijra politicians are perhaps but a footnote to the political scene, but my effort here has been to sketch out a context to begin to think about the stakes in the operation as a critical political form, generally and with specific reference to persons constituted as both bioavailable and operable bodies. There are few happy endings, in anthropology or elsewhere, and though I would like to see some kind of redemption in Shabnam's election, the limits to operable citizenship turned on its head as radical political consciousness, this story is quickly crowded out by other critical events.

There are few happy endings, but against the authorization of exception that operates by collapsing bios and zoe into a fiction of relatedness, in 2000 and 2001 something else happened.

CODA: THE CONVIVIALITY OF OPERATIONS

Achille Mbembe (1992) famously troubled the adequacy of Bakhtinian celebrations of the carnal grotesque as responses to the massive verticality and monoglot order of the modern state of the iron cage. With Cameroon as the proximal referent, Mbembe suggested that to the extent that postcolonial governance has operated through a carnival mode of normalized exception, the social fact of carnival-from-below offers less an instance of "resistance" than of what he termed a *conviviality* of grotesques. One might call such a conviviality, after Agamben, a zone of indistinction, and it is increasingly less than obvious to me whether and how biopolitical and postcolonial exceptionality differ under neoliberalism.

To end, therefore, with the hijra politician bearing the narrative burden of her operable difference may only reenact the limit to a certain stratagem. India's great booster of neoliberal transformation in the late 1990s was, after all, Andhra Pradesh chief minister Chandrababu Naidu, he of the imaginary Web site *saleofkidneys.com.* Naidu's response to his state's persistent, in many areas growing, rural poverty has been a return to sterilization targets, yoked to a contemporary regime of computer development and global outsourcing revenue. But lest he be accused of the usual political impotence—promising but not delivering on the sovereign's countergift to the people—Naidu has wrapped his ability to deliver on the gift around the ubiquity of the vasectomy, to the extent that on two occasions farmers in Guntur told me that the chief minister himself had been vasectomized. Though such a belief may not be widespread, it points to an oft noted effect of Naidu's publicity and program. In tours of the countryside beyond his urban political base, Naidu responds to local critics who ask about failed or nonexistent forms of education or infrastructure by repeatedly linking the state's ability to give to the population's self-limiting through vasectomy or tubal ligation. The operation becomes proof of one's status as a responsible neoliberal subject, individually and collectively. Unlike the direct coercion of Indira

Gandhi's Emergency and its aftermath, Naidu's focus on the operation and in particular the vasectomy is predicated upon the necessity of *choosing* it.

Hijras may claim Vajpayee, the unmarried prime minister, as a brother, but Chief Minister Naidu, with his own phantasmatic vasectomy, offers the sign of the operation in confirming his claims upon the state. Here is the zone of indistinction, between Shabnam Mausi and Chandrababu Naidu, eunuch-turned-sovereign and sovereign-turned-eunuch. Here is the terrain where Mbembe suggests caution.

I have tried to suggest that what comes to matter in the resurrection of the sovereign in the form of the eunuch is not the usual lack assumed in the castration—for the logic of the operation displaces its effects—but a different, and salutary, lack. What is at stake is the possibility of an ascetic body and of imagining a social world outside the frequently grotesque demands of neoliberal welfare and its intimacy with violent cuttings, the operative stakes of caring and being cared for. Hijras, within and only within the contingent logic of recent political form, are the other to the asymmetrical care of the state, to the promise and fear of operable citizenship by sterilization, for they hold open the election of a surgery beyond necessity.

Notes

This chapter has benefited from critical comments received during its three successive airings: at the SAR advanced seminar "The State at Its Margins," at the University of Toronto, and at the University of Chicago. Particular thanks are due to Veena Das, Deborah Poole, the other seminar participants, and the two SAR Press reviewers, and at home at Berkeley and UCSF to Warwick Anderson, Stephen Collier, Eugene Irschick, Andrew Lakoff, Donald Moore, Aihwa Ong, Anand Pandian, Paul Rabinow, Lucinda Ramberg, Tobias Rees, and Nancy Scheper-Hughes. My beginning to think about the operation as a critical form is indebted above all to the work of Cecilia Van Hollen.

1. In a work-in-progress, Scheper-Hughes is working through both the metonymic and metaphoric relations of these three modes of exchange—that is, both how they differ from and supplement one another and how they are structurally interchangeable effects of an emergent logic of bodily fragmentation.

2. I offer this reworking of the stakes in subsumption, drawing on Prasad's

engagement with Etienne Balibar, with recognition of my limits in Marxist conversation. I choose *subsumption* to mark the operative stakes in assemblage here against, for example, *hybridity* (Gupta 1998). A disjuncture of orders of reason and being appears at stake, and creative efforts to perform modern citizenship in this context involve the wound of one's operability and not the supplementable graft one might associate with hybrid technologies.

3. Agamben draws on Hannah Arendt in foregrounding the classical distinction between bios, life within the polis, and zoe, the bare life all living matter lays claim to. The modern predicament involves the extension of the zone of indistinction, where these two kinds of life are not distinguishable, to encompass more and more of the world and its institutions.

4. Hijras are a staple of anthropological writing, including my own. Often self-defined in terms of an intersexed third gender, hijras are far more often a set of communities organized around ritual and sex work and a secret operation encompassing castration and penectomy. The explosion of sex research that has followed the circulation of global AIDS welfare capital in India and Bangladesh has both expanded more complex and subtle classifications of hijra identification and promoted new transgendered articulations (Cohen n.d.). I use *eunuch* interchangeably with *hijra* for a number of reasons. First, *eunuch* is the primary term of the dominant English-language Indian news media and, as such, demands the translatability of the position of the hijra and its commensurability with a dense assemblage of colonial and contemporary Western forensic and scientific reference. Second, *eunuch* is used as a self-referential term by many hijras, in effect marking their position in relation to such mediascapes. I have earlier taken up some of the referential stakes in the category of hijra (Cohen 1995b) but without sufficient attention to these metropolitan demands. I mean the exchangeability of *hijra* and *eunuch* in this chapter to represent the social fact of these demands and neither an accession to nor refusal of them. One might argue that insistence on the translatability of *hijra/eunuch* neutralizes its function as a colonial and postcolonial site of Indian exceptionality. Third, and most relevant to my purpose here, I utilize *eunuch* as I am arguing that the postoperative status (as opposed to feminization in itself) of the represented hijra matters to the articulation of her political will.

8

Productivity in the Margins

The Reconstitution of State Power in the Chad Basin

Janet Roitman

How is it that when one travels to the edge of the desert in the midst of austerity, one finds a stronghold of movement and mobility? How is it that the recent history of deregulation and privatization in this no-man's-land created by long-standing political neglect and ongoing factional fighting has not decimated the possibilities for livelihood? These questions about the incommensurability between dispossession and wealth creation nagged me throughout my stay in the Chad Basin.[1] They are central to the following reflections on productivity in the margins of state power in that same region, where we witness both conflict over regulatory authority and its dispersion through knots of power relations tied through cords of unregulated economic activity that span national borders. These borders have been critical to the current reconfiguration of state power in the Chad Basin and on the African continent more generally.

One of the most striking things about the landscape of the Chad Basin is the intense movement that takes place under the blazing sun and through the hot, dry air, along dusty paths aligned with thorny bushes and down steaming tarmac roads. This physical movement includes caravans of young men on bicycles, who pedal the long blistering routes and cross the mountain passes between Cameroon and Nigeria in their quest for black-market petrol, which they bring back to the cities in large plastic containers, attached behind them in potentially explosive towers. These young men are joined by streams of blue Suzuki motorcycles imported from Nigeria and in the service of all kinds of commerce, from transporting contraband to serving as clandestine taxis. This movement also includes old-style caravans, now composed of hefty six- to ten-wheel trucks, which ply the Sahara piled high with merchandise, dry goods, foodstuffs, and men, the occasional Kalashnikov poking out from under a mass of white robes and canvas bags. Some of the movement best qualifies as exchanges and transformations, or value conversions. The most obvious of these are constant monetary conversions, mostly inspired by currency differentials between franc-zone monies and the Nigerian naira, as well as the need to move from nonconvertible currencies, such as the franc CFA, to convertible ones. But these exchanges also involve the swapping, counterfeiting, and accumulation of national identity cards, voter registration cards, high school and university diplomas, and birth certificates.

Generally interpreted as beyond the state or even antistate, these activities are often quite misleadingly called "the informal economy." However, while they often share the characteristic of circumventing state economic regulation, these economic activities cannot be described or understood as marking out a realm distinct from state power, either in terms of their organization or their functioning (for a critique of the concept of the informal economy, see Roitman 1990; Hibou 1996). To the contrary, such activities are fundamentally linked to the state and are even essential to the very recomposition of state power in present conditions of extreme austerity. The tactics of mobility and misdemeanor inherent to activities associated with unregulated markets circumscribe targets of wealth, etching out new economic spaces, and constitute, in themselves, objects of economic regulation. In this latter capacity, they are at the heart of the postcolonial state's endeavor to fill its coffers and finance its constituents. By underscoring that point, this presentation of productivity in the margins does not necessarily confirm predictions about the demise of state power on the African continent. Nor does it demonstrate ways in which unregulated economic activities are potential bases for capitalist economic activity (de Soto

1989), shadow economies that sometimes surpass nodes of state power (Nordstrom 2001), or parallel economies that undermine internal state legitimacy but not juridical sovereignty (Reno 2001).

Over the past decade, African states have been generally depicted in academic research and media commentary as "weak states" (Migdal 1988; Kaplan 1994; Zartman 1995; Reno 1995), a view often interpreted in terms of their failure to adhere to the Weberian model of the rational-legal state. In short, these kinds of states are characterized as having limited capacity with respect to resource extraction, social control, and policy implementation. Thus, they lack authority and legitimacy in the domestic realm, often leading to a loss of control over territories and populations. Likewise, and following from that depiction, African political economies have been interpreted as increasingly marginalized from the international political economy (see Callaghy and Ravenhill 1993; Bach 1998; Castells 1998:70–165). This portrayal maintains, somewhat tautologically, that state failure results from the state's incapacity to control resources, commercial and financial activity, and regional trade.

Contrary to these accounts, my experience in the Chad Basin was not lacking in testimony to the strengths of certain African states, such as Cameroon, Nigeria, and Chad. These states have crushed rebellions and opposition movements not only through brute force but also through savvy political maneuvering, proving their respective abilities to monopolize the means of violence and to command central parts of the bureaucratic apparatus. Yet, the efficacy of these states is also generated out of what Michel Foucault described as the capillary effects of state power, or the effective constitution of the very field of "the state" through forms of power that exceed the state bureaucracy or its central institutions. Our intuition is that states produced through highly effective forms of capillary power are "strong" states, and those that resort to the exercise of power through "right of state" and violence are "weak" states, whose legitimacy is in question. But in the Chad Basin, the emergence of unregulated economic activities and violent methods of extraction, such as economic appropriation through seizure, indicate that violent practices can also be produced as a legitimate mode of the exercise of power. That is, violence can be part of the very legibility of power.

To home in on this problem, I make a distinction between state power and state regulatory authority. This seems a more precise manner of taking on the state as an anthropological object, and it helps make sense of the paradox between the increasing intensity of unregulated activities and the persistent efficacy of state infrastructures. In other words, the conceptual and practical distinction between state regulatory authority and state power accounts, in some respects, for the contradiction between the expansion of unregulated activities, which seems to indicate a loss of state control, and the continuity of state power in spite of it all. It also has allowed me to inquire more specifically into the modalities by which state regulatory authority is contested, subverted, and even abetted. I was able to do so during my stay in Cameroon in the early 1990s, when there was much protest over regulatory authority. Although widespread, this movement against certain interventions in people's economic lives cannot be described as a mass struggle against state regulatory authority or a matter of "society against the state" (Clastres 1989). Instead, during this time, Cameroonian citizens questioned and debated the very intelligibility of the exercise of state regulatory authority and fiscal relations. This was not a question of simple—meaning absolutely oppositional—resistance to state appropriations or even to state regulation in and of itself. What was at issue, rather, were the criteria upon which regulation is defined (that is, targets, modalities, ends), which implies conflict over the very relationships produced in and through regulation, as well as the rights and obligations inhering in those relationships. In this sense, because the *relationship* produced out of regulation and not merely the fact of regulation was at issue, the very production of the fiscal subject—or the effects of truths about that relationship and the concepts and categories it presupposes—was at the heart of conflict over the intelligibility of regulatory authority.

This chapter examines the concomitant contestation of regulatory authority and its redeployment. One of the chapter's central themes is that this latter form of power can be both unstable yet highly effective. It stems from the point that state regulation of the economy entails constant efforts to govern the frontiers of wealth creation, including the literal frontiers of the country, as well as the conceptual frontiers of the economy. This process is such that in the Chad Basin the pluralization of figures of regulatory authority goes hand in hand with the reconstitution of state power and explains to a large degree how in recent times, economic and social mobility have been produced out of situations of extreme austerity.

MAKING MONEY IN THE CHAD BASIN

The general question of productivity in marginal spaces of the global economy speaks to the subthemes of how marginality is central to the generation of states of power and how it is constitutive of the very legibility of power. Although once linked to the international economy via first the slave trade and then the colonial cotton and peanut economies, those living in the Chad Basin now suffer economically from the fairly recent collapse of these latter markets. Furthermore, the region has no industrial base and is not even an industrial periphery. How, then, does one make money in the Chad Basin? How does one connect into the global economy from the edge of the periphery? How does one eke out a livelihood when one has no recourse to significant natural resources, a viable industrial base, or even service sector employment? Recourse to subsistence farming is evidently one solution. Yet most people are not returning to their villages, despite the fact that prospects for gainful employment have dwindled in the towns and cities. As in many places, the prospect of economic security through family ties and farming does not compete these days with the lure of profits to be had in regional and ultimately transnational markets. This shift is partially due to the demise of world markets for certain primary products and the recent rearrangement of industrial production that privileges labor markets in Southeast Asia, South Asia, and Latin America.

In the Chad Basin, "emerging markets" retrace the trails of the old trans-Saharan and east-west Sahelian economies, reproducing certain historical forms of finance and distribution while generating novel resources from international markets. The end of the cold war and the deregulation of both world and local markets, which precipitated the increased circulation of small arms, drugs, mercenaries, and private security personnel on the African continent, have facilitated this process. More specifically, arms flow from Eastern Europe, China, South Africa, Angola, and the independent republics of the former Soviet Union through the Sudan, Libya, Chad, Cameroon, Nigeria,

Niger, and Algeria. Mercenaries from Chad, Sudan, and Pakistan circulate throughout the region, while American, French, and British private security companies contribute to this movement of guns and men (Bayart, Ellis, and Hibou 1997; Friedman 1993; *Le Figaro* 1997; Harding 1996; Banégas 1998). Likewise, trade in gold, diamonds, ivory, and drugs finance war and ongoing factional fighting. At a more mundane level, trade in petrol, hardware, electronics, grain, cement, and stolen cars or four-wheel-drive trucks supplies factions and conflicts in Niger, Chad, the Central African Republic, and the Sudan (Soudan 1996; Dorce 1996; Bennafla 1997).

The privatization and downsizing of national administrations and armed services, which have swollen the ranks of those seeking alternative forms of enrichment, have abetted the expansion of these economic activities. Between 1992 and 1997, 27,000 Chadian military personnel were slated to be demobilized and disarmed (*Le Progres* 1997; *N'Djamena Hebdo* 1997; Teiga 1997; Bennafla 1996). This military demobilization campaign has incited newly unemployed soldiers to enter into small-arms trafficking, for which they have contacts and expertise. They "enter the bush," as they say, where they join up with organized groups of road bandits, especially those coming from Cameroon, Nigeria, Niger, the Central African Republic, and the Sudan. Furthermore, formal commercial concerns have linked up with these seemingly renegade networks. The urban-based merchant class, which produced its rents through debt financing until the late 1980s (Bayart 1989), has been forced to reorient its economic activities with the contraction of bilateral and multilateral aid. Having worked as transporters and suppliers for public works projects, the merchant elite's convoys now plow desert paths and mountain roads running through Nigeria, Cameroon, the Central African Republic, Chad, Libya, and the Sudan. They form critical links in smuggling operations and the illegal trade in petrol and serve as financial backers of highly organized gangs of road bandits.

Although these merchant networks, which are essentially urban, have managed to sustain predominance over the countryside by reinventing modalities for enrichment, such strategies are now accompanied by, and increasingly dependent upon, those pursued by the unemployed and recently dispossessed. No doubt, the unemployed have been keen to follow the paths of these commercial convoys, working as transporters, guards, guides, and carriers along national borders. Their activities presuppose collusion with recently unemployed or extremely underpaid military personnel, customs officials, and other government figures who control safe passage and regulate entry into this lucrative economic sector. However, the urban economy, the political and social base of the merchant elite and military personae, is in many ways now subservient to what I will call the "economy of the bush." No longer simply the agrarian sector comprising rural and agricultural activities, the economy of the bush encompasses fundamental commercial, financial, and monetary activities. Its vitality is attested to by a report on the monetary situation in the franc zone, which notes the "urban exodus" of bank bills and coinage that have followed the flows of trade in the hinterlands and especially along national borders (*L'Autre Afrique* 1997).[2] In that sense, "entering the bush" is not just about parallel or shadow economic and political activities. Nor is it a space of regressive attitudes toward money and international links that procure wealth.[3] The economy of the bush may have its covert or even insurgent aspects, but it is equally a realm of well-known strategies of accumulation, where claims to the right to wealth are now articulated and enacted.

CLAIMS TO WEALTH: *"INCIVISME FISCALE"*

The dismissed, dispossessed, downsized, and under- or unemployed who have taken to the bush, highways, and borders are making claims to wealth and even to the very right to wealth. Many unemployed youths have some form of education, yet they find themselves obliged to scavenge for money. The economy of the bush provides them with cash and gives them a means to counter what they feel is the state's monopoly over surpluses. They have aired this sentiment consistently over the last decade, arguing that their activities are a manner of exercising claims to wealth. These opinions were heard most clearly during the 1990s, when, just after the legalization of independent political parties, a widespread political movement took hold of the main cities in Cameroon. In May 1991, this movement culminated in the Opération Villes Mortes campaign. Organized by the National Coordination of

Opposition Parties and Associations, it involved a strategy of civil dis-
obedience implementing general strikes, work boycotts, economic
blockades, and clandestine services—such as motorcycles that served
as "hidden" taxis—to deny taxation (Champaud 1991; *New York Times*
1991, *Africa Confidential* 1991a, 1991b; Monga 1993; Kom 1993;
Roitman n.d.). The strategy of this campaign was explicit: its aim was
to undermine the fiscal base of the regime. Indeed, Opération Villes
Mortes crippled the Cameroonian economy. It resulted in an estimated
40 percent decrease in economic activity, which represented four
billion CFA per day for the state, including taxes and fees (Diallo
1991:18), or the equivalent of the preceding year's revenues (van de
Walle 1993:381). Those who participated in the movement expressed
their criticism of the regime's exactions and levies, which ultimately
finance the ruling party and the political elite; the state's methods
of extraction, which are often heavy-handed; and the regime's failure
to provide economic opportunities and economic security to local
populations. In turn, the regime dubbed Opération Villes Mortes and
the general refusal to pay taxes *"incivisme fiscal,"* which was intended to
typify the movement as "uncivil" or beyond the pale of civic behavior.

As I observed this struggle between the state and its citizens unfold,
it became clearer to me that the pertinent question was not the outright rejection of regulatory or fiscal authority, but rather disagreement
over the intelligibility of the exercise of that authority. In the marketplace in the town of Maroua (population 120,000), I spoke with people
both during calm moments and just after clashes between demonstra-
tors and the police. My conversations indicated that there was no consensus among local people as to the significance of the movement. I
will not quote them at length here, but most people I spoke to basically
agreed on the need to deprive the regime of its fiscal base so as to force
it to respond to certain demands. Yet, some insisted that this response
should entail increased and effective regulation to combat the extension of unregulated markets, whereas others underscored the liberat-
ing effects of the movement and the desire to throw off the shackles of
state regulation. One merchant echoed the feelings of many others,
insisting on the role of the state as guarantor of the market and economic security, which he viewed as threatened by foreign influences.
He explained:

With the crisis, workplaces are closed; merchants hardly sell anymore. Companies are closed, and functionaries are two or three months without salaries. With these months without salaries, they have debt. We don't sell, and some merchants can't pay their licenses. Nigerians ["Nigerians" refers to those peddling wares from Nigeria, regardless of national origin] go door to door with merchandise, through the neighborhoods, along all the paths, they hawk their wares. They sell cheaper. They don't pay for licenses, no taxes; the administration does not take care of the problem.... Nigeria is killing Maroua. People don't want to consume Cameroonian products. Money is going out of the country ...the state must make order; it must cover me....If the state has its profits, I'll have mine.

Another merchant concurred, saying, "I'm obliged to pay taxes, and I don't earn anything. If the state obliges me, I must do it. The administration must take its responsibilities in hand...they must eliminate the ambulatory sellers."

Many merchants who see foreign economic operators and those who evade regulation, such as ambulatory sellers, as problematic also condemn the state for its inaction. However, they hone in on civil servants, who are no longer the principal source of capital for extended families and networks of redistribution and who contribute to capital flight by purchasing goods in neighboring markets in Nigeria. Merchants thus find themselves in the contradictory position of having to "work the bush" (meaning unregulated markets) and pay taxes. As an angry merchant declared firmly:

There is no market; there is no money. The civil servants don't earn money like before. Firms are shut; people are bankrupt; companies have no work. The problem is capital flight. I pay taxes, and they go to the exterior; there is no more money in Cameroon. We're obliged to work the markets in the bush—and to pay licenses. The government is the source of these problems. I sell at a loss because things are cheaper in Nigeria.

Another man repeated the view that civil servants, being both the primary consumers and those who mainly buy abroad, are undermining the Cameroonian economy and fueling unregulated exchanges: "There is no market because there is contraband. I buy merchandise in Douala [Cameroon], not in Nigeria.... Contraband is breaking us. There are a lot of taxes on us; commercial licenses *[la patente]* are too expensive. The state functionaries go to Banki [Nigeria] for everything, even for household items and food. Who are we going to sell to?"

On the other hand, not everyone depicted the porous border and unregulated economic activities as problems of state. Some people made immediate reference to "democracy" as the force behind the demonstrations in the marketplace and the population's newfound refusal to pay taxes. Thus, when I asked why people are now willing to confront the authorities in the marketplace, I was told:

> The state must function; they [merchants] have to pay their *droits* [taxes and duties]. The problem is Nigeria: the border is permeable; the smugglers must be countered. They [Cameroonian merchants] can't sell their products, and they don't want to pay for a license. They're selling at a loss. They'd be willing to pay if the smugglers were stopped, if they could sell their own products. They refute the authorities in the market because they're threatened by Nigeria, and they hold the authorities responsible. Or it's because of democratization; it's democratization misunderstood *[la démocracie mal comprise]*—that's why they live this ambiguity.

A municipal administrator put forth this same view: "They burned the controllers' post and the police post in the marketplace. Now they say it's democracy, and it spills over and it's anarchy. Even when the police whistle, they say they're free, it's democracy. It's an adjustment.... People don't want to pay [taxes], they say it's democracy."

When asked what happened just after a violent confrontation between security forces and civilians in the main marketplace, one young man repeated this view, albeit from the perspective of the opposition:

> The police encircled the city and the market. People

decided to stay at home. The police were asking for tax receipts; if you didn't have it, they put you in a truck. No one came to the market. There was great disorder. People burned tires; they prevented anyone from circulating, even the police. We haven't paid for a year now. We have entered into politics. Politics helped us refuse to pay. It's democracy. If we pay taxes, it finances the RDPC [Rassemblement Democratique Du Peuple Camerounais]. Forty-nine million remains to be paid. It's their problem; this government doesn't interest us. We used to be obliged; now it's democracy, we're no longer obliged.

"But why do people have the courage to refuse now?" I asked.

"The [authorities] are afraid of the vandals; they'll come burn them alive, in their houses and in their cars. The state doesn't have any means. It's the population that has the means; they can sell from their homes."

While insisting on the state's responsibilities, many see the generalization of unregulated exchanges as a democratizing force because it has brought down barriers to economic mobility: black-market petrol is everywhere, everyone has access. As one person put it, "The petrol trade is not clandestine anymore, not only because the gendarmes and customs officials are all involved, but also because it has been democratized: anyone can do it and everyone does."

Another man concurred, underscoring again that this is not a matter of society versus the state because state agents are all implicated in the effervescence of unregulated traffic:

> People are willing to confront the authorities because they have petrol. They can burn things, and the gendarmes are afraid of being burned alive in their cars or in their houses. And all the people have petrol; it's everywhere because of the traffic with Nigeria; it's all over the streets and in every house. And the gendarmes can't do anything because they [themselves] are all involved in the traffic.

Generally speaking, my conversations with the foot soldiers of the economy of the bush always came back to the idea that—in spite of strong nationalist and especially protectionist sentiments—the expanding trade in unregulated goods is a source of economic freedom and empowerment. Associated with the right to engage in commerce regardless of means, those who smuggle petrol on the Nigerian-Cameroonian border often described their activities as part of "democratization" because "anyone can participate." Moreover, their supply kept gas prices low, thus aiding the impoverished consumer. Yet, democratization—a topic I will not dwell on here [4]—was evidently being reduced to the question of establishing freedom from tax. It was also interpreted as a means to negate or rectify exclusions heretofore established through economic regulation, such as licensing. However, as many people noted, the police, gendarmes, and customs officials are involved in unregulated commerce, thus making the opposition between "them" and "us" obscure (see Roitman n.d.). The fact that people are living "ambiguity" is an astute point made by one man cited above. Ultimately, there was much uncertainty about the very field of positive knowledge in which state interventions in citizens' lives have been conceptualized and enacted. This debate has centered upon certain interrogations: What is the ultimate source of wealth? And, as a corollary, what does "les droits"—meaning taxes as well as rights and obligations—refer to? Responses to this last question are dependant upon the first, and they thus vacillate, depending on whether wealth is primarily localized as something generated by and within the state, the market, the consumer, the civil servant, the citizen, or something else. This interrogation of wealth and rights involves reflection about the ways in which fiscal targets are qualified as such and the manners through which the fiscal subject emerges in the field of regulation.[5]

THE RIGHT TO WEALTH, THE RIGHT TO TAX

In Cameroon, the incivisme fiscal movement was often summarized as the refusal to pay la patente, or commercial licenses. These were imposed upon all merchants owning shops and businesses, as well as petty traders selling wares or pieces of cloth spread on the ground or on old wooden planks set up at the edges of the marketplace. As a form of tax, la patente enters into the general category of droits, which in French signifies, depending on the context, duties, fees, and taxes, as well as entitlements and rights of entry and access. From my experience, those who pay taxes in northern Cameroon—including Europeans—generally refer to droits in terms of rights of access: one pays taxes for the right to access certain markets, or for the privileged relationships that ensure exchanges and commercial relationships.[6] Tax is often signified in local parlance as a "price" *(le prix)*; it is the price one pays for the right of access. Today, the tension between obligations and entitlements that forms the spinal column of "rights" (les droits) has become quite taut. Thus, the chief of a butcher's market *(sarki pawa)* in Maroua insisted that one "pays for rights" and that unregulated trade in cattle and the proliferation of neighborhood butchers who work in back streets, backyards, and the bush are a negation of rights of access in both economic and political terms:

> Before, to be a butcher, you had to have the paper....Now they go get the paper—the license *[la patente]*...but they no longer slaughter under my eye....If they have their papers, they have paid for certain rights. I explain that they must see me, they must respect the rules. Ten years ago, it wasn't like that....They're not in agreement now; it's not democracy yet.

During the so-called incivisme fiscal movement, the Paul Biya regime sought to establish a homologous relationship between sources of political disorder and sources of economic disorder, between, for instance, "antinational" activity and the so-called informal economy— what one merchant cited above referred to as "markets in the bush." Consequently, terms of debate about economic citizenship, or the nature of rights and responsibilities inherent in the fiscal relationship, have been restricted for the most part to the question of security *through* the state versus security *from* the state. And this question basically involves, as the Opération Villes Mortes movement itself articulated, rights to security either through the fiscal actions of the state or from the fiscal actions of the state. Therefore, although paying taxes has been construed historically as requisite for—or even constitutive of—the status of "free citizen," in the present context, the constitution of the "free citizen" is construed less in terms of a founding economic transfer than in terms of the conditions that allow for that transfer. The merchants' remarks quoted above are exemplary of this general viewpoint insofar as they state that those conditions include security from foreign economic and political influences, as well as access to a market.

Yet, merchants now contest the idea of paying for the right to trade, or paying for access to the market *(le droit du marché)*, by making claims to "the right to a market"—*le droit au marché*, often referred to as le droit du marché —or to the very conditions that would allow one to pay tax. The general public's very willingness to confront the authorities in a concerted manner was consistently explained to me as a matter of access to and control of petrol: *"Nous avons zoua-zoua; c'est le feu public"* ("We have zoua-zoua; it's the public fire [or the public's fire]").[7] Calls for le droit du marché (or le droit au marché) were thus both appeals for state protection of national markets and concomitant assertions of the freedom to engage in commerce regardless of means, which counters the gatekeeping functions of entitlements construed as rights of access. In this sense, one might argue that "the right" (le droit) to wealth, which involves both entitlements and duties, was not being constructed in the specific name of the "consumer" or the "producer" or the "worker," but rather as the fiscal subject.

The constitution of the fiscal subject is, of course, inherently related to the status of citizenship, a point underscored at a meeting between high-level administrators and the merchants of Maroua in April 1993. This gathering was an attempt by the regime to bring insurgent traders and businessmen into the fold of "civic behavior," which involved the formation of a special commission to investigate tax evasion and regulation of the main marketplace. At this time, the local prefect took the opportunity to remind the merchants,

> You are the ones who fostered the presence of Nigerians, Chadians—you benefit from their presence. The networks are very, very complicated. The Nigerians and Chadians rent stores from you....[T]hey're in the parallel and informal circuits that you have initiated....The commission [on taxes and the marketplace] cannot work freely....No one will reveal their profit margins. You say you have only four cartons of soap [in your store], and you're riding around in a Mercedes. We know that the command "Refuse!" [to pay

tax] runs through the market. But you tell me that foreigners are the ones who tell the youth to attack the people from the Ministry of Finances....Lots of activities take place in the form of traffic. Traffic was never the life of a country *[faire vivre un pays]*. And where that is the case, like in the Gambia, it was organized by the agents of the state itself. But if you have houses and cars...and the state has nothing, what can you do for Maroua? The roads must be tarred, public works are stopped; they must continue, but there is no money....If you don't pay taxes, the country will die. The country is on its knees because its sons *[les fils du pays]* don't pay their taxes....It's no use to use a whip, it simply means that you are not free men.

Many merchants responded that they were not opposed to state regulation of their economic activities, but they did object to the state's manners of appropriation, as well as the presupposition that they were the ultimate sources of wealth, the foundations of the state treasury. Just after the meeting, one shopkeeper explained to me,

We are not against licenses; before, we paid without force, without the police. They say that if you trade in the market, you need a license, at 37,000 CFA....The prefect says it's not a political problem. They warn us to pay because the civil servants don't have any money. If we pay the licenses, will that suffice to pay the civil servants? The prefect gave 120,000 CFA to 120 policemen to come massacre the market. If we don't pay, they close down our shops.

An older man, who had a small shop, added,

Before, they came to the market to collect money—it was paid in installments, and we got a receipt. They came every Monday. Even if the government sent a crazy man, we did what they asked. Now, the people who come are not children; they are big. If you say you have nothing, they close your shop....For five years now, they shut us down, chain our stores, and they leave. If they close your store and you stay in the market, they say, "Go steal."

In many ways, the incivisme fiscal movement expressed—and even served to develop—interrogations about the legitimate foundations of state wealth, the forms of wealth to be subject to state appropriations, the distinction between licit and illicit commerce, the integrity of the contours of the nation-state, and the nature of national identity. The present regime has insisted that the dramatization of citizenship should take place primarily through the fiscal relationship, an assertion that, of course, presupposes a stable representation of national affiliation. National wealth rests upon national unity, which is construed as an objective reality. During the 1990s, various regional groups, including members of the opposition, some of whom have called for decentralization and federalism, and the secessionist movement in the Anglophone northwestern and southwestern provinces, explicitly contested the very idea of national unity. The idea was also implicitly challenged by ongoing conflicts between various communities spanning international borders, such as the Kotoko and Arab Choa communities in the north (Socpa 2002; Bah and Issa 1997), and the intensification of unregulated cross-border trade and its attendant forms of affiliation (Bennafla 1998, 2002; Roitman 1998). Historically speaking, national unity has been localized in the national treasury as opposed to ethnic, racial, or religious authenticity, which has perhaps mitigated tendencies toward decentralization, fragmentation, adversity between nationals, and regionalization. In his address to the merchants of Maroua and their political representatives, the prefect thus insisted, through circular reasoning (and in a tone quite reminiscent of colonial forms of truth): "The treasury is the unity of the country...the unity of the country depends on the coffers of the state." These remarks were made in specific reference to the idea that tax receipts in the various provinces contribute to the central government's ability to pay civil servants everywhere in the country.

In recent times, efforts to ensure the continuity of the foundations of wealth—in the slave, in dependents, in the head of the family, in the consumer, in the civil servant, in the salary, in development aid, in the national treasury—have intensified. This process has brought the question of "national unity" to the fore. Since the time of colonization by the French, redistribution has occurred nationally through salary payments ensured via external financing. These have underpinned the burgeoning civil service and parastatal sectors, providing the material means for national distribution and the construction of dependency relations through patronage networks and extended families. As everywhere, the salary system structures social stratification. But following in the traces of the colonial state, the Cameroonian postcolonial state is the nexus of the great majority of salaried activity. Therefore, because the salary creates relations of dependency and debt between the state and recipients (and their dependents), it is constitutive of, and reflects, a particular notion of citizenship. In Cameroon, salaries are most often construed as "privileges" as opposed to simple remuneration for productive activity. This attitude is evident to anyone who witnesses the pleadings of those who arrive, day after day for months on end, at the barred windows of the public offices where salaries might (eventually) be distributed. This perception of the salary as a privilege and not a right is the combined result of the deployment of the salary as part of a disciplinary apparatus establishing relations of dependency and indebtedness between the state and its subjects, as well as historical understandings of the relationships that bind wealth, work, and the state.

Without expanding on that last point, which has been developed elsewhere (Mbembe and Roitman 1995; Roitman n.d.), what I wish to highlight here is that the materiality of the civil link between the state and its subjects has been realized through taxes and welfare services—as in many parts of the world—as well as through wealth, *or even simply money,* produced in state infrastructures. By the early 1990s, that mode of financing national unity was no longer guaranteed. Thus, wealth and work have been sought out elsewhere. An "ex"–road bandit who participated in gang-based organizations that attacked cars, trucks, and caravans explained that his exploits were a form of work. When asked whether what he did was theft, he replied, "No. I didn't steal, I was working."

I insisted, "Yes, but stealing is not working!"

"You don't understand anything. The thief is like a liar. The liar wastes his spit for nothing; he talks to earn nothing. The thief steals out of reflex; he takes everything that passes in front of him, even useless things."

"You seem to be proud that you were a different kind of thief."

"Are you trying to insult me? I'll say it once more: when there is a salary at the end, you're not a thief. Me, I work the road."

This man went on to describe "small work operations," insisting that work involves not only attacks on targets of wealth for the salary but also the clearing out of small groups of "thieves" who encumber the roads and prevent the professionals from carrying out their "work." As he said, "I'm sure that few people know that there are moments when we attack other groups to eliminate the thieves so that we can work."

Ultimately, debate about foundational terms, such as national wealth, have occasioned cross-examinations of certain established truths, such as what constitutes wealth and work. People have interrogated the status of wealth produced through seizure and raiding performed by both agents of the state and the local populace. They have also probed the status of limit zones, such as borders and the bush, where such wealth is produced. This cross-examination of established truths might be thought of as a moment that has engendered supplementary definitions of licit wealth and legitimate manners of appropriation. In other words, contrary to "economic crisis" or "legitimacy crisis" readings of such moments in many parts of Africa, the destabilizing effects of this recognition of the inconsistent nature of these seemingly invariable referents have not simply led to a loss of sense and meaning in the world.[8] With the expansion in the field of "the economic," so also the fiscal subject has come to signify new things. These are engendered through a complex genealogy, which cannot be told here. But what we can see from this short exposé is that the very presupposition that citizens are the source of the state's wealth—that they are to pay for access to entitlements and that the salary constitutes the privileged link between the state and its citizens—has been scrutinized. As a productive moment, incivisme fiscal, or the process of questioning it entailed, gave rise to transformations in the discursive field in which "wealth" and "the national" are figured, as well as the material effects of that discursive domain on contemporary practice.

One of those effects is the novel arrangements between official and unofficial forms of regulatory authority that have become institutionalized in the region. These relationships involve more than the establishment of monopolies over new forms of wealth; they entail the normalization of particular definitions of licit wealth and manners of appropriating such wealth. Thus, while recourse to these networks of accumulation and acquiescence to their associated figures of authority may be inspired by a contraction in material wealth and access to such wealth (the "marginalization of Africa" thesis), they also transpire from the extension of the discursive field in which wealth and value are figured. "Spoils," for instance, is now an ambivalent sign in the regional lexicon of wealth: once associated with war and asocial forms of wealth creation, it now signifies the disavowal of particular social obligations, such as tax and debt (Roitman 2003). As with fraudulent commerce, what is seized cannot be taxed. And for those living in a web of international and local debt relations, seizure is a means of interfering in the social order implied by such obligations. Furthermore, "spoils" now signifies a new sociability of exchange insofar as it is a new means of redistribution. Although tax collection was described and thus denounced as a form of seizure, many people, especially demobilized soldiers and dispossessed youths, have inverted this power equation by seizing spoils themselves.

In the end, seizure has become generalized as a mode of enrichment: financial regulators chain merchants' stores shut, haul merchants to prison, confiscate goods, and exact fines. Customs officials and gendarmes skim off of trucks and travelers, usurping contraband and often going poaching themselves, and gangs of professional road bandits hijack cars and attack road convoys. Ultimately, "tax" can be effected in sites outside the limits of the state-citizen bind. This view was put to me during a visit to Cameroon in 2001–2003, long after the demonstrations associated with incivisme fiscal had subsided. In response to criticism for not having paid his official taxes, a young motorcycle-taximan, a member of the Association des Moto-Taximen, declared,

> We pay our taxes every day! Whether we have all the right
> papers for the motorcycle or not, we pay taxes to the police
> and gendarmes. In fact, it's become a reflex. The policemen
> of Ngaoundéré don't stop me anymore. I'm all old hand in
> the moto-taxi business. I've driven moto-taxis for people in
> high places, for men in uniform [who own fleets of clandestine motorcycles]. Furthermore, often even when the police
> don't stop me, I go to them to pay the tribute [in a monetary
> sense].[9]

During the same conversation, another moto-taxi driver added:

> The police and the moto-taximen, we're partners. We know
> that if we are disposed to giving them a bit of money from
> time to time, we can work together. Together—that is, the
> police and the moto-taximen—we exploit illegality. Even
> when you have all your papers in order, you're in illegality
> because the motorcycle is illegal. Not even 15 percent of the
> motorcycles are painted yellow.[10] We have imposed our
> vision of things on the authorities. The police themselves
> close their eyes; they can always find an infraction to ticket....
> So that the system can continue to function properly, it's
> important that there are people in violation, because if
> everyone was in line with the law, the authorities—the
> police—wouldn't gain their share, and then they would sup-
> press the motorcycles on the pretext that they cause acci-
> dents, that we are hoodlums, etc. Today, maybe we are
> hoodlums, but we are hoodlums who help sustain families
> and contribute to the well-being of agents of the force of
> law. Long live the tolerant police *[la police compréhensive]!*

When asked whether they considered their activities "licit" or
"illicit," there was general agreement that "anything that can move a
poor man from hunger and begging is licit." But one young man
argued that

> we struggle in domains that force you to circumvent the
> law—with all the risks. For example, we sell contraband
> petrol and medicines, etc., which are officially forbidden.
> But what do you expect? Often, those who are supposed to
> see that people respect the law are our sponsors; they give us
> our original financing. A customs official who finances a
> petrol smuggler is not going to attack him [the smuggler] or
> the protégés of his colleagues! And without us, the work of
> the policeman, the customs official, the taxman, the head of
> the gendarmes would have no interest for those who do it.
> Thanks to us, they have no financial problems.

> "But that's corruption!"

That's not corruption. When you give 10,000 or 20,000 CFA to a policeman or a customs official to get your merchandise through, what does that change for the national economy? Corruption is when one sells the Régie Nationale des Chemins de Fer [rail company], the SNEC [water company], the SONEL [electric company], etc. Everyone knows that that's negotiated; there are big commissions. One single person can earn in a privatization more than all of Touboro [a town known for contraband] can produce, save in a decade. Us, we give with pleasure, and the police receive with pleasure, just like the customs official. They've become family.

Until now, the desire to move from the payment of tax as a fee for access—or as a founding economic transfer—to the payment of tax as an act that transpires from entitlement—or from the assurance of economic and political security—has not been achieved by those who now exercise claims to wealth. Regardless of transformations in representations, for those who engage in the emergent regional and transnational economies, making transfers to their associated figures of regulatory authority in order to secure their livelihood, the question of payment for access is being merely transposed onto another field of action. In other words, young petrol traffickers might envision the commissions and tariffs they pay to their patrons as the price of "democratized" business, because "anyone can participate regardless of means," but they are still the fiscal subjects of national entities. Nonetheless, their representations of those transfers and their associated exchanges contribute to the institutionalization of practices of wealth creation through unregulated activities and figures of power associated with those transfers in the Chad Basin.

THE PLURALIZATION OF REGULATORY AUTHORITY, THE RECONFIGURATION OF STATE POWER

In the Chad Basin, new figures of regulatory authority have appeared in tandem with revived or newly founded networks of exchange. This power is exercised by controlling access to possibilities for accumulation, hence determining the right to employment and enrichment. This activity takes place at the highest levels of business through commissions on deals, right-of-entry taxes, tribute and royalty payments, protection fees, and even payment for safe delivery of goods procured through customs fraud or for their "legal" passage through customs (see Hibou 1997). Likewise, it transpires at the everyday level of business through levies on local merchants; protection and entitlement fees paid by young men engaged as guards, guides, and runners; entry taxes paid at unregulated border markets; and tolls on roads near these economically sensitive outposts (see Bennafla 1998; Grégoire 1998).

Most often, those who direct the financing, labor recruitment, and material organization required by these regional networks of trade take part in commercial-military relationships that permit them to exercise their authority over regional economic activities, essential resources, and local populations. In Chad, these militaro-commercial figures are known as *les douaniers-combattants:* literally, "customs officials-soldiers" or, more prosaically, "fighting customs officials." They comprise leaders of factions or rebel groups, such as the Mouvement pour le Développement around Lake Chad, and military personnel who find rents on fraudulent commerce more attractive than their official (and often unpaid) salaries (on the military-commercial connection, see Faes 1997, Abba Kaka 1997, and Ngarngoune 1997). These authority figures compete with instances of national regulatory authority insofar as they become the final arbiters of enrichment and employment. Through levies and duties imposed on local populations, they establish an autonomous fiscal base. And in some respects, they have become guarantors of economic security and access to wealth for local people, in spite of their association with violence.

Regional entrepôts and border settlements generate distinct regimes of violence, being highly militarized and often exercising control over residents and passersby through arms and attacks on roadways. However, these outposts also provide access to wealth and possibilities for accumulation, as well as protection and a blueprint for action at a time of insecurity and a sense of loss of possibility. Payments made to ensure access to international and regional markets, essential commercial and financial relationships, and protection serve to formalize various kinds of traffic, be it small arms crossing long distances or petrol smuggled through a mountain pass. This system makes such activities less unpredictable in terms of both logistics and revenues. Moreover, contributions to those who regulate access to and participation in these commercial and financial activities are not without services rendered. These services include protection and a formal cadre, but they also involve the redistribution that takes place through the financing of community facilities, such as mosques and churches, or through family demands, such as in times of illness, death, or misfortune.

The proliferation of these kinds of relationships, and the extractive and redistributive logics that go with them, is such that local people now find themselves implicated in relationships with numerous figures of regulatory authority. But this is not necessarily a matter of state regulation versus non-state regulation. Militaro-commercial alliances associate renegade militias, gendarmes, demobilized soldiers, customs officials, military officers, political administrators, wealthy merchants, and government ministers. Although this amalgam seems to represent merely the implication of members of government and the national military in illegal and informal mafia-style syndicates—which is sometimes the case—this is an oversimplification. Although *state regulatory authority* is surely challenged and imperiled by the ability of these new authority figures to extract from local populations, these new forms of power do not usurp state power. In fact, in some instances we can see how they even contribute to the restitution of state power in this time of debt and austerity.

As in many other places, although transnational phenomena present problems for state regulation, they nonetheless become part and parcel of the political logics of the state itself, contributing to its capacity to fulfill constitutive tasks, such as extraction or redistribution (see Sassen 1995 on the creation of new legal regimes and, more generally, Hibou 1999).[11] For example, the Cameroonian administration has seized upon the recently established market town of Mbaïboum as a new target of fiscal power. Mbaïboum mushroomed on the international borders of Chad, Cameroon, and the Central African Republic in 1987. It serves as a hub of unregulated commerce in locally produced and imported industrial goods (cement, textiles) and consumer items (salt, sugar, clothing, cassette players, hardware), as well as imitation or bogus pharmaceuticals, arms, gold, and diamonds. In 1992, just after commercial activities in Mbaïboum intensified, a Cameroonian customs station suddenly appeared. Although the state has provided neither water nor electricity to this "boomtown," it now manages to take in twenty million CFA a year through the sale of market duties *(droits de marche)* and licenses (Bennafla 1998:54, 68). Yet, this official presence does not mean the legalization of unregulated activity, nor has it eclipsed the power of the emergent regulators who were first on the scene. The unofficial (non-state) regulators of commerce at Mbaïboum still exercise their "rights" over local populations: they collect "entry and exit" duties in the market (5,000 to 10,000 CFA per vehicle) and tolls on incoming roads (10,000 to 50,000 CFA for trucks) (Bennafla 1998:68), not to mention commissions and protection fees on the more lucrative trade in gold, arms, diamonds, and rhinoceros horns.

In fact, the Cameroonian government has not taken any measures to subdue or extinguish unofficial regulation, and its own customs policy has been described as "accommodating" and even "encouraging," with low levels of taxation on goods and very little surveillance of the national identities of those passing across the borders (Bennafla 1999:66). In both Cameroon and Chad, official military escorts are sometimes used to protect both those traveling to trade at such outposts and those engaging in the fraudulent traffic that feeds them. For instance, Cameroonian military escorts protect merchants traveling between Mbaïboum and outlying cities from persistent road bandits. And in Chad, the Garde Nationale et Nomade is known to pack into Toyota pickup trucks and ride at "breakneck speed" through town, escorting vehicles containing smuggled goods to the marketplace (Abba Kaka 1997). The Chadian and Cameroonian states have every reason to facilitate border traffic and smuggling operations because they provide remuneration for under- and unpaid military personnel who convert to customs officials. Hence, they redeploy the salary through economico-political relationships that exceed the state, or through private means.

But such complicity does not necessarily mean that unregulated traffic is legalized. The state simply offers a legal structure for these activities while not altering the fact that they are still deemed either formally illegal or based on fraud. Hence, administrative documents that do not take into account the quantitative or qualitative nature of the commerce involved are produced. This amounts to providing a false legal status for merchants and smugglers—or what locals refer to as *un vrai-faux*. Common practice along the borders of all states in the Chad Basin—and perhaps everywhere in the world—this is just one way the state is at the heart of the proliferation of sub- and transnational networks of accumulation and power. Through this false legalization, under- and unpaid state administrators are "paid" through the commissions and rents they procure. Furthermore, the state's dire problems of financial liquidity are resolved through access to hard currency in contexts where local monies are nonconvertible. Traffic between the Chad Basin and the Sahara is one example. In Niger, the state is at the center of the organization of illegal trade in American cigarettes. Emmanuel Grégoire (1998:100) points out that "The Nigerian state has, in effect, set up a legislative framework which organizes this traffic and obtains significant customs receipts, estimated at about 6 billion francs CFA in 1994 and 1995, or the equivalent of a month and a half of functionaries' salaries, which are six months past due (January 1998). Operators act in perfect legality in Niger, with fraud transpiring only at the cost of neighboring states which prohibit imports of foreign cigarettes to protect its own industry (Nigeria) or tax them strongly for the same reason (Algeria and Libya)." In this case, state agents not only collude with but also depend upon intermediaries (for example, Tuaregs)[12] who control trade routes and provide security in dangerous zones, such as southern Algeria and the border between Niger and Chad. State administrators engage in these relations for personal profit, of course, but they are also a means to remedy the insolvency of the state and its associated political risks—which are constantly on the horizon, as is attested to by consistent demands put forth by unpaid bureaucrats, including members of the police and the army. Such an example partially answers the daunting question of how insolvent states somehow manage to function and even expand their administrations in spite of bankruptcy and indebtedness. In Cameroon, for instance, 20,000 administrators were added to the rolls between 1987 and 1997, despite the fact that there was no official recruitment during that time (Hibou 1997:150).

The state thus benefits from profitable situations produced by competing regimes of power. It sometimes also instigates the proliferation of unregulated, underregulated, or falsely regulated activities, and even becomes dependent upon those wielding power (for example, regulation of access) and expertise (for example, security) in sub- and transnational networks. Even though these endeavors potentially undermine state regulatory authority and national security, as noted above, they also contribute to the viability of the state through the production of new rents and possibilities for redistribution among strategic military, political, and commercial personalities. This results in a seemingly contradictory situation. For instance, the Cameroonian army claims to be fighting "a war" against organized groups of highway robbers and incursions of rebel groups from Chad, both of which include downsized and underpaid soldiers, but the proliferation of armed road bandits is neither spontaneous nor haphazard. In this "war," border towns have become rearguard bases as well as frontline posts. A Cameroonian soldier posted in the far north described what he and his colleagues referred to as "the front":

> These bandits are men like you and me. Very intelligent. They are very well informed of people's movements in this part of the country since they have their accomplices everywhere.... Their heads [faces] are always masked in turbans and they are specialists in rearward combat. After every assault, they withdraw in cascade, sweeping the [Cameroonian] soldiers with gunfire, and they retreat to Nigeria where they know we don't have the right to pursue them. (Pideu 1995:6)

In an eighteen-month span, "the front" was ravaged by the deaths of between 400 and 500 civilians, with five or six times as many injuries. The numbers are hard to gauge, of course, especially since graves are often uncovered in the bush (mostly in Nigeria) and many of the injured never report to officials. During a sixteen-month period around 1995, sixty "highway bandits" were killed, according to the Cameroonian military posted there. Five soldiers were said to be killed over the same period, which is more than the number killed in the military conflict with Nigeria over the oil-rich Bakassi region in the south (all estimations come from Pideu 1995). "You're there with your comrades, you see them leave in a truck. Thirty minutes later, they come tell you they were all killed," was how one soldier portrayed the impact of this "parallel army," which outpowers the Cameroonian forces (Pideu 1995:6). At the time, the latter had no telephone or radio links, were often immobilized for want of petrol, and suffered from insufficient funds for provisions. Their primary task of escorting convoys of commercial trucks and bus- or carloads of anxious travelers was compromised by this lack of infrastructure and materiel, which is often cited as a reason for their own participation in attacks. The state military is informed about the movements of these road gangs, which, being highly organized, are traceable. A Cameroonian soldier referred to state knowledge about these seemingly spontaneous acts of violence: "[E]very day, the military authorities in Maroua and Yaoundé are informed about the zones and villages in which the killers camp. In their villages, they work just like a regular army. They take guard every night and dispose of cars and motorcycles for their operations" (Pideu 1995:6). These regional contingents have their own villages in Cameroon; indeed, they have their own regions (for example, Waza to Dabanga). Their interventions, though explosive, are not sporadic. In the late 1990s, they distributed tracts advertising the day and time of future attacks, warning travelers to be equipped with at least 2,000 CFA *"nouveau format"* (referring to new banknotes issued in Cameroon around the time of the 1994 devaluation). Those who failed to produce the desired sum in the right form risked "loss of genitalia," according to descriptions of the tracts in Pideu (1995).

At any rate, this levy may be a form of spoils, but it is not necessarily simply haphazard theft. As reported in the local press:

> Certain dignitaries of this part of Cameroon think that these attacks are knowingly maintained by authorities in Yaounde *[le pouvoir de Yaounde]*, with well-defined ramifications for local administrative authorities. According to informants, a gold wristwatch belonging to an important person from Maroua *[un fils de Maroua]* was taken by highwaymen only to reappear later in the Sub-Prefect's possession in Kousseri. This provoked lots of commotion in town. Furthermore, locals complain that the bandits, once arrested and put in the hands of public authorities, are immediately released, thus inciting large-scale criminality in [the region]. (Pideu 1995)

One wonders, moreover, whether a truly marginal operation would insist on receiving only newly printed bills, at the time when old bills were generally recycled through informal or black-market exchanges without much difficulty. More recently, an "ex"–road bandit, a citizen of the Central African Republic who spends much of his time on the Cameroonian border, described his experience, which highlights this point and underscores the idea that "illegal" can be "licit":

> I participated in attacks in which I had different roles. I carded the sack of spoils *[le sac de butin]*. I took care of the leader's *[le chef]* security. I picked up the arms after an operation. I participated in the planning of an attack. I never commanded; I didn't have my own group. You know, to have your own group, you have to have the means and the relations.

> "What means, what relations?"

> You have to buy the arms, give something to the guys before going to the attack, pay for their food, lodge them for days somewhere, pay the informers who go to the marketplace to identify people who made a lot of money, etc.

> "And the relations?"

> [sigh of impatience] I told you that I don't know everything. The gang leader, sometimes it's even someone who I've never seen. My prison friends took me to the leaders, and after an attack, sometimes we'd never see one another again, even in the marketplace. In the Central African Republic, I had a gang leader who I found sometime later as my neighbor out in the [agricultural] fields! There were two guys with whom we'd worked who were cultivating his fields.

> "What relations does a gang leader need?"

> Are you naive, or are you doing this on purpose? Do you think that you can do this kind of work without protection? For example, the leader [of an attack previously described] and myself, in one operation we got a lot of money. I don't know how much exactly, but between the money we found, the jewelry, the watches, etc., the booty *[le butin]* came to

something in the millions [CFA]. We were fifteen or twenty people, I can't remember. I got 150,000 CFA. Since we attacked cattle herders and cattle merchants, well, it's sure that the leader got one over on us, since for himself he kept millions. But afterward, when I saw him in the fields cultivating, I understood that it was the man in the car who kept most of it.

"Wait a minute. Who is the man in the car?" This was not the first time I had heard people talk about a man who comes in a car just after an attack.

"Oh! I can't really say. In any case, we threw all the arms and the spoils in the trunk of the car. Those who had military uniforms also threw them in. We dispersed, and then I got my part in the evening, at the rendezvous."

"And the man in the car?"

"I never saw him again. But I'm certain that he went back to the city."

"Because he lives in the city?"

"Obviously! If it was someone from one of the villages around here, I would know him! A car in a rural area, that doesn't go unnoticed."

"What does the man in the car, who comes from the city and makes you risk your life for a pittance, represent for you?"

"You're the one who says that it's a pittance! Do you know what a civil servant's salary is in the Central African Republic? The 150,000 CFA that I got allowed me to spend a peaceful Ramadan and to clothe my family for the festivities. What work brings in 150,000 CFA for no more than a half-day's work?"

"Theft!"

"You also want to work the road? Allah carries out everyone's prayers. Those who don't want to give over the *zakkat* [Muslim charity payment recognized by the state, one of the five pillars of Islam], we take up the responsibility to take it from them. It's a charity payment on their fortune, a revenue tax."

"So you replace the state tax services! Is that legal? Is it legitimate?"

"Legal? Surely not! As for legitimacy, it is not for you, nor anyone else, to tell me how I should assure my survival. You, the civil servants, you have your 'benefits' on the side. Is that legitimate? When people are named to a position of responsibility, they bring along their close relations, members of their tribe. What happens to those who don't have relations in high places? In any case, for me, the ends justify the means, and long live the man with the car."

"The man in the car" or "the man from the city" signifies members of the state bureaucracy, including district governors, prefects, and military officers, as well as high-placed commercial figures, who are frequently one and the same. The entrepreneurial pursuits include strategies for the reconstitution of politico-financial networks. These networks may etch out autonomous political spaces vis-à-vis state power, constituting what was described as a parallel—illegal but licit—tax system, but their activities serve to finance political patrons through transfers that move up the hierarchy. This system ultimately prevents the emergence of a counterelite or counterpower, thus clarifying how this country, marked by severe inequalities, extreme poverty, and "ethnic" tensions, has avoided civil war. It is a matter of the very formation and maintenance of a dominant political class—or the stability of a regime.[13]

However, beyond political commissions and payouts, and underwriting political stability, rents (or wealth) produced in this way are essential to "an extremely complex system of revenue transfers from formal and official circuits to parallel ones, from urban households to rural ones, from the richest to the most dispossessed (via allocations to families; social expenditures and diverse benefits such as school fees, health, funerals, participation in customary ceremonies)" (Mbembe 1993:367–68). These forms of redistribution are a primary mode of the exercise of state power. Appropriating rents associated with sub- and transnational networks of accumulation—and thus collaborating with

and managing their associated figures of financial power and regulatory authority—means creating wealth for off-budget activities, such as
hiring private security companies or financing political parties, and
state functions, such as paying administrative salaries or financing
external conflicts. In this sense, the regional networks described herein
are a resource that contributes to the political logics of predation that
define the historical exercise of state power in Africa.[14] Yet, this is not
to reduce this situation to a historical-cultural necessity: similar situations obtain in Colombia, Peru, Algeria, and Russia, where tributary
relations between the state and sub- and transnational networks of
wealth and power prevail. Moreover, although this form of mediation
between state power and emergent figures of power may be interpreted
as in keeping with certain historical continuities (for example, the role
of intermediaries in the Atlantic slave trade or in the enactment of
colonial power), its specificity arises out of the contemporary global
political economy.

Many observers (Hibou 1999; Vallée 1999; Reno 2001) have
described how state consolidation on the continent is now taking place
via indirect, or nonbureaucratic, means. This is in large part due to the
emergence and deregulation of particular markets (for example, small
arms, mercenaries, private security companies), as described above.
But is this manner of exercising power via indirect mediations a novel
aspect of state power in Africa? Recourse to private, foreign agents, for
example, is a long-standing manner of ensuring the effective exercise
of state power. In Africa, this method has involved the use of external
alliances, such as the cold war powers, or external resources, such as
foreign aid, to manage internal conflicts and the demands of factions
constituting the basis of state power (Bayart 1989; Reno 1995; Hibou
1997, 1999). In that sense, the reconfiguration of power on the continent today is less a matter of new practices of the exercise of state
power than of novel ways of negotiating the changing world economy
or managing extraversion. In the Chad Basin, sub- and transnational
regimes of accumulation are critical connections to today's external
rents; they are another means of insertion in the world economy.
Figures of regulation associated with these regimes are critical to the
consolidation of state power, even though they work to undermine
state regulatory authority. They represent, through the production of

wealth on the frontier, one place where the tentacular effects of state power are redeployed in the state's quest for the means to redistribute and produce new targets of wealth.

Evidently, a particular historical fiscal subject is produced in and through relationships with these new forms of regulatory authority. This fiscal subject, or subjectivity, is not produced primarily through the forms of rationalization and individuation associated with modern liberalism and bureaucratization. Nor does it result from a seemingly autonomous and oppositional "moral economy"[15] that has emerged in the margins of state failure. Insofar as the generalization and intensification of unregulated economic activities and violent modes of appropriation have led to the process of questioning the status of licit versus illicit practice, it is surely the basis for the reconfiguration of governmental relationships. Yet, these processes do not establish the bases for new forms of sovereign power, understood as a condition of unqualified power. For one thing, the possibility of such forms of power is, as Michel Foucault argued, nonsensical, or at least an irrelevant question, because such totalizing, coherent, and unitary situations do not obtain (Foucault [1978] 1990: esp. 93–97, 1980:82–102). More significantly, it is not at all clear that the domain inscribed by the realm of unregulated exchange and the pluralization of regulatory authority challenges this juridical representation of power: To what extent is the intelligibility of the very idea of sovereignty destabilized? To what extent can we discern changes in the production of valid statements about what the sovereign is or is not? It is clear that the definition and circumscription of new realms of thought and action give rise to unprecedented possibilities for the organization of economic and political life, leading to the pluralization of regulatory authority in the Chad Basin today. But the ultimate question is whether such changes result from transformations in the organization of knowledge or in the prevailing manner of producing valid statements such as "this is (legitimate) regulatory authority" or "this is a (legitimate) sovereign."

Notes

I thank the SSRC-MacArthur Foundation Program on Peace and Security Fellowship; the Ciriacy-Wantrup Fellowship of the University of California, Berkeley; and the MacArthur Foundation Program on Global Security and

Sustainability for their kind support. I also thank Hamidou Bouba and Saïbou Issa for their help and Mariane Ferme and Deborah Poole for their critical input. All language translations are my own.

1. I lived in this region (Maroua, Cameroon, and N'djamena, Chad) during various periods from 1992 to 2002. "The Chad Basin" is a fairly vague geographical concept, but I use the term here to refer to what are today northern Nigeria, northern Cameroon, Chad, and the Central African Republic. This is a working definition based on my research preoccupations.

2. de Boeck (1999) describes how young Zairian urbanites have migrated to rural areas along the Angolan border to partake in the diamond economy. This migration has led to their inclusion in a "dollarized" economy, the bush economy—as opposed to the urban economy—becoming the very source of tokens of wealth and consumption.

3. Contrary to Ferguson (1999), who describes how certain signifying practices associated with representations of rural life, denoted as "localism," are contrasted with those associated with urban life, or "cosmopolitanism," in Zambia. For debate over his book, see Fardon et al. (2001).

4. Although the reference to "democratization" is widespread in these quotations, it is best to think of the actual process as multiparty politics.

5. The question of uncertainty in the field of positive knowledge in which economic regulation is conceived and justified is an immense topic that merits a genealogical perspective, which is attempted in Roitman (n.d.).

6. When trying to understand people's use of the term *price* when referring to what I would call *tax,* I was surprised to discover that many European business-men conflated price and tax, putting forth the same reasoning that I received from Cameroonians: tax is a price because it is a right of entry or access. On the significance of the conflation between tax and price as part of a technology of power, see Roitman (2003, n.d.).

7. *Zoua-zoua* is the term used to signify illegal petrol.

8. As is implied by James Ferguson's recent (1999) and otherwise interesting reading of the situation in the Zambian copper belt. For a critique of the "disenchantment" reading of contemporary economic phenomena, see Bayart (1994).

9. I thank Saïbou Issa for carrying out these conversations.

10. In the regime's effort to quell incivisme fiscal, which it did with some success, the regime insisted, among other things, that clandestine motorcycle

taxis enter into officialdom through a new tax called the *impôt libératoire,* vehicle registration, vehicle insurance, and so forth, and that they be painted yellow. Drivers are now supposed to wear helmets and gloves, neither of which I have ever seen.

11. Some might argue that although the continuity of a *regime* might occur through the appropriation of modes of wealth creation established in transnational networks, the *state* is imperiled by transnational exchanges that evade its authority. However, if these networks enable the state to perform its essential tasks (extraction, enabling productive economic sectors, redistribution, financing war), they perpetuate the viability of the state as a political institution as much as a particular regime.

12. Grégoire (1998:95, 101) notes that the Tuareg of Hoggar are especially known as *passeurs* between Algeria and Niger and that the Nigerian army often offers protection for convoys running illegal deliveries between Niger and Libya.

13. A good example in Cameroon is the Biya regime's tolerance—lest we not say *sanction*—of high military officials' involvement in the arms, drugs, and counterfeiting sectors.

14. On the multiple manifestations of the predatory logics of state power, see Bayart (1989), and on the *dédoublement de l'état* in the form of *conseils administrative,* for example, see Bayart (1977: esp. 64–67). On *dédoublement* as a mode of power, see Mbembe (1992).

15. For a critique of the concept of moral economy, see Roitman (2000).

9

The Signature of the State

The Paradox of Illegibility

Veena Das

Recent formulations on the genealogies of the state have taken inspiration from Benjamin's ([1978] 1986) discussion on the oscillation between the founding and maintaining violence of law, and especially his insight into the ways the legal form detaches itself from what it is supposed to "represent." While this approach has been extremely productive in showing the importance of states of exception as lying both inside and outside the law (Agamben 1998), it has also tended to render sovereignty as if it were best analyzed as a spectral relic of a past political theology. I argue in this chapter that an attention to the sociologics through which claims to sovereignty are made and sustained, on the one hand, and the authority of the state as literalized in everyday contexts, on the other, might help us see the state as neither a purely rational-bureaucratic organization nor simply a fetish, but as a form of regulation that oscillates between a rational mode and a magical mode of being. As a rational entity, the state is present in the structure of rules and regulations embodied in the law, as well as in the institutions for its implementation. But like many other writers in this volume, I do not regard law as a sign of the sovereignty of the state or as an institution through which disciplinary regimes are put into place. Rather, I approach the law here as a sign of a distant but overwhelming power brought into the framework of everyday life by the representation and performance of its rules in modes of rumor, gossip, mockery, and mimetic representation and also as a resource for seeking certain rights, although a resource whose use is fraught with uncertainty and danger. Apart from instituting other modes of action in which states recognize *one another*, the state also acquires a different kind of presence, which I call magical, in the life of communities through these local practices. I deploy the notion of magic here, not to suggest that the state tricks the audience—a notion used by Fernando Coronil (1997) with great effect in his recent study of the state in Venezuela. Instead, I wish to make four specific claims in this regard. First, magic has consequences that are real; hence, I prefer to speak of the magic of the state rather than the fictions of the state. While I am perfectly aware that fictions belong to life, in characterizing magic as having consequences that are real, I am trying to stay close to the representations I encountered in the field. Second, the forces mobilized for performance of magic are not transparent. Third, magical practices are closely aligned to forces of danger because of the combination of obscurity and power. Finally, to engage in magic is to place oneself in a position of vulnerability. I hope to show the modalities by which the state in India is suspended between a rational and magical presence, but the ethnography I present, even at its dramatic moments, rests on everyday practices. This is why, instead of counting on theatrical performances of state rituals, the theater of kitsch, or the grotesque parodies of the double funeral as described by Taussig (1997), I look at the spectacular as nevertheless grounded in the routines of everyday life. And it is here that I find myself proposing that the idea of signature, tied as it is to the writing technologies of the state, may be useful in capturing this double aspect of the state.

WRITING AND SIGNATURE

We owe to Jacques Derrida the idea of writing as occurring in a context that is never fully saturated. Derrida (1988) has argued forcefully that in understanding writing, we need to go beyond the usual understanding of writing as an extension of oral communication. Writing, for him, is not only a means of communication with absent persons, but more importantly, it questions the very model of language as a system (or only as a system) of communication. In the critique of intentionality, which would tie consciousness in speech acts to the presence of the person and in writing to the appending of a signature, Derrida points to the force of breaking inherent in the act of writing itself. The notion of writing here does not follow from the logic of textual domination in performance of authority as in Messick (1993), but rather from the instability introduced by the possibilities of a gap between a rule and its performance.

Thus, if the written sign breaks from the context because of the contradictory aspects of its legibility and its iterability, it would mean that once the state institutes forms of governance through technologies of writing, it simultaneously institutes the possibility of forgery, imitation, and the mimetic performances of its power. This, in turn, brings the whole domain of infelicities and excuses on the part of the state into the realm of the public. One of the methodological observations that follow is that to study the state, we need to shift our gaze from the obvious places where power is expected to reside to the margins and recesses of everyday life, where such infelicities become observable. There is, of course, a paradox here, for it is in the realm of illegibility, infelicity, and excuses that one sees how the state is reincarnated in new forms. Whereas Taussig (1997) talks of the spasmodic recharge, the circulation of power between the dead and the living, the state and the people, I would like to start with certain inscriptions.

TWO EXAMPLES

Consider two different kinds of documents that I encountered during my work among survivors of the 1984 riots after the assassination of Mrs. Gandhi, then prime minister of India.[1] I found these documents intriguing. The first was a typical form of the First Information Report (FIR) filed in police stations after the riots had been brought under control in Mangolpuri and Sultanpuri, two adjacent localities in West Delhi where I worked with survivors. The second were divorce agreements drawn by the caste Panchayat (literally the "assembly of five," referring to the legislative and adjudicatory powers invested in caste or village elders) in these localities to formalize "divorces" between widows and their dead husbands—duly executed on stamped court paper. Let me revisit the scene of the riots in these two places after the assassination of Mrs. Gandhi and the way I came across these documents. What follows is not a chronology of the riots but certain scenes into which I entered.

After three days of killing and looting in the resettlement colonies of Delhi, the riots had been brought under control. Some survivors in Mangolpuri and Sultanpuri who had been shifted to relief camps in the city gathered enough courage to go to the police station to register criminal cases against those who had looted their property or killed a family member. They did this more to obtain official proof that these grievous events had indeed occurred, and that they had been affected by these events, than in any hope that the perpetrators would be caught or punished, because the survivors were well aware of the complicity of the police in the riots. The policeman on duty at the station insisted on dictating the framing sentences of the First Information Report, which is a normal practice in police stations (see Das and Bajwa 1994). The standard framing sentences, written in Hindi, ran as follows:

> Dinank 31.10.84 ko Bharat sarkar ke pradhanmantri Shrimati Indira Gandhi ki unke do suraksha karmachariyon dwara nirmam hatya karne ke karan Bharat ki rajdhani Dilli mein janta mein bhari rosh hone ki vajah se kai sthanon par janta nein majma khilafe kanoon banakar agjani, lootmar va katle aam kiya, vibhinn Gurudwaron Sikh gharon va unki dookanon ko loot liya.

> On October 31, 1984, due to the fact that the Prime Minister of India Mrs. Indira Gandhi was cruelly murdered by her two security guards, the people in Delhi, the capital of India, being enraged, engaged in illegal activaties of arson, looting, and mass killing. Several *gurudwaras,* Sikh families, and their shops were looted. (my translation)

The FIR then became specific in enumerating names of family members who had been killed or maimed and the property that had been looted or destroyed.

How is it, then, that the framing sentences of the FIR used language that attributed a certain subjectivity to the crowds, claiming that they had been *so maddened by anger* that they attacked people and property? After all, the victims were well aware that the attacks had been led or orchestrated by local politicians and were under the command of the local station house officer. First, when one went to the police station to register a complaint, one did so because local brokers of power (*dalals,* as they were known in the locality) had said that it would be difficult to claim any compensation for loss without legal proof. In the police station, an officer dictated the first part of the FIR to claimants. They were told that a complaint could not be registered without such a formal statement. Such formulaic modes of recording complaints are routine in police stations and are often oriented to the imagination of how the case will be presented in a court of law (Das and Bajwa 1994). In this case, though, a term such as *katle aam* (mass killing) evokes a historical imagery of chaos, in which invading armies kill local populations en masse. What is haunting in this case is that these FIRs, which encoded what one might call the lie of the state, were also required by other organizations engaged in relief work as proof of the victim status of claimants. For instance, even gurudwara (Sikh temple) committees, which offered pensions to widows of riot victims, demanded an FIR as proof that a woman's husband had died in the riots. Thus, ironically, those who were locked in a combative relationship with the state and who had direct evidence of the criminality of the state nevertheless ended up being pulled into the gravitational force of the state through the circulation of documents produced by its functionaries.[2]

My second example comes from documents known in the community as *talaqnamas* (deeds of divorce). These were executed by the caste Panchayat of the Siglikars (the major caste group I worked with in Sultanpuri) on stamped court paper. The documents recorded the agreement between the natal family of a man who had died in the riots and his widow, stating that they would divide the compensation received from the government equally. In addition, under this agreement, the parents of the dead man agreed to give a "divorce" to his widow. As I have described elsewhere (Das 1990), due to the custom of leviratic marriage in this community, there was strong pressure on a young widow to marry a brother of the dead man, if one were available. The government decision to award compensation for the death to the widow meant that many young women could get independent access to cash incomes. In addition, the gurudwara committees instituted a "pension" for the widows analogous to what widows receive from the government when their husbands die in the line of duty, as in war or in an accident. From the perspective of the community, the rightful heir of a dead man was his coparcener—that is, either a father or a brother. Even a man's mother was said to have a stronger moral claim on the money awarded in compensation for his death than his widow had. Hence, the conflict between these norms of inheritance and state norms caused considerable tension in the community. A resolution was sought in the nature of a compromise. If a widow refused to marry her deceased husband's brother or another suitable kinsman, she was given a "divorce," after the division of the compensation between her husband's father and herself, so that mutual claims with her affinal kin came to an end. I was not able to attend any of the Panchayat meetings because they were held at night, surrounded by an air of clandestine operation. Besides, because of various threats I had received from those engaged in the violence, it would have been foolhardy to risk going to the meetings at late hours. I was interested to learn, however, that even in arriving at a community consensus that violated state injunctions, the Panchayat had evoked the authority of the state. Equally stunning was that the Panchayat tried to make its decisions "legal" by evoking the authority of the very state that had perpetrated the terror.

I hope that these examples show the mode in which the state is present in the life of the community—its suspension between a rational-bureaucratic entity and a magical entity. As a rational entity, it is present in the structure of rules and regulations; community customs are made to appear valid in the shadow of these rules and regulations. But its magical qualities are apparent in the uncanny presence it achieves in the life of the community, even at moments of the community's defiance of the state—as though the community derives its own existence from a particular reading of the state.

I realize that using the term *community* here may give the impression that I am setting up a binary opposition between state and community. I hope that it is sufficiently clear from my descriptions that the life of the community was completely entangled with the forms of governmentality that were set in motion after the riots. However, it is important to keep in mind that the forms of governmentality are constituted here through sporadic, intermittent contact, rather than through an effective panoptic system of surveillance. Nor is the state dealing with isolated individuals. Urban neighborhoods, especially on the fringes of the city, are made up of migrants with strong kinship and caste networks; networks of related kin come to occupy contiguous housing units set up on land they have simply occupied or that has been allocated to them under different governmental schemes. These material conditions allow certain forms of community to be re-created,[3] but such communities can be maintained only by entering into various kinds of negotiations with agents of the state, such as policemen or state inspectors. The ability of people living in these neighborhoods to protect their houses from demolition, or their "illegal" household production from closure, depends upon their negotiations with these agents of the state—a point I elaborate on in later parts of this chapter.

I shall now go on to suggest that what sustains the double existence of the state between a rational mode and a magical mode is the state's illegibility.

READING THE LAW

Allow me to loop back to the devastation of the riots in a street in Sultanpuri. As I have described in my earlier work, the spatial distribution of the riots is best understood in terms of the anchoring of local hostilities to national events (Das 1996, 1998), but what interests me here is how the perpetrators evoked the image of law. The interpretation of events was not easy for the victims, for the distinction between the legal and the illegal was so blurred in their everyday lives that it was hard for them to read what was happening. My field notes describe the events in one street, A/4, on November 1. Crowds had gathered and were accompanied by a policeman, the station house officer (SHO) of that locality. The moment is frozen in my memory from the accounts I was given—it was described by many as the turning point, when violence moved from verbal abuse and pelting with stones to killing.

The crowd gathered outside the house of the A/4 *pradhan* (headman of the caste) and challenged him to come out. The pradhan came out with a gun. The SHO ordered him to take the gun back into the house. Some other Sikhs, hearing the noise, gathered near the scene. The SHO ordered all Siglikars to go back into their houses and threatened that otherwise they would be hauled off to the police station. Frightened and somewhat confused, they went back to their houses. When the pradhan came out again, this time accompanied by his two adult sons, the crowd started hurling abuses at him. I am not very clear as to the precise statements made at this time, but it seems that abuses and insults were a mixture of fragments from different kinds of discourses. There was continuing anger at the Siglikars having made good and the admonishment that now they would pay the price for having been so arrogant about their wealth. The charge referred to the fact that as craftsmen, some Siglikars had secured jobs in the Middle East and were wealthier than their neighbors who belonged to the Chamar (previously untouchable) caste. But the crowd hurled other abuses at the pradhan.

Frequent challenges *(lalkars)* hurled by the crowd were *"Khun ka badla khun"* ("Blood must be avenged with blood") and *"Tumne hamari ma ko mara hai"* ("You have killed our mother").[4] Crowds that had gathered outside the hospital where Mrs. Gandhi's body lay on October 31 had occasionally shouted these slogans, and they gained in intensity for the next few days while her body lay in state at the Nehru Museum. As pictures of her body and tributes paid to her were telecast, one could hear these same slogans in the background. It appears that in this locality, at the moment of violence, a certain "nationalist" discourse, picked up from images on television, began to speak through the body of the crowd gathered there. The pradhan and his sons were badly beaten, the crowd asking him to seek forgiveness, to apologize. Apologize for what? he asked repeatedly. For having abrogated privileges beyond the status of the Siglikars, for having killed "our mother." The more he tried to fight, the more the crowd beat him with *lathis* (sticks). His sons tried to come to his aid and were also beaten. Eventually, the leaders of the crowd, assisted by constables, poured kerosene over his beaten and bruised body and set fire to him. His two sons were killed in a similar manner. His wife, who was hiding inside, could not contain herself when she heard her sons calling out to her. The crowd threatened and warned her to stay inside, but she insisted on coming to her sons and was similarly killed. All the while, the bodies were burning, the dying persons were calling out for water, and the SHO was shouting that if anyone dared interfere with the law (*kanoon ke khilaf kisi ne hath uthaya*—raise a hand against the law), he would be shot dead. The crowd dispersed—no one could tell me when—but the SHO announced that all Siglikars had to stay within their houses if life was dear to them. The Siglikars in this locality said that at first they were stunned. Was this a legal operation? The SHO had evoked the authority of the law, even as people were being killed by the constables. Frightened that the crowds might come back, they wondered, should they try to escape in the cover of darkness? Escape where? When some people tried to sneak out to neighboring houses to consult (many neighbors were close kin), they discovered that a watch was being kept from the terraces of two houses. They were warned that if they did not return immediately, they would be shot dead.

Let me take the case of the *jhuggi* (shanty) dwellers in another street, P/1, located at the edge of the colony, with a park and a broad street dividing the *pucca* (cement) dwellings of the P block from the jhuggis. A little distance away, a sewage canal divided Sultanpuri from a *jhuggi jhopdi* cluster (a cluster of shanties and huts) in the adjoining colony. The jhuggi dwellers of the P/1 cluster, both Hindus and Muslims, had assured the Sikhs living with them that they would be protected at all costs. On November 1 and 2, when aggressive crowds, sometimes accompanied by policemen, had roamed the colony, the Sikhs in this block had hidden in their neighbor's jhuggis. On the third night, a police jeep had gone around announcing a curfew and threatening jhuggi dwellers that if they continued to give shelter to the Sikhs, their whole cluster would be set on fire. The police blatantly claimed that it was "illegal" to give shelter to any Sikh. Frightened by these threats to their neighbors and feeling a moral obligation not to endanger their neighbors' lives, the Sikhs decided to run toward the sewage canal that divided the colony from Mangolpuri. Some hoped to hide in the fields, but the police followed them and shot at them. Later, in the course of a police inquiry into these events, the SHO defended his actions by saying that the people he shot at were troublemakers who had tried to defy the curfew. Precise estimates are not possible, but at least twenty people died in this block, and the total number of Sikhs killed in this locality was close to a thousand.

The examples I give show how the documentary practices of the state, on the one hand, and the utterances that embody it, on the other, acquire a life in the practices of the community. It is the iterability of writing, the citability of its utterances that allows a whole realm of social practices to emerge that even in resisting the state reproduce it in new modes. The circulation of words such as *law* during the riots, and the fact that crowds were led in several instances by a policeman, showed the blurred lines between law and its violation. In recalling the events of November 1, people repeatedly stated that it was not clear whether the Sikhs were going to be punished for the assassination of Mrs. Gandhi and whether the crime was seen as committed on behalf of the community. Although many protested that they had nothing to do with the crime, their legal responsibility for the act was never very clear to them. Thus, even the question of which community they belonged to was tied to their reading of the law. Were they part of the local Siglikar community that had no connections to the militant movement, or were they now to consider themselves part of the larger Sikh community, which they believed was in some ways responsible for the assassination? The presence of the SHO in uniform, the evocation of "law" ("if anyone dares lift his hand against the law"), made the state present precisely where its absence as a rule-governed entity was most evident. The voice of the policeman evoking the authority of the law when the law was clearly dead was what announced the spectral presence of the state. It is this *illegibility* of the state, the unreadabilty of its rules and regulations, as well as the location of legitimacy of customary institutions such as the caste Panchayat in the ability to replicate the documentary practices of the state, that allows the oscillation between the rational and the magical to become the defining feature of the state in such margins.

ITS INTERNAL LIFE

The examples I have given might suggest that I am making a sharp distinction between the functionaries of the state and the members of a community to whom the state is illegible. In fact, it is my argument that many of the functionaries of the state themselves find the practices of the state to be illegible. I was not able to interview the SHO about his own role in the carnage, so I turn to other scenes.[5]

I interviewed other policemen about their roles in the counterin-surgency operations in the Punjab, and I found their way of talking about their roles in the maintenance of law to be shot with ambiva-lence. Rather than talk like state functionaries engaged in implement-ing rules and regulations, they occasionally talked as if they directly embodied the law. I suggest that a complicated entanglement of state and community makes them act as if they are direct embodiments of the state, especially in relation to harnessing the energies of the dead. Here are excerpts from an interview with Tej Singh, a senior police offi-cer in the Punjab who was directly involved in anti-insurgency opera-tions.[6] The same policeman was later shot dead by one of his own junior officials; I will give a brief account of the retelling of that event by another police officer later. I have to be somewhat circumspect in giving precise dates and locations because of the conditions of anonymity under which such information was offered.

Tej Singh was stationed in Amritsar, one of the centers of the mili-tant movement. During Operation Blue Star (the code name for the army operation against the militants in 1984), he was part of a team that surrounded the temple and was to give cover to army personnel as they moved into the temple. The army and police had sustained heavy losses in this operation, yet Tej bore little resentment about the risks he had been made to take. In fact, he deflected any discussion about the actual operation by describing instead a small local event in the police station about one week prior to Operation Blue Star. He spoke in Punjabi laced with occasional English phrases. Here he describes the atmosphere in the police station in those tense days and a visit by an astrologer, who regularly offered informal advice:

> The Pandit came to the police station—he used to come to collect some money, and we would ask him to predict the future[7]. So I said, "Pandta [a form of address], look at my hand and tell me what will happen." He studied my palm and shook his head, putting his hands on his ears, and said, "Parlay, parlay" [referring to a cosmic flood, mentioned in Hindu sacred texts, that ends an era in the cycle of time]. I said, "Stop this *bakbak* [nonsense]—tell me what you see." He said, *"Sahib, duniya khatam ho jayegi par tu bachuga"* ["Sahib,

the world will come to an end, but you will survive"]. When I was standing on the terrace of a house in the street giving cover and bullets were coming from all directions, one grazed my headgear, and I thought of the Pandit. (my translation)

This vignette shows in a small way how police officers may be charged with implementing the rules and regulations of the state, but they do not cease being members of local worlds with their own customs and habits. The weekly visit of the astrologer to the police station in the middle of extremely risky operations, though described with a sense of the absurd, points to these lines of connection. The next example, however, shows how the local imperatives within which the rationality of the state is embedded led Tej Singh to experience himself as the direct embodiment of these contradictory discourses that included reference to locality and caste. In this interview, he reflects on the militant movement and his own sense of being a police officer belonging to a previously "untouchable" caste:[8]

We know these boys—we know there are some to whom Khalistan [the imagined homeland of the Sikh militant discourse] means something and others for whom it is an occasion to indulge in liquor, drugs—we also know who are the big men who are using the young men to carry their own ambitions. The genuine leaders of the movement trust me, although we are on opposite sides. But these other kind— they really fear me. So they have been after my blood [this phrase was spoken in English]. So one day, as my driver and I are going on a high road at night, this truck bears down on us at high speed. The truck driver fled after hitting us—my driver was in a coma. I know who those buggers—excuse my language—were. My driver was in hospital for two months, but he recovered. By some miracle I escaped. Then, three months later, I was sleeping on the lawn of my house. My subordinate officer came and whispered to me that the man who had arranged for my "accident" was caught in an encounter. Now I know that the correct thing is to hand him over to the law, but I also know these buggers—they have bought the law. I told my subordinate not to wait till the morning but to bring him in the dark to this large public park. I then took a bath, wore a white *kurta* pajama, drank a whole bottle of whiskey, and then I went to the park. There I kicked this man till he was begging for mercy. He was a Jat [a high caste, a landowner]—I am a Chamar [untouchable], and I remember him boasting once, when have the Chamars wielded a gun independently? So when I kicked him to death, I showed him that he can buy up the upper castes in the police and the courts, but he cannot buy me, this low-caste Chamar.

I must confess that I was chilled by this story—not because I did not know that such framed encounters were not unusual, but because this police officer had the reputation of impeccable integrity, even among the militants. Having risen from the lowly caste of untouchables, he was widely respected in his village for his charisma across the different caste groups. A few months after these interviews took place, he was killed. I heard that the militants announced an informal cessation of hostilities for two days after his death so that the funeral could be conducted without any mishap. Ironically, he died not as he had anticipated—at the hands of a militant or on the orders of the mafia—but by a bullet mistakenly fired by his own gunman.

Another policeman told me later that one of his trusted gunmen, Sukkha Singh, was assigned to penetrate one of the militant organizations. Sukkha became very involved in its affairs and began to receive drugs and illicit money. He became a party to these transactions, either because he did not want to blow his cover or because he became greedy and began to accept money for himself. As the policeman explained to me, one could never say with certainty what kinds of transactions these were, for the boundaries between the licit and illicit are so thin. In any case, Sukkha Singh received a notice to face an inquiry. Because he was very close to Tej Singh, the latter told him that he would attend the inquiry and that he had nothing to fear. In fact, I was told that the previous evening, Tej himself had dictated a written response to the charges the policeman was to face. On the day of the inquiry, one of the senior police officers in charge asked Sukkha to hand over his service revolver. Having an accused policeman hand over his weapon is purely routine, and it would have been restored to him after he was cleared of any charges. However, for some inexplicable reason, Sukkha completely lost his cool. He responded angrily, "No one asks Sukkha Singh to hand over his weapon," and he pulled the trigger, first killing Tej Singh and then himself. Those present were certain that the shot was not intended for Tej, Sukkha's senior and friend, but that Tej had gotten in the way and was accidentally shot dead. Tej's last words were *"Sukkha tu?"* ("Sukkha—even *you?*"). So there was confusion, the police officer told me. Perhaps Tej Singh died with the thought that Sukkha Singh had been bought over by the militants after all.

The version of the story I relate here did not appear in the newspapers or official accounts. The police officer who told me this story did not treat it as exceptional. He insisted that this kind of misreading happened more often than could be admitted. Thus, the illegibility of the rules, and the human actions that embody these rules, appears to be part of the way that rules are implemented. It is not that the mode of sociality to be found in the institutions of the state is based on clarity of rules and regulations and that these become illegible to the poor or the illiterate, but that the very persons charged with implementing rules might also have to struggle with how to read the rules and regulations.

In the next section, I want to address the problem of the relationship between law and regulation in the context of the illegibility of the state, drawing from some work on the National Emergency in India in 1975, when draconian measures were taken both to reduce the population and to clean up cities by removing slum dwellers to the periphery. I follow that with examples of how similar processes are operative in low-income neighborhoods in a variety of contexts, even when the political situation seems "normal." Although this discussion might seem like a digression, I want to suggest that riots do not bring something entirely new into existence. The peripheral colonies, in which the poor have come to be "resettled," are scenes of the arbitrary nature of state regulations, so the everyday experience of the state is marked by all kinds of negotiations between the local functionaries and the residents. The policies on housing and sterilization came to be linked, of course, due to the special dispensation of the Emergency, and they were applied with special rigor in Delhi in 1975. They constitute an earlier link in the lives of the urban poor in their relation to the state, and though these policies are not linked anymore, one can see certain continuities in the mode of surveillance that I explore later. In the popular imagination, the Emergency was known as the time of *nasbandi* (sterilization). This period shows with stark clarity how the politics of the body lies at the intersection between law and regulation.

THE NATIONAL EMERGENCY AS THE TIME OF *NASBANDI*

Emma Tarlo (2000) offers an excellent analysis of the manner in which two administrative schemes that were part of the state's normal housing policies and family-planning services for the poor—the Resettlement Scheme and the Family Planning Scheme—came to be implemented during the National Emergency. The center of gravity in her analysis is the everyday ecology of fear and greed through which the poor ended up as partners in the coercive programs of the state.

The Emergency was a period when all fundamental rights were suspended on grounds that the country was in danger of falling into anarchy. It was also a period of great pressure to obtain results in the family-planning program, whose target was primarily the urban poor. Though numerical targets had always been part of family-planning policies in India, the Emergency was widely regarded as a period of crisis in which the government was able to exercise unbridled control over the implementation of these policies (Dayal and Bose 1997; Shah Commission 1978). As with most coercive and ill-planned programs, there was pressure at every level of the bureaucratic hierarchy to produce results, but it was the lower echelons of the bureaucracy that bore the brunt of this pressure to meet targets and produce results. The authoritarianism of Mrs. Gandhi's rule in this period and the destruction of institutions made it imperative for the bureaucracy to implement the policies of the government, not in accordance with rules and regulations but in accordance with bureaucrats' reading of the wishes of their superiors. The state was literally seen to be embodied in the person of Mrs. Gandhi and her younger son, Sanjay Gandhi, who became, as was widely acknowledged, the extraconstitutional center of power (Mehta 1978). It was common knowledge that instead of written orders, the bureaucrats received oral orders to implement policies (Shah Commission 1978). Rumors about the fate of those who defied these orders or implemented them in half-hearted ways made lower-level officials extremely anxious about their jobs. So on the one hand, normal bureaucratic procedures were suspended. On the other, it was widely acknowledged that Mrs. Gandhi's son, Sanjay Gandhi, was emerging as an important center of power and that the beautification of Delhi and the control of population were his favorite programs. Although all of this is generally known, Tarlo provides a meticulous examination of the files in the slum development department of one locality in Delhi where these schemes were implemented. She shows, first, how the poor were forcibly removed from their habitats in the city and, second, that their claims to housing in the peripheries of the city were made dependent upon the production of sterilization certificates. None of this was strictly legal, but the paraphernalia of recording claims, examining certificates for authenticity, and so on, gave it the aura of a legal operation. In other words, the life of documents continued as if it were "business as usual."

The government's unacknowledged ways of linking claims to housing with sterilization were translated at local levels into a structure of co-victimhood—people searched for poorer relatives or neighbors who could be induced to undergo sterilization for money. Poor migrants, beggars, and other homeless persons were also induced to undergo sterilization, and an informal market in sterilization certificates developed. Those who needed to show that they had motivated others to become sterilized, so that they could keep their jobs or their houses, bought the certificates. By portraying the poor as active participants in state policies of repression, rather than passive victims or noble resisters, Tarlo shows how the political regime of the National Emergency was able to use fear and greed to draw different sections of people into its implementation. The point is that neither the lower-level bureaucrats nor those who were relocated on production of sterilization certificates could draw a line between the legal and illegal. The certificates, once they became part of the normal bureaucratic operations of recording, became proof of the "legality" of the operations. In the local-level offices where housing was allocated, the processes of recording the certificates and enumerating claims sanctioned on these bases gave the whole operation an air of normalcy.

Although Tarlo states that there are lines of continuity between the state's normal practices and forms of governance during the Emergency, she does not provide us with any ethnography of the continuity of these practices at the time of her fieldwork in the urban neighborhood she studied. I take this opportunity to provide a brief description of the functioning of the state in everyday life, and especially how forms of governance and modes of surveillance are put in operation in the offices of petty bureaucrats or on street corners where police constables patrol neighborhoods. It is at these sites that bribes for running illegal home production in *karkhanas* (small industrial workshops) are negotiated, or new migrants who often occupy state-owned land learn how to avoid eviction, or the stealing of water or electricity is condoned in exchange for bribes, votes, or other services linked to the underlife of politics. My intention is not to romanticize these practices or to castigate the poor—for very similar processes operate in upper-income neighborhoods, where bribes are offered for the stealing of electricity or the running of factories in residential colonies. But under the conditions in which residents of jhuggi jhopdi colonies live, such negotiations become necessary to ensure economic survival. These sites, then, are particularly important for understanding how states manage populations at the margins, and also how those living in these margins navigate the gaps between laws and their implementation.

Let me take two examples of these processes in everyday life from a low-income neighborhood in Delhi, not very far from the resettlement colony Tarlo studied. When I initiated my present study in health practices and local ecologies in 1999, I was given directions to the house of the local pradhan, Nathu Singh (a fictitious name). I went to meet him and explain my study. Within a couple days, another man confronted me and said that *he* was the leader of the locality and warned me against those who had misled me into thinking that Nathu Singh was the pradhan. Over time, I was able to work out the contours of the complicated relations between these two men. It appears that the second person had been the caste leader but had been displaced from his position through a series of contests with Nathu Singh over who could offer better services to the local community by negotiating with the forces of the state. In brief, Nathu had proved to be more adept in dealing with the "outside world." As he told me how he secured leadership of the local community, Nathu attributed his ability to deal with new community problems to his earlier job as a "room boy" in a prominent hotel, which had propelled him outside his neighborhood into new kinds of experiences. Nathu had spent his childhood in the village from which many of his current neighbors had migrated, and he had studied till eighth grade in the village school. His father had migrated to Delhi sometime in the early fifties, so it was easy for him to leave the village and join his father in 1970. He then got the job in the hotel and learned how to talk to people, how to hold his own in conversations with educated people, and how, as he put it, to hold his head high. Further, he was able to put aside money from the tips he received from hotel guests. Then, in 1982, a number of people from the village put up jhuggis on the land they now occupy. This act led to serious disputes with earlier settlers in neighboring areas. The Gujjars (a caste of pastoralists) living in nearby areas were angry with this group—especially because of caste rivalries and the Gujjars' not wanting to live near "untouchables." One night, several men from the Gujjar community came to attack the new residents. Nathu was able to gather enough men to wage a fight and chase away the aggressors. This act gave him prestige in the eyes of local residents.

However, Nathu was worried about the security of their claims over the land they had occupied. So he negotiated with a policeman responsible for patrolling the area to provide them with security in exchange for a *hafta* agreement (an agreed-upon weekly bribe with almost the force of custom). He asked every household for two rupees (about four cents) a month as a voluntary contribution to deal with various kinds of state officials, though he claimed that the contributions were not steady. It gradually became clear to everyone that he was a more effective leader for the community than the caste pradhan. Similar to the mediators described by Tsing (1993), Nathu Singh displaced the traditional leader to become an effective negotiator with the new forces of the state. I give one example of the modality of state presence and the kinds of negotiations that have to be effected.

Because this colony is an unauthorized colony, there are no electric connections in the houses. However, every household has drawn lines from the electric pole in the street to its dwelling. Some years ago, it was rumored that if a dwelling unit had an electric meter installed, the meter would eventually become proof of occupation, so the government could not evict such households and reoccupy their land. In law, the land on which people have made their jhuggis is owned by the state. But the legal position is complicated because some years ago, Nathu Singh managed to get a stay order from the High Court that restrained the government from evicting residents from this land unless alternative housing was provided to them. With the help of a lawyer, Nathu had registered the residents as an official Society of Harijans (scheduled castes, who enjoy certain benefits under the Indian constitution because of their depressed position in society)—thus securing for them some kind of legal status. The judge used this provision to grant the stay order to the registered society. But even though the residents could not be evicted from their dwelling units, there was still a problem. Those who had installed meters but never paid the electricity bills found that subsequent to the recent privatization of electric supply in Delhi, they faced huge bills. They simply did not have the resources to pay these bills. This created a precarious situation for them.

On a recent visit to the locality in December 2002, I found the whole place plunged in darkness. When I made inquiries, Nathu Singh told me that he had heard rumors of a raid on the locality by government officials and that they might demolish those houses that had not paid their electricity bills. This would put all the households into jeopardy because they were all engaged in some illegal activity, and one thing could lead to another. Under earlier arrangements, local government officials understood this situation and condoned the infringements (helped by weekly bribes), but a new set of officials might put the whole arrangement under risk. To avoid this risk, all households decided to cut off their electric supplies so as not to give a pretext to any official to visit the area. I asked the residents how they were going to deal with this problem, since they could not live without electricity forever. I then learned that several pradhans from adjoining localities were going to hold meetings and were planning a *dharna* (sit-in) in front of the High Court. The residents were hopeful that because a general election was scheduled for 2004, and because they constituted important vote banks, they would be able to have their colony authorized. Recall that during the National Emergency, people were able to get legal claims over their houses by obtaining sterilization certificates.

Now it seemed that the struggle was to put pressure on the local government to grant legal status to the colony, and thus titles to the occupied land so that residents could get electricity, water, and sewage systems. I hope that these examples make it clear that the Emergency brought out the practices of governance in sharp relief but for the poor, such practices were not exceptional. The intermittent nature of governmental control, the illegibility of the law, and the negotiations around the thin lines between the legal and the illegal are part of the everyday life of these neighborhoods. The state is present in the form of rumor—its signature is read everywhere. It may be worth remembering Benjamin ([1978] 1986), who stated that the tradition of the oppressed teaches us that the state of emergency in which we live is not the exception but the rule. The precarious nature of the everyday in the neighborhoods I have described gives us grounds to believe that this is not a metaphysical statement, but one located in the conditions of life and labor in these areas.

LEGITIMACY AND THE QUESTION OF SIGNATURE

I hope the iterability of utterances and actions in which the signature of the state can detach itself from its origin and be grafted to other structures and other chains of signification is clear. How does the state then claim legitimacy in the face of obvious forgeries, corruption within its own procedures, and the mimesis of its structures? To understand this, I turn to the realm of excuses—a classical subject in Austin's (1962) analysis of language but not often used in understanding the realm of politics, although it has been used in legal literature in the battered-woman defense and the cultural-defense argument (see Kelman 1994 and Walker 1999).

In Austin's understanding, excuses point to the realm of infelicities when performative utterances fail. Utterances with illocutionary force are felicitous when the context is in place and our trust in conventions is secure. It is then we can say that accuracy and morality are on the side of saying that "my word is my bond" (Cavell 1994). However, my claim in this chapter is that fragility of context is built into the situation in which signature cannot be tied to what one might think of as the notion of utterances and actions of the state. It is this fragility that accounts for the oscillation of the state between the rational and the magical modes. Excuses then provide us entry into a region of language in which we confront the vulnerability of human actions, as well as vulnerability of human utterances. My *actions* are vulnerable because of the limitations of the human body, and my *utterances* become vulnerable because my words may be transfigured elsewhere (see Cavell 1994). In ordinary life, this is the region of human vulnerability—I may be quoted out of context, my words can be reproduced in a mood of irony, or they may be infused with another affect. In the life of the state, that very iterability becomes not a sign of vulnerability but a mode of circulation through which power is produced.

The examples of FIRs, talaqnamas, sterilization certificates, ration cards, and hundreds of other such documents show how the state comes to be present in the everyday life of its subjects. Because it can be multiplied, literalized through court papers, certificates, and forged documents, it can enter the life of the community. But as Jeganathan, Ferme, and Poole have argued in their respective chapters in this volume, the subject's identity can never be fully assumed in the encounter with the state. It is precisely because the documents can be forged and used out of context, and because the bureaucratic-legal processes are not legible even to those responsible for implementing them, that the state can penetrate the life of the community and yet remain elusive.

In its turn, the bureaucratic rationality of the state can always evoke the very facts of its illegibility to the poor as the major form of its defense. Consider, for instance, that bureaucrats withhold information in any crisis on the grounds that because people are illiterate or ill informed, they have a tendency to panic. Elsewhere I have analyzed the way this excuse is routinely evoked in the management of epidemics (see Das and Dasgupta 2000). Adam Ashforth has analyzed the way in which the HIV/AIDS epidemic in South Africa poses a tremendous threat to the legitimacy of the state. What I would like to show is how bureaucratic logic displaces notions of irrationality and panic to a credulous public and thus constructs itself as "rational" in its deliberate absence of transparency.

PANIC AND BUREAUCRATIC RATIONALITY

The concept of panic to signify the nature of the collectivity to be managed by a rational bureaucracy finds an interesting genealogy in the field of public health, especially in the management of epidemics. Here is an early example of how management of life and exercise of sovereignty were mutually constructed in the margins of the colonial state. The details presented below come from Misra (2000) and from my own notes at the India Office Library.

The year was 1893, when the first laboratory-produced vaccine against cholera was to be tested in the field in India. Haffkine had arrived in India, having officially obtained permission to test his vaccine in the nation's choleric districts. There was considerable trepidation in official circles about the advisability of giving Haffkine permission to test his vaccine. The role of rumor in the mutiny of 1857 had not been forgotten, and officials were cautious in insisting that the government bureaucracy should not be seen as actively supporting this mission. Thus, in a dispatch of March 16, 1893, Surgeon General W. R. Rice evoked the notion of a "popular mind," arguing that though scientifically proven to be effective, the vaccine was not considered harmless in the popular mind (Misra 2000). Rumor was said to play a very important role in the fear of the new vaccine. For instance, in the Serampore municipality of Calcutta, where cholera had broken out, a team was sent to inoculate people on the request of residents, but the operation had to be suspended the next day because of "rumors" of the ill effects of the vaccine. The report on this incident stated, "No doubt some degree of panic was natural among the low caste people who work in the mills, but it is surprising that stories, however intrinsically absurd and improbable, should have been accepted by educated Natives and English managers without any attempt at enquiry" (cited in Misra 2000). There was also much discussion in the newspapers that Hindus would be incensed that animal products of a polluting nature had been injected into them, and one official noted that "native credulity" could be unscrupulously "played upon," jeopardizing the legitimacy of the government.

The deployment of the concepts of panic, rumor, and native credulity shows how the question of sovereign power was linked to the management of populations and especially the management of public order in the face of rumors and panic. The bureaucracy could establish itself to be rational in contrast to the native population. Thus, government abandoned the project of vaccinating the population, justifying it on grounds of native credulity. It is interesting that justification and

excuses that called upon risks of causing panic among native populations were acceptable modes of explaining the actions of the bureaucracy and thus defined the realm of the civil.

The example of Haffkine and the position of the government of
India toward the field trials in 1893 shows that bureaucracies construct
their actions as *vulnerable* in a field of enunciations that is overdeter-
mined by human passions—these passions are projected to other
agents, such as native credulity. As part of the distribution of expectations, bureaucracies are expected to "manage" these popular passions.
The play between law and regulation and the "management of life" was
not only evident in the case of epidemics but also in the case of other
disruptions to "order." The form of reasoning that attributes distur-
bance of order to popular passions was evoked repeatedly in the case of
riots, too, as these were seen as embodiments of "popular passion" (see
Pandey 1990).

The stability of these representations became evident to me when I
was part of a 1984 delegation in Delhi petitioning the lieutenant governor to publicly acknowledge the number of Sikh men who had died in
the riots. We were told that to publicize these facts would lead to a flar-
ing of public passion, which could lead to more deaths. Similarly, the
Srikrishna Commission, set up by the government of India in 1994 to
investigate riots in Mumbai in December 1992 and January 1993, found
that accusations about the complicity of the police were explained away
by senior police officers as "communal bias" on the part of the lower
rungs of the police force. Senior officials claimed that members of the
lower rungs were not fully educated and hence were subject to sectar-
ian prejudices. For instance, referring to the deposition of one Ramdeo
Tyagi, the joint commissioner of police, Justice Srikrishna, stated the
following:

> To a pointed question as to whether in his assessment there
> was any communal bias on the part of the constabulary in
> handling the riot situation, he also diplomatically replied
> that in any society, *unless people are fully educated,* there is bound
> to be a hidden bias in the mind of every person belonging
> to one community against the other and that such bias
> must have surfaced. However, when it came to opening
> fire the police had been impartial though complaints had

been made to him by the Muslims that their establishments
were attacked and damaged in the very presence of police
personnel. (Srikrishna 1998:214; emphasis added)

Thus, in explaining why more Muslims died in police firing, the
officer resorts to claiming that the general level of education of the
population was responsible for contaminating the police force. The
bureaucracy institutes *itself* as rational by characterizing the *people* as
credulous and irrational. It is notable, though, that the lower rungs of
the police are assimilated into this fold of the "uneducated public."
The whole realm of acceptable excuses creates the realm of the civil, in
which the very illegibility of the state to its citizens becomes the mode
of establishing its legitimacy.

In his reflections on the Srikrishna Commission Report, Hansen
argues that such reports are in the nature of state spectacles that provide a kind of public catharsis and try to represent what he calls the
"sublime" dimensions of the state—"its fairness, rationality, tolerance
and justice" (Hansen 2001:158). Hansen is rightly skeptical whether
such state spectacles would be able to maintain this "myth" of the state
as rational and just, because the broader conditions under which a violence of hatred takes place have taken root in all kinds of ways in India.
He exhorts us that "We thus need to rethink what the state means and
how it presents itself in everyday life, and explore how governance has
become organized around competing languages—bio-political rationalities as well as various forms of sovereignty (legal, political, etc.)—
both within and beyond the state" (Hansen 2001:233).

My own contention is that despite Hansen's good intentions, his
emphasis on state spectacles as a route toward generating understanding of sovereignty and everyday life is theoretically flawed because of its
allegiance to the idea of the state, at least theoretically, as an order-
generating mechanism. This idea fails to address the issue of how the
practice of sovereignty itself operates, especially in relation to the production of "killable bodies" (Agamben 1998). Hansen's formulation of
politics asks for special attention to spectacles in public spaces and
looks to theatricality, rather than a descent into the everyday, as a site
for understanding how law itself becomes constitutive of various forms
of sociality, away from its official sites. I have argued instead that if we

understand the everyday as a ground from which we move toward the official sites of law (such as courts of law and inquiry commissions), then we can get better insight into the force of law. The performative, not as settled convention but as that which breaks from context, as in the examples of vulnerability we saw, stands in tense relation to the pedagogic (Bhabha 1994b). The importance of looking at excuses is that it immediately draws attention to the margins as places that are managed but that also insert themselves in gaps and fragilities of context. It is here that new modalities of rule are initiated in the search for survival. In the next section, I argue that margins are important for understanding the functioning of the state, not only in postcolonial societies but in metropolitan centers—for states, like nations, are by definition unfinished projects everywhere.

COMPARATIVE OBSERVATIONS

From the descriptions and examples I have used in this chapter, one might be tempted to conclude that the state becomes illegible in non-Western countries because it is an import from the West. I want to argue, on the other hand, that it is part of the logic of the state that it constructs itself as an incomplete project, because there are always margins on which people have to be educated to become proper subjects of the state. I would then like to offer a digression, shifting my gaze to recent developments in cultural-defense arguments used in US courts on behalf of Asian immigrants, to give us an insight into this issue.

Leti Volpp (1994) has argued that the assumption behind the cultural-defense argument in US courts is that immigrants are not fully integrated into the nation: hence, a person is not fully constructed as an agent responsible for his or her actions in the eyes of the law. Thus, recent immigrants are distinguished from earlier immigrants, who are seen as fully integrated into American culture. In her analysis of *The People* v. *Dong Hu Chen,* in which Dong Hu was accused of killing his wife because he suspected her of having a relationship with another man, Volpp shows how the case constructs the immigrant as the average person belonging to a particular culture, versus a reasonable person who is seen to be universal. The defense lawyer in this case had cited the hold of Chinese culture on the defendant as constituting attenuating circumstances for the act. The court had called for expert testimony from an area expert, a Professor Pasternak. In soliciting the expert testimony, the court was interested in finding out how a hypothetical average mainland Chinese man would behave in such a situation, as opposed to a typical American man. Pasternak argued that in his experience, an average highland Chinese man would be compelled to kill his wife under these circumstances. In fact, Pasternak compared the pressure of the community to "voices in the head." In holding Dong Hu Chen as not fully responsible for his action, the judge displaced the notion of agency from the person of the defendant to the voices of the community. How are we to understand the judge's construction of context here?

It is notable first that while receiving the cultural plea defense, the judge did not make any inquiry about either contemporary family structure in China or Chinese jurisprudence on these issues. Clearly, what was at stake in the judgment was the concern with the role of law in creating the American nation. The judge made many asides on the openness of American values and that exposure to these values would transform immigrants into the reasonable men of American law.[9] In other words, the defense plea was accepted in this case because of the assumption that values embodied in American law are not transparent to the immigrant. In other cases, courts rejected the cultural-defense argument when it seemed to violate what are seen as basic human values. It is interesting that on the one hand, by accepting the idea of culture as a source of value and allowing agency of the defendant to be displaced onto the community, the court expands the realm of the civil, while on the other hand, by positing this "deviant" behavior as a result of the failure to read American society correctly, the court also creates peripheries that are "educable" and hence capable of being brought into the center at some future time. The immigrant communities become, thus, a site in the United States on which the idea of the rationality of the American way of life is cited, thereby also creating the "normalcy" of patterns of racial discrimination.

CONCLUDING THOUGHTS

I have suggested in this chapter that the concept of signature is important for understanding the presence of the state in the life of the community, both as a bearer of rules and regulations and as a spectral presence materialized in documents. I claim that the rationality effect is created through a whole field of enunciations that come to the fore in the management of crises—thus, management of epidemics and breakdown of law and order belong to the same field of enunciations, legislative practices, and techniques of control through which the state comes to construct itself as rational in opposition to a credulous public. I suggest a series of concepts—rationality, magic, legibility, legitimacy, vulnerability of action, and vulnerability of utterance—to capture the life of the state in the margins. Vulnerability and power are not opposed here. Instead, through an exchange between the real and the imaginary as in notions of panic, rumor, and credulity, the domain of the civil is instituted and controlled. There are then neither pure victims nor noble resisters—to use Tarlo's (2000) felicitous phrasing—but a series of partnerships through which state and community mutually engage in self-creation and maintenance. This does not mean that we cannot engage with questions of justice and rights or that communities formed through suffering are delegitimized. The place from which these engagements occur, though, is not that of the moral space of innocent victimhood but of the rough-and-tumble of everyday life.

Notes

Earlier versions of this chapter were presented to the Center for Developing Societies in Delhi; School of Oriental and African Studies, London; Sociological Research Colloquium, Delhi School of Economics; American Anthropological Association, Washington, D.C.; and the advanced seminar "The State at Its Margins" at the School of American Research in Santa Fe. I am very grateful to participants in these seminars for the stimulating discussions and especially to Talal Asad, who, with characteristic generosity, brought many dispersed ideas into shaper focus in his comments during the seminar at Santa Fe.

1. For earlier accounts of this work, see Das (1995, 1996, 1998).

2. Among the various reports produced by civil rights organizations, see especially PUDR/PUCL (1984) and Citizen's Commission (1984) for evidence of the complicity of various politicians and the police in the riots.

3. I thank Peter Geschiere for this point. For details of the caste composition in these neighborhoods, see Das 1996.

4. The use of this term is interesting because it locates the act in a structure

of feud relations (Das and Bajwa 1994). It is imperative in a feud that a person who has been ambushed and is about to be killed must be given the reason in the form of a challenge. Although the media reported such locutionary forms as political slogans, they occupy a hybrid position as both part of the traditional repertoire and part of the modern democratic right to protest.

5. Because I assisted the People's Commission and the Police Inquiry Commission in gathering evidence and, along with NGOs working in this area, helped get compensation for victims by doing their paperwork, the police officer could easily identify me. Besides, in the atmosphere of fear and suspicion, any attempt to even talk to local police officers could have caused fear among survivors.

6. The names of policemen are fictitious. Though there is no way for me to directly acknowledge their help in this study, I want to express my profound gratitude to the policemen and lawyers who extended their help to me.

7. Pandit is a Brahmin subcaste. But in the Punjab, unlike many other regions in India, the Brahmins do not enjoy a high status. They are considered dependents of powerful landowning castes. Though their purity is not in question, they are more figures of fun than of awe. In this case, the Pandit was a small-time astrologer and palmist.

8. Forms of civility and legal requirements in India do not permit the use of such terms as *untouchable* or *Chamar* because of their stigmatizing connotations. In most contexts, I would use an officially acceptable term such as *scheduled caste*, or one that is coined by these castes *(Dalits)*. Here I am using the terms Tej Singh himself used, because much of the force of his affect would be lost if I substituted these terms with others.

9. In a recent paper, Sita Reddy (2002) argues that when it comes to women defendants accused of filicide, the courts deploy the idea of universal maternal emotional motives that any reasonable traditional woman would have in any culture. Reddy makes a bold move in suggesting that at the heart of the cultural-defense argument is the therapeutic state that assumes that the ills of the alien culture will be cured over time. I regret that I came across this paper only after I had completed the present chapter and hence cannot take up her argument in greater detail, but it points to ways in which managing life and exercise of sovereignty come to be linked in the margins.

10

Contesting Displacement in Colombia

Citizenship and State Sovereignty
at the Margins

Victoria Sanford

Control will be strict in the frontiers of the future,

Only the survivors will be admitted.

—*Mario Bendetti,* Inventario

On my first trip to Colombia in October 2000, I visited Barran-cabermeja in the department of Santander in the region referred to as Magdalena Medio—a lush, green river valley located in the hills east of Antioquia, west of Venezuela and north of Bogotá. Barranca, with a population of some 300,000, is an urban center. It also forms one of the many internal frontiers where we can see how the mechanisms of state control are reconfigured in relation to displaced communities. I argue in this chapter that such communities are not only objects of state control but are actively involved in shaping their futures in relation to the state. With assistance from the United Nations High Commissioner for Refugees (UNHCR), I went to Barranca to interview internally displaced Colombians who struggle with what it means to be Colombian while living a disjointed existence, disarticulated from their communities and pushed to survive at the margins of the Colombian state (Das et al. 2000:1–19). The UNHCR office is located in Barranca's one high-rise building, the Estrella, which has twelve floors. From the UNHCR balcony, one sees a large oil refinery to the far left. To the right is a densely treed neighborhood where oil company administrators live. Adjacent to the headquarters is a large army base, and directly in front are the grid streets of Barranca. Beyond the grid, the horizon holds the numerous unpaved barrios of the city's poor and working people. During my stay, music from discos floated up into the night, and the streets were filled with traffic and nightlife, despite the fact that for more than two months, at least two bombs had exploded each week. Just beyond the street cafés and discos, the town abruptly stops at the river to the right. On the other side of the river and down its banks, FARC (Revolutionary Armed Forces of Colombia) guerrillas control the territory.[1]

On my first day, I traveled across internal frontiers of the state, demarcated in Barranca by army checkpoints, to one of the poor barrios. My guide was Esmeralda, a local leader of displaced communities now precariously resettled in the peripheral barrios. Our taxi driver had been assigned to us by the Popular Feminine Organization (OFP), a local NGO working with displaced women in poor barrios. Our driver was *de confianza* (trustworthy) and was directed by an OFP leader to "stay with them at all times and bring them back safely." We traveled out to the barrios to meet with displaced women and visit OFP barrio projects.[2] At one project, a local youth leader said, "Our work is difficult. We open a space here so that youths have a place to distract themselves from the violence that surrounds us. We hope that this violence will end. We struggle for life" (author's interview October 2000).

As we left her barrio, we came upon twenty-four professional soldiers at a military checkpoint. The exact status of this checkpoint within a legal-administrative framework was unclear. On the one hand, these spaces are set up presumably to protect citizens against threats of terror, but on the other hand, the military or paramilitary personnel at these checkpoints may unleash violence on people they consider "suspect" (see also Jeganathan in this volume). The barrio checkpoint that stopped us is one of the many frontiers that crisscross Barranca and the rest of the country. Three vehicles were stopped ahead of us. The bicycles and mopeds of five youths were strewn over the street. On our right, four of the youths had their hands on a wall and stood spread-eagled as four soldiers frisked them roughly. Two other soldiers pushed another youth toward the wall as they took his schoolbag. They laughed as they emptied the bag's contents onto the street. The soldiers appeared to be pushing the youths into the wall as they asked them questions. A large, black personnel tank with no windows on the sides towered over the stopped vehicles in front of the checkpoint. *La Policia en Busqueda de Paz,* "The Police in Search of Peace," was written on the side of the tank in large white letters. The rest of the soldiers pointed their machine guns at the youths, at the people in the cars in front of us, and at us. To our left, the commander stood in the middle of the road, laughing as he aimed his machine gun at each vehicle. All these soldiers, including their commander, fingered the triggers of their machine guns.

This checkpoint was manned by professional soldiers. They were easy to distinguish from the eighteen-year-old recruits who had nervously reviewed our papers at other army checkpoints. The professionals were in their late twenties to early thirties. They were large and muscular, as opposed to the skinny kids who fill the ranks. These soldiers wore black bandanas around their heads and belts of machine gun ammunition crisscrossing their chests in what Colombians refer to as "Rambo-style."

As we pulled up to the commander, our taxi driver tensed the muscles in the back of his neck. Esmeralda trembled. When we neared the commander, machine gun barrels entered the open car windows. We stopped in front of him, and the soldiers stepped back. The commander continued laughing. He pointed his machine gun inside our car, first through the driver's window, nearly touching the driver's temple, then into my window, waving us along as the barrel touched the hair on the side of my head. We drove off in silence. When we were out of sight of the soldiers, we began to talk about our powerlessness and inability to help the detained youths. "There is nothing to be done," said the taxi driver. "They would just finish off all of us."[3] At the OFP office, I was asked to make an official complaint about the army's behavior to the Defensor Publico (Public Defender's Office). After I gave the public defender specifics about the incident, he told me that he would write a letter to the local army base commander. He also told me that the professional soldiers were elite troops, trained by the United States in counterinsurgency, and that in the two weeks since the elite troops had arrived, there had been many problems in the barrio. "The problem is, they believe they can do whatever they want, because they can," he explained.

Academic and policy analysts commonly point to Colombia as a weak or "failed" state, citing the inability of state agencies to fulfill administrative mandates (such as the public defender's inability to do anything more than write a letter to the army base commander) (CPDH 1991; DP 1999). My research, however, suggests that Colombia is neither a failed state nor a state lacking in functioning infrastructure. Rather, it is a state in which the actions of the elected government, bureaucratic agencies, and legal apparatus are, in large part, determined by the reconstitution of the state and its infrastructure at its margins through the army's use of surveillance and state-sanctioned violence, including the use of proxy paramilitary forces. Moreover, many who argue that Colombia is a failed state also favor strengthening the Colombian army, which indicates a more than implicit recognition of the army as integral to state power. At the same time, this argument contradicts the failed-state thesis. In this chapter, I want to explore how the state exercises power in marginal areas over which it claims to have little control, yet in which it maintains or strengthens its centralized base of power through the use of violence and surveillance— at least temporarily and at great cost to its citizens. Michael Hardt and Antonio Negri (2000:39) suggest that "the sovereignty of Empire itself is realized at the margins, where borders are flexible and identities are hybrid and fluid. It would be difficult to say which is more important for Empire, the center or its margins." Though Hardt and Negri refer to the sovereignty of a globalized, post–nation-state empire, their point about sovereignty being realized at the margins is applicable to the nation-state's constitution and reconstitution of sovereignty as well.

Building on Walter Benjamin's belief that the "state of exception" is the rule in which we live, Giorgio Agamben identifies the sovereign as "having the legal power to suspend the validity of law" and thereby the power to be legally "outside the law" (1998:55). In this sense, the notion of sovereignty is tied to the ability of the state to resort to a "state of exception," "state of siege," and/or suspension of citizen rights, which, in turn, enables it to exercise violence that is both inside and outside the law. If the location of power was limited to the nation-state, so, too, would be the constitution and reconstitution of sovereignty. But Michel Foucault challenged traditional juridico-institutional conceptions of power, and thus sovereignty, by arguing that rather than look for a "central form" of power, one must seek to recognize power in its "multiplicity" of forms and study these forms as "relations of force that intersect, interrelate, converge, or, on the contrary, oppose one another or tend to cancel one another out" (1997:59). Writing on "state-making" and the recent trials of Pinochet and Milosevic, Jacques Derrida observes the announcement of "a transformation" and "major event" in which the "sovereignty of the State, the immunity of the head of state are no longer in principle, in law, untouchable" (2001:57). My own understanding of sovereignty is based on both Benjamin's and Agamben's theorizing that the "state of exception" is a marker of sovereignty, without losing Foucault's recognition of the multiple locations of power and Derrida's observation that the sovereignty of the state is no longer absolute. This framework provides an opportunity to "move beyond the unbounded borders of the nation-state" by acknowledging the nation as a contested space in which citizenship and state sovereignty are reconstituted at the margins (Angel-Ajani, n.d.:5). Further, it allows for examination of the relationship between citizenship and state sovereignty, recognizing that power rests in the citizens, as well as the state, and that the power of each is mutually constituted (even, and perhaps even more so, during a "state of exception").

I consider the lived experiences of Colombians who have been displaced inside their country in order to understand the role of these marginalized actors in the complex processes that both challenge and reconstitute state sovereignty at its cultural and political margins. I understand the practice of displacement to be a key military strategy of war, rather than a byproduct (Sanford 2001). Thus, I want to problematize and investigate the interrelationship of the replication of this and related practices by the army, insurgent forces, and paramilitaries in their struggle for dominance and hegemonic power.

We can observe how the surveillance mechanisms of the state in Colombia slide into violence at a variety of frontiers: between urban and rural, between Colombia and neighboring states. My experience at the Colombian army's urban checkpoint in Barranca helped me understand the multiple internal frontiers and margins of Colombia. In particular, when I visited the Peace Communities of the Urabá-Chocó region in 2000 and 2001, the army's urban checkpoint called my attention to the exercise of state power through army and paramilitary checkpoints along the Atrato River and its tributaries. The struggle for dominance in this region is both a means and an end for the army, the paramilitaries, and the guerrillas because the river and its tributaries are strategic pathways for the smuggling of guns, money, and cocaine.

In this chapter, I focus on Colombia's fifty-nine self-proclaimed Peace Communities, which I suggest challenge and reconstitute citizenship and state practices (with important implications for sovereignty) by constituting new domains for the production of truth —domains in which Foucault found the very "practice of true and false" to be transformed (1980:131–32). Moreover, these new domains represent new sites on which the state is sought to be made transparent and accountable to its citizens, even as they face the kind of power tactics deployed by the army and paramilitary that I have described. In the Peace Communities, these sites are constituted at the local level within the communities themselves; at the regional level, through the accretion of truth when expressed by the collectivity of communities; at the national level, through involvement of the Catholic Church, national and international NGOs, and unarmed agents of the state itself; and at the international level, through the political brokering of the UNHCR, international NGOs, and international observers.

In the summer of 2001, while international and urban Colombian hopes for resolution of the armed conflict through peace negotiations remained high, the peace process had no visible or experiential impact on state surveillance and violence, or on the state and paramilitary confrontations with FARC guerrillas, which had become a quotidian factor of peasant life in the Peace Communities. Describing the Urabá-Chocó region of Colombia, Father Leonides Moreno said, "Here there is no peace process. Here there is dominion and the territorial advance of armed actors" (author's interview July 5, 2001). Indeed, until 1996, Chocó had been the dominion of the FARC for two decades. In 1996, the FARC's domination of the region was challenged by paramilitaries (who have long-standing and close ties to the Colombian army and trace their roots to serving as hired guns for plantations, factories, and drug lords). Many who today occupy high-ranking positions in the Colombian army were material and intellectual authors of paramilitary violence in the 1980s. As commanders of the armed forces, they have ties to the paramilitaries, including coordination of army/paramilitary maneuvers.[4] In the words of one international functionary, "It took the paramilitaries less than four years to conquer the territory it had taken the FARC two decades to occupy" (author's interview October 2000). The key to paramilitary success in gaining control of the region was to attack river communities, violently displacing more than 45,000 people. The fifty-nine Peace Communities that exist today represent some 12,000 displaced people who have returned to their lands. Urabá-Chocó is one of the many embattled margins of the Colombian state. It is precisely because margins function like states of exception that they become important sites for understanding the way in which notions of sovereignty and exception are tied together. The use of paramilitary forces to control checkpoints highlights the manner in which control is vested into agents who are in one sense outside the law but in another sense are inside the law, for they are able to function precisely because they enjoy the protection of the state. This situation makes the rural and urban margins the terrain from which such agents, functioning both within and outside the state, can establish, consolidate, and advance their exercise of power (HRW 1998b). Thus, as in the cases discussed by Poole and Roitman in this volume, it is also at these margins that the privatization of state violence is revealed.

THE PEACE COMMUNITY OF CACARICA

My experience in Colombian Peace Communities began in October 2000 when I participated in the UNHCR-coordinated accompaniment of the displaced residents of Cacarica on their return to their village. Paramilitaries had displaced the residents in February 1999. In addition to the UNHCR, the displaced were also accompanied by representatives of Peace Brigades International, Justicia y Paz (Justice and Peace), Humanidad Vigente (Vigilant Humanity), the Ministry of Health, the Ministry of the Interior, the vice president's office, the Defensor Público, the Human Rights Ombudsman, and the Red de Solidaridad Social (Social Solidarity Network, also a government organization).

Cacarica is a Peace Community. Peace Communities are small, mostly rural river villages that have organized to assert their neutral, nonviolent stance in the face of the surveillance, control, and extreme violence of the army, paramilitaries, and guerrillas. By declaring their village a Peace Community, residents are demanding that armed groups stay out of their village.

Cacarica is located in the Urabá zone in northern Chocó and northwestern Antioquia. Urabá is a strategic area located on the Panamanian frontier. To reach Cacarica, we traveled by boat from the port city of Turbo across the Gulf of Urabá for about two hours until we reached the Atrato River. At the Atrato, we entered the jungle. We traveled the river for about four hours, then traveled along a small tributary for another two hours to reach the path to Cacarica. From the start of the path, it is a two-hour hike through the jungle to the actual village. Paramilitaries dominate the rivers and tributaries here. Both guerrillas and paramilities use the Atrato to move weapons from Panama. Cacarica is closer to Panama than to any other Colombian town.

The entire Urabá area is rich in natural resources desirable to international businesses and local elites. Both national and international companies have amassed great wealth via the extraction of wood here. In addition, many people believe that the region contains oil. Urban elites in Urabá-Chocó also talk about a new canal being built through this area, as well as the development of lucrative African palm oil tree plantations. Indeed, a December 6, 2001, article in the Colombian newspaper *El Tiempo* noted international interest in both a canal and oil extraction in this region.[5] Moreover, the Atrato and Sucio Rivers, their tributaries, and the surrounding jungle are principal corridors for moving armed columns, weapons, cocaine, and money.

The location and geography of both guerrillas and paramilitaries in this region highlight the intense competition for control of the rivers and river communities that form the physical, cultural, political, and economic frontiers of the state. This is not to suggest that the river communities are the only frontiers or margins of the state. On the contrary, geographical, political, economic, and cultural frontiers and margins of the state can be found throughout Colombia, including but not limited to urban peripheries, rural communities, indigenous and Afro-Colombian communities, as well as the shadow economies and cultures of coca growing, drug trafficking, gunrunning, and money laundering. The colonization of these rivers was the focus of the most recent waves (late 1970s to early 1990s) of state-sanctioned migration, development, and frontier expansion. In the Urabá-Chocó region, guerrilla expansion in the zone paralleled colonization until the early 1990s, when the paramilitaries, in tandem with the Colombian army, began attempts to regain state control of the rivers. This increasing occupation by paramilitaries ultimately displaced overt army control (or made it unnecessary). Nonetheless, to travel the rivers of the jungle, one must pass through numerous Colombian army checkpoints. While this region has been considered historically an economic, territorial, and social frontier of the state, these checkpoints, and the columns of paramilitaries and guerrillas one comes upon between them, point to the overlap and tension between the concepts of frontiers and margins. The rivers represent the margins of state sovereignty, where the violence and regulatory powers of the state become clearly privatized in both guerrilla and paramilitary maneuvers and checkpoints. In this sense, the rivers are more than territorial or social frontiers. They are margins that run through the spectral state. For example, though the Colombia-Ecuador border is patrolled by Colombian and Ecuadorian state agents (immigration, customs, armed forces), the massive "illegal" movement of arms, armed columns, drugs, money, and undocumented immigration constitutes a margin of the state as well.

Like most displacement in Colombia, the February 1999 Cacarica displacement was not the first or the last in the region. In the Cacarica area, paramilitaries displaced 2,000 people (civilians) in 1997 (author's interview August 2001). The alleged strength (or alleged civilian support) of the guerrillas was used to justify development of paramilitaries as a strategy to retake territory. The paramilitaries consolidated their control using displacement as the principal tactic to empty the zone of any possible guerrilla support.

According to those who have been displaced, displacement operations are joint maneuvers between the paramilitaries and the army. The army frequently uses planes and helicopters to bomb civilian areas, forcing inhabitants to flee while paramilitaries carry out ground maneuvers, destruction of the physical community, threats to and assassinations of those deemed subversive or potentially so, and sometimes full-scale massacres (author's interviews 2000 and 2001). A paramilitary who had recently returned from combat confirmed survivor testimonies. Specifically about massacres, he told me, "Human rights are a problem. Now we can't massacre everyone, we have to kill them one by one, one by one" (author's interview August 7, 2001).[6]

In February 1999, paramilitaries entered Cacarica and ordered community members to displace themselves within twenty days. They were told to go to Turbo, where they were to be received by the police. For the residents of Cacarica, who have only heavy wooden boats with small outboard motors, this trip took around eight hours. However, the trip takes only two hours in the high-powered boats available to only UN, Peace Brigade, and Colombian military personnel.

When Cacarica residents reached Turbo, the local police were waiting for them. The newly homeless were taken to the local soccer field, where the police told them to set up camp. At the field, there were no services whatsoever—no running water, no sanitation, no shelter— nothing but a field. At this juncture, the Catholic social justice group Justicia y Paz became involved with the community.[7] Justicia y Paz, a Bogotá-based Catholic social justice organization, pushed for the provision of basic health care, water, sanitation, food, and other humanitarian services. It was able to considerably improve the basic quality of life for displaced Cacarica residents with the assistance of Oxfam, Doctors without Borders, and the International Red Cross. However, it is important to keep in mind that the displaced of Cacarica represent only 2,000 of the 280,000 civilians displaced by violence in 1999.

THE STATE AND ITS PROXY FORCES

In the Urabá area, paramilitaries control the northern part of Urabá, Antioquia, and Córdoba; paramilitary leader Carlos Castaño dominates this area. Paramilitaries in Urabá and elsewhere support local economic powers and move freely from north to south in their areas of control (except for mountainous areas dominated by guerrillas). At the state's multiple margins, these aspects of state practices become evident through army maneuvers and paramilitary checkpoints. Indeed, in Apartadó, army soldiers patrol the streets—guarding the restaurants and bars where off-duty paramilitaries eat, drink, and dance. Traveling from Apartadó to the beach town of Necocli on public transportation, our bus was stopped and/or waved through five times at paramilitary checkpoints, as army vehicles moved up and down the highway and army platoons patrolled the highway at the periphery of each town less than a kilometer from each paramilitary checkpoint. The infrastructure of Colombian army patrols, troop maneuvers, and security checkpoints lends protection to the paramilitaries and allows them safe freedom of movement and action. Once revealed, this relationship between the army and the paramilitaries, which is mutually beneficial on a strategic level, makes legible a relationship of power intended to remain illegible by proxy paramilitaries of the state operating in the anonymity of the margins of the state. Thus, what at first glance appears to be simply a privatization of state violence is revealed in practice as state violence by proxy.

Displacement in the Urabá area can be traced back to the founding of the paramilitaries between 1994 and 1995 (Comisión Andina de Juristas Secional 1996; Garciá 1996). Indeed, the largest barrio in Apartadó is Barrio Obrero, founded by civilians displaced by paramilitaries between 1995 and 1997. Today Barrio Obrero is controlled by paramilitaries and *sicarios*, or hired thugs. In this way, marginalized communities on the urban peripheries also become margins of the state and sites of contention where state sovereignty is made visible through violence and surveillance. As is the case in other areas, it is the use of proxy paramilitary forces that shows how sovereignty stands both inside and outside the law.[8]

The paramilitaries have used displacement as their central military tactic in rural areas. On the urban peripheries, paramilitaries most often use threats, disappearances, and assassinations in their exercise of state power. While agents of the state may assert little to no control within these communities, in fact, the ranks of the paramilitaries comprise poor young men recruited shortly after completing military service in the Colombian army (and therefore they are trained by the Colombian army prior to joining the paramilitaries). Moreover, on the streets of Apartadó in broad daylight, I witnessed an older man in plain clothes giving orders to a group of soldiers on the street. I also witnessed an army official in uniform giving orders to a group of young men, who, as they say in Apartadó, *tenían pinta de paramilitares* (had the paint [or mask] of paramilitaries), referring to their carriage, style, and dress.

Operación Limpieza (Operation Social Cleansing) is a parallel system of justice that paramilitaries have established in the urban areas now claimed in their dominion. In this parallel system of justice, it is safe to leave items in one's car in Apartadó, for example, because a person seen stealing will be shot. Indeed, this system is part of the phenomenon of social cleansing targeting drug users, street children, prostitutes, and petty thieves. Social cleansing also targets NGO leaders and members, as well as other poor individuals, who are killed if they try to organize a union or protest injustice. One example of this parallel system of justice took place in the spring of 2001 near Apartadó. A mayor called a community meeting with local leaders, who were organizing for the rights of banana plantation workers. He offered to facilitate communication between the plantation and the workers. He passed around a sign-up sheet for the meeting, which was scheduled to take place the following week. Within one week, all but one person who had signed the list had been killed. As the individual who recounted this story on condition of anonymity pointed out, "Now the victims sign their names to the death lists" (author's interview August 6, 2001). Actions such as this are carried out in the name of "citizen security," which depoliticizes structures of state terror by placing them outside the framework of international human rights and humanitarian law.

This social cleansing needs to be discussed in terms of human-rights violations, and the victims of social cleansing need to be included in inventories that quantify victims of political assassinations. The killings constitute political means and have political ends—they create and sustain terror among those who most need to organize to defend their rights. At the same time, social cleansing provides a level of assurance to the middle and upper classes, who may feel protected from crime and view the victims of social cleansing as something less than human, living on the margins of society. Indeed, one international human-rights worker commented, "It's nice to be able to leave the doors unlocked and the windows open when I am not home—it's a benefit of the paras" (author's interview July 2001).

Theoretically, we need an idiom to argue that these are political killings because they are not common crime: they are systematic because they target specific populations. If victims of social cleansing are not included in the quantification of human-rights violations, a commentator will speak about the number of political killings (5,000 per year) and then point out that the number of "nonpolitical" assassinations (25,000 to 30,000 per year) was actually higher. This simplification of an incredibly complicated political situation allows for the conclusion that Colombia is simply a "violent" country and Colombians are "by nature" violent people, or that they have a "culture of violence" (comments I have heard both inside and outside Colombia) (see Poole ed. 1994). In addition to the obvious racism and ethnocentrism, this type of conclusion is especially problematic because it negates the political character of the conflict and implies that there can be no political solution because these people and this culture are "by nature" simply violent.

In Urabá today, the paramilitaries control municipalities through alliance with, or representation of, local economic power interests. They act in ways consistent with racketeers or mob bosses, charging for protection and operating like Pinkertons with carte blanche. The guerrillas dominate the mountains; the paramilitaries control the rivers and municipalities. The guerrillas are around the rivers, and the paramilitaries are around the mountains. The Colombian army is present at checkpoints on the rivers, in helicopters flying overhead, and in ground maneuvers around (and often through) Peace Communities. The civilians are everywhere in between the guerrillas, the paramilitaries, and the army.

NEW SITES OF STATE LEGIBILITY

Between 1997 and 1998, Justicia y Paz sought support from international human-rights NGOs and foreign embassies to pressure the Colombian government to broker the safe return of the displaced residents of Cacarica to their homes. With support from the UNHCR and international and national NGOs, the displaced were able to formalize their efforts in December 1999 in agreements with the Colombian government that allowed their safe return to their lands as Peace Communities. These agreements contained several key guarantees from the government pertaining to the security, protection, education, health care, and documentation (including land titles and personal identification) of the displaced people from Cacarica.

For security, a Casa de Justicia (local house of justice or small court) was to be established, with a civilian representative from the national government reinforcing the community's position of neutrality with the armed actors, including the paramilitaries, guerrillas, and army. The actual Casa de Justicia building has been constructed, and a government representative is now residing in the community.

A particularly significant point in the agreements is that no armed entity (legal, illegal, or extralegal)—including the army, guerrillas, and paramilitaries, respectively—may enter the territory of the community. Indeed, at the entrance to Cacarica, a hand-painted sign in the Peace Communities' rainbow colors states: "We are a Peace Community. We are special because we do not carry any weapons. No armed actors, whether legal or illegal, are permitted in our community." Further, the agreements guarantee that there will be no collaboration with any armed groups. This guarantee is among the central concerns of all communities in zones of conflict, because if the army enters a community, the residents become guerrilla targets, and if guerrillas enter a community, the residents become targets of the paramilitaries and the army. Thus, the Peace Communities do not want any armed actors entering their territories. This provision is particularly significant for female peasants, who are often forced to provide food and lodging to armed men passing through their communities. Though pressured to give support, the act of doing so makes the women military targets for the next group that comes through.

The agreements between Cacarica and the Colombian government are significant for Cacarica residents because they allowed residents to return to their homes. The agreements are also viewed as a model for other displaced residents seeking to return home, as well as those seeking to consolidate their independence from armed actors. The agreements also represent the possibilities for mutually reconstituting state sovereignty and citizenship at the margins of the state. While state violence and surveillance at the margins continue to reconstitute state power and sovereignty, the agreements reached with the Peace Communities suggest that subaltern agency, by asserting citizenship rights and creating new sites for political action through local, national, and international alliances, also plays a role in the constitution of state sovereignty and state legibility (see Coronil 1997; Dirlik 2000; Sassen 2000; J. Scott 1998; Das this volume). The agreements reached with the Peace Communities, as well as the actual existence of the Peace Communities, represent a new form of subaltern contestation to the armed ambition of the Colombian army, paramilitaries, and guerrillas. This contestation challenges the power of the armed actors by offering a new terrain of engagement without recourse to violence. The agreements represent subaltern engagement in the reconstitution of the state at its margins, making the presence of the state more legible on the frontiers of the Peace Communities and, indeed, transforming the state itself (for an interesting comparison, see Roldán 2002).

Of course, the agreements are only the beginning of the process. The implementation will determine its success or failure. The government representative in Cacarica is from the Ministry of the Interior. Ostensibly, it is his job to ensure that no armed groups enter the community's territory. Of course, one wonders how one man from the Ministry of the Interior is going to implement such a monumental task. In addition, issues that at first seemed clear suddenly appear murky. For example, where does the territory of the community begin and end? Who decides? Is it a violation if an armed group is outside the community? surrounding it? walking through it? What if an armed group makes threats to community members farther down the river? Who is responsible to adjudicate? How will the government respond? What if the soldiers sent in response are among the 12,000 professional soldiers trained by the United States in counterinsurgency tactics? A Colombian army official, when asked about the paramilitaries, said, "The enemy of the paramilitary is my enemy. So the paramilitary is my friend" (author's interview December 2001). Will army soldiers protect villagers from paramilitaries when the paramilitaries claim that the villagers are "subversives" or support the guerrillas?

Particularly worrisome is the diffuse structure of justice between the responsibilities, obligations, and powers of the Human Rights Ombudsman, Ministry of Interior, Defensor Público, and prosecutor's office. The Casa de Justicia can receive a complaint and advise the various ministries of the complaint, but it can take no penal action. The Human Rights Ombudsman can investigate and sanction, but it mostly focuses its energies on prevention of human-rights violations. The public defender's office promotes and distributes information about human rights; it also provides technical assistance to people seeking redress. The prosecutor's office investigates rights violations but can take no preventative actions on behalf of human rights. What does this convoluted structure mean when an armed group violates the agreements by entering the territory of Cacarica? Which office is responsible for which aspect of a claim? How are the residents to know? And doesn't this situation make inaction (due to confusion and/or fear) easy for functionaries?

Further, the Canadian government donated a speedboat and a satellite communication system for the Casa de Justicia so that the government representative can notify the army, police, and Ministry of the Interior if an armed group enters the community. This equipment arrived in July 2000. In mid-October, the Defensor Publico and Human Rights Ombudsman were still fighting about who was responsible for the maintenance and upkeep of the equipment; the boat was not in use because they had not yet determined who would pay for gas. The Social Solidarity Network was helping both offices reach an interinstitutional agreement outlining responsibility for maintenance and upkeep of the equipment. The Social Solidarity Network folks are familiar with this dilemma—they, too, had a boat but no resources to pay for gas. In sum, the Casa de Justicia in Cacarica has a rustic house, one staff person, equipment that is still not up and running, no house for the representative to live in, no computer, and an extremely complicated, dangerous, and ill-defined mandate to carry out.

It is also important to note that the agreements are being carried out with accompaniment and implementation of programs by representatives from the national government (not the local government, because it is dominated by paramilitaries). Still, despite a convoluted mandate, the agreements have established limits to the way the state can operate on the margins. The new administrative sites are amplified from local to international domains through the presence of national and international NGOs. Representatives of Justicia y Paz, Peace Brigades, and other national and international groups are living in Cacarica with retornados (the returned) to increase their safety and security. Justicia y Paz continues to seek safety and peace for other displaced communities, and Peace Brigades now has four offices throughout the country. Each group provides regular updates to the international community through Web sites, e-mail lists, speaking tours in the United States and Europe, and international observation tours in Colombia. It is through this process, and through their collectivity as Peace Communities and their administrative relationships to unarmed state actors, that each Peace Community transcends its locality as a mere village on a river in Colombia and becomes a site for the reconstitution of state sovereignty. Moreover, the constitution of Peace Communities becomes a new site from which the international community can judge the Colombian state and put pressure on it regarding the way the state exercises power.[9] In this way, river communities, though still geographically isolated margins of the Colombian state, are no longer simply sites of state surveillance and violence for the reconstitution of state power and sovereignty but are also new sites of state legibility presenting possibilities for subaltern transformation of state sovereignty and citizenship.

Finally, though the displaced of Cacarica were able to return to their homes, this return did not mark an end to displacement in the area, nor did it finalize state sovereignty or citizenship. In September 2000, just two weeks prior to the Cacarica return, paramilitaries displaced 1,300 indigenous people in nearby Carepa. The precarious situation of the displaced and the Peace Communities is further deteriorating with the increased militarization that Plan Colombia has brought to the countryside. Thus, even though Peace Communities are now players in the exercise of power at the state's margins, this contested space is a cartography of Hardt and Negri's margins "where the borders are flexible and identities are hybrid and fluid" (2000:39).

DISPLACEMENT AND CITIZENSHIP

For Peace Community members, current paramilitary attacks and displacement of nearby communities become part of a continuum in the *present* of memories of their own displacement in the *past*. Alfonzo, who fled his community of Camelias in 1997, recalled, "Helicopters were bombing, and paramilitaries were firing machine guns. To go to the river to cut bananas was to risk one's life. They burned our village, and we lost all our rice. When the army would come, they would say, 'Don't be afraid of us, have fear of those who come after,' meaning the paramilitaries. They had no respect for our lives. We had to leave" (author's interview August 2001). Those internally displaced found themselves jobless and homeless, living in displacement camps scattered on the peripheries of Apartadó, Turbo, and San Jose Apartadó.

The politico-military shift of responsibility from the army to the paramilitaries has had dire consequences for the political and social well-being of Colombian society. Displacement is not a new phenomenon in

Colombia, but in the 1980s it was individuals who were displaced by targeted threats. Along with the entry of paramilitaries into the field of gross human-rights violations via political killings, forced displacement also increased drastically when the paramilitaries entered the politico-military theater in 1990. By 1995, there were 130,000 displaced; in 1996, another 180,000 people were displaced; in 1997, another 250,000 people were displaced; in 1998, 300,000; in 1999, 280,000; in 2000, more than 300,000 people were displaced. In total, that is more than 360 people fleeing their homes each day (CCJ 2000). According to UNHCR functionaries in Colombia, estimates for displacement in 2001 exceed the 300,000 displaced the preceding year (personal communication July 5, 2001). In 2003, human-rights groups report more than 1,000 people fleeing their homes each day (Hagen 2003:66). Though the government recognizes only 400,000 displaced people, humanitarian aid organizations counted 1.5 million displaced people as early as 2000 (CCJ 2000).

Hannah Arendt suggested that the term *displaced persons* was expressly invented for the liquidation of the category of statelessness ([1951] 1973:279), which paved the way for the loss of rights of citizenship, creating a category of the persecuted as rightless people. Significantly, she stated, "The more the number of rightless people increased, the greater became the temptation to pay less attention to the deeds of the persecuting governments than to the status of the persecuted" (294). Moreover, she pointed out that this shift from the deeds of the government to the needs of the displaced constituted an innocence, "in the sense of complete lack of responsibility," which "was the mark of their rightlessness as [much as] it was the seal of their political status" (295), because as rightless people, she wrote, "their freedom of opinion is a fool's freedom, for nothing they think matters" (296).

Mateo, a Peace Community leader, explained to me last summer, "When one is displaced, one loses the feeling of being Colombian, a citizen with rights and responsibilities. After many community meetings of the displaced, we decided to return together in 1999. We decided to live in the middle of the conflict because if we waited for it to end, we would never return to our lands. We opted for pure nonviolence. They should respect the decision of the people. If they want to fight with each other, they can—but not on our land and we won't fight with them. As the peace communities, we have a life of peace, not violence. Our goal is to support peace, not war" (Sanford 2001).

While staying in the Peace Community of Costa de Oro during July and August 2001 with Asale Angel-Ajani and Kimberly Theidon, we witnessed the tremendous pressures on the communities. On a humanitarian mission with a social service team from the diocese of Apartadó, accompanying the displacement of the communities of Andalucia and Camelias from a combat zone to Costa de Oro, we were stopped by guerrillas several times. Usually, there were two or three irregular forces. That is, they were not the regular uniformed combatants of the FARC but rather local recruits. Though armed, they did not brandish their weapons in a menacing way. We were also forcibly removed from our boats at gunpoint by several dozen paramilitaries, who twice detained our group—once for about an hour and once for about thirty minutes. The first time, when the paramilitaries commanded us to beach our small boats on the riverbank, they ordered us into a corridor they had cut into the jungle and shouted at us to "run like cattle." As we ran into the jungle, some fifty-three paramilitaries with machine guns and mortar launchers said, "Here are the cattle. What shall we do with them?" However, when they saw our three international faces, they began to say, "Good morning, don't worry. We won't do anything to you." This did not stop them from attempting to separate several young men from our group, however. Father Honelio intervened, telling the commander that if they wanted to talk with one of us, they would have to talk to all of us—effectively informing him that if they wanted to kill one of us, they would have to kill all of us. As Honelio explained, "We will not be separated as a group." At this, the commander ordered a dozen or so paramilitaries to engage the guerrillas on the other side of the river in an exchange of mortar and machine gun fire. Had the guerrillas responded, the paramilitaries would have had more choices of how to handle us—because civilians often die in crossfire. Fortunately, the guerrillas did not respond.

This is not to paint the guerrillas as innocent actors. We were frequently told, "Both sides kill. The paras kill everyone; the guerrillas are more selective." Indeed, when we were there, the paramilitaries were seeking to gain territorial dominion by displacing the Peace Communities, and the guerrillas were seeking to regain territorial dominion by prohibiting villagers in the war zone from displacing. The state is not absent from this area, and paramilitary actions are not without an army presence. After twice being detained by the same paramilitary regiment (all in shiny new uniforms), we had spent nearly two hours with the same paramilitaries. On one occasion, when we returned to Apartadó, we ran into two paramilitaries at an ice cream store. As the wave of recognition passed over us, they began to smirk, and we made the ambiguous salutation *"Buenas tardes"* and kept walking. On another occasion, at an army checkpoint on the river, the commanding soldier was giving our papers the usual review. Though we had not previously seen him at an army checkpoint, Dr. Angel-Ajani and I recognized him—as one of the paramilitaries who had detained us. Once back on the river after clearing the checkpoint, we commented on how the paramilitary uniforms and weapons were so much newer than those of the army. Part of what made the commanding officer stand out was our memory of him in a new paramilitary uniform with new weaponry. At the checkpoint, his army uniform was shabby, faded, and frayed, and his belt and holster were worn and cracked.

Shortly after our departure in August, the paramilitaries seized control of several key communities, entered Costa de Oro, and occupied Curvarado—the last town you pass as you head upriver to the Peace Communities in the heart of the war zone. Paramilitaries killed several Curvarado functionaries, including a municipal secretary who had participated in one of the accompaniment missions. In early September, the paras seized Peace Community lands and killed four residents of Puerto Lleras, claiming the land while threatening to kill anyone who challenged them. Also in September, the guerrillas tightened control on tributaries under their command—including prohibiting the diocese teams from entering some communities. In late October, the paras forcibly recruited two boys from Costa de Oro, and the guerrillas ambushed a platoon of paramilitaries, killing at least thirty of them and reclaiming the territory and populations that the paras had conquered in September. In Curvarado, the guerrillas killed a peasant branded as a paramilitary collaborator. In late October, residents of Costa de Oro were very worried because one of their leaders was on the FARC's list of people to be assassinated. On November 10, Father Honelio and another priest were prohibited from entering

Costa de Oro, then under definitive guerrilla control. At the time, one observer expressed fear that the paramilitaries would respond to the guerrillas with an even more severe attack on the communities. Indeed, on December 5, 2001, the guerrillas and the paramilitaries had a major battle in the town of Rio Sucio. Several hundred civilians were killed in the battle, which caused another wave of displacement of those fearing even greater retaliatory battles. On Christmas Day 2001, the guerrillas killed two youth leaders in Costa de Oro. At the time of this writing, in April 2003, the army has more checkpoints than ever along the Atrato River, and Peace Community movement along the river and its tributaries is restricted by the army, paramilitaries, and the FARC.[10] The FARC controls all river tributaries and access to Peace Communities and towns except Curvarado (which remains a contested space) and Rio Sucio (which continues as a dominion of the paramilitaries). The diocese continues to accompany Peace Community residents, although the FARC sometimes impedes their movement on tributaries or prohibits entry into some Peace Communities.

I want to close by suggesting that despite the surveillance, control, and extreme violence experienced by the communities at the hands of the army, paramilitaries, and guerrillas, the fifty-nine Peace Communities continue because those who were rendered rightless by displacement made a decision to reassert their citizenship and their human rights by reclaiming their lands and reconstituting themselves as Colombian citizens in Peace Communities, thereby reconstituting state sovereignty from below. While the army, paramilitaries, and guerrillas continue to fight for hegemony through territorial dominion, and control of the population through displacement or infringement of freedom of movement, the Peace Communities create new domains for peace that can only be revealed in practice as a negation of war. By drawing administrative agencies and juridical representatives into their practices, the Peace Communities expose the contradictions of the state and especially the violence of its army and proxy forces. Borrowing from Giorgio Agamben, truth is revealed as "a taking-place of the false, as an exposure of its innermost impropriety" (1993:13). And this is possible because truth is an entity of the world that Foucault noted "is produced only by virtue of multiple forms of constraint" and that "has regular effects of power" (1980:131).

I am not suggesting that life in the Peace Communities is some kind of romantic postmodern experience in which peace is achieved by virtue of being sought or that the Colombian state is magically transformed. However, my research and continued contact with the Peace Communities suggest that these effects of power are experienced in the everyday life of the community despite its current cycle of occupation by armed actors (who filter in and out of Peace Communities with fluidity) and that the reconstitution of citizenship has explicit effects on state sovereignty. Moreover, by establishing a new domain for the community practice of peace and human rights, the effects of this community power challenge not only the paramilitaries and guerrillas but also the spectral presence of the state, the state's production of a truth that defines the war as a drug war, and a state that makes and remakes sovereignty with legible and often illegible surveillance and violence. Remember Mateo's words: "We decided to live in the conflict." He also told me that "neither side is going to win, because they have lost the people" (author's interview August 2001). Father Leonides said, "It shouldn't be that those who make war define peace" (team interview July 5, 2001). The Peace Communities challenge military definitions of peace by constituting the rights of citizenship during the everyday experiences of those whom the state would reduce to "bare life" in the midst of conflict (Agamben 1998). Moreover, while surveillance and violence remain central state practices, by forcing the state to assert its power at the margins through administrative acts of law and service provision, these rights of citizenship reconstitute the state and the role of the citizen-subject on the very terrain upon which state sovereignty is realized.

EPILOGUE

In August 2002, Alvaro Uribe Velez was inaugurated as president of Colombia. Uribe ran his election campaign as a referendum against terrorism. Yet, his first actions after taking office only served to further institutionalize the militarization of the Colombian state. Among his key strategies for "democratic security," Uribe has (1) invoked emergency powers and declared a "state of internal unrest" that allows him to rule by decree in areas of extreme conflict that he has designated "Rehabilitation and Consolidation Zones," severely limiting outside contact to civilian populations in these areas; (2) begun training part-time soldiers to form a "peasant army"; and (3) formed a national network of civilian informants, with the intention of involving one million Colombian citizens in spying on their neighbors. Each of these projects further blurs the distinction between paramilitaries, militias, and the state army.

Although the election of Uribe has increased the impunity of paramilitaries, the Peace Communities continue to create new modes of everyday life grounded in the enactment of a collective moral imagination of communities committed to peace. In October 2002, more than 2,000 representatives of fifty-six peace communities and several hundred national and international observers participated in the fifth anniversary celebration of the founding of Peace Communities. This gathering, held in the river town of Curvarado, reaffirmed the success and commitment of the 12,000 displaced Colombians who have returned to their lands in the combat zone to construct new lives as Peace Communities. A mass was held to celebrate life and remember those who gave their lives for peace. Ambassadors from Spain, Holland, and Sweden participated in the event, as did several delegations of international observers and representatives from national and international NGOs. At the close of the four-day celebration, internationals attending the gathering accompanied participants back to their communities, passing army, paramilitary, and guerrilla checkpoints along the way. In Costa de Oro, community member Don Rafael said, "We are still here. Peace is not an alternative. Peace is our only option."

When I returned to Costa de Oro in February 2003, residents reported the continued presence of the FARC and paramilitaries in the jungle and rivers outlying their community. They also reported that there had been no violence against Costa de Oro residents since July of the preceding year. Resident Don Alvino explained, "They know that people are watching out for us and that what happens here doesn't end here. And we don't travel alone on the river anymore. We don't send our young men out to the crops alone. We always travel in groups. They will never again have the opportunity to grab two or three of our youths or kill a leader traveling alone. Maybe they now know, finally understand, that we are not going to leave our lands. We live for peace. We live for our lands. These are the lands of our children. The peace communities are what our children will inherit, the example of living in peace. My God, I hope my children see peace."

Notes

This chapter draws on research in the Urabá-Chocó region of Colombia in October 2000 and fieldwork conducted on the Ecuadorian-Colombian border with Asale Angel-Ajani and Notre Dame students Mariela Rodriguez, Jessica Scanlan, Kristi Green, and Karen Callan in May and June 2001. During July and August 2001, Dr. Angel-Ajani, Kimberly Theidon, and I conducted field research and accompanied the Peace Communities of Urabá-Chocó. I am grateful to the Institute for Scholarship in the Liberal Arts, Undergraduate Research Opportunity Program, Graduate Student Proposal Writing Fellowship, and Strake Fellowship at the University of Notre Dame, as well as the Institute for Human Rights Policy and Practice, for supporting collaborative work with my students and colleagues on this project. I especially thank Veena Das and Deborah Poole for including me in the SAR advanced seminar "The State at Its Margins," which helped me better problematize the margins of the state. Michael Bosia carefully analyzed several drafts of this chapter with a political scientist's eye to understanding the state. Asale Angel-Ajani, Leon Arredondo, Shannon Speed, and Scott Appleby offered extremely thoughtful commentary on this work-in-progress. I especially thank Leon Arredondo for his very close read of this chapter and insightful comments about the historical conceptualization of these frontiers within the Colombian imaginary. Scott Appleby and Hal Culbertson gave me a welcome opportunity to present a draft of this chapter to my colleagues at the Kroc Institute. Roberta Culbertson gave me a quiet, supportive space in which to write and invited me to present this work at an international symposium on violence at the Virginia Foundation for the Humanities. This research project would not have been possible without the kind collaboration of Leyla Lima and Maria Paz Bermejo of the United Nations High Commissioner for Refugees, who made possible my participation in the accompaniment. Finally, I benefited from support of the diocese of Apartadó, the accompaniment teams, and the Peace Community members themselves. Unless otherwise specified, all interviews were conducted under the condition that I respect the informant's anonymity. Any errors are, of course, my own.

1. The FARC is the largest and oldest guerrilla organization in Colombia, with some 18,000 armed combatants. For more on the history of guerrillas in Urabá-Chocó, see Comisión Andina de Juristas Colombianas (1994) and Beltran (1996).

2. OFP barrio projects include daily, low-cost midday meals for poor and working people, free meals for children, tutorials for children, microenterprise projects for women, recreational activities for children, and community support groups.

3. This same taxi driver shared fears of being assassinated, naming nine drivers who had recently lost their lives to violence. Like others I interviewed in Barrancabermeja, the taxi driver requested anonymity.

4. In author interviews, current and former paramilitaries in Ecuador and Colombia repeatedly confirmed communication and planning between paramilitaries and Colombian army officials. For more on Colombian paramilitaries, see Human Rights Watch (1996a, 1996b, 2000).

5. The Permanent Consultation on Internal Displacement in the Americas considers plans for the construction of a new canal to be central to the conflict in the Chocó region in general and the Atrato River area in particular. See Inter-American Commission on Human Rights (1999).

6. The soldier agreed to a taped interview on condition of anonymity. At a spring 2001 Kellogg Institute forum, Curt Kammen, former US ambassador to Colombia, also spoke of human-rights efforts as a hindrance to US policy in Colombia.

7. For more on camp conditions in Turbo, see Human Rights Watch (1998a).

8. Field research in Colombia indicated that this is the case in marginalized barrios of Apartadó, Bogotá, and Barrancabermeja. Testimonies from Colombian refugees in Ecuador confirm these practices in Medellín, Cali, Barranquilla, Nariño, and Putumayo, among other places.

9. I use the term *international community* to mean the international NGOs, UN agencies, and churches working for peace within Colombia, as well as those in other countries.

10. These restrictions remain constant but with variation—sometimes reflecting military maneuvers and confrontations between the armed actors and sometimes reflecting the whim of the commander at the checkpoint. On any given day, an accompaniment boat from the diocese may be allowed to enter a Peace Community, be denied entry, or have entry delayed.

11

Where Are the Margins of the State?

Talal Asad

In their thoughtful introduction to this rich collection of essays, Veena Das and Deborah Poole question the definition of the state in terms of centralized control over a determinate territory, and they propose that we explore the state's "margins"—that is, the places where state law and order continually have to be reestablished. For state power, they insist, is always unstable, something best seen when one moves away from the "center." They proceed to identify three ways in which the state's margins may be imagined: first, as peripheries or territories in which the state has yet to penetrate; second, as "spaces, forms, and practices through which the state is continually both experienced and undone through the *illegibility* of its own practices, documents, and words"; and, finally, as the "space between bodies, law, and discipline." Each of the splendid essays brought together here traces one of these ways of imagining the state's margins.

The overall argument that seems to emerge from the introduction is that the state's margins can be viewed differently precisely because "the state" itself is not a fixed object. This argument is enormously suggestive, and I want to think a little along these lines.

The term *state* is, of course, used in a number of different discourses. These include (but are not exhausted by) the discourse of sovereign states (whether princedoms or republics) facing one another in war and peace; the discourse of state governance (in the regulation of behavior, the acquisition and distribution of resources, the care of populations, the maximization of security); and the discourse of state politics (the struggle to establish a nation-state; competition over policy). Such discourses invoke languages of law, of justice, of raison d'état, of benefit—languages that define and redefine the foundations of sovereignty and the obligations of obedience, the criteria of citizenship and nationality, the rights of self-defense and punishment. The boundaries of "the state" vary accordingly, as does its internal morphology: the different ways of determining membership and inclusion, inside and outside, the law and the exception.

The modern idea of the "state" has a complicated Western history, and a contested one at that.[1] In the late Middle Ages, the Latin word *status* and the vernacular equivalents *estat, stato, state* had a variety of political meanings, but mainly these words referred to the standing of rulers. According to medieval legal theories, the ruler possessed or even embodied the government. In Renaissance Italy, histories and advice books for magistrates (as well as the mirror-for-princes literature to which these eventually gave rise) initiated a tradition of practical political reasoning in the context of new city republics that gave a novel sense to the terms *status* and *stato*.

The writers in this tradition were concerned above all with the conditions for the successful maintenance of these republics—especially after their widespread usurpation by hereditary princes. Because they considered the ability to secure a particular *kind* of government (over and above the person of the ruler) to be essential, these writers tended to use the terms *status* and *stato* to refer to it. Among the conditions necessary for successful maintenance of the government was the defense of territory over which the ruler had authority—and so the land itself came to be denoted by the same words. But perhaps the most significant extension of the term *state* was its reference to the structures of administration and force by which the prince controlled his domain (*regnum* or *civitas*).

It seems to have been the humanist republicans who originated the idea of a sovereign authority that would regulate the public affairs of an independent community. And it was they who first used the word *status* or *stato* to refer to the apparatus of government that rulers were obliged to maintain. But they attained to only half the doubly abstract notion of the state as it is widely understood today. For according to the modern concept, the state is an entity with a life of its own, distinct from both governors and governed. And because of this abstraction, it can demand allegiance from both sides. For the humanist republicans, in contrast, the state (or "commonwealth" and "political society," as they preferred to call it), being an expression of the powers of the people, could not be quite detached from the entire community. Of course, they distinguished between the apparatus of government and those temporarily in charge, but they always regarded the powers established by the community in such apparatuses as essentially the powers of the community as a whole. However, the fully abstract idea of the state was developed by those who argued against this tradition of popular sovereignty, most famously Hobbes ([1651] 1968).

In this conception, the state dominates and defends the community, orders and nurtures its civil life. The state, independently of the entire population, embodies sovereignty. Far from being a myth, the state's abstract character is precisely what enables it to define and sustain the margin as a margin through a range of administrative practices. (In the republican tradition, by contrast, the sovereignty of the state is delegated by rather than alienated from its subjects. This, in a sense, makes the governing state a margin of the citizen-body it represents.)

In some critical literature on the state (especially in anthropology), one finds the word *fetish* used to suggest that because the state has an abstract character, it is merely an ideological construction and its claim to solidity and power is therefore empty. This allusion to Marx's ([1867] 1961) famous account of the commodity as a fetish seems to me unhelpful. For Marx, it will be recalled, the fetishism of commodities refers to the fact that "a definite social relation between men... assumes, in their eyes, the fantastic form of a relation between things." This points us, he argued, toward the imaginary world of religion. "In that world the productions of the human brain appear as independent beings endowed with life, and entering into relation both with one another and the human race. So it is in the world of commodities with the products of men's hands. This I call the fetishism which attaches itself to the products of labour, so soon as they are produced in commodities, and which is therefore inseparable from the production of commodities" ([1867] 1961:72). However, the reification of social relations of production that characterizes the commodity is quite different from the abstract character of the modern state. The commodity form *hides* the productive power of the laborer. It is merely inert material falsely taken to be alive. The abstract structure of the state, on the other hand, is the essential condition for the exercise of specific kinds of legal power—whether they are claimed by government or by citizens. Although officials and politicians may lie and deceive, the state's abstract character hides nothing. It is not an illusion.

This may seem all very theoretical, but part of the point I want to make is that abstraction is a necessary feature of both the state and the citizen precisely because they are concepts in modern political discourse. Abstractions are inevitably used in everyday discourse, and they inform everyday practices. When we abstract a term from one context and employ it in another, we treat something in the two contexts as equivalent. Historian of statistics Alain Desrosieres puts it thus: "The only way of understanding the recurrent opposition in politics, in history and in science between on the one hand contingency, singularity and circumstance and on the other hand generality, law, regularity and constancy is to ask: 'for what purpose?' The question is not: 'Are these objects *really* equivalent?' but: 'Who decides to treat them as equivalent and to what end?'" (1990:200–201). The idea of abstraction is necessary to the notion of equivalence, and both are integral to the modern liberal state.

Thus, political theorists often claim that the liberal state is required to treat all citizens with equal concern and respect. For example, Ira Katznelson argues that "what is distinctive to liberalism, as compared to other political theories, is the type of equality it values: 'the requirement that the government treat all those in its charge *as equals*' (Dworkin 1978:125), that is, with equal concern and respect. The issue of who gets included 'in its charge' may be contested but not the standing of liberal citizens" (Katznelson 1994:622). But the principle of *legal* equality doesn't depend on attitudes of "concern and respect." Nor, conversely, does the expression of concern and respect presuppose the principle of legal equality. On the contrary, the strict application of the principle requires that citizens be treated with absolute *indifference*. For only indifference enables citizens to be counted as equivalents. Yet, when individuals are treated as *really equivalent,* a bureaucrat may judge them as he pleases. In other words, when faced with *substitutables* from among whom he has to choose, his choice is by definition completely free and therefore uncertain. He may tend to choose a white over a black in the United States, a Muslim over a Copt in Egypt, a Jew over an Arab in Israel—so long as, in each case and on every occasion, the pair are representable as "equal" in the sense of being *the same.* Only a tally of the choices reveals the structure of bias in the statistical sense against a political category that is taken by critics to be *different.* (For example, of immigrants applying for French citizenship in 1997, 35 to 50 percent of Africans did not qualify, compared with 20 percent of North Africans and 8 percent of southern Europeans.)[2] The uncertainty of choice is expressible in probabilities, but even the statistical structure of bias does not prove that a biased decision was made in a particular case. To determine *that* probability, a profile of decisions must be constructed for each bureaucrat.

If it is the case that people in society are never homogeneous, that they are always constituted by different memories, fears, and hopes, that they have different histories and live in different social-economic conditions, then the official who chooses or judges may be held accountable for who, how, and why he categorizes. But the act of categorizing always involves abstraction from one context and its application to another context—and it is always, in a sense, uncertain.

Equality, generality, and abstraction thus rest on uncertainty. They define the margins of the state, where immigrants abstract themselves from one "national body" and seek to enter another, where they are aliens and where they confront officials who apply the law.

Let us take France, with its intense political demands to reject elements of "foreignness" from the national body. The suspicion these demands encourage among officials and the powers given to them to pursue their suspicion whenever it is aroused make for uncertainty about who can be a national. Here is a case reported in a recent article:

> Jacques R was annoyed back in 1995 when he left his identity card in a jacket that he had sent to the cleaners, but he wasn't worried; he thought that he could pick up a duplicate

card from police headquarters. To his surprise, the clerks asked him to prove that he was French, so the next day he returned with a pile of papers, and was even more surprised when they were immediately confiscated. He lost his temper, asked whether they thought he was a forger and told them again that he needed his ID card urgently. They assured him he would get it soon. Three months later, on Christmas Eve, he got a summons from the state prosecutor, which explained that in 1953 his father had been awarded French citizenship by mistake (Jacques had been born in 1954). As his father now counted as a foreigner and as Jacques had not applied for French nationality before the age of 18, he was not French either, and proceedings were under way to confirm this. The court later ratified the prosecutor's decision. Jacques was not French. He could not understand. He had always lived in France; he had studied there, had done his military service, married a Frenchwoman, and ran a shop. He had never been in trouble with the police, and had already renewed his ID successfully. Fortunately he was able to prove that he had lived in France for more than 10 years, and that the authorities had always considered him to be French, so he was entitled to right of abode at least. Two years later, the court accepted his plea and, at the age of 43, he at last became French. But his children, with their "foreign" father, lost their French nationality, and the family had to initiate legal proceedings to establish that the children too were entitled to right of abode. (Maschino 2002)

No one, the writer goes on, can now be sure of avoiding this treatment.

The nationality law in France is not complicated. A person is French if at least one parent is French. Children born in France of foreign parents can opt to be French at the age of eighteen. People may also become French by naturalization. However, because only official documents can confirm the required facts needed to acquire French nationality, the possibility always exists that they are forged. So in recent years, officials have been told to follow the rules carefully to lessen the likelihood that immigrants will be able to circumvent the law. Under these rules, the applicant must produce his or her own birth certificate and one for each parent and grandparent. He or she must also submit a *livret de famille* (an official document recording births and deaths in each family), as well as *livrets* of parents, in-laws, and grandparents, and marriage certificates for everyone. Finally, applicants must produce personal military service records and work testimonials. All these documents are essential before a certificate of nationality can be issued. The printed instructions that enumerate these requirements warn applicants that this is "a provisional list, to which other items may be added following an initial review of the application."

Now there is nothing *arbitrary* about any of this. The rules (an abstraction) are being strictly followed. Officials use the nationality law to defend the idea of "being French." At stake are the conditions necessary for the application of the law. The most important of these is the elimination of any suspicion of a material irregularity in an applicant's case. This calls for careful probing, the asking of personal questions that many people find offensive (What kind of food do you normally eat [or language do you normally speak] at home? Who are your friends? Why do you wear that headscarf?).[3] Particular officials use particular words in particular places in obedience to the rules and to the state's law (an abstraction).

Suspicion (like doubt) occupies the space between the law and its application. In that sense, all judicial and policing systems of the modern state presuppose organized suspicion, incorporate margins of uncertainty. Suspicion is like an animal, "aroused" in the subject, it covers an object (a representation or person) that comes "under" it. Suspicion seeks to penetrate a mask to the unpleasant reality behind it: the unauthorized creation of an authorizing document, a hidden motive to commit a crime, a latent disease, a terrorist in disguise. Suspicion initiates and is an integral part of *an investigation,* and the investigation ends when suspicion is put to rest—when a "reasonable" person comes to a conclusion, one way or the other, on probable evidence. Suspicion opposes and undermines trust (Khan 2002).

It is worth remembering that the origins of the modern (secular) state are connected to the concern for agreement among "reasonable" men and thus to the creation of a margin to which "religion" (and other forms of uncertain belief) properly belonged.

The truths of religion and morality, so it was argued in the sixteenth and seventeenth centuries, could not be known for certain. This position was not confined to religious skeptics. Even religious believers like Locke could point to an important fact: that political conflicts over religious doctrines appeared to be incapable of final solution by rational means, whereas everyone could agree that such things as social unrest and political persecution were sources of harm to life, limb, and property in this world. In delimiting the realm of legitimate politics— so Locke and others reasoned—let us therefore attend to the harms of this world about which we can all be certain, rather than the harms of the next world, on which we shall never agree.[4] The plausibility of this argument was important in facilitating the subordination of the religious domain to the practical and ideological power of the early modern state.

By the twentieth century, however, it became increasingly evident that the truths not merely of the hereafter but also of this world are not knowable with certainty. Society, in particular, is increasingly constructed, apprehended, and represented by statistical probability. Yet, this has not resulted in arguments for excluding social and psychological facts from the realm of legitimate politics or the administrative activity of the state. On the contrary, what we find is increasingly widespread argument over how knowledge of a commonly shared social world is to be politically interpreted, and therefore how aspects of that world are to be defended or changed. The fact that these arguments—just like seventeenth-century theological arguments—seem to be incapable of being rationally concluded is no longer regarded as a good reason for declaring them "outside politics." In modern liberal societies, public arguments over the economy, racial discrimination, multiculturalism, medical ethics, pornography, gender identity, religious education, and a host of other questions are not only endless, they are each carried out through statistical discourses in which figures and their meanings are presented and contested and policies formed. Certainty gives way to contestable estimates of probability. Does the margin therefore now pervade the entire state?

This wonderful collection of articles sensitizes us to such questions. By analyzing in different ways the margins of the modern state where uncertainty obtains, they make us aware that "the modern state" does not always possess the firmness that many commentators assume to be essential to it. Veena Das, in her brilliant contribution, alerts us to the uncertainty of legal rules: Does a written rule apply in a particular case, and if so, how should it be applied to practice? Does the rule conflict with other rules, and if so, how can they be reconciled? Where does the authority of laws lie? The answers to such questions, to the doubts generated by them, must be given authoritatively—that is to say, *from beyond the written rules*. It is this *alien* authority and not the written rule itself that constitutes the law of the state. The authority of the law seeks to make things *definite* within the continuous flow of uncertainty by imposing itself from outside, as Freud would say. In liberal democracies, the theory is that citizens make the law their own by collectively willing it. But *authority* is always prior to acts of submission, whether they are coerced or consented to. The *force* of the law therefore derives from beyond the general will of citizens.

Das's sensitive discussion of the illegibility of legal rules seems to get to the heart of the question of how we can best conceive of the margins of the state. Her answer, in effect, is this: In order to identify the margins of the state, we must turn to the pervasive uncertainty of the law *everywhere* and to the arbitrariness of the authority that seeks to make law certain.

This brings me to my final comment. As a mode of addressing social uncertainties, statistical arguments are now widely used in administration, legislation, and the judiciary. The language of statistics has become integral to the modern mode of government, which has learned to thrive on probabilities and risks—that is to say, on marginal spaces. That is why—as Das has argued—the entirety of the state is a margin. Or rather, the sovereign force of the law is expressed in the state's continual attempts to overcome the margin.

Notes

1. The comments that follow rely on Quentin Skinner (1978).

2. See Maschino (2002). The ministry subsequently stopped mentioning the country of origin of unsuccessful applicants.

3. "It is not unusual for clerks to ask personal questions designed to detect 'foreignness.' A barrister of North African origin was asked how many times she ate couscous, whether she often visited Morocco, what nationality her friends

were and which newspapers she read. A Tunisian was asked why he had twice made the pilgrimage to Mecca. A Serbian academic, whose children were preparing for the entrance exam for France's top teacher training college, was asked which language she spoke at home. Clerks even query levels of education. Small details influence the decision and an application may be adjourned because the person is too openly foreign (that headscarf), has family ties outside France, or seems 'fundamentalist'" (Maschino 2002).

4. I draw this interpretation of Locke's views on toleration from Ashcraft (1992), Dunn (1984), Mendus (1989), and McClure (1990).

References

Abba Kaka, A.
1997   Cette fraude qui tue! *Le Temps* 69 (April 9–15):8. N'Djamena, Chad.

Abélé, Marc
1990   *Anthropologie de l'etat.* Paris: Armand Colin.

Abrams, Phillip
1988   Notes on the Difficulty of Studying the State. *Journal of Historical Sociology* 1(1):58–89.

Abt Associates
2000   *The Impending Catastrophe: A Resource Book on the Emerging HIV/AIDS Epidemic in South Africa.* Johannesburg: Henry J. Kaiser Foundation.

ADA. *See* **Archivo Departmental de Ayachucho.**

Adams, Abigail
1996   Gringas, Ghouls, and Guatemala: The 1994 Attacks on North American Women Accused of Body Organ Trafficking. *Journal of Latin American Anthropology* 4(1):112–33.

1998   Word, Work, and Worship: Engendering Evangelical Culture in Highland Guatemala and the United States. Ph.D. diss., University of Virginia, Charlottesville.

Africa Confidential
1991a   Cameroon: Crisis or Compromise? October 25.
1991b   Cameroon: Biya Besieged. July 26.

Agamben, Giorgio

1993   *The Coming Community.* Minneapolis: University of Minnesota Press.

1998   *Homo Sacer: Sovereign Power and Bare Life,* translated by D. Heller-Roazen. Stanford, CA: Stanford University Press.

2000   *Means without End: Notes on Politics.* Minneapolis: University of Minnesota Press.

2001   Sovereignty. Paper presented at the annual meeting of the American Anthropological Association, Washington, DC.

Akbar, Syed

2000   Naidu's Portal Hosts a New Website—Saleofkidneys.com. *Indian Express.* May 19.

Aljovín de Losada, Cristóbal

2000   *Caudillos y Constituciones: Perú: 1821–1845.* Lima: Universidad Católica and Fondo de Cultura Económica.

Althusser, Louis

1971   Ideological State Apparatuses (Notes Towards an Investigation). In *Lenin and Philosophy and Other Essays,* pp. 127–88. New York: Monthly Review Press.

Americas Watch

1992   *Peru under Fire: Human Rights since the Return to Democracy.* New Haven, CT: Yale University Press.

Anandan, Sujata

2001   Quit If You Differ with Us, BJP to Sena Chief. *Hindustan Times.* March 2.

Angel-Ajani, Asale

n.d.   Negotiating Small Truths: Incarcerated African Women and Other Forms of State Violence. Unpublished manuscript.

Appadurai, Arjun

1996   Numbers in the Colonial Imagination. In *Modernity at Large: Cultural Dimensions of Globalization,* pp. 114–39. Minneapolis: University of Minnesota Press.

Arce Vilar, César, and Manuel del Solar Retamozo.

1998   La Conciliación: A propósito del Centro de Conciliación de Ayacucho. *El Peruano.* March 12.

Archivo Departmental de Ayachucho (ADA)

1920   Causa criminal seguida contra Hernan Carrillo, Avelino Núñez y Zaragoza Aspur por el delito de flagelcion. Archivo Departamental Ayacucho, Corte Superior, leg. 372, cuad. 18; 86 fs.

Arendt, Hannah

[1951]   *The Origins of Totalitarianism.* New York: Harcourt Brace.
1973

Asad, Talal

2003   *Formations of the Secular: Christianity, Islam, Modernity.* Stanford, CA: Stanford University Press.

Ashcraft, Richard

1992   The Politics of Locke's Two Treatises of Government. In *John Locke's Two Treatises of Government: New Interpretations,* edited by E. J. Harpham. Lawrence: University of Kansas Press.

Ashforth, Adam

1998a   Reflections on Spiritual Insecurity in a Modern African City. *African Studies Review* 41(3):36–67. Soweto, South Africa.

1998b   Witchcraft, Violence, and Democracy in the New South Africa. *Cahiers d'Études Africaine* 38(2–4):505–532.

2000   *Madumo: A Man Bewitched.* Chicago: University of Chicago Press.

Associated Press

2001   S.F. Will Pay for Sex Changes. *Wired News,* May 1. http://www.wired.com/news/politics/0,1283,43462,00.html.

Auslander, Mark

1993   "Open the Wombs!" The Symbolic Politics of Modern Ngoni Witchfinding. In *Modernity and Its Malcontents: Ritual and Power in Postcolonial Africa,* edited by J. Comaroff and J. Comaroff, pp. 167–92. Chicago: University of Chicago Press.

Austin, John L.

1962   A Plea for Excuses. In *Philosophical Papers.* 3d ed., edited by J. M. Urmsom and G. J. Warnock, pp. 175–205. Oxford: Oxford University Press.

al-Azhar University

1991   *A Documentary Synopsis about al-Azhar University.* Cairo: al-Azhar University Press.

Bach, D., ed.

1998   *Régionalisation, mondialisation et fragmentation en Afrique subsahariene.* Paris: Karthala.

Bah, T., and Issa, S.

1997   Relations inter-ethniques, problématique de l'intégration nationale et de la sécurité auzabords sud du Lac Tchad. In *Regional Balance and National Integration in Cameroon,* edited by P. Nkwi and F. Nyamnjoh, pp. 280–88. Yaoundé, Cameroon: ASC and ICASSRT.

Bakhtin, Mikhail

1984   *Rabelais and His World.* Indianapolis: Indiana University Press.

Balandier, Georges

1951   La situation coloniale: approache théoretique. *Cahiers internationaux de sociologie* 11:44–79.

Baldwin, Peter

2001   *Contagion and the State in Europe, 1830–1930.* Cambridge: Cambridge University Press.

Balibar, Etienne

1991   Citizen Subject. In *Who Comes after the Subject?* edited by E. Cadava, P. Connor, and J. Nancy, pp. 33–57. London: Routledge.

1994   "Rights of Man" and "Rights of the Citizen": The Modern Dialectic of Equality and Freedom. In *Masses, Class, Ideas,* translated by J. Senson, pp. 39–59. London: Routledge.

Banégas, R.

1998   De la guerre au maintien de la paix: le nouveau business mercenaire. *Critique internationale* 1(Autumn):179–194.

Banton, Michael, ed.

1966   *The Social Anthropology of Complex Societies.* ASA Monograph 4. London: Tavistock.

Basadre, Jorge

1931   *Perú: Problema y posibilidad.* Lima: Rosay.

1997   *Historia del Derecho.* Lima: Universidad Nacional Mayor de San Marcos.

Bastos, Santiago, and Manuela Camus

1995   *Abriendo Caminos: Las Organizaciones Mayas desde el Nobel hasta el Acuerdo de Derechos Indígenas.* Guatemala City: FLACSO.

2003   *Entre el mecapal y el cielo: Desarrollo del movimiento Maya en Guatemala.* Guatemala City: FLACSO and Cholsamaj.

Bataille, Georges

1989   *The Accursed Share.* New York: Zone Books

Bayart, Jean-François

1977   *L'État au Cameroun.* Paris: Fondation nationale des sciences politiques.

1981   Le Politique par le bas en Afrique noire. *Politique Africaine* 1:53–83.

1989   *L'Etat en Afrique.* Paris: Fayard.

1993   *The State in Africa.* London: Longman.

1994   L'invention paradoxale de la modernité économique. In *La réinvention du capitalisme,* pp. 9–43. Paris: Karthala.

Bayart, Jean-François, Stephen Ellis, and Béatrice Hibou

1997   *La criminalization de l'État en Afrique.* Bruxelles: Editions Complexes.

Beltran, Harvey

1996   *Uraba—Region, Actores y Conflicto.* Bogotá: Gente Nueva Editorial.

Bendetti, Mario

1990   *Inventario: Poesia Completa (1950–1985).* Madrid: Visor Editores.

Benjamin, Walter

[1978]   Critique of Violence. In *Reflections: Essays, Aphorisms, Autobiographical*
1986   *Writings*, edited by P. Demetez, translated by E. Gephcott, pp. 277–301.
          New York: Harcourt Brace Jovanovitch.

Bennafla, Karine

1996   Rapport sur les échanges transfrontaliers informels au Tchad.
          Unpublished paper.

1997   Entre Afrique noire et monde arabe. Nouvelles tendances des échanges
          informels tchadiens. *Revue Tiers Monde* 38(152):879–96.

1998   Mbaïboum: un marché au Carrefour de frontiéres multiples. *Autrepart*
          6:53–72.

1999   La fin des territories nationaux? *Politique Africaine* 73 (March):42–49.

2002   *Le commerce frontalier en Afrique Centrale.* Paris: Karthala.

Bentham, Jeremy

[1830]   The Constitutional Code. In *The Works of Jeremy Bentham*, vol. 9, edited
1962   by John Bowring, pp. 14–18. New York: Russell and Russell.

Berglund, Axel-Ivar

1976   *Zulu Thought-Patterns and Symbolism.* Bloomington: Indiana University
          Press.

Bhabha, Homi K.

1994a   By Bread Alone: Signs of Violence in the Mid-Nineteenth Century. In *The
          Location of Culture*, pp. 198–212. London: Routledge.

1994b   *The Location of Culture.* London: Routledge.

Boone, James A.

1999   *Verging on Extra-Vagance: Anthropology, History, Religion, Literature,*
          Arts...Showbiz. Princeton, NJ: Princeton University Press.

Bose, Sugato, and Ayesha Jalal, eds.

1997   *Nationalism, Democracy and Development: State and Politics in India.* Delhi:
          Oxford University Press.

Bradford, Phillips Verner, and Harvey Blume

1992   *Ota Benga: The Pygmy in the Zoo.* New York: St. Martin's Press.

**Bradshaw, Debbie, Rob Dorrington, David Bourne, Ria Laubscher,
Nadine Nannan, and Ian Timaeus**

2001   AIDS Mortality in South Africa. Paper presented at the Aids in Context
          Conference, University of the Witwatersrand, Johannesburg.

Brandt, Hans-Jurgen

1986   *Justicia Popular: Nativos Campesinos.* Lima: Fundación Friedrich Naumann.

Brown, Wendy

1995   *States of Injury: Power and Freedom in Late Modernity.* Princeton, NJ:
          Princeton University Press.

Burga, Manuel, and Alberto Flores Galindo

1987   *Apogeo y Crisis de la República Aristocrática.* Lima: Rikchay Perú.

Burrell, Jennifer

2000   Update: The Aftermath of Lynching in Todos Santos. *Report on Guatemala* 21(4):12–14.

Butler, Judith

1987   *Subjects of Desire: Hegelian Reflections in Twentieth-Century France.* New York: Columbia University Press.

1993   *Bodies That Matter: On the Discursive Limits of "Sex."* London: Routledge.

Callaghy, Thomas, and Ravenhill, John, eds.

1993   *Hemmed In: Responses to Africa's Economic Decline.* New York: Columbia University Press.

Castells, Manuel

1989   *The Informational City: Information Technology, Economic Restructuring, and the Urban-Regional Process.* Oxford: Basil Blackwell.

1998   *End of Millennium.* London: Blackwell Publishers.

Cavell, Stanley

1994   *A Pitch of Philosophy: Autobiographical Exercises.* Cambridge, MA: Harvard University Press.

CCJ. *See* **Colombian Commission of Jurists.**

CEH. *See* **Comisión de Esclarecimiento Historico.**

Cesaire, Aimé

1972   *Discourse on Colonialism.* New York: Monthly Review Press.

Champaud, Jacques

1991   Cameroun: au bord de l'affrontement. *Politique Africaine* 44:115–20.

Chatterjee, Partha

1997   *State and Politics in India.* Delhi: Oxford University Press.

Chavunduka, G. L.

1980   Witchcraft and the Law in Zimbabwe. *Zambezia* 8(2):129–47.

Citizen's Commission

1984   *Report of the Citizen's Commission.* Delhi: Citizen's Commission.

Clastres, Pierre

1974   *Société contre l'etat.* Paris: Les Editions de Minuit.

1989   *Society against the State.* New York: Zone Books.

Cohen, Lawrence

1995a   Holi in Banaras and the *Mahaland* of Modernity. *GLQ* 2:399–424.

1995b   The Pleasures of Castration: The Postoperative Status of *Hijras, Jankhas,* and Academics. In *Sexual Nature, Sexual Culture,* edited by P. R. Abramson and S. D. Pinkerton, pp. 276–304. Chicago: University of Chicago Press.

1998   *No Aging in India: Alzheimer's, the Bad Family, and Other Modern Things.*
Berkeley: University of California Press.

1999   Where It Hurts: Indian Material for an Ethics of Organ Transplantation.
Daedalus 128(4):135–65.

2001   The Other Kidney: Biopolitics beyond Recognition. *Body and Society*
7(2–3):9–29.

n.d.   The *Kothi* Wars. In *The Moral Object of Sex: Science, Development, and Sexuality
in Global Perspective,* edited by V. Adams and S. L. Pigg. Chapel Hill, NC:
Duke University Press, in press.

Cohn, Bernard

1987   Census, Social Structure, and Objectification in South Asia. In *An
Anthropologist among the Historians,* pp. 224–54. Delhi: Oxford University
Press.

Cojtí Cuxil, Demetrio

1991   *Configuración del Pensamiento Maya.* Quetzaltenango, Guatemala: Academia
de Escritores Mayas.

1995   *Ub'anik Ri Una'ooj Uchomab'aal Ri Maya' Tinamit: Configuración del
Pensamiento Político del Pueblo Maya,* pt. 2. Guatemala City: Cholsamaj.

1996   The Politics of Maya Revindication. In *Maya Cultural Activism in Guatemala,*
edited by E. F. Fischer and R. McKenna Brown, pp. 19–50. Austin:
University of Texas Press.

Colombian Commission of Jurists (CCJ)

2000   *Panorama de Derechos Humanos y Derecho Humanitario en Colombia. Informe de
Avance Sobre 2000.* Bogotá: CCJ.

Comaroff, John L.

1998   Reflections on the Colonial State, in South Africa and Elsewhere: Factions,
Fragments, Facts and Fictions. *Social Identities* 4(3):321–61.

COMISEDH. *See* **Comisión de Derechos Humanos.**

Comisión Andina de Juristas

1999   *Gente que hace justicia: La Justicia de paz.* Lima: Comisión Andina de Juristas.

2000   *Manual de Capacitación en Justicia de Paz.* Lima: Comisión Andina de
Juristas.

Comisión Andina de Juristas Colombianas

1994   *Uraba-Informes Regionales de Derechos Humanos.* Bogotá: Comisión Andina
de Juristas Colombianas.

Comisión Andina de Juristas Secional

1996   *Colombian, Uraba, Beltrán, Uraba and Clara Inés Gracia. Uraba-region, Actores y
Conflicto, 1960–1990.* Bogotá: CEREC.

Comisión de Derechos Humanos (COMISEDH)

1990   *Informe Estadístico Sobre la Desaparición Forzada de Personas en el Perú,
1983–1989.* Lima: COMISEDH.

Comisión de Esclarecimiento Historico (CEH)

1999 Guatemala: Memory of Silence. http://hrdata.aaas.org/ceh/report.

Comisión de la Verdad y Reconciliación

2003 Comisión de la Verdad y Reconciliación Web site. www.cverdad.org.pe.

Commission of Inquiry into Witchcraft Violence and Ritual Murders

1996 *Report of the Commission of Inquiry into Witchcraft Violence and Ritual Murders in the Northern Province of the Republic of South Africa (Ralushai Commission).* Northern Province, South Africa: Ministry of Safety and Security.

Commission on Gender Equality

1998 *The Thohoyandou Declaration on Ending Witchcraft Violence.* Johannesburg: Commission on Gender Equality.

2000 *Decrease in Witchcraft Killings and Violence.* Johannesburg: Commission on Gender Equality. http://www.cge.org.za/press/2000/22-7-2000.4.htm.

Consejeria Presidencial para los Derechos Humanos (CPDH)

1991 *Justicia, Derechos Humanos e Impunidad.* Bogotá: CPDH.

Cooper, Frederick

2002 *Africa since 1940: The Past of the Present.* Cambridge: Cambridge University Press.

Coordination of Organizations of the Pueblo Maya of Guatemala (COPMAGUA)

1995 *Acuerdo Sobre Identidad y Derechos de los Pueblos Indígenas.* Guatemala City: Cholsamaj.

COPMAGUA. *See* **Coordination of Organizations of the Pueblo Maya of Guatemala.**

Coriat, Percy

1993 *Governing the Nuer: Documents in Nuer History and Ethnography, 1922–1933.* Oxford: Jaso.

Coronel, José

1999a Actores sociales: Sociedad Rural Ayacuchana y Comunidad Campesina. In *Actores Sociales y Ciudadanía en Ayacucho,* pp. 9–20. Ayacucho: USIS.

1999b Seguridad Ciudadana en el área rural de Ayacucho. Unpublished paper.

2000a *Diagnóstico de Levantamiento de Línea de Base para la Instalación de los Núcleos Rurales de Administración de Justicia en el Distrito de Huambalpa.* Ayacucho: IPAZ.

2000b Sociedad rural ayacuchana e institucionalidad. Unpublished manuscript.

Coronil, Fernando

1997 *The Magical State: Nature, Money, and Modernity in Venezuela.* Chicago: University of Chicago Press.

Cover, Robert

1995 Nomos and Narrative (1983). In *Narrative, Violence and the Law: The Essays of Robert Cover,* edited by M. Minow, M. Ryan, and A. Sarat, pp. 95–172. Ann Arbor: University of Michigan Press.

CPDH. *See* **Consejeria Presidencial para los Derechos Humanos.**

Das, Veena

1989   Subaltern as Perspective. In *Subaltern Studies VI*, edited by R. Guha, pp. 345–99. New Delhi: Oxford University Press.

1990   Our Work to Cry: Your Work to Listen. In *Mirrors of Violence: Communities, Riots, and Survivors in South Asia*, edited by V. Das, pp. 345–99. Delhi: Oxford University Press.

1995   *Critical Events: An Anthropological Perspective on Contemporary India.* Delhi: Oxford University Press.

1996   The Spatialization of Violence: A "Communal" Riot in Delhi. In *Unravelling the Nation*, edited by K. Basu and S. Subrahmanyam, pp. 46–64. Delhi: Penguin Press.

1998   Official Narratives, Rumor, and the Social Production of Hate. *Social Identities* 4(1):109–30.

Das, Veena, and R. S. Bajwa

1994   Community and Violence in Contemporary Punjab. In *Purusartha: Violences and Non-Violences in India*, edited by D. Vidal, G. Tarabout, and E. Meyer, pp. 245–61. Paris: Editions de l'école des etudes hautes en sciences sociales.

Das Veena, and Abhijit Dasgupta

2000   The Cholera Vaccine: Trajectories in Contemporary Bengal. *Economic and Political Weekly* 35:625–33.

Das, Veena, Arthur Kleinman, Margaret Locke, and Mamphela Ramphele

2001   *Remaking a World: Violence, Social Suffering and Recovery*, edited by P. Reynolds. Berkeley: University of California Press.

Das, Veena, Arthur Kleinman, Mamphela Ramphele, and Pamela Reynolds

2000   *Violence and Subjectivity.* Berkeley: University of California Press.

Dayal, John, and Ajoy Bose

1997   *For Reasons of State: Delhi under Emergency.* Delhi: Ess Ess Publications.

de Boeck, Filip

1999   Domesticating Diamonds and Dollars: Identity, Expenditure and Sharing in Southwestern Zaire. In *Globalization and Identity: Dialectics of Flow and Closure*, edited by P. Geschiere and B. Meyer, pp. 177–209. Oxford: Basil Blackwell.

Defensoria del Pueblo (DP)

1999   *Contra Viento y Marea—Conclusiones y Recomendaciones de la ONU y la OEA para Garantizar la Vigencia de los Derechos Humanos en Colombia.* Bogotá: DP.

Degregori, Carlos Iván

1989   *Que Difícil es ser Dios: Ideología y Violencia Política en Sendero Luminoso.* Lima: El Zorro de Abajo.

Degregori, Carlos Iván, José Coronel, Ponciano del Pino, and Orin Starn
1996   *Las Rondas Campesinas y la Derrota de Sendero Luminoso.* Lima: Instituto de Estudios Peruanos and Universidad Nacional de San Cristóbal de Huamanga.

de la Cadena, Marisol
2000   *Indigenous Mestizos: The Politics of Race and Culture in Cuzco, Peru, 1919–1991.* Durham, NC: Duke University Press.

Deleuze, Gilles, and Felix Guattari
[1972]   *Anti-Oedipus: Capitalism and Schizophrenia,* translated by R. Hurley.
1983   Minneapolis: University of Minnesota Press.
1987   *A Thousand Plateaus: Capitalism and Schizophrenia,* translated by B. Massumi. Minneapolis: University of Minnesota Press.

Delius, Peter
1996   *A Lion Amongst the Cattle.* Johannesburg: Ravan Press.

Department of Health, Directorate of Health Systems Research and Epidemiology
2000   *Summary Report: National HIV Sero-Prevalence Survey of Women Attending Ante-Natal Clinics in South Africa.* Johannesburg: Department of Health.
2001   *Summary Report: National HIV Sero-Prevalence Survey of Women Attending Ante-Natal Clinics in South Africa.* Johannesburg: Department of Health.

Department of Justice
1997   Designation of Sierra Leone under Temporary Protected Status. *Federal Register* 62(213):59736–37. http://www.sierra-leone.org/tps.html.

Derrida, Jacques
1988   Signature Event Context. In *Limited Inc.,* edited by G. Graff, pp. 1–25. Evanston, IL: Northwestern University.
1992   Force of Law: The Mystical Foundation of Authority. In *Deconstruction and the Possibility of Justice,* edited by D. Cornell, M. Rosenfeld, and D. Carlson, pp. 3–67. New York: Routledge.
2001   *On Cosmopolitanism and Forgiveness.* London: Routledge.

DESCO
1989   *Violencia Política en el Perú, 1980–1989.* 2 vols. Lima: DESCO.

de Soto, Hernando
1989   *The Other Path: The Invisible Revolution in the Third World.* New York: Harper and Row.

Desrosieres, Alain
1990   How to Make Things Which Hold Together: Social Science, Statistics and the State. In *Discourses on Society,* vol. 15, edited by P. Wagner, B. Wittrock, and R. Whitley, pp. 200–21. Boston: Kluwer Academic Publishers.

Dhareshwar, Vivek

1995a   Our Time: History, Sovereignty, Politics. *Economic and Political Weekly* 30(6):317–24.

1995b   The Postcolonial in the Postmodern: Or, the Political after Modernity. *Economic and Political Weekly* 30(30):104–12.

Diallo, M.

1991   Qui gouverne le Cameroun? *Jeune Afrique* 1595 (July 24–30):18.

Dirks, Nicholas

2001   *Castes of Mind: Colonialism and the Making of Modern India.* Princeton, NJ: Princeton University Press.

Dirlik, Arif

2000   *Postmodernity's Histories: The Past as Legacy and Project.* Lanham, MD: Rowman and Littlefield.

Dorce, F.

1996   Cameroun: cette guerre qui cache son nom. *Jeune Afrique économie* 229 (November 18):54–56.

Douglas, Mary, ed.

1970   Introduction: Thirty Years after Witchcraft, Oracles and Magic. In *Witchcraft Confessions and Accusations,* pp. xiii–xxxviii. London: Tavistock.

DP. *See* **Defensoria del Pueblo.**

Driscoll, Mark

2000   Erotic Empire, Grotesque Empire. Ph.D. diss., Cornell University, Ithaca, NY.

Dumézil, Georges

1956   *Aspects de la function guerriere chez les Indo-Europeans.* Paris: Presses Universitaires de France.

Dunn, John

1984   *Locke.* New York: Oxford University Press.

1995   *Contemporary Crisis of the Nation State?* Oxford: Blackwell Publishers.

Dworkin, Ronald

1978   Liberalism. In *Public and Private Morality,* edited by H. Stuart. Cambridge: Cambridge University Press.

Engels, Friedrich

[1884]   *The Origin of the Family, Private Property and the State.* New York: Pathfinders
1972   Press.

Evans-Pritchard, E. E.

1937   *Witchcraft Oracles and Magic among the Azande.* Oxford: Clarendon Press.

1940   *The Nuer: A Description of the Modes of Livelihood and Political Institutions of a Nilotic People.* Oxford: Clarendon Press.

Faes, G.

1997   Le dernier maqui. *L'Autre Afrique* 1 (May 21–27):64–69.

Fanthorpe, Richard

2001   Neither Citizen nor Subject? "Lumpen" Agency and the Legacy of Native Administration in Sierra Leone. *African Affairs* 100:363–86.

Fardon, Richard, James Ferguson, F. Nyamnjoh, and Janet Roitman

2001   Autour d'un livre. *Politique Africaine* 81(March):177–95.

Farmer, Paul

1992   *AIDS and Accusation: Haiti and the Geography of Blame.* Los Angeles: University of California Press.

Farrand, Dorothy

1988   *Idliso: A Phenomenological and Psychiatric Comparison.* Johannesburg: University of Witwatersrand.

Federal Register

2003   Termination of the Designation of Sierra Leone under the Temporary Protected Status Program; Extension of Employment Authorization Documentation. http://a257.g.akamaitech.net/7/257/2422/ 14mar20010800/edocket.access.gpo.gov/2003/03-22488.htm.

Feldman, Alan

1991   *Formations of Violence. The Narrative of the Body and Political Terror in Northern Ireland.* Chicago: University of Chicago Press.

Ferguson, James

1994   *The Anti-Politics Machine: "Development," Depoliticization, and Bureaucratic Power in Lesotho.* Minneapolis: University of Minnesota Press.

1999   *Expectations of Modernity: Myths and Meanings of Urban Life on the Zambian Copperbelt.* Berkeley: University of California Press.

Ferguson, James, and Akhil Gupta

2002   Spatializing States: Toward an Ethnography of Neoliberal Governmentality. *American Ethnologist* 29(4):981–1002.

Ferme, Mariane C.

1998   The Violence of Numbers: Consensus, Competition and the Negotiation of Disputes in Sierra Leone. *Cahiers d'Études Africaines* 150–152:555–80.

2001   *The Underneath of Things: Violence, History and the Everyday in Sierra Leone.* Berkeley: University of California Press.

Ferme, Mariane, and Danny Hoffman

2002   Combattants irréguliers et discours international des droits de l'homme dans les guerres civiles africaines. Le cas des «chasseurs» sierra-léonais. *Politique Africaine* 88:27–48.

Figueroa Ibarra, Carlos

1991   *El Recurso del Miedo: Ensayo Sobre el Estado y el Terror en Guatemala.* San Jose, Costa Rica: Editorial Universitaria Centroamericana.

Filmer, Robert

1949   *Patriarcha and Other Political Writings,* edited by P. Laslett. Oxford: Blackwell.

Fischer, Edward F., and R. McKenna Brown, eds.

1996   *Maya Cultural Activism in Guatemala.* Austin: University of Texas Press.

Fitzpatrick, Peter

1988   The Rise and Rise of Informalism. In *Informal Justice?* edited by R. Matthews, pp.178–211. London: Sage Publications.

2001   Bare Sovereignty: Homo Sacer and the Insistence of Law. *Theory and Event* 5(2):67–81.

Foucault, Michel

1970   *The Order of Things.* New York: Vintage.

1976   *The History of Sexuality. Volume 1: An Introduction,* translated by R. Hurley. New York: Random House.

[1978]   *The History of Sexuality. Volume 1: An Introduction.* New York: Vintage Books.
1990

1979   Governmentality. *Ideology and Consciousness* 6:5–21.

1980   *Power/Knowledge: Selected Interviews and Other Writings 1972–1977,* edited by C. Gordon. New York: Routledge.

1991   Governmentality. In *The Foucault Effect: Studies in Governmentality,* edited by G. Burchell, C. Gordon, and P. Miller, translation by R. Braidotti, revised translation by C. Gordon, pp. 87–104. London: Harvester Wheatsheaf.

1994   The Punitive Society. In *Michel Foucault: Ethics, Subjectivity, and Truth, the Essential Works of Foucault 1954–1984,* vol. 1, edited by P. Rabinow, pp. 22–37. New York: New Press.

1997   *Ethics: Subjectivity and Truth,* edited by P. Rabinow. New York: New Press.

2003   *Society Must Be Defended: Lectures at the College de France, 1975–1976,* translated by D. Macey. New York: Picador.

Fried, Morton

1967   *The Evolution of Political Society.* New York: Random House.

Friedman, M.

1993   Kalachnikov: trente années de rafales. *Jeune Afrique 1701–1702* (August 12–25):98–101.

Fuller, Christopher J., and John Harris

2000   For an Anthropology of the Modern Indian State. In *The Everyday State and Society in Modern India,* edited by C. J. Fuller and V. Bénéï, pp. 1–31. New Delhi: Social Science Press.

Fuss, Diana

1995   *Identification Papers.* New York: Routledge.

Fyfe, Christopher

1962   *A History of Sierra Leone.* Oxford: Oxford University Press.

Galy, Michel

1998   Liberia, machine perverse. Anthropologie politique du conflit libérien. *Cahiers d'Études Africaines* 150–152(2–4):533–53.

Gamarra, Jefrey

2000   Conflict, Post-Conflict and Religion: Andean Responses to New Religious Movements. *Journal of Southern African Studies* 26(2):271–86.

Garciá, Clara Inéz

1996   *Uraba-region, Actores y Conflicto, 1960–1990.* Bogotá: CEREC.

García Sayan, Diego

1987   Perú: Estados de Excepción y su Estado Jurídico. In *Comisión Andina de Juristas, Estados de Emergencia en la Región Andina,* pp. 93–126. Lima: Comisión Andina de Juristas.

1996   Reforma Judicial: El Beneficio de la Duda. *Debate* (September–October):16–17.

Gcabashe, Lindelihle

2000   The Involvement of Traditional Healers in TB and HIV Efforts in South Africa. AF-AIDS. http://www.hivnet.ch:8000/africa/af-aids/viewR?666.

Geertz, Clifford

1980   *Negara: The Theater State of Nineteenth Century Bali.* Princeton, NJ: Princeton University Press.

Geschiere, Peter

1997   *The Modernity of Witchcraft: Politics and the Occult in Postcolonial Africa.* Charlottesville: University of Virginia Press.

Geshekter, Charles

1999   A Critical Reappraisal of African AIDS Research and Western Sexual Stereotypes. Rethinking AIDS Homepage. http://www.virusmyth.com/aids/data/cgstereotypes.htm.

Gilman, Sander

1985   Black Bodies, White Bodies: Toward an Iconography of Female Sexuality in Late Nineteenth-Century Art, Medicine, and Literature. In *Race, Writing, and Difference,* edited by H. L. Gates Jr., pp. 204–38. Chicago: University of Chicago Press.

Gilroy, Paul

1993   *The Black Atlantic: Modernity and Double Consciousness.* Cambridge, MA: Harvard University Press.

Gledhill, John

1994   *Power and Its Disguises: Anthropological Perspectives on Politics.* London: Pluto Press.

Gluckman, Max

1963   *Order and Rebellion in Tribal Africa.* London: Cohen and West.

1965   *The Ideas of Barotse Jurisprudence.* New Haven, CT: Yale University Press.

Godelier, Maurice, and Marilyn Strathern, eds.

1991   *Big Men and Great Men: Personifications of Power in Melanesia.* Cambridge: Cambridge University Press.

González, Matilde

2002   *Se Cambió el Tiempo: Conflicto y Poder en Territorio K'iche' 1880–1996.* Guatemala City: AVANCSO.

González Ponciano, Jorge Ramon

1999   Esas Sangres No Están Limpias: Modernidad y Pensamiento Civilizatorio en Guatemala. In *Racismo en Guatemala? Abriendo el Debate sobre un Tema Tabú,* edited by C. A. Bianchi, C. R. Hale, and G. Palma Murga, pp. 15–46. Guatemala City: AVANCSO.

Gootenberg, Paul

1989   *Between Silver and Guano: Commercial Policy and the State in Post-Independence Peru.* Princeton, NJ: Princeton University Press.

Government of Sri Lanka

[1972]   A Reprint of the Registration of Persons Act, No. 32 of 1968, as Amended
1998   by Acts Nos. 28 of 1971 and 37 of 1971. Colombo: Government Printer.

Gow, David, and Joanne Rappaport

2002   The Indigenous Public Voice: The Multiple Idioms of Modernity in Native Cauca. In *Indigenous Movements, Self-Representation and the State in Latin America,* edited by K. Warren and J. Jackson, pp. 47–80. Austin: University of Texas Press.

Gramsci, Antonio

1989   *Selections from the Prison Notebooks,* edited and translated by Q. Hoare and G. Nowell Smith. New York: International Publishers.

Grandin, Greg

2000   *The Blood of Guatemala: A History of Race and Nation.* Durham, NC: Duke University Press.

Green, Linda

1999   *Fear as a Way of Life: Mayan Widows in Rural Guatemala.* New York: Columbia University Press.

Grégoire, Emmanuel

1998   Sahara nigérien: terre d'échanges. *Autrepart* 6:91–104.

Grundlingh, Louis

2001   A Critical Historical Analysis of Government Responses to HIV/AIDS in South Africa as Reported in the Media, 1983–1994. Paper presented to the AIDS in Context Conference, University of the Witwatersrand, Johannesburg.

Guha, Ranajit

1983   *Elementary Aspects of Peasant Insurgency in Colonial India.* Delhi: Oxford University Press.

Gupta, Akhil

1995   Blurred Boundaries: The Discourse of Corruption, the Culture of Politics, and the Imagined State. *American Ethnologist* 22(2):373–402.

1998   *Postcolonial Developments: Agriculture in the Making of Modern India.* Durham, NC: Duke University Press.

Hagen, Jason

2003   Uribe's People: Civilizations and the Colombian Conflict. *Georgetown Journal of International Affairs* 4(1):65–71.

Hale, Charles R.

1997   Consciousness, Violence, and the Politics of Memory in Guatemala. *Current Anthropology* 38(5):817–38.

Hansen, Thomas Blom

1999   *The Saffron Wave: Democracy and Hindu Nationalism in Modern India.* Princeton, NJ: Princeton University Press.

2001   *Wages of Violence: Naming and Identity in Postcolonial Bombay.* Princeton, NJ: Princeton University Press.

Hansen, Thomas, and Finn Stepputat, eds.

2001   *States of Imagination: Ethnographic Explorations of the Postcolonial State.* Durham, NC: Duke University Press.

Harding, J.

1996   The Mercenary Business. *London Review of Books* (August 1):3–9.

Hardt, Michael, and Antonio Negri

2000   *Empire.* Cambridge, MA: Harvard University Press.

Harnischfeger, Johannes

2000   Witchcraft and the State in South Africa. *Anthropos* 95:99–112.

Harrington, C. B.

1985   *Shadow Justice? The Ideology and Institutionalization of Alternatives to Court.* London: Greenwood Press.

Hegel, George Wilhelm Friedrich

[1807]   *Phenomenology of Spirit.* Oxford: Oxford University Press.
1977

[1821]   *Elements of the Philosophy of Right,* edited by A. W. Wood, translated
1991   by H. B. Nisbett. Cambridge: Cambridge University Press.

Henry, Doug

2000   Embodied Violence: War and Relief Along the Sierra Leone Border. Ph.D. diss., Southern Methodist University, Dallas.

Herzfeld, Michael

2001   *Anthropology: Theoretical Practice in Culture and Society.* Oxford: Blackwell Publishers.

Heyman, Josiah McC., ed.

1999   *States and Illegal Practices.* Oxford: Berg.

Hibou, Béatrice

1996   *L'Afrique, est-elle protectionniste?* Paris: Karthala.

1997   Le 'capital social' de l'État falsificateur, ou les ruses de l'intelligence économique. In *La criminalization de l'État en Afrique,* edited by J.Bayart, S. Ellis, and B. Hibou, pp. 105–58. Paris: Éditions Complexes.

2002   The Privatization of the State in North Africa. Paper presented at New York University.

Hibou, Béatrice, ed.

1999   *La Privatisation des états.* Paris: Karthala.

Hill, Michele B., and Greg Black

2002   The Killing and Burning of Witches in South Africa: A Model Community Rebuilding and Reconciliation. In *Culturally Responsive Interventions: Innovative Approaches to Working with Diverse Populations,* edited by J. Ancis. New York: Brunner Routledge.

Hindu

1998   Mafia, Middlemen Nexus in DDA. September 30.

2000   Failure to Curb Abkari-Official Nexus. November 8.

2003   HC Upholds Invalidation of Eunuch's Election. February 4.

Hindustan Times

2001   Will Eunuchs Rule Kaliyug? January 15.

Hobbes, Thomas

[1651]   *Leviathan.* London: Penguin Classics.
 1968

hooks, bell

1984   *Feminist Theory: From Margin to Center.* Boston: South End Press.

Hope, Stanley

1997   *The Degrading of Human Dignity. A Short History of British Immigration Acts 1962–1996.* Iona, Scotland: Wild Goose Publications.

HRW. *See* **Human Rights Watch.**

Hulme, Peter

[1986]   *Colonial Encounters: Europe and the Native Caribbean 1492–1797.* London:
 1992   Routledge.

Human Rights Watch (HRW)

1996a   *Colombia's Killer Networks: The Military-Paramilitary Partnership and the United States.* New York: HRW.

1996b   *Trafficking in Women to Italy for Sexual Exploitation*. Washington, DC: International Organization on Migration.

1998a   *Columbia Report 1998*. New York: HRW.

1998b   *War without Quarter: Colombia and International Humanitarian Law*. New York: HRW.

2000   *Colombia: The Ties That Bind: Colombia and Military-Paramilitary Links*. New York: HRW.

Humphrey, Caroline

2003   Stalin and the Blue Elephant: Paranoia and Complicity in Post-Community Metahistories. In *Transparency and Conspiracy: Ethnographies of Suspicion in the New World Order*, edited by T. Sanders and H. West, pp. 175–202. Durham, NC: Duke University Press.

Hutchinson, Sharon Elaine

1996   *Nuer Dilemmas: Coping with Money, War, and the State*. Berkeley: University of California Press.

IDL. *See* **Instituto de Defensa Legal.**

Inden, Ronald

1990   *Imagining India*. Cambridge: Basil Blackwell.

Instituto de Defensa Legal (IDL)

1999   *Justicia de Paz: El Otro Poder Judicial*. Lima: IDL and Unión Europea.

2000   *Justicia de Paz: Propuesta de Ley*. Lima: Comisión Europea and IDL.

n.d.   *Manual para jueces de paz*. Lima: IDL.

Inter-American Commission on Human Rights of 1999

1999   *Country Report: Columbia*. San José, Costa Rica: Organization of American States.

Inter-American Development Bank

1997   *Peru: Improving Access to the Justice System*. Washington, DC: Inter-American Development Bank.

IPAZ

1998   *Proyecto Acceso a la Defensa, Protección, Documentación y Titularidad de las Poblaciones Desplazadas por la Violencia de las Provincias de Huanta y Vilcashuaman*. Ayacucho: Prodev and Par-Union Europea and IPAZ.

n.d.   *Sistematización de la Experiencia de los Núcleos Rurales de Administración de Justicia*. Ayacucho: IPAZ.

Jeganathan, Pradeep

1994   The Task of Theory. In *An Introduction to Social Theory*, edited by R. Coomaraswamy and N. Wickremasinghe, pp. 7–22. Delhi: Konark Press.

Joint United Nations Programme on HIV/AIDS

1999   AIDS Epidemic Update: December 1999. http://www.unaids.org/hivaidsinfo/documents.html#wad.

Jonas, Susanne

2000   *Of Centaurs and Doves: Guatemala's Peace Process.* Boulder, CO: Westview Press.

Jordan, Bobby

2000   AIDS Deaths Rocketing in Johannesburg. *Sunday Times* (Johannesburg). May 28. http://www.suntimes.co.za/2000/05/28/news/gauteng/ njhb03.htm.

Kadetsky, Elizabeth

1994   Guatemala Inflamed: Accused of Stealing or Murdering Babies, American Women Are Attacked by Hysterical Mobs. *Village Voice.* May 31.

Kant, Immanuel

[1797]   *The Metaphysical Elements of Justice,* translated by J. Ladd. Indianapolis:
1965   Bobbs-Merrill.

Kantorowicz, Ernst H.

[1957]   *The King's Two Bodies: A Study in Mediaeval Political Theology.* Princeton, NJ:
1981   Princeton University Press.

Kaplan, R.

1994   The Coming Anarchy. *Atlantic Monthly* (February 2):44–76.

Katznelson, Ira.

1994   A Properly Defended Liberalism: On John Gray and the Filling of Political Life. *Social Research* 61(3):611–30.

Kaviraj, Sudipta

1988   A Critique of the Passive Revolution. *Economic and Political Weekly* 23(45–47):2429–44.

Kelman, Mark

1994   Reasonable Evidence of Reasonableness. In *Questions of Evidence: Proof, Practice, and Persuasion across Disciplines,* edited by J. Chandler, A. Davidson, and H. D. Harootunian, pp. 169–88. Chicago: University of Chicago Press.

Khan, M. Ali

2002   On Trust as a Commodity and on the Grammar of Trust. *Journal of Banking and Finance* 26(9):1719–66.

Kindra, Jaspreen

2001   "I Need to Keep People Fighting": Former KZN "Warlord" Thomas Shabalala's Tryst with Tragedy Is Helping Break the Stigma Attached to AIDS. *Mail and Guardian* (Johannesburg). March 30.

Kohli, Atul

1990   *Democracy and Discontent. India's Growing Crisis of Governability.* Cambridge: Cambridge University Press.

Kom, A.

1993   Trahison d'une intelligentsia. *Jeune Afrique Economique* 165(March):166.

Larson, Brooke

1988   *Colonialism and Agrarian Transformation in Bolivia, Cochabamba 1550–1900.* Princeton, NJ: Princeton University Press.

L'Autre Afrique

1997   Un billet de banque, ça peut couter cher. August 13–19.

Le Figaro

1997   Afrique: le nouvel empire des mercenaries. January 15.

Le Progres

1997   Armée: lumiére sur las démobilization et la réinsertion. May 13. N'Djamena, Chad.

Lock, Margaret

2002   *Twice Dead: Organ Transplants and the Reinvention of Death.* Berkeley: University of California Press.

Locke, John

[1690]   *Two Treatises of Government,* edited by P. Laslett. Cambridge: Cambridge

1988   University Press.

Lomnitz, Claudio, ed.

2000   Introducción. In *Vicios Públicos, Virtudes Privadas: La Corrupción en México,* pp. 11–30. México City: CIESAS.

Loucky, James, and Marilyn M. Moors, eds.

2000   *The Maya Diaspora: Guatemalan Roots, New American Lives.* Philadelphia: Temple University Press.

Loveman, Brian

1993   *The Constitution of Tyranny: Regimes of Exception in Spanish America.* Pittsburgh: University of Pittsburgh Press.

Maine, Sir Henry Sumner

[1866]   *Ancient Law.* New Brunswick, NJ: Transaction Press.

2002

Malkki, Liisa

1995   *Purity and Exile: Violence, Memory, and National Cosmology among Hutu Refugees in Tanzania.* Chicago: University of Chicago Press.

Mamdani, Mahmood

1996   *Citizen and Subject: Contemporary Africa and the Legacy of Late Colonialism.* Princeton, NJ: Princeton University Press.

Manrique, Nelson

1988   *Yawar Mayu: Sociedades Terratenientes Serranas, 1879–1910.* Lima: Instituto Francés de Estudios Andinos and DESCO.

1989   La Década de la Violencia. *Márgenes* 3(5–6):137–82.

Mariátegui, José Carlos

1925   El Proceso del Gamonalismo. *Amauta* 25 (July–August): 69–80.

Martin, Emily

1994   *Flexible Bodies: Tracking Immunity in American Culture from the Days of Polio to the Age of AIDS*. Boston: Beacon Press.

Marx, Karl

[1867]   *Capital*, vol. I. Moscow: Foreign Languages Publishing House.
1961

Maschino, Maurice T.

2002   Are You Sure You Are French? *Guardian Weekly*. June.

Maurer, Bill

1997   *Recharting the Caribbean: Land, Law and Citizenship in the British Virgin Islands*. Ann Arbor: University of Michigan Press.

Mavhungu, Khaukanani

2000   Heroes, Villains, and the State in South Africa's Witchcraft Zone. *African Anthropologist* 7(1):114–29.

Mbembe, Achille

1992   Provisional Notes on the Postcolony. *Africa* 62(1):3–37.

1993   Épilogue: Crise de légitimité, restauration autoritarie et déliquescence de l'État. In *Itinéraries d'accumulation au Cameroun*, edited by P. Geschiere and P. Konings, pp. 343–74. Paris: ASC and Karthala.

2000   At the Edge of the World: Boundaries, Territoriality, and Sovereignty in Africa. *Public Culture* 12(1):259–84.

2001   *On the Postcolony*. Berkeley: University of California Press.

Mbembe, Achille, and Janet Roitman

1995   Figures of the Subject in Times of Crisis. *Public Culture* 7(2):323–52.

McAllister, Carlota

2002   Good People: Revolution, Community and *Conciencia* in a Maya-K'iche' Village in Guatemala. Ph.D. diss., Johns Hopkins University, Columbia, Md.

McClure, K. M.

1990   Difference, Diversity, and the Limits of Toleration. *Political Theory* 18(3):361–91.

McKie, Robin, and David Beresford

2000   Africa's AIDS Fate Hangs in the Balance. *Daily Mail and Guardian*. May 8. http://www.mg.co.za/mg/news/2000may1/8may-aids.html.

Mehta, Vinod

1978   *The Sanjay Story*. Bombay: Jaico Publications.

Meillassoux, Claude

[1975]   *Maidens, Meals and Money*. New York: Cambridge University Press.
1981

Mendus, Susan

1989   *Toleration and the Limits of Liberalism*. Atlantic Highlands, NJ: Humanities Press International.

Messick, Brinkley

1993   *The Calligraphic State: Textual Domination and History in a Muslim Society.*
        Berkeley: University of California Press.

Migdal, Joel

1988   *Strong Societies and Weak States: State-Society Relations and State Capabilities in
        the Third World.* Princeton, NJ: Princeton University Press.

Minaar, Anthony, Marie Wentzel, and Catherine Payze

1998   Witch Killing with Specific Reference to the Northern Province of South
        Africa. In *Violence in South Africa: A Variety of Perspectives,* edited by
        E. Bornman, F. van Heerden, and M. Wentzel, pp. 175–99. Pretoria:
        Human Sciences Research Council.

Ministerio de Justicia del Perú

1994   *Foro: Nuevas Perspectivas para la Reforma Integral de la Administración de
        Justicia en el Perú.* Lima: Ministerio de Justicia.

2000   *Guía de Consulta del Juez de Paz.* Lima: Secretaría Ejecutiva del Poder
        Judicial.

Misra, Kavita

2000   Productivity of Crisis: Disease, Scientific Knowledge and the State in India.
        Economic and Political Weekly 35(43–44):385–97.

Mitchell, Timothy

1988   *Colonising Egypt.* Cambridge: Cambridge University Press.

Mitchell, Timothy, ed.

1999   Society, Economy, and the State Effect. In *State/Culture: State-Formation after
        the Cultural Turn,* edited by G. Steinmetz, pp. 76–79. Ithaca, NY: Cornell
        University Press.

2000   *Questions of Modernity.* Minneapolis: University of Minnesota Press.

Monga, Célestine

1993   Les derniéres cartes de Paul Biya. *Jeune Afrique Economique*
        165(March):166.

1996   *The Anthropology of Anger: Civil Society and Democracy in Africa,* translated by
        L. L. Fleck. London and Boulder, CO: Lynne Rienner Publishers.

Montesquieu, Charles-Louis

[1748]   *The Spirit of Laws,* edited by David Wallace Carrithers. Berkeley: University
 1977   of California Press.

Moore, Henrietta, and Todd Sanders

2001   *Magical Interpretations; Material Realities.* London: Routledge.

Moran, Mary, and Anne Pitcher

2003   Women and the Negotiation of Peace and Reconstruction in Liberia and
        Mozambique. Paper presented at the annual meetings of the Association
        of American Geographers, New Orleans.

Morgan, Lewis Henry

1877   *Ancient Society.* New York: H. Holt.

Mukerjee, Sutapa
2001   Flamboyant Indian Eunuch Takes on Chief Minister in State Polls. *Agence France Presse.* April 6.

Mukwaya, A. Kabweru
1997   The Political Economy of the Asian Question in Uganda's Relations with Britain, 1895–1972. *Makerere Papers in Social Research* 1(1):110–34.

Nader, Laura, ed.
1969   *Law in Culture and Society.* Chicago: Aldine Press.

National Immigration Law Center (NILC)
2002   AG Extends TPS for Nationals of Sierra Leone. http://www.nilc.org/ immlawpolicy/asylrefs/ar102.htm.

National Institute of Allergy and Infectious Diseases
2000   *The Relationship between the Human Immunodeficiency Virus and the Acquired Immunodeficiency Syndrome.* Bethesda, MD: Office of Communications and Public Liaison, National Institute of Allergy and Infectious Diseases, National Institutes of Health.

N'Djamena Hebdo
1997   Lorsque démobilization rime avec développement. *N'Dajmena Hebdo* 281(May 15):6–7.

Nel, C. J., T. Verschoor, F. J. W. Calitz, and P. H. J. J. van Rensburg
1992   The Importance of an Anthropological Perspective in Relevant Trials of Apparently Motiveless Murders. *South African Journal of Ethnology* 15(3):85–92.

Nelson, Diane M.
1988   *Guatemala Polos de Desarrollo: El Caso de la Desestructuración de las Comunidades Indígenas,* vol. 2. Mexico City: CEIDEC.

1999   *A Finger in the Wound: Body Politics in Quincentennial Guatemala.* Berkeley: University of California Press.

2003   "The More You Kill the More You Will Live": The Maya, "Race," and the Biopolitical Economy of Peace in Guatemala. In *Race, Nature, and the Politics of Difference,* edited by D. Moore, J. Kosek, and A. Pandian, pp. 122–46. Durham, NC: Duke University Press.

New York Times
1991   Strike Aims to Bleed Cameroon's Economy to Force President Biya's Fall. August 5.

Ngarngoune, S.
1997   Alerte au Sud. *N'djamena Hebdo* 280(May 8):4.

Niehaus, Isak A.
1997   *Witchcraft, Power, and Politics: An Ethnographic Study of the South African Lowveld.* Johannesburg: Department of Social Anthropology, University of the Witwatersrand.

NILC *See* **National Imigration Law Center**

Nordstrom, Caroline

2001   Out of the Shadows. In *Intervention and Transnationalism in Africa: Global-Local Networks of Power,* edited by T. Callaghy, R. Kassimir, and R. Latham, pp. 216–39. Cambridge: Cambridge University Press.

Nordstrom, Caroline, ed.

1995   *Fieldwork under Fire.* Berkeley: University of California Press.

O'Donnell, Guillermo

1999   Polyarchies and the (Un)Rule of Law in Latin America: A Partial Conclusion. In *The (Un)Rule of Law and the Underprivileged in Latin America,* edited by J. Méndez, G. O'Donnell, and P. Sérgio Pinheiro, pp. 303–37. Notre Dame, IN: University of Notre Dame Press.

Oglesby, Elizabeth

2001   Politics at Work: Elites, Labor and Agrarian Modernization in Guatemala, 1980–2000. Ph.D. diss., University of California, Berkeley.

Ong, Aihwa

1999a   Clash of Civilization or Asian Liberalism? An Anthropology of the State and Citizenship. In *Anthropological Theory Today,* edited by H. Moore, pp. 48–72. Cambridge: Polity Press.

1999b   *Flexible Citizenship: The Cultural Logic of Transnationality.* Durham, NC: Duke University Press.

Oosthuizen, Gerhardus C.

1992   *The Healer-Prophet in Afro-Christian Churches.* Leiden: E. J. Brill.

O'Phelan Godoy, Scarlett, ed.

2001   *La Independencia del Perú: De los Borbones a Bolívar.* Lima: Universidad Católica and Instituto Riva-Agüero.

Ortiz de Cevallos, Gabriel

1999   Reforma Judicial: La Administración de la Justicia. *Debate* (September–October):18–21.

Own Correspondents

2001a   AIDS "Far Deadlier Than Apartheid." *Daily Mail and Guardian* (Johannesburg), March 22. http://www.mg.co.za/za/archive/2001mar/22maram-news.html.

2001b   AIDS Cure Ploughed up as a Weed. *Weekly Mail and Guardian* (Johannesburg), March 15. http://archive.mg.co.za/nxt/gateway.dll/DailyNews/MGO2001/3lv03128/4lv03324/.

Pandey, Gyanendra

1990   *The Construction of Communalism in Colonial North India.* Delhi: Oxford University Press.

Pantham, Thomas

2003   The Indian Nation-State: From Precolonial Beginnings to Post-Colonial Reconstructions. In *The Oxford India Companion to Sociology and Social Anthropology,* edited by V. Das, pp. 1413–46. Delhi: Oxford University Press.

Pásara, Luís

1979   La Justicia de Paz. *Derecho y Sociedad* (1979):219–31.

1982   El Campesinado Frente a la Legalidad. *Derecho y Sociedad* (1982):73–112. Lima, Peru.

1988   *Derecho y Sociedad en e Perú.* Lima: Ediciones El Virrey.

Patwardhan, Anand, dir.

1994   *Father, Son, and Holy War.* New York: First Run/Icarus Films.

Peña Jumpa, Antonio

1998   *Justicia Communal en los Andes del Peru: El Caso de Calahuyo.* Lima: Universidad Católica.

People's Union of Democratic Rights, and People's Union of Civil Liberties (PUDR/PUCL)

1984   *Who Are the Guilty? Report of a Joint Inquiry into the Causes and Impact of the Riots in Delhi from 31 October to 10 November.* Delhi: PUDR and PUCL.

Perrot, Jean Claude, and Stuart J. Woolf

1984   *State and Statistics in France, 1789–1815.* New York: Harwood Academic Publishers.

Petryna, Adriana

2002   *Life Exposed: Biological Citizens after Chernobyl.* Princeton, NJ: Princeton University Press.

Pideu, K.

1995   Une province abandonee auz coupeurs de route. *La Nouvelle Expresión* 243(March 28–31):6.

Planas, Pedro

1998   *La Descentralización en el Perú Repubicano (1821–1998).* Lima: Municipalidad Metropolitana de Lima.

Poole, Deborah

1988   Landscapes of Power in a Cattle-Rustling Culture of Southern Andean Peru. *Dialectical Anthropology* 12:367–98.

1994   Performance, Domination, and Identity in the Tierras Bravas of Chumbivilcas. In *Unruly Order: Violence, Power and Cultural Identity in the High Provinces of Southern Peru,* pp. 97–132. Boulder: Westview.

Poole, Deborah, ed.

1994   *Unruly Order: Violence, Power and Cultural Identity in the High Provinces of Southern Peru.* Boulder: Westview.

Poole, Deborah, and Gerardo Rénique

1992   *Peru: Time of Fear.* London: Latin America Bureau.

Prasad, M. Madhava

1998   *Ideology of the Hindi Film: A Historical Construction.* Delhi: Oxford University Press.

PUDR/PUCL. *See* **People's Union of Democratic Rights, and People's Union of Civil Liberties.**

Rabinow, Paul

1989   *French Modern: Norms and Forms of the Social Environment.* Chicago: University of Chicago Press.

1999   *French DNA.* Chicago: University of Chicago Press.

2002   Midst Anthropology's Problems. *Cultural Anthropology* 17(2):135–49.

Radcliffe-Richards, Janet

1998   A Dangerous Superstition. *Clinical Transplants* (1998):345–47.

Radcliffe-Richards, Janet, Abdullah S. Daar, Ronald D. Guttmann, Raymond Hoffenberg, Ian Kennedy, Margaret Lock, Robert A. Sells, and Nicholas L. Tilney

1988   The Case for Allowing Kidney Sales. *Lancet* 351(9120):1950–52.

Ram, Kalpana

1998   *Na Shariram Nadhi,* My Body Is Mine: The Urban Women's Health Movement in India and Its Negotiation of Modernity. *Women's Studies International Forum* 21(6):617.

Rao, Aparna, and Michael J. Casimir

2002   Movements of Peoples: Nomads in India. In *The Oxford India Companion to Sociology and Social Anthropology,* edited by V. Das, pp. 219–62. Delhi: Oxford University Press.

Reddy, Sita

2002   *Temporarily Insane: Pathologising Cultural Difference in American Criminal Courts.* Sociology of Health and Illness Monograph 8. Philadelphia: Center for Bioethics, University of Pennsylvania.

Remijnse, Simone

2002   *Memories of Violence: Civil Patrols and the Legacy of Conflict in Joyabaj, Guatemala.* Amsterdam: Rozenberg Publishers.

Reno, William

1995   Corruption and State Politics in Sierra Leone. Cambridge: Cambridge University Press.

1997a   African Weak States and Commercial Alliances. *African Affairs* 96(383):165–85.

1997b   War, Markets, and the Reconfiguration of West Africa's Weak States. *Comparative Politics* 29(4):493–510.

1998   Warlord Politics and African States. Boulder, CO: Lynne Rienner.

2001   How Sovereignty Matters: International Markets and the Political Economy of Local Politics in Weak States. In *Intervention and*

Transnationalism in Africa: Global-Local Networks of Power, edited by T. Callaghy, R. Kassimir, and R. Latham, pp. 197–215. Cambridge: Cambridge University Press.

Riles, Annelise

2000   *The Network Inside Out.* Ann Arbor: University of Michigan Press.

Rivadeneyra Sánchez, Juan

1991   Los Sistemas Informales de Administración de Justicia en el Perú. *Revista Vasca de Derecho Procesal y Arbitraje* 3(3):341–51.

Roitman, Janet

1990   The Politics of Informal Markets in Sub-Saharan Africa. *Journal of Modern African Studies* 28(4):671–96.

1998   The Garrison-Entrepôt. *Cahiers d'Études Africaines* 37(2–4):297–329.

2000   Économie morale, sujectivité et politique. *Critique internationale* 6 (Winter):48–56.

2003   Unsanctioned Wealth, or the Productivity of Debt in Northern Cameroon. *Public Culture* 15(2):211–37.

n.d.   *Incivisme Fiscale: An Anthropology of Economic Regulation and Fiscal Relations in the Chad Basin.* Princeton, NJ: Princeton University Press, in press.

Roldán, Mary

2002   *Mary, Blood, and Fire: La Violencia in Antioquia, 1946–1953.* Durham, NC: Duke University Press.

Rose, Jacqueline

1996   *States of Fantasy.* Oxford: Clarendon Press.

Rosenthal, Franz trans.

1969   *The Muquddimah: An Introduction to History,* by Ibn Khaldûn. Princeton, NJ: Princeton University Press.

Rousseau, J. J.

[1762]   *The Social Contract.* London: Penguin Books.
1981

Sanders, Todd, and Harry West, eds.

2002   *Transparency and Conspiracy: Ethnographies of Suspicion in the New World Order.* Durham, NC: Duke University Press.

Sanford, Victoria

2001   Peace Communities in Colombia and the Renegotiation of Displacement, Relief, and Anthropology. Paper presented at General Anthropology Division invited session "Anthropological Encounters with Humanitarian Relief," American Anthropological Association, Washington, DC.

2003   *Buried Secrets: Truth and Human Rights in Guatemala.* New York: Palgrave Macmillan.

Sassen, Saskia

1995   *Losing Control? Sovereignty in an Age of Globalization.* New York: Columbia University Press.

1998   *Globalization and Its Discontents: Selected Essays 1984–1998.* New York: New Press.

2000   *Cities in a World Economy.* Thousand Oaks, CA: Pine Forge Press.

Scheler, Max

1961   *Ressentiment,* translated by W. W. Holdheim. New York: Free Press.

Scheper-Hughes, Nancy

1996   Theft of Life: The Globalization of Organ Stealing Rumours. *Anthropology Today* 12(3):3–11.

2000   The Global Traffic in Human Organs. *Current Anthropology* 41(2):191–224.

Schirmer, Jennifer

1998   *The Guatemalan Military Project: A Violence Called Democracy.* Philadelphia: University of Pennsylvania Press.

Schmitt, Carl

[1922] *Political Theology: Four Chapters on the Concept of Sovereignty,* translated by
1985   George Schwab. Cambridge, MA: MIT Press.

Scott, David

1999   *Refashioning Futures: Criticism after Postcoloniality.* Princeton, NJ: Princeton University Press.

Scott, James C.

1985   *Weapons of the Weak: Everyday Forms of Peasant Resistance.* New Haven, CT: Yale University Press.

1998   *Seeing Like a State: How Certain Schemes to Improve the Human Condition Have Failed.* New Haven, CT: Yale University Press.

Select Committee on Social Services

1998   *Report of the Select Committee on Social Services on Traditional Healers.* No. 144-1998. Cape Town: Parliament of the Republic of South Africa. http://www.polity.org.za/govdocs/parliament/papers/ta/1998/ta1111.html.

Shah Commission

1978   *Shah Commission of Inquiry: Third and Final Report.* Delhi: Government of India Publications.

Singh, Sudhir K.

2000   Politicians Wake Up to Voters' Ire as Eunuchs Romp Home. *Times of India.* February 29.

Skinner, Quentin

1978   *The Foundations of Modern Political Thought.* Cambridge: Cambridge University Press.

Sluka, Jeffrey A.

2000   *Death Squads: The Anthropology of State Terror.* Philadelphia: University of Pennsylvania Press.

Smith, Carol, ed.

1990   *Guatemalan Indians and the State: 1540 to 1988.* Austin: University of Texas.

Smith, Gavin

1999   Overlapping Collectivities: Local Concern, State Welfare and Social Membership. In *Confronting the Present: Towards a Politically Engaged Anthropology,* pp. 195–227. Oxford: Berg.

Smith, Richard S.

1996   *Rule by Records: Land Registration and Billage Custom in Early British Punjab.* Delhi: Oxford University Press.

Socpa, A.

2002   Democratisation et autochtonie au Cameroun. Ph.D. diss., University of Leiden.

Soudan, F.

1996   La guerre secréte. *Jeune Afrique 1871*(November):13–19.

South Africa

2000   *HIV/AIDS/STD Strategic Plan for South Africa.* Pretoria: Government of South Africa. http://www.gov.za/documents/2000/aidsplan2000.pdf.

South Africa Department of Health

1997   *White Paper for the Transformation of the Health System in South Africa.* Pretoria: South Africa Department of Health. http://www.polity.org.za/govdocs/white_papers/health.html.

South Africa Public Protector

1995   *Report in Terms of Section 8(2) of the Public Protector Act 23 of 1994: Report No 1(Special Report) Investigation of the Play* Sarafina II. Cape Town: House of Assembly. http://www.polity.org.za/govt/pubprot/report1b.html.

South African Press Association

2000

Spivak, Gayatri

1988   *In Other Worlds: Essays in Cultural Politics.* New York: Routledge.

Srikrishna, Justice B. N.

1998   *Report of the Srikrishna Commission Appointed for Inquiry into the Riots at Mumbai during December 1992 and January 1993.* Mumbai: Jyoti Punwani and Vrijendra.

Statesman

2000   Shabnam Mausi Learns the Rules of the Game, Blasts Politicians. March 6.

Stern, Steve

1983   The Struggle for Solidarity: Class, Culture and Community in Highland Indian America. *Radical History Review* 27:21–45.

Stern, Steve, ed.

1998   *Shining and Other Paths: War and Society in Peru, 1980–1995.* Durham, NC: Duke University Press.

Stoler, Ann

1995   *Race and the Education of Desire: Foucault's History of Sexuality and the Colonial Order of Things.* Durham, NC: Duke University Press.

Stuart, Graham H.

1925   *The Governmental System of Peru.* Washington, DC: Carnegie Institution.

Tarlo, Emma

2000   Body and Space in a Time of Crisis. In *Violence and Subjectivity,* edited by V. Das, A. Kleinman, M. Ramphele, and P. Reynolds, pp. 242–71. Berkeley: University of California Press.

Taussig, Michael

1996   The Injustice of Policing: Prehistory and Rectitude. In *Justice and Injustice in Law and Legal Theory,* edited by A. Sarat and T. Kearns, pp. 19–34. Ann Arbor: University of Michigan Press.

1997   *The Magic of the State.* New York: Routledge.

Tedlock, Barbara

1992   *Time and the Highland Maya.* Albuquerque: University of New Mexico Press.

Teiga, M. B.

1997   Une armée, certes, mais combine de divisions. *L'Autre Afrique* (December 17–23):14–15.

Thomas, Jeremy, Lehihi Masego, and Victor Khupiso

2001   The Grim Reaper. *Sunday Times* (Johannesburg). January 28. http://www.suntimes.co.za/2001/01/28/business/news/news01.htm.

Times of India

2000a   Vajpayee Is Like a Brother to Me: Shabnam Mausi. November 17.

2000b   Gorakhpur Ministers Hear the Clap Loud and Clear. November 27.

2000c   Great Experiment in Gorakhpur. November 27.

2000d   Eunuch to Run in Assembly Polls. December 18.

Torpey, John

2000   *The Invention of the Passport: Surveillance, Citizenship and the State.* Cambridge: Cambridge University Press.

Trouillot, Rolph

2001   The Anthropology of the State in the Age of Globalization: Close Encounters of the Deceptive Kind. *Current Anthropology* 42(1):126–38.

Tsing, Anna

1993   *In the Realm of the Diamond Queen: Marginality in an Out-of-the-Way Place.* Princeton, NJ: Princeton University Press.

UNAIDS

2000   *South Africa: Epidemiological Fact Sheet on HIV/AIDS and Sexually Transmitted Infections: 2000 Update.* Geneva: UNAIDS/WHO Working Group on Global HIV/AIDS and STI Surveillance. http://www.unaids.org/hivaidsinfo/ statistics/june00/fact_sheets/pdfs/southafrica.pdf.

UNAIDS and World Health Organization

1998   *Epidemiological Fact Sheet on HIV/AIDS and Sexually Transmitted Diseases: South Africa.* Geneva: UNAIDS and WHO. http://www.unaids.org/hivaidsinfo/ statistics/june98/fact_sheets/pdfs/southafrica.pdf.

USAID

1999   *Congressional Presentation for Peru, FY 2000.* Washington, DC: USAID.

Vallée, O.

1999   La dette privée est-elle publique? Traites, traitement, traite: modes de la dette africaine. *Politique Africaine* 73(March):50–67.

van de Walle, N.

1993   The Politics of Nonreform in Cameroon. In *Hemmed In: Responses to Africa's Economic Decline,* edited by T. Callaghy and J. Ravenhill, pp. 357–97. New York: Columbia University Press.

Van Hollen, Cecilia Coale

1998   Birthing on the Threshold: Childbirth and Modernity among Lower Class Women in Tamil Nadu, South India. Ph.D. diss., University of California, Berkeley.

Verryn, Trevor

1981   "Coolness" and "Heat" among the Sotho Peoples. *Religion in Southern Africa* 2:11–38.

Vincent, Joan

1990   *Anthropology and Politics: Visions, Traditions, and Trends.* Tucson: University of Arizona Press.

Volpp, Leti

1994   (Mis)Identifying Culture: Asian Women and the "Cultural Defense." *Harvard Women's Law Journal* 17:57–101.

Vries, Hent de

2002   *Religion and Violence: Philosophical Perspectives from Kant to Derrida.* Baltimore: Johns Hopkins University Press.

Walker, Charles F.

1999   *Smoldering Ashes: Cuzco and the Creation of Republican Peru, 1780–1840.* Durham, NC: Duke University Press.

Warren, Kay

1998   *Indigenous Movements and Their Critics: Pan-Maya Activism in Guatemala.* Princeton, NJ: Princeton University Press.

Watanabe, John M.
1992   *Maya Saints and Souls in a Changing World.* Austin: University of Texas Press.

Weber, Max
1978   *Economy and Society,* edited by G. Roth and C. Wittich. Berkeley: University of California Press.

Wilkinson, D., L. Gcabashe, and M. Lurie
1999   Traditional Healers as Tuberculosis Treatment Supervisors: Precedent and Potential. *International Journal of Tuberculosis and Lung Disorders* 3(9):838–42.

Willis, R. G.
1970   Instant Millennium: The Sociology of African Witch-Cleansing Cults. In *Witchcraft Confessions and Accusations,* edited by M. Douglas, pp. 129–39. London: Tavistock.

Wilson, Richard
1995   *Maya Resurgence in Guatemala: Q'eqchi' Experience.* Norman: University of Oklahoma Press.

Wolf, Eric
1982   *Europe and the People without History.* Berkeley: University of California Press.

Yamba, Bawa
1995   *Permanent Pilgrims: The Role of Pilgrimage in the Lives of West African Muslims in Sudan.* Washington, DC: Smithsonian Institution Press.

Zartman, I., ed.
1995   *Collapsed States. The Disintegration and Restoration of Legitimate Authority.* Boulder, CO: Lynne Rienner.

Zappi, Sylvia
2003   Zones d'Attente: La Police accusée de violences. *Le Monde.* March 15.

Žižek, Slavoc
1989   *The Sublime Object of Ideology.* London: Verso.
1992   *Enjoy Your Symptom! Jacques Lacan in Hollywood and Out.* New York: Routledge.

Zook, Darren Christopher
1998   Developing India: The History of an Idea in the Southern Countryside, 1860–1990. Ph.D. diss., University of California, Berkeley.

Zur, Judith
1998   *Violent Memories: Mayan War Widows in Guatemala.* Boulder, CO: Westview.

Index

Abstraction, and concept of state, 29–30, 281–83

Africa: and "economic of legitimacy crises," 208; and political theory of the state, 81–83, 193; privatization and state sovereignty in, 92–93; refugees and passage across borders, 109–10; state consolidation and reconfigurations of power in, 221; and use of term witchcraft, 162n6. *See also* Cameroon; Chad; Sierra Leone; South Africa

Agamben, Giorgio, 11–13, 15, 25, 30, 178, 190n3, 256, 257, 273

AIDS: and hijra identification in India, 190n4; and witchcraft in post-apartheid South Africa, 141–61

Algeria, and regional networks of wealth and power, 221

Alvarado, Velasco, 44, 51

American University of Cairo (AUC), 96, 107, 108

ANC (African National Congress), 144, 145, 146–47, 158

ancestors, and belief systems in South Africa, 155–56

Angel-Ajani, Asale, 271, 272

Angola, and informal economy of border regions, 223n2

anthropology: history of concept of state, 4–5, 8, 31n3; and recent literature on law, margins, and exception, 11–19; rethinking of state from perspective of margins, 4–11, 19–30; and violence as object, 69–70. *See also* ethnography; margins; state

apartheid, in South Africa, 145–46

Arendt, Hannah, 190n3, 270

Asad, Talal, 29–30

Ashforth, Adam, 21–22, 24–25, 27, 123, 130, 245

Austin, John L., 244–45

authority: and judicial system in margins of Peruvian state, 43, 63n4; and state power in Chad Basin, 194–222; state and figures of local, 14–15. *See also* power; sovereignty

autonomy: and indigenous peoples in Guatemala, 136; and local judges in Peruvian legal system, 42 al-Azhar University (Egypt), 95, 101, 115n4

Baldwin, Peter, 26
Balibar, Etienne, 78, 79, 80n6, 189n2
Banco Metropolitano (Guatemala), 134
Basadre, Jorge, 61
Bataille, Georges, 31n3
Bayart, Jean-François, 224n14
Benjamin, Walter, 11, 12, 225, 244, 256, 257
Bentham, Jeremy, 62n1
Bhabha, Homi, 122
Bhengu, Ruth, 162n5
bioavailability, and organ transplantation in India, 168–72, 179
biopolitics: and bioavailability at margins of state in India, 172; concept of in anthropological discussions of state and margins, 10; and ethnographic literature on state and margins, 25–30; and management of populations and territory in Sierra Leone, 81–114
Biya, Paul, 203, 224n13
body: concept of margins and production of biopolitical, 10; and legal concept of habeas corpus, 12; and management of life as object of politics, 28–29; and politics in postwar Guatemala, 137–38
borders: and biopolitical management of populations in Sierra Leone, 81–114; exclusion and documentary practices of state, 17–18; and relationship of checkpoints to state in Sri Lanka, 75
British Nationality Act (1948), 103–106, 112

Cameron, Edwin, 162n5
Cameroon: and carnival as metaphor for postcolonial state, 188; and reconstitution of state power in Chad Basin, 191–222
Canada, and Peace Communities in Colombia, 268
carnivals: in Guatemala, 122, 124–25, 138; and postcolonial state in Cameroon, 188. See also sideshow
Carrel, Alexis, 168
Castaño, Carlos, 262

Catholic Church, and displaced communities in Colombia, 258, 262
Cavell, Stanley, 32–33n8
Central African Republic, and informal economy of Chad Basin, 213, 218–19
Centro de Conciliación (APENAC), 55–56
Chad: informal economy and reconstitution of state power on margins of, 20–21, 191–222; refugees and border crossing between Sudan and, 102
checkpoints: and border crossings in Africa, 110; and boundaries of state in Sri Lanka, 67–79; and military violence in Colombia, 254–55, 257–58, 261–63, 272, 277n10
China, and immigrants to U.S., 249–50
citizenship: and Agamben's theory of sovereignty, 12–13; displacement and state sovereignty at margins in Colombia, 253–76; and informal economy of Chad Basin, 204–205, 206; and margins of state in Sierra Leone, 81–114. See also exclusion/inclusion; populations
class, and citizenship in Sierra Leone, 108
Clastres, Pierre, 5, 31n3
Clinton, Bill, 183
Cohen, Lawrence, 18, 24, 27, 28–29
Cojtí Cuxil, Demetrio, 120
Colombia: citizenship and state sovereignty at margins of, 14, 18, 21, 27, 253–76; and regional networks of wealth and power, 221
colonialism: and arbitrariness of law in Sierra Leone, 83–86; and formation of Peruvian state, 39–40, 63n5–6; historical legacy of in African politics, 81; and immigration policy in U.K., 105; and rethinking of concept of state in anthropology, 6. See also postcolonialism
Comaroff, John L., 86
Commonwealth Immigrants Act (U.K.), 104–105
communication: rumor as subaltern form of, 24–25; writing and theory of, 226–27
community: and concepts of equality and sovereignty, 78; and illegibility of state in India, 230–31; and judicial system

in Peru, 57–59, 64n11; role of women in Peruvian, 64n12; and social impact of AIDS in South Africa, 153, 157, 158–60, 161

Conciliation Centers (Peru), 53

constitution, of Peru, 40–41

COP-MAGUA (Guatemala), 132–33

Coronil, Fernando, 226

corruption: and privatization of power in Peru, 62n1; and rethinking of political theory of state in Africa, 81

Costa Rica, and Mayan rights movement, 132

Cover, Robert, 50

creativity, margins as spaces of, 19–25, 33n10

culture: and cultural defense arguments in U.S. courts, 249–50, 252n9; and cultural-rights movement of Maya in Guatemala, 125, 133–34

Das, Veena, 14–15, 23, 24, 27, 126, 279, 287

De Alwis, Malathi, 80n3

death, and social impact of AIDS in South Africa, 152–56. See also mortality rates

de Boeck, Filip, 223n2

Deleuze, Giles, 31n3, 82, 89, 100, 113, 115n2

democracy: and AIDS epidemic in South Africa, 157–61; regulatory authority of state and economy of Chad Basin, 200. See also politics

Derrida, Jacques, 226–27, 257

Desrosieres, Alain, 282

development, and modernization in India, 166

Devi, Asha, 187

Dhareshwar, Vivek, 80n5

discourses, and use of term state, 280

divorce agreements, in India, 227–28, 229–30

Doctors without Borders, 262

documentary practices: and illegibility of state in India, 245; and immigration policy in U.K., 103–106, 112; and immigration policy in U.S., 100–102, 115n5; and international traffic in visas and passports, 99, 109, 115n6; and justice on margins of Peruvian

state, 35–36, 38, 59–62, 62–63n2, 63–64n8; national identity and theories of sovereignty, 15–19, 32–33n8, 284–85; and state control of populations and territories, 111; and tax receipts in Sierra Leone, 94. See also citizenship; exclusion/inclusion; immigration; national identity

domestic violence, and judicial system in Peru, 55, 64n10

drift, and image of Peruvian state, 42, 48, 60, 62–63n2

Dumézil, Georges, 32n6

duplicity and duping, and state in postwar Guatemala, 117–39

Economics and economy: and indigenous peoples in Guatemala, 127–28; margins and conceptual boundaries of, 20–21; and organ transplant scandal in India, 181–82; and Peace Communities in Colombia, 260; and social impact of AIDS in South Africa, 153–154; state power in Chad Basin and informal, 192–93, 195–211; and structural adjustment in Sierra Leone, 93–94. See also labor; privatization; taxation

Ecuador, and paramilitaries, 277n4

Egypt, and refugees or migrants from Sierra Leone, 95–96, 101, 103, 106–107, 112, 114, 115n4

encomienda, and colonialism in Peru, 39–40

engaño, and the state in Guatemala, 117, 118, 129–31

England. See United Kingdom

epidemics, literature on state formation and, 26–27. See also AIDS; public health

equality: of citizens in liberal theory, 30, 282–83; and concepts of citizenship and sovereignty, 78

essentialism, and social/cultural identity in Sri Lanka, 77

ethics, bioavailability and organ transplantation in India, 176

ethnography: and images of duplicity in postwar Guatemala, 121; impact of war and violence on conduct of work in, 11; and problem of origin of law,

15; and recent literature on biopolitics of state and margins, 25–30; rethinking of concepts of state and margins, 4–11. *See also* anthropology; Cameroon; Chad; Colombia; Guatemala; India; margins; Peru; South Africa; Sierra Leone; Sri Lanka; state

eunuch, and hijra identification in politics of India, 184–89, 190n4

Evans-Pritchard, E. E., 5, 6, 162n6

exception, organ transplantation in India and logic of, 172–80

exclusion/inclusion: and concept of margins in ethnography, 10–11; gender and state effect in Sierra Leone, 112–13; and immigration policy in U.K., 105; indigenous peoples and inclusion of marginal populations in national identities, 9; Mayan organizers and Guatemalan state, 125–26; national identity and documentary practices of state, 15–19; and reform of judicial system in Peru, 54–55; refugees and nature of state sovereignty, 91; territorializing languages and nation-state formation in Latin America, 37. *See also* citizenship; documentary practices; national identity; refugees

Family: and judicial authority in Peru, 63n4; and organ transplantation in India, 173–74; and social impact of AIDS in South Africa, 153–154. *See also* divorce agreements

family planning, and housing policy in India, 239–41. *See also* sterilization

Fanthorpe, Richard, 115n3

FARC (Revolutionary Armed Forces of Colombia), 254, 258, 273, 275, 276n1

fascism, and social/cultural identity, 77

Ferguson, James, 178, 223n3, 223n8

Ferme, Mariane, 16, 21, 123–24, 245

fetish, and ideological construction of state, 281–82

Foucault, Michel, 25–26, 27, 29, 30, 78, 88–89, 118, 193, 222, 256–57, 258, 274

France: and politics of national identity, 283–85, 287n3; and *zones d'attente* at

airports, 98, 110

Freud, Sigmund, 287

frontier, and judicial system in Peru, 43, 65n14

Fujimori, Alberto, 52, 64n8

Fuss, Diana, 136

Galy, Michael, 115n2

gamonal and *gamonalismo*, and forms of power in Peru, 43–46, 51–59, 63n5, 65n14

Gandhi, Indira, 227, 228–29, 239

Gandhi, Sanjay, 239, 240

Gazi, Costa, 146

gender: and hijra operation in India, 167, 184–89, 190n4; role of women in Mayan cultural-rights movement, 133–34; role of women in Peruvian communities, 64n12; state effect and exclusion in Sierra Leone, 112–13; violence and power in Peru, 43–44

geography, and control of rivers in Colombia, 260–61, 265, 269. *See also* landscape

Geschiere, Peter, 162n6

Godelier, Maurice, 14

González, Domingo, 120

Great Britain. *See* United Kingdom

Grégoire, Emmanuel, 215, 224n12

Guatemala, Mayan rights movement and margins of state in postwar, 22–23, 117–39

Guatemalan Mayan Language Academy (ALMG), 120, 126, 131

Guattari, Felix, 31n3, 82, 89, 100, 113, 115n2

guerillas. *See* FARC; military

Guha, Ranajit, 25

Guinea, and refugees, 91

Gulf War (1991), 95

Habeas Corpus Act of 1679, 12

Hansen, Thomas, 171–72, 178, 248–49

Hardt, Michael, 256, 269

health. *See* epidemics; medicine; public health

Hegel, George Wilhelm Friedrich, 7, 14

hijra operation, third-gender status and politics in India, 167, 184–89, 190n4

Hobbes, Thomas, 8, 281

Homo sacer, and problem of sovereignty

and exception, 11–13, 15, 25, 29
Hong Kong, and international traffic in
    passports, 99–100, 109
hooks, bell, 118
housing policy, and National Emergency
    in India, 239–41
Humanidad Vigente (Vigilant Humanity),
    259
human rights: and checkpoints in Sri
    Lanka, 80n3; and displaced commu-
    nities in Colombia, 261–62, 263–65,
    267–68, 270; indigenous peoples and
    abuses in Guatemala, 125, 127. *See
    also* exclusion/inclusion; NGOs;
    refugees; violence
Humphreys, Caroline, 33n10
Hupuarachichi, Amara, 80n3

Ibarra, Carlos Figueroa, 124
identity cards, and checkpoints in Sri
    Lanka, 72–74, 75–77, 79; and power
    of state in Sierra Leone, 86. *See also*
    documentary practices; national
    identity
illegibility. *See* legibility/illegibility
imagination: and arbitrariness of law in
    Sierra Leone, 87; judicial system and
    margins of Peruvian state, 49–50; and
    refugees from Sierra Leone, 91–92;
    sovereignty and relative position of
    center and periphery, 29–30
immigration, and citizenship in Sierra
    Leone, 94–114; and cultural plea
    defense in U.S. courts, 250, 252n9;
    and policy in U.K., 103–106, 112; and
    policy in U.S., 100–102, 115n5;
    process of in Guatemala, 133–35. *See
    also* documentary practices; refugees
incivisme fiscal movement (Chad Basin),
    197–98, 203, 206, 208, 209, 223n10
inclusion. *See* exclusion/inclusion
Inden, Ronald, 80n4
India: illegibility and violence at margins
    of state, 226–51; and surgical opera-
    tions at margins of state, 18–19,
    23–24, 28–29, 165–89
indigenous peoples: and inclusion of
    marginal populations in national
    identities, 9; margins, state, and
    duplicity in Guatemala, 117–39
Inter-American Development Bank, 52

internally displaced persons (IDPs), 90.
    See also refugees
international community, use of term,
    277n9
International Monetary Fund (IMF), 92
Iran, and organ transplant sales, 183–84
isidliso, and witchcraft in South Africa,
    141–42, 148–50, 151, 162n7
Italy, and history of concept of state, 280

Jeganathan, Pradeep, 15, 17, 18, 245
justice: concept of state and demands for
    popular, 8; and community in mar-
    gins of Peruvian state, 35–62; and cre-
    ativity of margins, 21–24; exclusion
    and documentary practices of state,
    17; and social impact of AIDS in
    South Africa, 154, 157–61. *See also* law
    and legal systems; mediation
Justicia y Paz (Justice and Peace), 259,
    262, 265, 268

Kafka, Franz, 110–11, 114
Kammen, Curt, 277n6
Kant, Immanuel, 7–8, 14, 49, 50, 65n14
Kantorowicz, Ernst H., 137
Katznelson, Ira, 282
Kaviraj, Sudipta, 172
Khomeini, Ayatollah, 183–84
Kishore, R. R., 173

Labor: control of and border crossing
    between Chad and Sudan, 102–103;
    and indigenous peoples in
    Guatemala, 127–28
landscape, of Chad Basin, 191–92. *See also*
    geography
languages: and documentary practices of
    Peruvian state, 59; and identity cards
    in Sri Lanka, 76–77; and image of
    dual oppositions in Peru, 41; and
    indigenous peoples in Guatemala,
    119–20, 140n1; and organ transplan-
    tation in India, 173–74; and spatial
    marginality, 37–38, 41; and witchcraft
    in South Africa, 141, 152, 162n6–7
law and legal systems: arbitrariness of in
    Sierra Leone, 83–94; and continuous
    attempts of state to overcome mar-
    gins, 279–87; and *gamonalismo* in
    Peru, 46–51; and history of concepts

of state and margins, 8; and illegibility of state in India, 231–39; lived experience on margins and concept of, 22–23; and recent anthropological work on margins and exception, 11–19, 33n11; and spatial language of sovereignty in Peru, 41–42; and traditional forms of punishment in Peru, 63n3; and witchcraft in South Africa, 159–60. *See also* justice

legibility/illegibility: checkpoints and identity cards in Sri Lanka, 75; and concept of margins and the state, 9–10, 279, 287; displaced communities and Colombian state, 265–69; and documentary practices of state, 16–19, 24; and frontier justice, 65n14; and geographic borders of Sierra Leone, 87–88; and violence on margins of state in India, 225–51

legitimacy, and illegibility of state in India, 244–45

liberal theory and liberalism: equality and substitutability of citizens in, 30, 282–83; and point of origin of state, 50; transcendent character of state and monopoly over violence, 32n6. *See also* neoliberalism

Liberation Tigers of Tamil Elam (LTTE), 67

Liberia: and civil war, 81–82, 89, 115n2; and refugees on territorial borders, 91

life expectancy, and AIDS epidemic in South Africa, 144

Lock, Margaret, 168

Locke, John, 8, 286, 288n4

Lomnitz, Claudio, 62n1

Magic, and illegibility of state in India, 226. *See also* witchcraft

Maine, Henry Summer, 5

Malkki, Liisa, 91

Mamdani, Mahmood, 114

maps of anticipation, and checkpoints in Sri Lanka, 17, 68, 72, 79

margins: abstraction and concept of state in contemporary thought, 29–30, 281–83; and recent anthropological work on law and exception, 11–19; and recent anthropological work on

reconfiguration of state, 19–25; recent ethnographic literature on biopolitics of state and, 25–29; School of American Research advanced seminar on state and, 3–11; social uncertainties of and view of state, 279–87. *See also* anthropology; Chad; Colombia; ethnography; exclusion/inclusion; Guatemala; India; periphery; Peru; Sierra Leone; South Africa; Sri Lanka

Marriott, McKim, 179

Martin, Emily, 118, 139

Marx, Karl, 80n5, 137, 281–82

Mausi, Shabnam, 187, 189

Mayans, and image of duplicity in postwar Guatemalan state, 117–39

Mbeki, Thabo, 145, 161n4

Mbembe, Achille, 85–86, 92, 97, 113, 188, 220

mediation: and judicial reforms in Peru, 56; and witchcraft accusations in South Africa, 159

medicine: and AIDS epidemic in South Africa, 150–52; and organ transplantation in India, 165–89. *See also* epidemics; public health; traditional healers

Mejia, Anastasia, 132–33

Messick, Brinkley, 227

Mexico, and migration process in Guatemala, 134–35

military: and regulatory authority in Chad Basin, 196, 212–13, 214, 216–17; and states of emergency in margins of Peru, 56–57; violence and displaced communities in Colombia, 255–76

Misra, Kavita, 246

Mitchell, Timothy, 82, 85, 113

mobility: and border-making practices of state, 17–18; and duplicity in postwar Guatemala, 136–37, 139. *See also* immigration; refugees

modernity and modernization: biopolitics and management of populations, 27; and checkpoints in Sri Lanka, 74; and judicial reforms in Peru, 52–55; planned development and population control in India, 166

Monga, Célestine, 31n1

Montesquieu, Charles-Louis, 5

Moreno, Leonides, 258, 274
mortality rates, and AIDS epidemic in South Africa, 143–44. See also death
Mouvement pour le Développement (Chad), 212
Mukherjee, Sutapa, 187
Musa, Solomon, 99–100, 109, 115n6
Mutwa, Credo, 163n9

NAFTA (North American Free Trade Agreement), 136
Naidu, N. Chandrababu, 183, 188–89
National AIDS Co-Ordinating Committee of South Africa (NACOSA), 144
National Coordination of Opposition Parties and Associations, 197–98
National Emergency (India, 1975), 238–44
national identity: and checkpoints in Sri Lanka, 67–79; and documentary practices of state, 24, 32–33n8; and ethnicity in Guatemala, 127; indigenous peoples and inclusion of marginal populations in, 9; and politics in France, 283–85, 288n3; and refugees from Sierra Leone, 89–90; and theories of sovereignty, 15–19
nature, and concepts of state and margins, 8
Ndungane, Njongonkulu, 146
Negri, Antonio, 256, 269
Nelson, Diane M., 22, 23–24
neoliberalism, and judicial reforms in Peru, 52, 54
NEPAD (New Partnership for African Development), 93
Netherlands, and Peace Communities in Colombia, 275
nexus, and social theory in India, 179–80, 181
NGOs (non-governmental organizations): and civil war in Sierra Leone, 92, 96; and displaced communities in Colombia, 254, 258, 259, 265, 268, 275
Nigeria: and reconstitution of state power in Chad Basin, 191–222; and refugees from Sierra Leone, 106
Nucleos Rurales de Administracion de Justicia (NURAJ), 57–59, 64n12

Oglesby, Liz, 134

operability, and organ transplantation in India, 168–72, 176–77
Operación Limpieza (Operation Social Cleansing), 263–64
Opération Villes Mortes campaign (Cameroon), 197–98, 203
order, and rethinking of state in ethnography from perspective of margins, 5–8
organ transplantation, and margins of state in India, 165–84, 189
ORPA (Revolutionary Organization of the People in Arms), 132
Oxfam, 262

Pan-Africanist Congress, 146
paramilitary. See FARC; military; Shining Path
passenger registries. See documentary practices
passports. See documentary practices
PCP-SL (PCP-Sendero Luminoso), 39, 57, 63n3, 64n11
Peace Accord on Indigenous Identity (1996), 133
Peace Brigades International, 259, 268
Peace Communities (Colombia), 257–76
People v. Dong Hu Chen (U.S.), 249–50
periphery: idea of margins as, 9; imagination of sovereignty and relative positions of center and, 29–30. See also margins
Peru: local and state authority in administration of justice, 14, 18, 22, 35–62; and regional networks of wealth and power, 221
Pideu, K., 217
pluralization, and regulatory authority in Chad Basin, 211–22
politics: and AIDS as witchcraft in South Africa, 143; checkpoints and identity cards in Sri Lanka, 76, 79; and hijra operation in India, 184–89; and human-rights violations in Colombia, 264–65, 270; management of life as object of, 28–29; and margins as space of creativity, 21; Mayan movement in Guatemala and transnational indigenous-rights activism, 126; and national identity in France, 283–85, 288n3; and organ transplantation in

India, 178. *See also* biopolitics; democracy

Poole, Deborah, 16–17, 18, 22, 24, 123, 126, 137, 245, 259, 279

Popular Feminine Organization (OFP), 254, 277n2

populations: biopolitical management of in Sierra Leone, 81–114; and surgical operations in India, 165–89. *See also* citizenship; family planning; life expectancy; mortality rates

postcolonialism: and rethinking of concept of state in anthropology, 6; and state in Cameroon, 207; and state in Sierra Leone, 86, 89. *See also* colonialism

power: borders and biopolitical regimes, 89; and colonialism in Sierra Leone, 85–86; and concepts of state and margins in ethnography, 9; and Foucault's theory of biopower, 26, 27; judicial system of Peru and personalized forms of local, 43–46, 50–51, 62n1, 63n6; and postcolonial state in Sierra Leone, 86; of traditional healers in South Africa, 150–51; and witchcraft paradigm in South Africa, 161. *See also* authority; sovereignty

PPPs (public-private partnerships), 93. *See also* privatization

primitive, and history of concept of state in anthropology, 4–5

privatization: and informal economy of Chad Basin, 196; and power of state in Peru, 62n1; and state sovereignty in Africa, 92–93

public health: and AIDS epidemic in South Africa, 142, 143–47; and concept of panic in India, 245–47. *See also* epidemics; medicine

Race, and immigration policy in U.K., 104, 112

Radcliffe-Richards, Janet, 175

Ralushai Commission (South Africa), 160

Ram, Kalpana, 171

Ramachandran, M. G., 183

rationality, and illegibility of state in India, 245–49, 251

Red Cross, 101, 262

Red de Solidaridad Social (Social Solidarity Network), 259, 268

Reddy, Sita, 252n9

reforms, of judicial system in Peru, 51–55, 63–64n8–10

refugees: and citizenship in Colombia, 253–76; and citizenship in Sierra Leone, 94–114; civil war and violence in Sierra Leone, 91–92, 93; and territorial borders in contemporary political debates, 90–91

Registration of Persons Act (Sri Lanka), 73–74

religion, and political conflicts over truth, 286. *See also* Catholic Church

Reno, William, 81–82, 102

Rigoberta Menchú Foundation, 132

Rios Montt, Efraín, 129, 131

Rithambara, Sadhvi, 184

rivers, control of in Colombia, 260–61, 265, 269

Roitman, Janet, 14, 20–21, 259

Rousseau, Jean Jacques, 8

rumor: and public health policy in India, 246–47; as subaltern form of communication, 24–25

Russia, and regional networks of wealth and power, 221

Sanford, Victoria, 18, 21, 27

Sarafina II (anti-AIDS musical), 144, 161n2–3

Saudi Arabia, and migrants from Sierra Leone, 95, 107

Scheper-Hughes, Nancy, 167, 169, 189n1

Schmitt, Carl, 11, 12, 87–88, 112

School of American Research, and seminar on state and margins, 3–11

Scott, David, 80n4

Scott, James, 20, 126

Sekhar, Saye, 180–81, 182

Shabalala, Thomas, 147

shadow states, of Africa, 81–82, 86. *See also* state effect

Sharma, Rakesh, 186

Shining Path (Peru), 39, 57, 63n3, 64n11

sideshow, as metaphor for state in Guatemala, 118, 123–25, 135, 138. *See also* carnivals

Sierra Leone, citizenship and margins of state, 16, 81–114

signature, and illegibility of state in India, 226–27, 244–45, 250–51 slavery, and British colonialism in Sierra Leone, 84

Smith, Carol, 127

social cleansing, and human-rights violations in Colombia, 263–65

South Africa, AIDS epidemic and suspicions of witchcraft in post-apartheid, 21–22, 24–25, 27, 141–61

sovereignty: displaced populations and margins of state in Colombia, 253–76; and equality of citizens, 78; figure of *Homo sacer* in Agamben's theory of, 11–13; and Foucault's theory of biopower, 26; imagination of and relative position of center and periphery, 29–30; and judicial system in Peru, 41; language of popular in Peruvian constitution, 40–41; national identity and theories of, 15–19; and relationship between Peruvian state and margins, 51; and suspension of law, 87–88. *See also* power; state

space and spatial models: biopolitical body and concept of margins, 10; and concepts of state and margins, 33n10; language and concept of territorial margin, 37–38, 41

Spain: and colonial history of Peru, 39–40; and Peace Communities in Colombia, 275

Srikrishna Commission (India), 247–48

Sri Lanka, checkpoints and political identity in, 17, 67–79

state: abstraction and concept of in contemporary thought, 29–30, 281–83; and recent anthropological work on law, margins, and exception, 11–19; recent anthropological literature on reconfiguration of at margins, 19–25; and recent ethnographical literature on biopolitics and margins, 25–30; School of American Research advanced seminar on margins and, 3–11; and social uncertainties of margins, 279–87. *See also* anthropology; Chad; Colombia; democracy; ethnography; Guatemala; India; legibility/ illegibility; politics; Peru; shadow states; Sierra Leone; South Africa; sovereignty; Sri Lanka; state effect

state effect: and citizenship in Sierra Leone, 82, 86, 110, 111–14; and indigenous peoples of Guatemala, 123–24, 125–26. *See also* state

stereotypes, of indigenous peoples in Guatemala, 122, 124, 127

sterilization, and population control in India, 167. *See also* family planning

stigma, of AIDS in South Africa, 155, 156–57

Strathern, Marilyn, 14

Structural Adjustment Programs (SAPs), 93–94

subaltern theory: and Peace Communities in Colombia, 266–67, 269; and rethinking of concept of state in anthropology, 6; and rumor as form of communication, 24–25

subjection and subjectivity: and citizenship in Sierra Leone, 114; and checkpoints in Sri Lanka, 75, 78–79

Sudan, and migrant labor, 102–103

Sweden, and Peace Communities in Colombia, 275

Tanzania, and refugees, 91

Tarlo, Emma, 239–41, 251

Taussig, Michael, 32n6, 227

taxation: and concept of price, 223n6; and documentary practices in Sierra Leone, 94, 115n3; and informal economy of Chad Basin, 202–11

temporary protected status (TPS), 98–99, 100, 111, 115n5

Thackeray, Bal, 184, 187

thanatopolitics, and biopolitics, 25

Theidon, Kimberly, 271

Tiruchelvam, Neelan, 68

Tiwari, Madhu, 186–87

Toledo, Alejandro, 52

traditional healers, and AIDS in South Africa, 149–52, 153, 154, 157, 158, 162n9

Transplantation of Human Organs Act of 1994 (India), 173, 178

truth: Colombian state and production of, 273–74; political conflicts and concept of certainty, 286

Tsing, Anna, 32n5, 33n10

tuberculosis, and AIDS epidemic in South Africa, 149–50

United Kingdom: and colonial administration of Sierra Leone, 84–86; and colonialism in India, 171–72; immigration policy and migrants from Sierra Leone, 103–106, 112

United Nations: and civil war in Sierra Leone, 92; Commission for Historical Clarification in Guatemala, 125; High Commissioner for Refugees (UNHCR) and displaced communities in Colombia, 253, 258, 259, 265, 270; and Joint Programme on HIV/AIDS in South Africa, 144

United States: and airports as checkpoints, 74, 75; and cultural-defense arguments in courts, 249–50, 252n9; and immigrants from Sierra Leone, 97, 98–99, 100–102, 111, 114, 115n5; and migrant labor from Guatemala, 134

Urbie Velez, Alvaro, 274–75

URNG (Guatemalan National Revolutionary Unity), 117

USAID (United States Agency for International Development), 52, 120

Vajpayee, Atal Behari, 187, 189

Van Hollen, Cecilia, 171

violence: checkpoints and political identity in Sri Lanka, 67–79; and civil war in Guatemala, 117, 119; and civil war in Sierra Leone, 92; and illegibility of state in India, 231–41, 247; and masculinity as feature of power in Peru, 43–44; and military in Colombia, 254–76; and panic behavior in indigenous regions of Guatemala, 130–31; and regulatory authority in Chad Basin, 200–201, 212–13, 216–17; and rethinking of concept of state from perspective of margins, 6–8; and states of exception, 11; transcendent character of state and monopoly over, 32n6. *See also* human rights

visas. *See* documentary practices

Volpp, Leti, 249–50

Weber, Max, 7, 8, 22, 32n7

witchcraft: and AIDS in South Africa, 141–61; use of term in Africa, 162n6. *See also* magic

women. *See* gender

World Bank, 52, 92, 126

writing, and theory of communication, 226–27

Yamba, Bawa, 102–103

Zaire, and informal economy of Angolan border, 223n2

Zambia, and representations of rural and urban life, 223n3

Žižek, Slavoj, 138

zones d'attente (France), 98, 110

Zook, Darren, 171

School for Advanced Research Advanced Seminar Series

PUBLISHED BY SAR PRESS

CHACO & HOHOKAM: PREHISTORIC
REGIONAL SYSTEMS IN THE AMERICAN
SOUTHWEST
Patricia L. Crown & W. James Judge, eds.

RECAPTURING ANTHROPOLOGY: WORKING IN
THE PRESENT
Richard G. Fox, ed.

WAR IN THE TRIBAL ZONE: EXPANDING
STATES AND INDIGENOUS WARFARE
R. Brian Ferguson &
Neil L. Whitehead, eds.

IDEOLOGY AND PRE-COLUMBIAN
CIVILIZATIONS
Arthur A. Demarest &
Geoffrey W. Conrad, eds.

DREAMING: ANTHROPOLOGICAL AND
PSYCHOLOGICAL INTERPRETATIONS
Barbara Tedlock, ed.

HISTORICAL ECOLOGY: CULTURAL
KNOWLEDGE AND CHANGING LANDSCAPES
Carole L. Crumley, ed.

THEMES IN SOUTHWEST PREHISTORY
George J. Gumerman, ed.

MEMORY, HISTORY, AND OPPOSITION UNDER
STATE SOCIALISM
Rubie S. Watson, ed.

OTHER INTENTIONS: CULTURAL CONTEXTS
AND THE ATTRIBUTION OF INNER STATES
Lawrence Rosen, ed.

LAST HUNTERS–FIRST FARMERS: NEW
PERSPECTIVES ON THE PREHISTORIC
TRANSITION TO AGRICULTURE
T. Douglas Price &
Anne Birgitte Gebauer, eds.

MAKING ALTERNATIVE HISTORIES:
THE PRACTICE OF ARCHAEOLOGY AND
HISTORY IN NON-WESTERN SETTINGS
Peter R. Schmidt & Thomas C. Patterson, eds.

SENSES OF PLACE
Steven Feld & Keith H. Basso, eds.

CYBORGS & CITADELS: ANTHROPOLOGICAL
INTERVENTIONS IN EMERGING SCIENCES AND
TECHNOLOGIES
Gary Lee Downey & Joseph Dumit, eds.

ARCHAIC STATES
Gary M. Feinman & Joyce Marcus, eds.

CRITICAL ANTHROPOLOGY NOW:
UNEXPECTED CONTEXTS, SHIFTING
CONSTITUENCIES, CHANGING AGENDAS
George E. Marcus, ed.

THE ORIGINS OF LANGUAGE: WHAT
NONHUMAN PRIMATES CAN TELL US
Barbara J. King, ed.

REGIMES OF LANGUAGE: IDEOLOGIES,
POLITIES, AND IDENTITIES
Paul V. Kroskrity, ed.

BIOLOGY, BRAINS, AND BEHAVIOR: THE
EVOLUTION OF HUMAN DEVELOPMENT
Sue Taylor Parker, Jonas Langer, &
Michael L. McKinney, eds.

WOMEN & MEN IN THE PREHISPANIC
SOUTHWEST: LABOR, POWER, & PRESTIGE
Patricia L. Crown, ed.

HISTORY IN PERSON: ENDURING STRUGGLES,
CONTENTIOUS PRACTICE, INTIMATE
IDENTITIES
Dorothy Holland & Jean Lave, eds.

THE EMPIRE OF THINGS: REGIMES OF VALUE
AND MATERIAL CULTURE
Fred R. Myers, ed.

CATASTROPHE & CULTURE: THE
ANTHROPOLOGY OF DISASTER
Susanna M. Hoffman &
Anthony Oliver-Smith, eds.

URUK MESOPOTAMIA & ITS NEIGHBORS:
CROSS-CULTURAL INTERACTIONS IN THE ERA
OF STATE FORMATION
Mitchell S. Rothman, ed.

REMAKING LIFE & DEATH: TOWARD AN
ANTHROPOLOGY OF THE BIOSCIENCES
Sarah Franklin & Margaret Lock, eds.

TIKAL: DYNASTIES, FOREIGNERS,
& AFFAIRS OF STATE: ADVANCING
MAYA ARCHAEOLOGY
Jeremy A. Sabloff, ed.

GRAY AREAS: ETHNOGRAPHIC ENCOUNTERS
WITH NURSING HOME CULTURE
Philip B. Stafford, ed.

PLURALIZING ETHNOGRAPHY: COMPARISON
AND REPRESENTATION IN MAYA CULTURES,
HISTORIES, AND IDENTITIES
John M. Watanabe & Edward F. Fischer, eds.

AMERICAN ARRIVALS: ANTHROPOLOGY
ENGAGES THE NEW IMMIGRATION
Nancy Foner, ed.

VIOLENCE
Neil L. Whitehead, ed.

LAW & EMPIRE IN THE PACIFIC:
FIJI AND HAWAI'I
Sally Engle Merry & Donald Brenneis, eds.

ANTHROPOLOGY IN THE MARGINS
OF THE STATE
Veena Das & Deborah Poole, eds.

THE ARCHAEOLOGY OF COLONIAL
ENCOUNTERS: COMPARATIVE PERSPECTIVES
Gil J. Stein, ed.

GLOBALIZATION, WATER, & HEALTH:
RESOURCE MANAGEMENT IN TIMES OF
SCARCITY
Linda Whiteford & Scott Whiteford, eds.

A CATALYST FOR IDEAS: ANTHROPOLOGICAL
ARCHAEOLOGY AND THE LEGACY OF
DOUGLAS W. SCHWARTZ
Vernon L. Scarborough, ed.

THE ARCHAEOLOGY OF CHACO CANYON: AN
ELEVENTH-CENTURY PUEBLO REGIONAL
CENTER
Stephen H. Lekson, ed.

COMMUNITY BUILDING IN THE TWENTY-
FIRST CENTURY
Stanley E. Hyland, ed.

AFRO-ATLANTIC DIALOGUES:
ANTHROPOLOGY IN THE DIASPORA
Kevin A. Yelvington, ed.

COPÁN: THE HISTORY OF AN ANCIENT MAYA
KINGDOM
E. Wyllys Andrews & William L. Fash, eds.

THE EVOLUTION OF HUMAN LIFE HISTORY
Kristen Hawkes & Richard R. Paine, eds.

THE SEDUCTIONS OF COMMUNITY:
EMANCIPATIONS, OPPRESSIONS, QUANDARIES
Gerald W. Creed, ed.

THE GENDER OF GLOBALIZATION: WOMEN
NAVIGATING CULTURAL AND ECONOMIC
MARGINALITIES
Nandini Gunewardena & Ann Kingsolver, eds.

IMPERIAL FORMATIONS
*Ann Laura Stoler, Carole McGranahan,
& Peter C. Perdue, eds.*

OPENING ARCHAEOLOGY: REPATRIATION'S
IMPACT ON CONTEMPORARY RESEARCH AND
PRACTICE
Thomas W. Killion, ed.

NEW LANDSCAPES OF INEQUALITY:
NEOLIBERALISM AND THE EROSION OF
DEMOCRACY IN AMERICA
*Jane L. Collins, Micaela di Leonardo,
& Brett Williams, eds.*

SMALL WORLDS: METHOD, MEANING, &
NARRATIVE IN MICROHISTORY
*James F. Brooks, Christopher R. N. DeCorse,
& John Walton, eds.*

MEMORY WORK: ARCHAEOLOGIES OF
MATERIAL PRACTICES
Barbara J. Mills & William H. Walker, eds.

FIGURING THE FUTURE: GLOBALIZATION
AND THE TEMPORALITIES OF CHILDREN AND
YOUTH
Jennifer Cole & Deborah Durham, eds.

TIMELY ASSETS: THE POLITICS OF
RESOURCES AND THEIR TEMPORALITIES
*Elizabeth Emma Ferry &
Mandana E. Limbert, eds.*

DEMOCRACY: ANTHROPOLOGICAL
APPROACHES
Julia Paley, ed.

CONFRONTING CANCER: METAPHORS,
INEQUALITY, AND ADVOCACY
Juliet McMullin & Diane Weiner, eds.

WRITING CULTURE: THE POETICS
AND POLITICS OF ETHNOGRAPHY
*James Clifford &
George E. Marcus, eds.*

THE COLLAPSE OF ANCIENT STATES AND
CIVILIZATIONS
*Norman Yoffee &
George L. Cowgill, eds.*

THE ANASAZI IN A CHANGING ENVIRONMENT
George J. Gumerman, ed.

REGIONAL PERSPECTIVES ON THE OLMEC
Robert J. Sharer & David C. Grove, eds.

THE CHEMISTRY OF PREHISTORIC HUMAN BONE
T. Douglas Price, ed.

THE EMERGENCE OF MODERN HUMANS: BIOCULTURAL ADAPTATIONS IN THE LATER PLEISTOCENE
Erik Trinkaus, ed.

THE ANTHROPOLOGY OF WAR
Jonathan Haas, ed.

THE EVOLUTION OF POLITICAL SYSTEMS
Steadman Upham, ed.

CLASSIC MAYA POLITICAL HISTORY: HIEROGLYPHIC AND ARCHAEOLOGICAL EVIDENCE
T. Patrick Culbert, ed.

TURKO-PERSIA IN HISTORICAL PERSPECTIVE
Robert L. Canfield, ed.

CHIEFDOMS: POWER, ECONOMY, AND IDEOLOGY
Timothy Earle, ed.

RECONSTRUCTING PREHISTORIC PUEBLO SOCIETIES
William A. Longacre, ed.

NEW PERSPECTIVES ON THE PUEBLOS
Alfonso Ortiz, ed.

STRUCTURE AND PROCESS IN LATIN AMERICA
Arnold Strickon & Sidney M. Greenfield, eds.

THE CLASSIC MAYA COLLAPSE
T. Patrick Culbert, ed.

METHODS AND THEORIES OF ANTHROPOLOGICAL GENETICS
M. H. Crawford & P. L. Workman, eds.

SIXTEENTH-CENTURY MEXICO: THE WORK OF SAHAGUN
Munro S. Edmonson, ed.

ANCIENT CIVILIZATION AND TRADE
Jeremy A. Sabloff &
C. C. Lamberg-Karlovsky, eds.

PHOTOGRAPHY IN ARCHAEOLOGICAL RESEARCH
Elmer Harp, Jr., ed.

MEANING IN ANTHROPOLOGY
Keith H. Basso & Henry A. Selby, eds.

THE VALLEY OF MEXICO: STUDIES IN PRE-HISPANIC ECOLOGY AND SOCIETY
Eric R. Wolf, ed.

DEMOGRAPHIC ANTHROPOLOGY: QUANTITATIVE APPROACHES
Ezra B. W. Zubrow, ed.

THE ORIGINS OF MAYA CIVILIZATION
Richard E. W. Adams, ed.

EXPLANATION OF PREHISTORIC CHANGE
James N. Hill, ed.

EXPLORATIONS IN ETHNOARCHAEOLOGY
Richard A. Gould, ed.

ENTREPRENEURS IN CULTURAL CONTEXT
Sidney M. Greenfield, Arnold Strickon,
& Robert T. Aubey, eds.

THE DYING COMMUNITY
Art Gallaher, Jr. & Harlan Padfield, eds.

SOUTHWESTERN INDIAN RITUAL DRAMA
Charlotte J. Frisbie, ed.

LOWLAND MAYA SETTLEMENT PATTERNS
Wendy Ashmore, ed.

SIMULATIONS IN ARCHAEOLOGY
Jeremy A. Sabloff, ed.

CHAN CHAN: ANDEAN DESERT CITY
Michael E. Moseley & Kent C. Day, eds.

SHIPWRECK ANTHROPOLOGY
Richard A. Gould, ed.

ELITES: ETHNOGRAPHIC ISSUES
George E. Marcus, ed.

THE ARCHAEOLOGY OF LOWER CENTRAL AMERICA
Frederick W. Lange & Doris Z. Stone, eds.

LATE LOWLAND MAYA CIVILIZATION: CLASSIC TO POSTCLASSIC
Jeremy A. Sabloff & E. Wyllys Andrews V, eds.

Participants in the School of American Research advanced seminar "Anthropology in the Margins of the State," Santa Fe, New Mexico, April 22-26, 2001. From left standing: Adam Ashforth, Veena Das, Pradeep Jeganathan, Mariane Ferme, Diane Nelson, Janet Roitman, Talal Asad. From left seated: Lawrence Cohen, Deborah Poole, Victoria Sanford.

Made in the USA
Lexington, KY
06 January 2012